Tears of the Silenced

A True Crime And an American Tragedy;
Severe Child Abuse and Leaving the Amish

Misty Griffin

"When I despair, I remember that all through history the ways of truth and love have always won. There have been tyrants and murderers, and for a time, they can seem invincible, but in the end, they always fall. Think of it—always."

— *Mahatma Gandhi*

"If you have a dream, don't just sit there. Gather courage to believe that you can succeed and leave no stone unturned to make it a reality."

— *Roopleen*

CONTENTS

DEDICATION

I would like to dedicate this book first and foremost to my husband who has shown me what it feels like to be loved.

I would also like to dedicate this book to all the silenced Amish victims. May they someday find a voice and be heard.

IMPORTANT NOTE

The following account is based on the real true life story of Misty Griffin. A girl held captive and severely abused most of her life by her mother and step-father. As a young child her family started to dress and live like the Amish. In her early twenties she became a baptized member of the Amish church. It is estimated that less than 100 people have ever joined the Amish from the outside world. Misty and her sister were adopted into the Amish community because they had been raised under harsher and stricter conditions than most Amish children. They knew to obey without question. Later she would report the bishop of her community to the authorities for sexual assault.

Given the severity of the author's life story she was cautioned and advised to disguise the identity of all persons, events and communities involved. It is not her intent to put anyone in harms way, but rather to tell her life's story in an attempt to prevent such tragedies from happening in the future.

Disclaimer: <u>The following account is based on the real true life story of the author. Names, locations, identifying characteristics and details have been partially altered, added and or withheld. A few instances of abuse were to traumatizing for the author to relive and they have been omitted. Any supposed likeness to any persons, communities, or specific locations should be reconsidered since some details have been modified.</u>

PREFACE

Foremost I would like to stress that not every single Amish community is the same as the one I lived in. My community was one of the strictest sects and belonged to the stricter half of the Amish.

While the fundamentals in all Amish communities are much the same, it can be said that the level of abuse becomes greater depending upon the strictness of that particular group. Some of the most progressive Amish have taken pains to raise awareness about the issue of sexual assault and child abuse. The more modern the church is, the more likely something will be done which usually is some form of counseling for the victim and rapist.(In rare cases the authorities have been contacted.) While this may not be much, it is, at least, some form of acknowledgment for the victim.

But the reality remains. Most Amish rape or child abuse victims have no resources. It is a scary reality, a place where the Amish rules outweigh any form of crime; sexual violence and animal abuse run rampant, and the worldly outside authorities may not be called. Shunning is the only punishment, but a few weeks shunning is such a light sentence for a rapist and from what I have seen it never works.

In light of these facts, there are many Amish, who actually wish to change these things but are afraid to go against the church rules for fear they will go to hell or be shunned. Thus, the cycle continues, the good people are forced to suffer in silence or leave, those are the only two options.

In conclusion: I did not write my life's story to point the finger at certain individuals or only at the Amish. Rather it is an attempt to raise awareness about child abuse and sexual assault. One person, acting at the right moment can save someone from a world of pain and even death. I hope child abuse and sexual assault survivors will take heart from my story and move past their pain to embrace their dreams. May everyone be encouraged and never turn a blind eye towards child abuse. Please be a hero and report, you may be that child's last chance.

Prologue

"There are moments when even to the sober eye of reason, the world of our sad humanity may assume the semblance of Hell."

— *Edgar Allan Poe*

I trembled as I walked into the police station. It was very small and appeared to have only two or three rooms in it. The town had less than two thousand residents, so I figured there must be a low crime rate as well. I walked through the front door and went over to a heavy wooden counter where a middle-aged policewoman sat at a computer. She looked up as I stood there watching her. I saw a surprised look on her face as she took in my appearance.

I imagined I was very different from most of the people that normally walked up to her desk. I was a young Amish woman, just a little over five feet tall, wearing an ankle-length, plain, teal-colored dress and apron. I had on knee-length black socks and black shoes, and my coat was of homemade denim with a high collar and hooks and eyes to hold the front closed. On my head I wore a stiff, white Amish kapp that covered nearly all my reddish-brown hair and it was tied in a small bow under my chin. I was shaking as I stood there, looking at the woman. I tried to get up enough courage to say something, but my mouth was so dry I could not form any words.

"Can I help you with something, honey?" the woman asked me as she took off her reading glasses.

I stared into her bright blue eyes, which crinkled up on the sides when she smiled. *She seems like a nice lady*, I thought, and I felt a little better.

"Um," I swallowed hard as I tried to block out the mental image of possibly being put in the Bann(shunned). "Um," I said again. I placed my trembling hands on the counter top.

"Yes, dear. What is it?" the woman asked.

8

"Um…" I said again. "Um… I would like to talk to the police, please," I pressed my hands down on the counter to stop them from shaking.

"Okay, In regards to what?"

"Um…" I hesitated. "I need to talk to someone because the bishop of my church attacked me and is threatening to kill me, and I think he is also poisoning his wife and molesting his daughters."

The woman raised her eyebrows in shock. After looking at me for another moment, she got up and came around the counter.

"Are you okay, honey?" she asked as she reached out to put an arm around my shoulders.

I backed up, not wanting her to touch me. I saw her nod as if she had seen this reaction before.

I was confused and not sure I was doing the right thing or not. I had witnessed so much abuse and so much pain in my life and I just felt I could no longer keep silent.

If an Amish man in my church confessed to rape or molestation he would only be shunned by the church for six-weeks. Going to the police was strictly frowned on and anyone who did so was risking being placed in the Bann (shunned) or would at least be stigmatized as untrustworthy for life.

I trembled, the Bann never worked for these sort of crimes. The offenders would unusually continue to offend after the dust settled or sometimes even still while in the Bann. If I did not report the bishop of my church to the authorities I knew there would be other victims, many more.....

THE BEGINNING OF A NIGHTMARE

"A belief in a supernatural source of evil is not necessary; men alone are quite capable of every wickedness."

- Sir William Neil

My story starts early one November morning in Phoenix, Arizona. I was born to a rather unusual couple; my mother was the seventeen-year-old girlfriend of her former stepfather, who was only twenty-eight-years-old himself. I was not their first child, in fact, I was the brand new sister to a two-year-old boy. Surprisingly enough, my grandmother was there to witness my birth—standing next to her former husband and the daughter she accused of stealing him away from her.

On that November day, some thirty-odd years ago, I became the newest member of this dysfunctional family. It included my grandmother, who appeared to be the head of the household. She was a crafty and vicious woman, disliked by all who knew her. She was also a mastermind at cheating the system for money so she never had to work, and while she was nearly illiterate, she was most certainly not stupid. She believed in taking advantage of people whenever possible. My mother, although not illiterate was quickly learning her mother's trade. Lastly, there was my father, for whom I have only a few vague memories.

And so I came into this world, a small, unwanted bundle. My birth however, would ensure that one more government check would be coming in the mail and was probably the spawning of my mothers government schemes as I grew older. But thank God I did not know that then; I was merely a small little bundle reaching out for food and comfort while I basked in the innocence of my state.

The first four years of my life were much like those of any child born into an unstable home environment. When I was one-year and ten-months-old, my sister was born. At that time, we were all living in Kansas and were on the run from the police. There was an arrest warrant out for my parents as they had taken my four-year-old brother across state lines when my grandmother had sole custody of him. My mother had only been fifteen when he was born, so she had signed over custody to her mother. One morning the FBI stormed into our small apartment and took my brother, kicking and screaming, out of the house.

Soon after this incident, my parents divorced, and my mother took my sister and I back to northern Arizona to live with our grandmother so she could be near my brother. My father moved to Phoenix, and my parents shared custody of my sister and me, although we ended up living with my father most of the time. For the most part, I felt safe with my father, and while memories are hazy, I can recall his small, yellow house that sat on a busy street. The smallest bedroom had two twin-size beds with matching bedspreads—one for me and one for my little sister, Samantha. I can remember my father taking us to the local swimming pool and letting us float around with child floaters on our arms. Those days were fun for my sister and I. We would laugh and splash each other in the warm Arizona sunshine. Little did I know that happy days such as these would soon disappear...like the leaves falling from a tree in autumn...but I would always remember those days with tears in my eyes. If I could have talked to my four-year-old self, I would have whispered,

"Run! Run like hell and don't look back!"

But of course, this is only wishful thinking, as one cannot turn back the hands of time—no matter how much one may wish to do so.

MY LIFE changed abruptly one night when I was four-years-old. My sister and I were spending the night with my aunt. I remember that we loved to stay at my aunt's; she had a giant greyhound that my sister and I always loved to play with.

Even at four-years-old, I am told that I was more mentally well-developed than other children my age. I felt like I was the mother to my little sister, who was now two-years-old. Even at my young age, I could sense that we were two very different little individuals. I was a quiet, calm little girl who tried to save every animal and bug I came across while my sister was a very angry child. She screamed constantly if she did not get her way; she would claw and bite people, her target was most usually me. While I was tall for my age, I was extremely thin and pale; my sister was very short, chubby and had freckles everywhere. Even though we were so completely different, we were still sisters, and I loved her dearly and I know she loved me.

Now, to return to the night that would change my life. It was nighttime at my auntie's house; the lights were off, and everyone was asleep. My aunty and her husband were asleep in one of the bedrooms while my sister and I were nestled down in the foldout sofa bed. It was a big, fluffy bed that my sister and I always begged to sleep on whenever we stayed over. I remember that night quite clearly. It was a dark night in Tucson, Arizona, but there was a hint of moonlight filtering in from the screen door on the porch, and a soft breeze was blowing. I heard a rustling sound and knew it was Aunty getting up to go to the restroom. I called out to her to wait for me, but she did not hear me. I jumped out of bed and ran down the hall after her. Suddenly, I heard a tremendous roar and felt myself falling forward. As I looked down, I saw a giant mouthful of teeth; I tried to grab for something to hold onto, but to no avail. I fell, head first into the dog's open mouth, and the rows of razor-sharp teeth clamped down hard on my small head.

The next thing I remembered was waking in a hospital room and looking up at my mother, who was standing over me. I remember feeling surprised, knowing that I had not seen her in a long time (I would later learn I had been unconscious for a couple of days). She was looking down at me and yelling at my father who was sitting next to me. I looked at them but I was unable to say anything, I just smiled.

Shortly afterward I was released from the hospital, but I was never the same after that accident. I had a long scar running from my left temple to my mid-cheek, another directly under my right eye, one running along my right temple and another under my chin. I also had several stitches on the back of my head where the dog's upper eye-teeth had sunk in. I felt different after I left the hospital. My speech was not very good and my coordination seemed slightly off. I could no longer remember things as well as I once had; I was very tired all the time and plagued with headaches.

One afternoon soon after I was released from the hospital, I was sitting on the sidewalk with my sister, who was tearing up grass by the roots and eating the dirt. I remember watching her, holding my pounding head and thinking that Dad had been acting strange the past few days. He kept hugging us and telling us that he loved us. When I asked him if everything was okay, his only answer was, "Somehow I always manage to screw things up."

That morning as I sat there, I watched a yellow jeep pull up into the driveway. My mother was in the passenger's seat, and in the driver's seat was a man with long, gray hair. I smiled and waved a tired wave; their radio was blasting loud rock music and I remember how much it hurt my head. My father yelled for my sister and me to go into the house. I grabbed my little sister and started walking to the house. The man in the Jeep frightened me with his intense stare. It unnerved me even though I was used to people staring at me. In spite of my scars people would often say that I had a kind smile. But somehow the gray-haired man's stare was different, I hated how he was staring at me—it was very unsettling, so I ran toward the house with my sister, but the man jumped out of the jeep and grabbed my arm.

"Where are you going, gorgeous?" he asked with a grin.

"My dad is calling me," I stuttered.

"That's okay," the man said. "My name is Brian, and you are going to be my daughter now."

I looked at him in confusion. Why would I be his daughter?

My dad was yelling at my mother and pushing past her toward us. My mom was holding papers that I assume were custody papers. Brian pulled me and my sister over to the jeep and pushed us inside. My mother got into the front seat and Brian started the engine. I watched in confusion as my father went over to Brian's window and yelled at him to let us out, but Brian drove past him into the street. I waved to my father and he waved back with a sad look on his face. I was crying and my sister was mumbling gibberish as she always did in stressful situations. That would be the last time I saw my father, and although I know he was not a perfect man, I felt loved and protected when I was with him...something I would never feel again for the rest of my childhood.

FOR THE next three hours, we drove north into the Bradshaw Mountains of northern Arizona. I sat quietly in the middle of the back seat while forty-eight-year-old Brian asked me question after question. He got angry when I did not answer his questions, so I replied with short sentences. He told me he was a gold miner in the mountains, and that he and Mamma lived there in a tiny trailer. He kept nodding his head as he told me that we were all going to live there together, hunting for gold and serving the Lord. I listened, not knowing what he was talking about. My head still hurt and he was a stranger. My stomach felt tense and I just wanted to go home. I listened, wide-eyed, as Brian told me that Mamma had said I was very intelligent, and that he was going to expect a lot from me. I looked over at my mother, who was just listening without saying anything. She did not even seem very interested in the fact that Samantha and I were there. Once or twice she yelled at Samantha to stop mumbling. Instinctively I reached out for my little sister, who eventually fell asleep in my lap.

When we arrived at the mine, Mamma got out and opened a heavy metal gate. We crossed a creek and then drove about a half-mile up a hill to a small flat place in the road. There I saw a tiny thirteen-foot trailer sitting next to a tall mine shaft. I woke Samantha and apprehensively followed Mamma and Brian inside the trailer. It was so small, there was barely enough room to stand. After a minute of everyone just standing in the middle of the room, Brian picked Samantha and me up and set us on the top bunk.

"Okay girls, go to sleep," he said.

Still in my day clothes, I fixed my sister a place and then lay down myself. My stomach was all knotted up, and I had an uneasy feeling about what was happening to us. I could hear Mamma and Brian talking outside as I drifted off to sleep. My life was about to become a living nightmare— one from which I would not be able to awaken for many years.

LIFE WITH Brian was a rude awakening for me and my sister. He believed in the strictest discipline and held to the notion that children were to be seen and not heard. He was very confusing at times. At night he would read us stories, Samantha and I loved stories, but we always listened tensely, knowing the slightest thing could send him into a wild rage. Sometimes we would all go on mining excursions or hike to the lake behind the mine, but all of this was laced with an undercurrent of fear as Brian began laying out one rule after another. One of the worst of his rules was that my sister and I were not allowed to talk to each other, or to strangers. The only time we were allowed to talk was when we raised our hands and were given permission. We were also not allowed to play with other children who might accompany their parents on the mining expeditions that we sometimes went on.

The days would draw out, sad and long, and I would find myself jumping at the slightest touch or sound. Every tiny mistake, whether it was forgetting to close a door, dropping a dish, not coming immediately when called or talking without permission, would earn us a severe switching or belting. I had learned to count and would sometimes count the blows when we were punished, to keep my mind off the pain; usually, the average was fifteen licks. If Samantha and I cried, Brian or Mamma would beat us until we stopped, many times we merely collapsed. Brian's favorite stance for us when he beat us was to have us bend over and touch our toes. If we fell over or stopped touching our toes, the beatings would continue until we complied.

These punishments took place about three times a day for each of us. The worst part was that my mother would either participate in the punishment or just stand by and watch. Sometimes I would run to her for help, only to have her shove me back at Brian, who would be angrily grabbing at me. I would get angry when Brian beat two-year-old Samantha. This would usually earn me a slap across the face, but I would not stop. My little heart was breaking into a million pieces, and there was nothing that could glue it back together.

And so my new life with Brian and my mother began. Isolated on that desolate mine that no one ever visited. Sometimes I would still be shaking from a recent beating when Brian would start reading us our nightly story. I would listen to the story and wish he were like that all the time. It almost seemed like he thought that the stories could absolve him, but they didn't, a story could never wash away the pain that we suffered on a daily basis.

Summer came and went in the Bradshaw Mountains, giving way to fall, and then to a snowy winter. Although we lived in Arizona, the winters were frigid in the mountains and especially in the thirteen-foot trailer. Days blurred into weeks, and the fond memories I had of living with my father were soon obliterated, replaced with trying to find ways to avoid Brian's wicked temper. Brian forced us to call him Dad. I hated it, but I had no other choice than to comply. In the summer, Brian and my mother would work the mines and take the gold ore to southern Arizona to be assayed. This was the mid-1980s, and gold was at its ultimate peak in price. In the winter, we would drive farther up into the mountains where Brian and Mamma would cut down oak trees for firewood to sell in town.

My sister and I would accompany them and sit quietly nearby, or wander off and silently play house. We invented our own sign language that we would use for playing, but sometimes we would forget and start laughing and talking. Usually, within a few seconds, Brian or Mamma would appear behind us with a switch in hand. I would watch angrily as tears welled up in Samantha's eyes. Although I never protested with anything other than my angry gaze, I could tell it made Brian angry because he always gave me a few extra lashes.

On Sundays we would sometimes go to the church in town. Brian would always warn us to not talk to anyone about our home life and only answer questions when asked. We were the two most quiet little girls in the church. I am so surprised that no one thought of our strange withdrawn behavior. Couldn't they see our sad eyes and the angry looks that Brian shot at us, or did they notice and just did not know what to do?

ONE SUMMER day, about a year after we came to live at the mine, Mamma told me to undress and go outside and stand next to the five-gallon bucket to wait for my bath. She always stood us in a five gallon bucket and gave us our baths before we went into town. I did not want to undress and stand outside since Brian always came over and talked to me as he stared me up and down. Whenever I tried to turn away from his stares, he would get angry and tell me I was an ungrateful, selfish little girl. Although I was not a perfect child, I was certainly not selfish, and his saying so made me sad and confused.

On this particular day, I stood next to the bucket for a few minutes, trembling as Brian started inching his way over. When I could no longer stand his staring, I asked him if I could play in the sawdust pile until Mamma was ready for me. He just shrugged, so I ran over to the giant sawdust pile and covered myself with the sawdust.

A couple of minutes later, Mamma came out of the trailer yelling for me. I ran back to the five-gallon bucket and found that she was very angry because I had fine sawdust all over me. I tried to tell her that Brian had given me permission to play in the sawdust, but she grabbed me and started shaking me. She said I had the devil in me and that she was going to beat it out of me. I started screaming, half hoping someone would hear and save me, but of course there was nobody to hear. Brian came over and grabbed me. He put my upper torso between his legs and squeezed as hard as he could. I struggled for breath as his knees squeezed my five-year-old diaphragm. My mother began hitting me with a big leather belt. Finally, I couldn't stand it any longer, so I tried to break free. Brian squeezed harder and harder with his legs and Mamma said the pain was just the devil trying to come out. I screamed and screamed, but only my echo heard me. My mother laughed an evil laugh with every blow, and Brian goaded her to keep going. When I finally quit struggling, Brian let me go. I went limp and sank to the ground. I tried to get up, but I could not. I had a horrible, piercing pain in the left side of my rib cage, and every breath was torturous.

Mamma wiped me down roughly and dressed me. Tears rolled down my cheeks, but I was too weak to scream anymore. After Mamma had dressed me, Brian came over and put me in the back of the pickup truck with the canopy on it. I lay in the back as the truck bounced across ruts in the road on the way into town. My little sister tried to hug me. I think she sensed there was something very wrong with me. The pain was so great I could not breathe. I put a hand on my upper left rib cage. I believe I had three broken ribs. I was in terrible pain, and the motion of the truck was making it even worse. Eventually, I could not help but scream. Brian opened the divider between the cab and the back and told me to shut up, or he would come back there and give me something to scream about. Samantha put her chubby hand over my mouth, and I gritted my teeth and cried softly into her long, curly red hair.

When we got into town, Brian parked at the far end of a shopping area like he always did. He got out and came to the back of the truck; he told us not to make a sound. Then he and Mamma walked off into the store. They

16

usually came back hours later with groceries or tools or clothes. Sometimes they would return in the middle of the day to take us in to use the restroom, and then they would leave again, but most of the time my sister soiled herself and I would just hold it for hours on end. We sometimes had a couple of old dolls to play with, but we did not have many toys because they would make noise and someone might hear us.

Staying in the truck was better than the times we had to go with them. On the rare occasions that we got to come out of the back of the truck, Brian would make us carry a belt with us so that other people could see what bad children we were.

In the back of the truck, I would get up on my knees and stare out through the cracks in the canopy. I would see children walking by with their parents, little girls in pretty dresses, mothers laughing and hugging them, and I would imagine that I was them for a short while. But I was not; I was only a small girl with bright green eyes and dirty blonde hair. I was peeking out at the world from the back of a pickup truck. People passed by within a few feet of Samantha and I, yet they never knew we were there. We were two little girls that did not exist—two sad, frightened little girls at the mercy of two merciless individuals.

On this particular day, however, I could not move. I was in so much pain that I just lay there. Samantha sat next to me, whispering stories meant for her ears only. I listened as she made up her bizarre stories. Sometimes I got tired of hearing her whispering to herself, but on this day it was comforting. She played with my long, blonde hair as she whispered; when her voice got too loud, I put a finger to my lips to quiet her. Brian or Mamma would often stop by to see if we were talking or being too noisy. We could never be sure when they might show up, so we could never talk. As I lay gritting my teeth in pain, I could hear people talking in the distance. A tear rolled down my cheek. Why did Samantha and I matter so much less than other children?

THAT SUMMER slowly turned into winter. My ribs never healed quite right. It felt like they bunched together and became a small knot, and even to this day, when I am running, I still feel pain in that knot. As time progressed, Brian and Mamma became more and more irritated. It was 1988, and the gold mining industry was suddenly experiencing an upsurge of activists protesting in front of the mines and in the surrounding towns.

These people were against the use of dynamite because of how it disturbed the animal habitats. Due to this, Brian was finding it harder and harder to get mining permits from the state. His frustration was turned back on my sister and I in a big way. Sometimes we were left alone in the trailer and I would scrounge up something for us to eat from the ingredients in the cupboard.

One day in late spring, Mamma put a sucker in both of our flannel shirt pockets. This made me very happy, and my little sister clapped joyfully. We loved candy. However, Mamma said that she was testing our obedience and that if we did not open the suckers before she gave us permission, we could have them. We both nodded, fully intending not to disappoint Mamma. However, as the day dragged on we grew hungrier and hungrier. Many times my sister started to eat her sucker, but I put it back in her pocket.

After awhile, we both could not think of anything else. I hesitated for a moment, but then I unwrapped the suckers so we could each have just one lick. Afterward, I carefully put the suckers back in the wrappers, not realizing the wet suckers would stick to the plastic. Later when Mamma inspected the suckers she saw what we had done, she was furious and told us that we were possessed by the devil. Brian stormed over angrily and grabbed the suckers. I watched sorrowfully as he threw them out into the bushes, and I began to tremble as I watched Mamma coming back towards us with two switches.

She handed one to Brian. I felt ready to pass out because I was so scared. Little Samantha cried, and I closed my eyes as I felt the switch grab at my flesh. I was surprised to find that I felt strangely numb. *How much pain could a person take before she did not feel it anymore?* I wondered. I believe this was the day they lost the permits to Brian's mining company.

Shortly afterward, we began packing our things. We didn't have much, but these things were all we had. Brian set fire to the tools and the mine shaft so the man that took over the mine would have great difficulties. Brian said we were moving to Washington State to stay with his dad, who had a small shop there. My sister and I were excited. We felt we were beginning a new life and it might be better because we would no longer be so isolated. Brian bought a new trailer that was a little bigger, and we packed everything inside.

On the day before we were to leave, we came back to the trailer and found it had been broken into. Brian was very angry and grabbed his pistol out of the truck and ran up into the thick manzanita brush. He came back with a teenage boy. He had the gun pressed to the kids head. Brian yelled at the boy to tell him where our stuff was or he said he would kill him. I remember standing in front of them, frozen, unable to move, and thinking that if he shot and missed, I was in the direct line of fire. The teenager was screaming, "Don't shoot! Don't shoot! Your stuff is up in the brush."

Brian laughed and said, "I should just shoot you anyway."

Brian finally let the boy go, but he chased after him, firing the gun in the air. I will never forget that day. It is etched into my mind forever. I was so scared, Brian seemed so cold and dangerous.

We left a few hours later and hit the road for Washington State. Brian seemed to be in a lighter mood as we traveled, and he told us stories of growing up in the Evergreen State. It took us about three days to reach Seattle. Sometimes Samantha and I got to sit in the cab rather than the truck bed. I would stick my head out the window and feel the wind whip through my hair as I smelled the new scent of the ocean. Samantha and I pointed out exciting new sights to each other, although we were careful not to make a sound.

As we traveled during the day and camped by night, things seemed nicer. Mamma and Brian were preoccupied and did not feel the need to beat us so much. For those few days, I told myself that things might not be so bad and that everything was going to get better. Little did I know that a dark cloud was looming in front of me, the extent of which I could not possibly comprehend at so young an age. It was a dark and ominous cloud that threatened to totally engulf me, and when it did, it would not leave even a trace that I had ever existed.

ENGULFED BY A SHADOW

"The most terrible poverty is loneliness, and the feeling of being unloved."

-Mother Teresa

We arrived in Washington one sunny summer day in June. I was six and a half years old, and my sister would turn five in August. I felt like an animal let out of a cage. I was so excited to smell and hear the ocean. I dreamed that I would catch a baby seal and make it my pet—not very practical, but so it is with children. Our journey came to an end at Brian's dad's bicycle and locksmith shop in a little town not far from Seattle. It was a small shop that they had worked in together when Brian was a teenager. After Brian left, his father continued focusing most of his attention on the locksmith part of the business before eventually retiring. When we arrived, the lower part of the building was being rented out to small business tenants, and the upper level was where Grandpa lived.

As we drove up in the back alley behind the shop, I watched curiously as Grandpa came out to greet us. He was a kind, older gentleman and I was very surprised when I met him. I had expected an older version of Brian, but Grandpa was just the opposite. While Brian was loud, chubby and just plain mean most of the time, Grandpa was extremely gaunt and very quiet. He gave Samantha and me each a big hug. We instantly loved this seventy-seven-year-old man. Samantha and I each grabbed one of his hands and followed him upstairs.

The upstairs loft was quite spacious with two bedrooms, a living room, a kitchen and a large bathroom. We moved into the bedrooms, and Grandpa said he would sleep on a foldout bed in his living room.

That afternoon Brian's older sister came by to visit. She seemed angry that she had not seen Brian for nearly ten years. She was dressed in a suit and had short, stylish hair. She walked with an air of confidence, and I could feel that Brian resented her.

Aunty Laura owned a small, successful business just a few blocks away, and when I asked her if she could stop by every day and visit us, she laughed and said she would try. I was so excited that I clapped my hands happily, but when I turned around I saw my mother's angry face glaring at me. After aunt Laura left, Mamma and Brian cornered me in my new room and began slapping me and backing me into a corner.

"Don't you ever talk out of turn like that again!" Brian yelled at me. "In fact, do not talk to her at all! She is only here to see what kind of bad things she can find out about me through you girls."

I suddenly felt my heart sink—maybe there was no new life; maybe it was the same game with only a few extra innocent players. Mamma and Brian brought my sister into the room, sat us both down on the bed and began laying out the rules. We were not to make any noise when we were being punished, we were not to tell anyone when we had been punished, and we should always appear to be happy when we were around others. If we were caught pouting or complaining for any reason, we would be severely punished. We were also not to disturb Grandpa for any reason or go anywhere with him.

That was how our new life began. Brian joined the union and worked local construction jobs; Mamma stayed at home with us and took care of the house. Sometimes after the work was done we would walk to the park that was only a few blocks away. Samantha and I liked these outings but we were awkward around the other children and usually just played with each other. We would stay for about half an hour, then walk back to the apartment above the shop. I always dreaded it when I would see the shop in the distance. It was like a prison and my heart would always flip flop as my feet crossed the threshold. Sometimes I wondered if the other kids I saw at the park were so scared to go home. In the afternoons we were allowed to go outside and play in the alley behind the shop. We loved playing in the alley, it was a great place to escape. In the evening when Brian came home it was even worse. He always found a reason to beat us and they were never light beatings, he always used the full force of his strength.

They would still beat us without mercy or make us stand in the corner for more than eight hours at a time, but it was usually in their bedroom, out of sight. Since we were not allowed to cry when we were being belted or beaten with a stick grandpa usually did not know what was going on, but sometimes we could not help it and cried anyway. Grandpa sort of pretended he did not notice our tear streaked faces, but sometimes I could see a disturbed look on his face.

21

OVER THE summer aunty Laura popped in unexpectedly all the time; her cheery presence was like a ray of sunshine that lit up the dreary flat. Grandpa usually stayed in the living room, reading his vast selection of western novels and watching television. He was very nice to us, but eventually, he began to lose interest in talking to us since we only responded by nodding or shaking our heads.

As you might imagine, Aunty Laura and my mother did not like each other one bit. I believe Aunty Laura found my mother quite odd. Mamma had been raised in the Mississippi backwoods and was not as refined as Aunty Laura. My mother did have emerald green eyes, however, and was quite pretty when she was not angry or irritated. Unfortunately, that was not very often.

One day Aunty Laura popped in and asked Mamma if she was going to enroll me in school that year since I was nearly seven. Mamma shook her head and said that she and Brian believed schools were evil.

Aunty Laura stared at her blankly. "Well, then how is she going to learn anything?"

"I am teaching her," Mamma snapped back.

Aunty Laura shook her head. "What are you teaching her? You don't know anything."

From then on Mamma and Aunty Laura were sworn enemies, but Mamma started focusing more on teaching me to read. That is something for which I will always be grateful to my Aunty Laura, if she hadn't pushed my Mamma so hard, I might never have learned to read as well as I did. Soon I was borrowing books from Grandpa and losing my sad little self in the western novels and historical books that he collected. As I skipped over the big words, I would imagine myself as the hero in the book, and I could forget for an instant that I was once again imprisoned by two people whose only joy in life seemed to be to inflict pain on the people around them. I was being held hostage in front of people who could have saved me had they known, but they did not know, and I could not tell them because I feared for my life. My sister and I were captives in plain sight, yearning for a rescuer that would never come.

AFTER THE INCIDENT with Aunty Laura, Mamma went on a quest to prevent her from coming to Grandpas. She informed Aunty Laura that she would have to call before coming over and told her to quit bringing things for Samantha and me. Aunty Laura told Mamma that it was not her house, it was Grandpa's, and she was free to come over if she wished. In the end,

Grandpa asked Aunty Laura to comply for the sake of peace. After that, we only saw Aunty Laura and her very kind family about every two weeks at family events that Brian was obliged to attend.

Once Mamma eliminated Aunty Laura, she began gaining more and more control of Grandpa, who was now very sick with colon cancer. She began controlling what he ate and where he went. At first, he did not want to comply, but Mamma told him he would get sicker and would have to go to a nursing home if he did not follow her instructions.

As the summer progressed, Brian began to act even stranger than usual; he ordered a bunch of books on a group of people called the Amish. I remember looking at the pictures of the odd-looking people and thinking that they looked like the characters from Little House on the Prairie. In the mornings Mamma would let us go into her bedroom and watch the show. I liked the show, but I did not understand why Brian was getting books on the people who dressed like them.

One morning, as we were eating breakfast, Brian announced that we were going to become real God-fearing people and obey the Bible in its entirety. He had Mamma take Samantha and me to a local class on crocheting so we could learn something that would keep us busy...like good little Amish girls supposedly were. We learned how to crochet in just a couple of days. Our teacher said she believed I was very talented with crafts and that made me smile.

After we had learned to crochet, my mother took us to the local thrift store and started buying a bunch of dresses for us. We were not used to wearing dresses, or anything nice for that matter. Being the little girls that we were, we had fun twirling around in our new full-skirted dresses. A few days later, Brian came home with some plain, white muslin dinner napkins. Mamma tied them around our heads and put one on hers as well. Brian stepped back to look at us and smiled.

"Not quite Amish yet," he said, "but pretty close."

From that day on, he took up reading the Bible to us every morning before he left for work. I liked the stories and listened attentively to the ones about the kind man called Jesus. I wondered why Brian was not more like him, especially since Jesus was God's son and we were supposed to be following God's word to the fullest.

Aunty Laura seemed to be in shock over our new way of dressing and argued about it many times with her brother. He told her she belonged to the wicked world that he was no longer a part of. It was clear that he enjoyed being the most religious and pious member in his family now. At first, my sister and I hated wearing the veils. They were itchy, and we both thought they looked ridiculous, but whenever we took them off, we were severely beaten and had to listen to Mamma or Brian read scriptures to us.

We were also told that we would burn in hell for our evilness.

Now Brian and my mother had a new avenue to make us comply with their every demand. Any supposed mistake was punishable with severe beatings that were supposedly for the good of our souls. One such mistake would be talking to anyone other than Mamma and Brian. We hardly ever said a word. We spoke so little during our childhoods. We were like ghosts who people barely seemed to notice.

Even at the young age of six, I knew there was something not quite right about what they were preaching to us because it did not fit with the scriptures they were reading to us. The stories about a loving Jesus did not fit with the way they used their anger to torment my sister and I.

I fell in love with the Bible and truly wanted to be a good girl. However, this seemed impossible because, according to Brian and Mamma, I was one of the evilest little girls ever born.

THAT SUMMER, one monotonous day followed another. As the season came to a close, Brian announced that we were going back to Arizona for the winter because he was going to be able to reopen one of the mines. My heart sank all the way down to my toes. I looked over at Samantha and saw the same emotion mirrored back at me. We did not want to go back to live at the mine where we would be all by ourselves with Brian and Mamma.

In the middle of September, as the cooler weather filtered down from the mighty Cascade Mountain Range, we said goodbye to Grandpa and Aunty Laura and her family. We packed our things into the trailer that had been parked in back of the shop all summer and headed south. Grandpa seemed sad, yet relieved to see us go. Now that Mamma was gone, Aunty Laura would be able to visit him like she used to.

As we drove back to Arizona that September, we looked very different from the family who had driven north only a couple of months earlier. Now we were plain people, set apart from the rest of the world. It was very confusing for a little girl. I did not want to go to hell, so I knew I had better comply with all of Brian and Mamma's commands. Whenever I messed up, they loved telling me that Jesus did not want such bad little girls in heaven and if I died I would most certainly go to hell. This made me cry, and I would tell them I was sorry for messing up, but they only shook their heads at me.

Mamma and Brian took turns driving. Samantha and I were ordered to crochet during the entire trip and told that there would be no talking and no breaks. When we finished our skeins of yarn, we were to unravel what we had made and start over. Brian said that we were preparing to own a farm someday and that we had to know how to work hard, so we would start here.

One day I made the mistake of looking up to see what my sister was asking Mamma. Brian flipped out and pulled the truck over to the side of the road. He reached into the back of the car, yanked me out of my seat and switched me with a blackberry branch he had picked from the side of the road.

"You are so lazy and worthless," he yelled at me. "Just like an Indian squaw, that's all you are—a good-for-nothing Indian squaw."

I tried not to scream as I listened in bewilderment to what he was shouting at me. I looked in the truck and saw that Mamma was studying a map. She was completely unconcerned that Brian was making welts and scratches all over my small frame. My great-grandfather had been a Cherokee Indian, and for some reason,, Brian hated Native Americans. I don't know why he only taunted me about it, but he did. I always thought he hated me the most because of my scars from the dog bite, but they were fading now and hardly noticeable. My pale white skin and blondish-brown hair did not look very Indian, but one never knew where Brian was coming from.

We arrived in Arizona after about three days of driving. We parked our trailer in a vacant lot just outside of Prescott. Brian was going to be working a different mine and starting his own mining company. This time, he hired some guys to work for him and, much to my relief he was gone most of the day. My sister and I were mostly confined to the trailer, crocheting, and cleaning. Sometimes we were allowed to go outside and quietly play around the trailer or read books. We were very lonely and sad little girls. Even though we were used to it we did not understand why we had to be so isolated.

Mamma had purchased some homeschooling books and kept them in a cupboard in case anyone from the state was ever to ask us if we were being educated. A few times a week she would give me a couple of school books, and I would read the instructions, trying to figure out how to do the lessons. Sometimes I was successful in following the instructions, but other times I just could not figure them out at all, and I felt like I was dumb. I also learned to write on my own by trying to copy letters. I never learned the formula for where to start a letter and then end it. My writing was more like art; while it resembled the letters, it was the product of drawing parts of letters and bunching them together.

It was now the late 1980s, and I can remember that I wanted to learn, but it was so hard to teach myself. I dreamed of growing up to be a great and famous missionary doctor that would save the world and find a cure for AIDS like the missionaries in Africa that I had read about in a National

Geographic. Once I mentioned as much, and Mamma and Brian looked at me like I had lost my mind.

"You are so dumb you will never be able to do anything useful in your whole life even if you try," Brian laughed.

My chin quivered, and I lashed back at Brian. "You don't know that!" I screamed at him. "Just because I want to do something useful and kind in life does not make me dumb."

Brian's mouth fell open for a moment, and then he slapped me so hard I flew backward against the wall. My small, seven-year-old frame was no match for that of a weathered miner, but I did not regret my words. The next day I was confined to the back of the trailer and only given bathroom privileges. I was told to stand in the corner and reflect on my rebellion, and that when I repented, I would be let go. I stood there for about twelve hours. Brian would come up behind me every so often and switch me and ask me if I felt so smart now. At the end of the day I passed out, no longer able to stand due to exhaustion and dehydration. Mamma put me in bed and I ran a fever for a couple of days. Eventually, the incident seemed to blow over, but Brian forever felt that I thought I was better than the rest of the family, and he took every opportunity to put me down and ridicule me.

FALL BLURRED into winter. My sister and I spent the days crocheting, looking at books or outside playing quietly around the trailer. Mamma began to get worried about getting in trouble with the government for not sending us to school, she collected welfare and food stamps for us children and was afraid someone might start asking us questions. Brian informed my sister and I that when he met Mamma she told him that she had no children and did not want to get us at all; but Brian found out about us and pressed her until she agreed to take us. Mamma and Brian did not get married. That way Mamma could collect our checks as well as get one for herself, claiming mental disability and citing Brian as her landlord.

Mamma finally got nervous that the state would notice I was not in school, and she ended up enrolling me. I was not used to being around other children, so I usually stayed at my desk. I could read better than the other first graders, but I was seriously behind in everything else and I looked very strange. Mamma had me wear normal clothes to school, but it was not long before the teachers asked to meet with Mamma and Brian to talk about my strange behavior. The teachers seemed bewildered when I did not race out to play like the other children, and I took little interest in playing or coloring. These were things I was not used to, and whenever I had wanted to play before, I was punished. I was just plain scared of everything and everybody and would shy away from the teacher when she tried to hug me. Needless to say, Brian got nervous about all the questions, so my time in school only lasted a couple of weeks.

Brian laughed at me and shook his head, telling me I was one dumb kid. It made me sad, but I did not know how to interact with anyone since I was not allowed to talk or have any kind of conversation at all. We were not allowed to play with other children, so when I was at school, all I did was sit at my desk. I felt self-conscious because I was so far behind the other first graders...I got most of the answers wrong. Unfortunately, all of my many bruises were well-hidden under my clothing, so no one ever saw them.

THAT FALL and winter my sister and I were allowed to go more places with Mamma and Brian because they were afraid we would be discovered if we were left in the truck and made noise. We were still not allowed to talk unless we raised our hands and were made to carry a belt with us wherever we went. My sister and I would take turns carrying the belt and pretending it was a toy to save ourselves from embarrassment. The reason no one ever called the authorities was probably because we were dressed so differently.

Wherever we went, people would ask us if we were Amish. Brian would proudly say that we were Amish-Mennonite because we drove a car but were pretty much the same as the Amish. On the occasions when Brian and Mamma would leave us by ourselves, Brian would place a tape recorder next to us and tell us that if we would so much as moved, he would know it and we would be in trouble. My sister and I developed other ways to communicate with each other; we had our own sign language, and we would sniffle and click between our teeth. One sniffle meant Brian was coming; two meant they were both coming, and three rapid ones meant they were in a bad mood and to look out.

When spring came, we traveled back to Seattle, and Brian took up construction again. We lived in various trailer parks and camping grounds in the area. I loved Washington State. It was so green and alive with wildlife and friendly people. It was an adventure when we traipsed through the surrounding thick forest and bushes every day.

Brian and Mamma both liked to fish and sometimes we would go to desolate beach areas for the weekend. Even though these places were more secluded, things were not quite as bad as the rest of the time. I think the fishing somehow relaxed them and they did not seem quite so hell bent on beating us. Samantha and I would walk around the beach when we were let out of the trailer. But we could never relax or be truly happy. We were still plagued by the no talking rule and most of the time we would quietly play in the waves or pick up sea shells. My stomach would be knots, as I waited for one of us to unknowingly make a mistake. Even though the no talking rule had been in place for years, we would still forget to raise our hands for permission to speak sometimes. I would feel so sad as I listened to Samantha's screams.

While Brian worked construction, Mamma would take care of the trailer, and she took cooking and canning lessons in town. Samantha and I were kept busy cleaning the trailer and crocheting and in the afternoon we were allowed to go outside and play in the thick woods. Most days of the week I would do a few pages from the homeschooling books. I had no order in how I did this and Mamma had not interest in teaching except when she was teaching Samantha to read. Most of the time I would only do one page of a lesson thinking that is how it was supposed to be done and since I did not really have a teacher most of my answers were wrong. Thus my progress was slow and almost non existent. I still continued to the next page though and did my best to figure out what I was supposed to do. Sometimes Brian would take an interest and look to see what I had done over the week. It was never much but since most of it was wrong he would yell at me and hit me on the head, then he would attempt to teach me just to show me how dumb I was. I never learned much from him though because I was so afraid of him.

The thing I hated most about this particular summer was that Brian made me his personal assistant. Every day when he came home I had to run to the front door, open it for him, take his lunch box and hard hat, and then take off his boots and socks. While he took a shower, I had to polish his boots for the next day. When he got out of the shower, he would inspect his boots. I would stand nearby with a knot in my stomach; if he found even one spot on the boots, he would sometimes rub my face on them and beat me with them. After the boot inspection, I would be forced to give him a full body massage. He would lay down and I would massage him from head to toe. My seven-year-old hands would tremble, I despised him so much, and I hated having to touch him. This ritual took about an hour. While Mamma prepared dinner, I would be on the bed at the back of the trailer with Brian, biting back tears of fear and trying to keep as far away from as possible so he could not fondle me.

My life was very sad at this point, but looking back, it is amazing to realize what a resilient spirit a child can have. When I was not being bothered by Mamma or Brian, I would dream of the future. In my dreams, I was always a missionary doctor that brought love and medical care to children all over the world. These were wonderful dreams that kept me going day after day.

Samantha still told herself stories and they seemed to calm her nerves. I often felt sorry for her because she was younger and much more babyish than I had ever been. I also worried because she had suffered terrible abuse as a toddler when she was being potty trained. I don't think she was much different than any other child her age but starting around age two Mamma and Brian had been convinced that she should have already been using the toilet by herself. As a result they did not put diapers on her when we were at home and whenever she would soil herself they would strip her naked a few feet from the creek and spank her little bottom with a stick as she ran towards the water. It was horrible and I would cry, even though I was only a little girl I knew this was wrong and sometimes I felt to vomit. This continued for about a year until Samantha was three.

LATER THAT summer, Samantha and I were allowed to spend a good part of our days in the bushes, picking huckleberries and blackberries. Although it was hot and we got into trouble if we did not pick enough berries, these outings got us away from Mamma and Brian. Mamma learned how to can in mason jars and made many jars of preserves as well as homemade bread and other baked goods. Brian believed we should follow Amish customs as much as possible, so we were truly living like the Amish in a trailer park.

Upon writing letters to Amish communities, Brian was informed that since he and Mamma were divorced they would never be allowed to fully join any Amish community. However, the Amish welcomed correspondence with people who wished to live a Plain lifestyle, and he was told he could get guidance from a bishop in Pennsylvania. The Bishop wrote Brian and told him he would not mentor him until we began conforming to full Amish dress code. He sent Brian the name of an Amish company that made things for 'plain people'. Brian happily ordered dresses, head coverings, aprons, shirts and broadfall trousers.

When the clothes arrived, my sister and I stared with dismay at the plain blue dresses and the uncomfortable-looking aprons and head coverings, but it did not take long before we got used to the uniform. Brian constantly admonished us on how utterly evil and prideful it was to have any form of print on our clothes. Mamma started taking sewing lessons again and was learning to make dresses and other items of clothing. Slowly but surely, Mamma and Brian were building an unbreakable barrier between us and the outsiders, a barrier few people would be willing to cross in order to save Samantha and me. I am sure there were people who had some idea how badly Samantha and I were being treated, but everyone looked the other way, all in the name of religious freedom.

We saw Aunty Laura and Grandpa that summer, but not very often. They were taken aback by our appearance, and they were embarrassed to go anywhere with us since people were constantly asking us if we were Amish. Grandpa was on the road to recovery after winning his battle with colon cancer, but he was still very weak and did not get out much.

When September came around, we pulled up stakes once again and headed south to Prescott. Brian looked after his mining operations, and I resumed the same routine whenever he came home. Many times I would pretend to be sick, but to no avail; he would tell me that good Amish women performed their duties whether they were sick or not. Brian felt that even though I was only eight, I was soon going to be a woman and should learn how to act like one. I learned to make bread, cook and clean the kitchen and was soon the main cook and baker in the house. My sister helped while Mamma oversaw us, beating us with the belt whenever we dropped something or made a mistake. A lot of times Mamma was worse than Brian. She would laugh fiendishly as she lashed the belt across our small frames. Sadly, the only times she gave us hugs or showed any affection at all was when other people were around to see.

One day while we were in Prescott, we saw some people dressed like us. I remember being surprised because we never saw people like us. Brian went over immediately and started talking to the man of the family, who seemed just as surprised to see us as we were to see him. There was the father, whose name was Gary, the mother, and their two daughters, who appeared to be in their early twenties. Brian found out that they, like us, had recently converted to the 'plain' lifestyle. The women said they would teach Mamma how to sew plain clothing, and they invited us to go to dinner at their house that evening. When we got to their place, we saw an old school bus stuffed full of all kinds of food and clothing parked in their front yard. When Brian asked what it was for, Gary informed him that they were hiding out because the government was after them. He did not mind sharing this with Brian because he knew Brian was also against the government.

I liked the daughters. They were very nice to Samantha and I. I especially liked the fact that Mamma did not beat me when we were at their house, and I always felt a little sleepy when I was there because I found myself relaxing. Mamma and I learned to sew from the girls and soon we were making our own plain clothing.

Only a few weeks after they met, trouble began to brew amongst the adults. Brian and Gary both wanted to be the leader of the group. Gary thought Brian should pay one-tenth of his income to him and that he should try to recruit new members, while Brian thought he should be the leader since he was older. Needless to say, they could not work things out, and we split company. One day before we parted ways, Mamma and I went to get some fabric from one of the bedrooms. As we entered, we noticed that one of the closet doors was open. I saw some hair sticking out from under the closet door and pulled on it; to my surprise, I found myself holding a blonde wig. I looked at it curiously while Mamma opened the large side door. My mouth fell open—there in front of us were a bunch of guns. Along the bottom of the closet, there were several boxes filled with

30

wigs, makeup and many different styles of clothes. Mamma quickly closed the closet and went to tell Brian that she had a headache and wanted to go home. The next day, Brian confronted them, and they argued for a while, and then we left. The next day when we drove by, they were gone, with their school bus full of supplies. Many times over the years I have wondered who they really were, but I suppose I will never know.

THE NEXT summer we went back to Washington just like the summer before...with the same routines and harrowing nightmares; so went the next summer as well. Brian loved shaming me by saying the only future he saw for me was as a prostitute. He told Mamma that I would try to seduce him all the time, and Mamma hated me for it. At eight and nine years old, I did not even fully understand what seducing was, but I still tried not to do it.

The winter I turned ten, we got a motor home and Brian officially quit the mining business. He could no longer get permits, and there were way too many people protesting mining in Arizona for him to try to continue. With some of the profits he made from selling the mine to a larger corporation, he bought woodworking tools and extra sewing machines. That summer we set up shop in the local trailer parks and began making things to sell. Mamma would sew Amish dolls while Samantha and I would sit for hours in the back of the motor home, stuffing the doll parts with cedar sawdust. We would work for eight to ten hours straight, stuffing and sewing doll parts. Mamma would sew the doll clothes for a while and then sit outside to sell them wherever we happened to be parked. These items sold pretty well, and due to this new found success, Samantha and I became a very valuable source of income. We never were given lunch breaks and rarely stepped outside of the motor home. I was still plagued with headaches, and the constant smell of cedar sawdust made them worse. Also the little school work we had been doing stopped. I had completed the second grade math book by this time and was attempting to start the third grade one, but because of my poor foundation I was not learning much.

Mamma put a divider up between the back and the front of the motor home. Samantha was sensitive to the heat, and on the very warm days the sweat would run down her face and become mixed with the fine sawdust that covered us. She would often cry for food since she was both anemic and had low blood sugar. We were not allowed out of the back until we had stuffed however many doll parts were needed. Sometimes I would watch Samantha as she ate the sawdust, she said it did not taste that bad. I would tell her that it was loaded with chemicals but she continued to eat it anyway.

And so the summers went, one exhausting day after the other. Mamma and Brian became our overseers while my sister and I did almost all of the work. They set time limits on how long it should take to do the dishes, sweep the floor, and make dinner. After we had stuffed a certain number of doll parts, we had to sew them together, cut out their clothes, and finally, we had to dress them. If we did not meet these outrageous deadlines we were beaten, often as many as three times a day. Brian's favorite way of punishing us was to pull down our underwear, and then while we bent over he would beat us so hard, we developed large blisters. That summer I reached puberty, and the shame he inflicted on me for that was despicable even for someone of his character.

During the evenings and on Sundays we would sometimes play checkers and other board games. Brian said he had played these as a kid and they seemed to make him sort of happy. Sometimes we would even have popcorn and Mamma would play too. Samantha and I would try to be happy, these were the most confusing of times. These people that kept us isolated from the world and beat us terribly would sometimes try and pretend that we were all normal and that we could have fun together. Samantha and I loved to play games and we would smile. Mamma and Brian would appear to be somewhat happy, and then, less than an hour later they would find some reason to beat us without mercy.

AT SUMMER'S end, we again headed back to Arizona, selling our wares as we traveled: Amish dolls, Brian's music boxes, cookbooks and so on. The daily rituals still took place every day. I still had to take off Brian's shoes, polish them and massage him. And the days dragged on, one after the other. Sometimes other camping families would visit us. Samantha and I were always happy when other people would stop by and sometimes we would walk over to their camps. There were other children in these camps and the people were really friendly and wanted us to be part of their camping community. Being the anti social type that he was Brian would periodically get irritated with the other campers and move us out in the middle of the desert for a week or so at a time.

A few other times we attended a Mennonite church. I think Brian liked the idea of walking into the church dressed Amish. It made him feel superior to the Mennonites and he would always argue with the men on how *worldly* their dress code was. I wished with all my heart that we could have stayed there or been more like them. Everyone there was very nice and friendly and often tried to ask Samantha and me questions, but we were not allowed to talk very much and after only a few weeks Brian got in an argument with the pastor and we were asked to never come back.

ONE DAY after dinner, Brian said we would all walk to the gas station to get milk. We were parked in a trailer park not far from Phoenix at the time. I remember thinking it was rather odd that we were all going to walk to the gas station together. Mamma and Samantha and I walked on ahead while Brian stayed back. Something was definitely amiss because when Brian caught up to us, he told us to hurry. About half an hour later, when we arrived back at the motor home, flames were leaping out of the windows, and the fire department was there. We lost everything in that fire except a few books and some clothes that were in the closets. Brian seemed happy, though. Not long after the fire we found out that we were being let out of the payments for the motor home and that the insurance would pay for everything we lost.

After the fire, Mamma contacted the Red Cross and they helped us out with food and clothing vouchers. Brian bought two large tents, and they became our new home. He also got a truck and sewing machines, and we started our business up again from the tents.

That March we headed back to Washington, where Brian and Mamma planned to buy a farm with the money they got from the insurance. Again, my life was taking a drastic turn. But as you will see, no matter how tragic the circumstances, with a little faith and perseverance anything is possible.

FORGOTTEN *BY THE* WORLD

"People speak sometimes about the 'bestial' cruelty of man, but that is terribly unjust and offensive to beasts, no animal could ever be so cruel as a man, so artfully, so artistically cruel."

— Fyodor Dostoyevsky

In March, we drove back to Washington State with the intent to buy land and start a farm. We packed the tents, the sewing machines and the rest of our belongings into a small hauling trailer Brian had bought, then we hit the freeway for the trek north. It was early spring, so we ran into some bad weather; it took us about five days to reach Bellingham, Washington. Once we arrived, Brian and Mamma went out with several real estate agents to look at land while Samantha and I shivered in the truck.

At that time land was very expensive, even the land in the middle of nowhere, due to the large number of dairy farmers in the area and the booming economy. One day Brian came across an ad in the paper; a local man was selling some land across the Cascade Mountains in eastern Washington. The land was located about forty minutes north of Omak, Washington. We drove across the mountains to see it. The property was nestled on a mountainside six miles outside of a small town with a population of only sixteen hundred people.

It was April now, but there were still snow flurries here and there, and the majestic mountains were capped with glistening crowns of snow. I sat in the truck with Samantha while Mamma and Brian went in to see the real estate agent. As I sat there, I saw ranchers and farmers walking by, and I was intrigued when I realized that we were in cowboy country. I thought to myself that this might actually be fun. Oh, for the innocence of childhood, unable to foresee the lurking danger ahead. With a hopeful, heart I would tell myself everything was going to be okay now. It never was of course, but in these situations one must hope or let their soul die, and I preferred the former.

We drove the six miles up the mountain on a dirt road. Along the way, we crossed over many cattle guards that prevented the cattle from walking down the road into town. The real estate agent explained to us that this area of Washington had a lot of what they called "open range," a term used by ranchers that let their cattle roam freely across the mountains. As we approached the six-mile mark, we suddenly veered off the county road and drove half a mile straight up the mountainside on a very rutted and muddy path.

"Just so you know," the cheery real estate woman told us, "in the winter the county does not plow this small section because it is a private road. The people who live up here mostly use tire chains and a prayer to get up the mountain in the winter."

"We have neighbors up here?" Brian asked with a frown.

The real estate agent smiled and nodded. "Oh, don't worry; you are not all alone up here. About two and a half miles up that way live the Farrows and about two miles beyond them live the Hawthorns. And," she carried on, "if you follow the county road a couple more miles up, there are a few more people scattered around."

I saw that Brian was not too happy at that news, and his forehead was furrowed in a frown as we drove up the steep road. Soon we arrived at what appeared to be a driveway leading to a huge parcel of land.

"Well, here it is—sixty acres of good quality ranch land," The real estate agent said as she flashed her big smile in Brian's direction.

I looked around at the acres of desolate, sagebrush-filled terrain. A few of the free-range cows she'd mentioned were munching grass in the distance, and two huge cottonwood trees swayed gently in the spring air. There were some flat areas, but the landscape was mostly made up of one hill after another. Mamma and Brian talked a lot, and my sister and I walked around a little. We discovered a creek across the road that was lined with tall aspen trees and green moss. We got back to the car just in time to hear Brian tell the agent that they wanted the land if they could agree on a price.

For a moment, my heart stopped. The land was beautiful, but it was in the middle of nowhere. There were no sounds from any other people; the quiet was only interrupted by the occasional cow mooing in the distance or the call of one bird to another. I remembered the Arizona mine and shuddered. I looked over at Samantha, and although we were not allowed to speak, I could see the same look of sheer terror in her eyes. What would happen to us here?

AFTER NEGOTIATING an agreeable payment plan with the owners, we moved up on the mountain. Even though Samantha and I had great misgivings about moving there, we were looking forward to not being cooped up in the truck and the tents so much; and Brian and Mamma would not have to worry about the people around us asking questions as to why we were not in school. As soon as we knew we were going to move, Mamma registered with the state to receive her disability, food stamps and the checks for Samantha and me. She registered in a different county 150 miles south in Wenatchee, Washington, and gave a fake address that was supposedly in that same county. How she never got caught is a mystery to me, but her scheme of listing Brian as her landlord and our bills as solely her own seemed to be working. When she had to go into the government office, she would change out of her Amish clothes and put on normal clothes.

Brian, too, was in hiding from the state. When he was in his late twenties, he had had charges filed against him for molesting a neighbor's eight-year-old daughter. When he got wind of the charges, he fled to Alaska for a couple of years. After that, he came back down to Arizona and started mining in the mountains. There, he married his second wife and had three children with her while living in a cabin deep in the Bradshaw Mountains. Eight years later, she fled the mountains to her parents' home in Phoenix, where she pressed charges against Brian for battery. She dropped the charges during the divorce when Brian agreed to give her full custody of the children with no contest.

After that, Brian kept a low profile in order to avoid paying child support; he had accumulated eight years of back payments. Every year when he filed taxes, his refund was taken by the IRS and given to his ex-wife. This made him very angry, and many times he muttered that he should have killed her when he had the chance. Now that we lived on the mountain, not even Aunty Laura or Grandpa knew where we were because Brian was afraid they might mention our location to his ex-wife.

The mountain was on the outskirts of a tiny ranch town, only three miles from the Canadian border. This proved to be the perfect place for Brian and Mamma to wallow in their paranoia about the evil government, while practicing their religious beliefs and torturing my sister and me.

The land had a small, flat area that was about an acre in size, and Brian said that was where we would build the house. In order to do so, we had to first clear away the sagebrush. In the meantime, we pitched our two big tents in the ravine, which looked like it had been a lake at one time but was now filled with tall grass and timothy hay. The giant cottonwood tree offered shade, and at night I could hear it swaying in the strong mountain wind that whistled through the trees on its way down one hill and up another. The winds would bring with them the call of one coyote to another and sometimes I would hear the distant scream of a panther. I would shiver on the blanket that was my bed and dream I was a little coyote romping around in the forest. That was much more fun than being me.

After we had pitched the tents, Brian announced that we would need a lot of money if we were going to try to build any sort of structure before winter set in. I shivered at the thought of winter; we would have to build a shelter or we would literally freeze to death. The winters on the mountain could range anywhere from zero degrees Fahrenheit to thirty degrees below zero. We learned this from an old, weathered rancher. He looked at my sister and I and shook his head.

"I remember tell of a family that lived up in these here mountains a few years back," He rattled in his mountaineer's way of talking. "One morning when the Mom and Pops went to wake their children who slept in the attic, they found the youngest, who was three, frozen to death and the five-year-old nearly frozen to death. Yep," He said, nodding his head, "you better not mess with these here mountains unless you know what you are doing, 'cause they seem beautiful, but I can tell ya, they show mercy for no man."

Brian informed the kind old rancher that he had lived in the Bradshaw Mountains of Arizona for many years. The rancher smiled and shook his head once again.

"Night and day, I tell ya, night and day. Be a shame for something happen to these pretty little girls," he said as he patted our heads.

I smiled up at him and looked into his leathery face, surprised to find bright blue eyes smiling back at me.

"Well, just warning you is all," he got back in his beat-up pickup truck. "I got to go check on some cattle on the back forty, heard tell there is a bobcat coming down and making some trouble with the newborn calves. You all be careful, and I will be seeing you around, I suppose,"He tipped his cowboy hat and drove away.

I shivered as I thought of the little kid who had frozen to death—how awful. Brian turned and looked at us angrily.

"I don't want you two talking or waving to that guy. You hear me? If you see his truck or any other truck coming, I want you to duck behind a bush. You hear me? I don't want anyone seeing you two, ever."

Samantha and I nodded silently. Of course; what else did we expect?

After the rancher left, Brian was very agitated. Samantha and I got nervous and began crocheting in the tent. We'd only been at it a few minutes when Brian stormed in and started screaming.

"Oh no you don't; you are on a farm now. No sitting around playing with yarn and such. I will expect a full day's work out of both of you."

Samantha and I looked at each other, not knowing exactly what we were supposed to be doing.

"Um... Sorry, Dad," My voice shook. "We do not know what you want us to do."

"Did I give you permission to speak?" Brian yelled as he started shaking me.

My head snapped back and forth, and my migraine suddenly exploded in my head.

"Don't you ever smart mouth me or speak out of turn again." He kept shaking me as hard as he could. "You hear, miss smarty pants? There is no one in this entire world that would miss you if I chopped off both of your heads right now and buried you under that tree over there." He threw me down on my blanket and then yanked me to my feet again.

"That's right," he whispered in my ear. "No one would know." He smiled down at me. "We could keep collecting checks; tell whoever asked where you were that you were at your grandparents." He paused to let the severity of what he was saying sink in. "But," he continued, "Who would even ask about you?"

I looked up at him, terrified, as he threw me back down on the floor of the tent. I quickly scrambled to my feet and went over to hug nine-year-old Samantha, who had started crying. As I tried to cover her ears, I saw Mamma laughing in the doorway.

"Come on, Brian," she laughed. "Quit scaring them and get them busy out here."

I did not cry. I glared back at Brian. I was so enraged, and not because he was threatening me, but because he had frightened my little sister so badly that she was trembling from head to foot. *How dare he?* I thought, my indignation boiling. Brian held my gaze for a moment, but I did not back down, almost daring him to do something. Surprisingly, he looked away and left the tent. I soon followed and vomited behind some sagebrush. My head hurt so badly, and I felt so dizzy I could hardly stand. I tried to see where Mamma and Brian were, but every time I looked up my head pulsed, and I saw three of everything. Head spinning, I walked back into the tent and passed out.

38

I was awakened a few hours later as Samantha shook me. I jumped up, afraid that it was Brian.

"Don't worry," Samantha was smiling. "Mamma and Brian went into town for tools. It takes about a half-hour there and a half-hour back on this dirt road, plus the time they'll be at the feed store, so we have about an hour and a half before they get back."

I stood up slowly. I felt better, although my head was still pounding. There had been something not quite right with my head ever since I was attacked by the dog, and whenever I tried to run, I could hear loud popping noises in my head. When Brian shook me and threw me into walls, the pops were even louder. I tried to shake the dizziness off, as I looked out the tent door. It was a beautiful, sunny day, and for the first time in a long time there were no tape recorders or adults to catch us talking.

"Come on," Samantha urged. "Let's look around."

We went for a walk around the ravine, looking at insects and birds that flew around, and we even tried to get close enough to pet a new calf that was standing with its mother. The mother would not let us get close, but she kept leading us farther and farther away from the tent. After a while, I told Samantha that we had better get back to the tents before Brian and Mamma got home. We hurried back and dove into the tent just as we heard the truck coming up the drive.

Brian and Mamma got out and pulled shovels, picks, and rope out of the truck.

"Here we go," Brian said as he started pulling things out of the truck bed. "We got a generator too, so we can start making things to sell again."

Samantha and I ran over to carry the new items into the tents. After we were done, we stood in front of the tent door, not knowing what we were supposed to do next. Brian came out of his tent, looking at a lumber catalog.

"You girls are going to start pulling sagebrush to clear a place for the house," He walked over to us, his face was stern. We walked to the clearing. "Here." He handed me a pick. "You grab them at the roots and bend them over, and then you start picking at them with this pick until they come loose, and you can pull them out."

I took the pick in both hands. My slight, eleven-year-old frame complained that it was too heavy, and I could see that Samantha's did as well. We each started picking at the roots of a sagebrush until Samantha sniffled once to let me know Brian was out of earshot.

"This is going to take months," I whispered to her.

39

"My arm hurts," she whispered back.

I nodded in agreement and then turned my attention back to the stubborn sagebrush bush as Samantha sniffled to let me know that Brian was sneaking up on us. He came to see what progress we had made in the last ten minutes—we had not even pulled one bush yet. We started pulling frantically, but the roots were stubborn and would not give.

"Okay, you two," Brian barked angrily, "you better step it up or you will be out here all night, and one of those bobcats might come down and pay you a visit!"

He went back to the tent, and Samantha and I watched tearfully as Mamma handed him a sandwich. I could hear Samantha's stomach growling, and I knew that she was suffering more than I was because of her low blood sugar and anemia.

"What if they do come and eat us tonight?" Samantha asked me frantically.

I smiled and shook my head. "Old Brian is full of it," I whispered. "All the westerns I have read say that wild animals are afraid of humans and only attack if they are cornered."

"Oh, okay." Samantha nodded, reassured.

I, of course, did not tell her about the stories of Panthers jumping out of trees and attacking cowboys and Indians. I often hoped that Brian and Mamma might happen upon said Panther, but then I felt bad for thinking it.

As dusk fell, Brian came out and said we could come in for the night. We had only cleared about five square feet but could do no more. Mamma gave us some soup, and we collapsed on our blankets and fell asleep to the lonely howl of coyotes that seemed to say, "You are all alone, so very alone...and defenseless."

THE NEXT morning, Samantha and I were awakened early by Brian, who told us to hurry and get some breakfast and then follow him. We did so as fast as we could; he led us back to the clearing to work on the sagebrush again. Brian informed us that we would work on the sagebrush until noon and then start making dolls to sell in Wenatchee during the afternoon.

Our muscles were still sore, and our hands were blistered from the work we had done the day before. Samantha started to cry saying that her back hurt. I tried to keep her quiet, but she was in a lot of pain. Brian came over and told her he was not going to have any slouches on his farm, and that she had better shape up, or he would show her what pain was. She ran over to me for protection, but I was in so much pain myself that I just told her to stop crying before we got in serious trouble. I told her to just pretend she was working and not use the pick. She obeyed, and I tried to work double time so Brian would not notice that Samantha was hardly doing anything.

Mamma did not help much. She mostly stayed in the tents, cooking and reading books on preserving foods. Brian would help us for a while, then go look at catalogs and take a nap. When he came back to work, he cheated by tying a rope around the bushes and pulling them out with the truck. Samantha and I watched jealously. It only took him a couple of minutes to pull a bush out with the truck, but it took us nearly eight minutes to do it by hand.

At noon, we trekked back to the tents to start working on the doll parts. Brian worked on making music boxes after he ate lunch. I will never know why we were not allowed to eat lunch since it would have enhanced our productivity, but we were not allowed any breaks during the day. Brian believed we had to learn to work hard, and he did not want us to be lazy.

The next couple of weeks passed with each day much like any other. Even when the spring rains came to the mountains and left Samantha and I soaked to the skin, we pulled up the sagebrush, while Brian and Mamma sat in the tent discussing plans or arguing—the latter of which they seemed to be doing all the time. Samantha and I often felt feverish at night, but Brian would tell us to quit faking it, and Mamma, as always, seemed indifferent to us.

It took us nearly two weeks to clear a big chunk of land, fifty feet wide by fifty feet long. While we were working, Samantha and I stumbled upon an old piece of cement that was sticking up from the ground. It turned out to be part of the basement to a house that belonged to a family that had lived on the land in the thirties. We were excited with our find, and ran down the cement steps into the tiny underground room which was only ten feet by ten feet. Of course, there was no hidden treasure, but it was still fun to see how old it looked. We did find a few mason jars of canned plums that still had their seal. Brian seemed pleased with our find and even let us eat the plums. To my surprise, they were absolutely delicious, even though they had been there, at least, sixty years.

Brian decided that we would build a small building on top of the basement and stay the winter there. However, lumber was expensive, so we would have to sell a lot of our crafts in town in order to buy the needed supplies. I remembered what the old rancher had said about the upcoming winter. If he was right, we only had four or five months before Jack Frost would return to visit the mountainside.

It was now May, and the mountains were beautiful with a rainbow of different colored wildflowers smiling out at us from every corner. They nodded their pretty heads cheerily in the warm spring air and brought a smile to my otherwise sad face. Along the county road, wild cherries were blossoming, and there were miles of apple, cherry, and peach orchards down in the valleys. All the way to Wenatchee, all you could see was orchard after orchard. When they were all in bloom, it was a masterpiece to behold. Springtime made everything look alive and beautiful, but there also seemed to be an air of urgency to prepare for the oncoming cold that would kill every form of life if it were given half a chance.

*T*HAT FIRST week of May, we loaded our wares into the truck and headed to Wenatchee to pick up Mamma's government checks. They did not come to the post office in our little town because the post office box had to be in the same city as her fake address. Every month, Mamma and Brian made this trip to pick up the checks and food stamps. Since Mamma did not have a job and the government did not know she was making money on the side with crafts, we qualified for virtually all kinds of government aid.

Just a few miles outside of Wenatchee, Brian and Mamma set up our table with Amish dolls, Amish cookbooks, and Brian's music boxes. A lot of people set up stands to sell their vegetables, so Mamma thought it might work to sell our items. Mamma put two chairs on either end of the table and told Samantha and I to sit there and try to sell something whenever someone came by. I was very nervous about talking to the customers because Brian had placed the small tape recorder under the table so he could hear what we said. I hated that infernal tape recorder; it seemed follow us everywhere.

After admonishing Samantha and me not to leave the table, Brian and Mamma went into town to take care of business. Samantha and I sat there along the freeway with our sun bonnets on, watching the cars go by and hoping someone would buy something so we would not get in trouble. Our prayers were answered, and many cars stopped, but most people just wanted to stare at us. A lot of people seemed shocked to discover that we were children, and when they asked where our mother was, we said that she had gone to buy some water.

We were selling the cookbooks for $15, dolls for $60 and the music boxes for $35. A lot of people said they collected unique things, and that our crafts would look nice in their houses. Samantha and I always got nervous when people stood around asking us questions such as where we lived, where we went to school, what grade we were in and so on. I often inadvertently glanced at the tape recorder that was whirling away under the table and just smiled at the questions. Why no one ever called the police, I will never know.

We did pretty well that day, and sold more than half of our items. Samantha and I were pleased with ourselves, and we did hand signals back and forth and pretended that we would run away with the money, but we didn't.

When Mamma and Brian came to pick us up, they were arguing, as usual. Brian grabbed the money box from me. He counted the money and said that it was not going to be enough for all the lumber we needed, but we went back into the city and bought a bunch of 2 x 4s to start building the frame for the shelter. Brian said we would have to make money faster in order to get the building finished because lumber was so expensive.

Samantha and I lay on top of the wood as we bounced our way home. It took about three hours to get from Wenatchee to our small town, and my sister and I were grateful that we did not have to crochet or work as we were gently rocked to sleep on our stacked lumber beds.

The next morning, Brian announced that we were going to go across the Cascade Mountains to the animal auction in Bellevue, Washington. He said we were going to buy pregnant goats very cheaply and then when the babies were a few months old, we would sell them to the orchard workers.

The following Tuesday found us at the auction, staring at rows of goats, cows, pigs and horses. I discovered that the baby goats were very playful and I wanted all of them, but Brian said that we had to be smart with our money and buy two for the price of one.

That day was sort of nice. Samantha and I petted and played with the animals as we walked past their pens, but we were always careful to follow Mamma and Brian and never do anything to upset them. It was so strange, their moods. Sometimes they almost acted sort of normal; For all appearances we were an Amish family at the auction looking for animals. Samantha and I would try and let ourselves be happy. At least this was something, at least we were out among people for awhile. Mamma and Brian liked the prospect of raising the animals and making money and were sometimes in a better mood. But we could never be sure how long these episodes would last and would always brace ourselves for the next blow, that would never fail to come.

We went home that day with four goats, two very pregnant ones and two small goats that were deformed but sweet-tempered. The little goats turned out to be three-month-old twins. They were not able to stand on their front hooves, so they walked on the sides of their legs instead. When Brian saw them, he said that they would make the same amount of meat as any of the others, and we bought them for next to nothing. Samantha and I played with them all the way home and squealed with happiness when they curled up in our laps for a nap.

Brian was sometimes nice to animals and other times unbelievably cruel. He and Mamma were both like that. I am so haunted by the cruel things I witnessed them doing to animals throughout my childhood. I have chosen to omit most of those instances. They are just to awful and haunting. I do not know how they could be nice to them sometimes and so cruel at other times. It does not make sense, but nothing they did really ever made sense.

That night when we got home, Brian was angry and grabbed the smallest one from my lap and threw him out of the back of the truck. As the little goat flew across the yard, I heard him cry out in pain. I jumped out and ran to him, tears running down my cheeks, to my horror, I discovered that one of his legs was broken. The goat looked up at me, pleading for me to help him. Brian kicked me and told me to get up. He said that the goat's leg was already damaged, so this was no big deal. I helped Samantha with the other goats, and then as everyone else ate supper, I sat with the goat and made a splint for his leg from some fabric and a straight branch that I had found. I struggled to fashion a splint that would allow the goat to move about and keep his leg bone in place. I had read in Grandpa's westerns about cowboys setting broken legs in this fashion and was going to try my luck. The goat, whom my mother had named Taco, cried when I pulled his leg to straighten the bone, but I think he knew that I was trying to help him, and I believe he was grateful.

When I was finished, I went back to the tent, expecting to get yelled at. But to my surprise, Brian did not look mad.

"Well, if it isn't the little nurse," he said with a strange smile. "Where did you learn to do that?"

"I read it in a book," I fidgeted nervously.

"Well, don't get attached to these animals. They are just dinner, you know." Brian was starting to get angry, but I thought I detected a sense of awe in his voice.

THE NEXT morning, with dawn barely peeking over the mountain ridge, I ran over to check on Taco and was pleased to find the splint still intact. I moved him away from the other goats and filled my ankle-length apron with dew-covered grass for his breakfast. After making a pile of grass in front of him, I sat next to him and told him my life's story as he munched. It almost seemed as if he were listening and nodding as he enjoyed his breakfast, but the companionship was short lived, as Brian emerged from the tent, shouting for me to quit playing around and get busy.

Mamma made breakfast while Samantha and me cleared more

sagebrush. At breakfast, Brian told us that things were going to change now that he had started building. Samantha and me would now have to get up before Brian and Mamma. We were to heat up water for coffee, make breakfast, put Brian's shaving things out and then wake them up. After breakfast, we would clean the two tents and then help Brian and Mamma with the building, pull sagebrush or take care of the animals.

I felt exhausted as Mamma and Brian kept adding to our list of chores. I was already tired, and my small frame was complaining loudly from all the heavy lifting it was required to do. I drifted off, thinking about how I could help Taco's leg heal faster, and barely listened as Brian's voice droned on and on. Brian said that I would be in charge of baking bread and sewing the clothes that were badly needed. My sister and I were in charge of virtually everything since Mamma had complained to Brian that she did not want to be stuck with the work around the tents. She believed that we were capable of doing more than we already were.

Samantha and I looked at each other with dread. Was there anything else they could possibly add to our day's work? Brian informed us that we would start right then, and no dawdling or we knew what we would get. Mamma set a timer for thirty minutes and said we had better have all the dishes done, dried, and put away and the tent floors swept and mopped by the time the timer went off. Of course, there was a huge stack of dishes and the tent was a mess.

"We're not going to make it," Samantha whispered to me.

I looked at her and nodded in agreement. To make things worse, we had to wait for the dish water to heat on the gas burner, and Mamma, who sat at the table watching us, would not let us use the water until it was near boiling. I complained that the water was too hot, but Mamma just shoved my hands into it while I screamed.

"You think you are such a smart girl" she muttered. "Well, you are not, because you don't even know how to wash dishes right."

Samantha and I cried as we did the dishes in the boiling water, and Mamma just laughed at us. When the timer went off, we were just starting to mop the floors. I felt my heart knot as I saw tears start to stream down Samantha's face. With pursed lips, I turned and looked at Mamma, who was clapping.

"Well done," she said with a fiendish glee. "For every minute it takes you to finish, you will get two lashes."

Samantha and I hurried as fast as we could, but we were still ten minutes late. Mamma went to the tent door and called Brian to come in. Samantha and I stood in the middle of the tent, trembling. I looked at Samantha's tear-stained face and bit my lip, trying to hold back my own tears. I had discovered it took some of their enjoyment out of beating me if I was not crying, and I was determined to give these two people as little joy as possible.

Brian stomped into the tent, grabbed me and dragged me outside the tents with Samantha following meekly behind. He made us both stand there, bent over with our underpants down and our dresses pulled up, while they went in search of switches. It happened that this was the time of my menstrual cycle, and I could not help letting a tear slip out as the blood trickled down my legs. When they came back, Samantha and I were both dizzy from bending over so long. Brian looked at me and laughed.

"I always knew you were a prostitute," he said as he nodded to himself.

I saw Mamma look over at me and make a disgusted face. The shame was so strong that I wanted to die right then and there. Samantha and I gritted our teeth as we received our twenty strikes. Samantha could not help but scream a few times, and it was all I could do to keep from joining her. After Brian and Mamma were done, they yelled at us to get back to work. I was not allowed to wash the blood from my ankles because Brian said that all Indian women just let their blood run everywhere like that, and if that was how I wanted to act, he would just let me walk around that way.

Mamma made another disgusted face at me, and I felt a knife go through my heart. It was very hard for me to understand why my mother treated me this way, and the only plausible explanation I could come up with was that the meaner Mamma was to my sister and I, the more attention Brian paid to her. It was a sick game for them, and although I had thought my life was miserable up to this point, the nightmare was really only beginning.

That day left me shaken and unsettled. It confirmed what I already knew to be true: I was living with crazy people. What was wrong with them? I did not know the answer, but I was afraid Samantha and I would die while they were beating us, either accidentally, or even intentionally. These were dark days for me, and I was very scared even though I refused to show it.

SUMMER FLEW by incredibly fast. My sister and I were so busy that we would sometimes collapse from exhaustion. We would awaken at around 5:30 am, and while I made breakfast and coffee, Samantha would boil water for Brian to shave and Mamma to wash up. Then she would quietly lay out their clothes for them. After this, we would tend to the animals by moving their tethers to fresh grass and hauling water for them from the creek. At 6:30, I would awaken Mamma and Brian, and while they got ready, Samantha and I would put breakfast on the table. For about thirty minutes after breakfast, Brian would read from the Bible and lecture us on what we had done to displease God the day before. Our sins were always along the same lines and usually were offenses such as wearing our dresses too tight, trying to seduce men or not obeying the time limit rules. Every morning there was always some reason God was angry with us. Samantha and I were very sad and would sit with our heads bowed, and even though I was not sure if what Brian was saying was true, he was very convincing, so I always told God how sorry I was throughout the day, just in case he was angry with me.

After breakfast, Samantha and I would run to and fro, trying to beat the horrible timers, but most of the time it could not be done, and Mamma and Brian happily dealt out beating after beating. After cleaning the tents, we ran to help with the new building, then frantically pulled sagebrush or chopped up ground for next year's garden. Around noon, we ran back to the tents. Samantha would start stuffing doll parts while I sewed either the doll's clothes or our own clothes. While I was sewing, I also had to make sure I had bread dough going and prepare something sweet for dessert. Brian loved sweets and got angry when I did not have time to make them.

When Samantha and I ran to the tents to start our afternoon work, Brian and Mamma would rest, and after Brian had taken his nap, he would call me into the sleeping tent to massage him. This was the worst part of my day, as he would fondle me even though Mamma was usually sleeping beside him.

Life at this point was numbing, and one day passed just like another. They seemed to blur into each other with no hope for change, and with every blow and every taunt, our souls became that much more scarred, until there seemed there was no room left for new scars, yet they still came at us hurtling with unrelenting force.

With the start of each day came dread and fear; the sheer sadness I felt as I crawled off my blanket to shut off the alarm was so suffocating I felt I could not get up. Quietly, I would wake Samantha, and we would dress in our solid-colored dresses and put on our black aprons, white head coverings, and black socks and shoes. We might add a black sweater if it was cold. This uniform set us so far apart from anyone around us; we felt as though we had a stamp on our foreheads proclaiming that we did not belong to normal society. We were not merely disadvantaged children—we simply did not belong, and whenever we were allowed to go into the city, we were looked upon with laughs and stares that made us feel even more ashamed than usual. However, we had been successfully brainwashed. We truly believed that if we did not strictly follow this dress code, we would go to hell. Add to all of this the fact that we were not allowed to talk unless we raised our hands and that we had no time in which to play or frolic about.

I do not wish for you, the reader, to feel sorry for us, but it is my wish to share the utterly helpless and miserable existence that my sister and I faced. Despite our terrible lot in life, I always had a strange feeling that my life was not meant to be like this. I felt I had some unforeseen destiny, and even when things seemed impossible, I would close my eyes tightly and pray to God to help me not lose all hope.

BY THE END of August, we had a herd of about twenty goats. Taco's leg had healed, and he hobbled after me on his bent hooves, getting into unspeakable mischief. The goats now herded together, and we let them roam the mountainside freely. They always returned at night to bed down in the ravine next to our tents. Many times, Taco popped his head in the tent door and snuggled next to me, and I would fall asleep with my arm around his neck. Unbeknownst to Brian, Samantha and I had made pets out of every one of the goats, and we also gave them all names.

The leader and most mischievous of the goats was named Cotton because she was pure white. Mamma called her 'Rotten Cotton', but she was a very nice big, white goat and she gave lots of milk. After Cotton, there was Shasta, Daisy, Elsie and quite a few others that followed Samantha and I wherever we went.

In the mornings, after Samantha and I milked the nine milk goats, we put the milk in canning jars and took it down across the dirt road to the creek. There we would place it in a tub we had anchored in the water that served as our way of refrigerating things. After that, we would haul several buckets of water back to the watering trough for the goats. Brian said we had to make sure that they had plenty of water so they could make a lot of milk for us.

During that summer, we went to farmer's' markets every weekend to sell our goods and were able to make enough money to complete a solid ten-by-ten-foot building on top of the old cellar. On the ground level, we put a gas stove and a table, and Brian built a loft with a ladder so that we could crawl up into it. It had just enough room for our cots. We filled the walls with sawdust, and Brian said that we would heat the room with the gas oven.

WITH MID-SEPTEMBER now upon us, old Jack Frost revisited the mountains. A shiver ran up my spine as I remembered the old rancher's words about the cold that was coming. I watched nervously as the geese flew south and the goats' fur became fluffier. During this time, Samantha and I waited anxiously for some sort of winter clothing to appear for us, afraid that if we were forced to go through winter in the clothes we had, we might not live to see spring.

Life in the new shack was tight, and Samantha and I were only allowed inside to sleep, cook and eat. Everything else was done under the giant cottonwood tree, which had a lean-to tarp nailed to it.

Life continued as usual, with the same grueling routine day after day. Brian preached to us from the Bible for an hour every morning, his eyes wild and spit falling from his mouth into his long, gray beard as he glared at us. We sat there in our long, plain-colored dresses, black aprons and white head coverings that covered most of our hair and were tied snugly under our chins. Brian wore plain white shirts and black broadfall pants with black suspenders. It was certainly true that we looked every bit like the Amish in the magazines. Brian had many books and many rules from the Bishop with whom he corresponded.

After breakfast, Samantha and I would start our usual work of milking the goats, making doll parts, sewing potholders, sanding music boxes, cleaning, cooking and pulling sagebrush. After all this time we still did not get lunch, and Samantha was not faring well. Eventually, Samantha and I started hiding small amounts of bread or pie in our dress pockets and would keep the food in a plastic bag behind the feed bags or under the tarp. This way, we could steal a few giant mouthfuls around noon without being seen.

While Samantha and I worked, Brian and Mamma often argued, and Mamma would storm off in the truck and go into town, leaving us alone with Brian, who would look for reasons to beat us. If they were not fighting, Mamma usually buried herself in one of her romance novels while Brian called me up to the loft for his daily message. Sometimes I would be so tired I could hardly keep my eyes open. To alleviate my sadness I traveled in my head, imagining that I was a nurse to some poor AIDS-stricken children in Africa. I even smiled sometimes because I was so lost in my daydream, which always included people depending on me to save them and find amazing cures.

Most of the time I couldn't even see Brian, a man I so despised. My mind just drifted away, very far away. Sometimes my daydreams were so real I could almost smell the jungle and hear the monkeys chattering to each other as they swung from tree to tree. It was a great fantasy, but not one that was attainable, or, at least, it didn't seem as if it was as I lay there in my faded, dark blue dress and long black apron with my white cap covering my head. I was someone who did not belong to the world which I so desperately longed for; I was an outsider, someone people of the world would only stare at when I walked by.

I honestly believed that in order to get to heaven, I had to dress this way. Still, I found it ironic that I was clothed from head to toe and supposed to be chaste and virtuous, yet Brian, the very one who preached this to me, would fondle me and make obscene gestures and remarks when he thought no one else was around. I was very confused, and as the days wore on the only happiness Samantha and I had was with our animals, the birds that fluttered above calling to each other, the sunsets that made a beautiful display from the mountaintops and our dreams which always consisted of being anywhere but on that terrible, lonely mountaintop.

ONE DAY IN October, Mamma came back from the welfare office with a worried look on her face. She told Brian that she had filled out her government paperwork stating that Samantha and I were being home schooled, and the state wanted us to come in for standardized testing. Mamma and Brian argued for a couple of days, and then Mamma dusted off some second-grade math and spelling books for Samantha and me. She told us that we would study in between our chores. Brian was angry and said that we were just being lazy, sitting around looking at books, but Mamma told him if they were not careful they could lose custody of us, and then they would not get their government checks; plus, we might talk to the authorities. She seemed very worried that they might go to jail for not having us in school. Sadly, their primary concern seemed to be that if they lost us, they would lose the six hundred dollars a month in governmental support, plus their food stamps and free slave labor.

I listened at the door with keen interest. What if they sent us to the school in town? That would be a dream come true. If that became a reality, we could make friends and would have a break from the grueling work we did every day. But, of course, there was no such luck. Brian reluctantly consented for us to study from the homeschooling books but said it should be for no more than an hour a day, and we had to get as much done as possible in that time.

Thankfully, Samantha and I were naturally very good readers, especially Samantha. Whenever she had to read something, she merely glanced at a page and seemed to have it read. When the motor home burned down and we didn't have much to do for once, I saw her read a five hundred page book in less than five hours. However, despite Samantha being an amazing reader and speller, she did not understand math very well, most likely due to her lack of interest in the subject and our lack of teachers. Unlike Samantha, I was excited to try to learn some math, because I figured doctors had to be pretty good at math. I had no idea what else they studied, but at least, this was something.

Teaching ourselves proved to be quite difficult for ten-year-old Samantha and my nearly twelve-year-old self. While we tried to follow the instructions in the book and checked our answers in the back of the book, it was very difficult, and we got most of the problems wrong. Whenever I asked Mamma for help, she would shrug and bury herself in her book, Brian would glare at me, just waiting for the hour to be up. Unfortunately, our school sessions only lasted about two weeks, because somehow, Mamma got around the state testing.

After that, we continued to do lessons sporadically just in case something ever happened, although I do not know how much it helped since we were not doing the lessons correctly or regularly. While I tried to figure out how to divide and do fractions, Samantha merely copied the questions from the lesson, got the answers from the back of the book and then put her name and the date on it. Mamma would then put the page away on the shelf where she kept all the work we did to show the state if they ever asked.

I never blamed Samantha for not caring about her studies, because we were so overworked; besides, she had no dreams that required her to study or to save the world. Her dream was to run away to Las Vegas and become a famous singer. She was an incredible singer with a soft, rich voice. She could sing anything after she heard it once, and she could carry the notes as perfectly as a well-trained singer. She did not sing very often, though, as there was nothing to sing about. The only time we had a chance to be happy was when Mamma and Brian ran errands into town and left us at home alone. Most of the time, Brian set up the tape recorder next to the place we were working, but we learned to sneak away from it and then come back later without him knowing it. It was always annoying when Brian came home because he would sit and look at a book while he played the tape recorder to see if we had been talking.

THAT OCTOBER, Mamma sold Taco and a few of our other goats to the orchard pickers from the valley below. I waved goodbye to Taco and could not help the tears that trickled down my cheeks—my sweet little friend was leaving. He looked at me from the truck bed with his sweet, innocent face, and I took some comfort in knowing that he had no idea what was going to happen to him.

The men that put him in the truck laughed and patted him and thought he was really cute. I was happy to learn later that Taco did not become dinner, but instead he became the family pet of the orchard foreman and was very spoiled by his three children.

After Taco left, I turned to my other goat friends. They loved hugs and pats on the heads and the treats that I would steal for them from the kitchen.

After selling Taco, Mamma came home one day with a puppy. He was a cute golden retriever and blue tick hound mix. He was brown with black spots scattered here and there and was very cute and cuddly. As soon as I saw him, I reached up to take him from Mamma, but Brian shook his head and said we couldn't play with him because he was going to learn to be a guard dog.

Mamma named him Buckwheat, and we called him Bucky for short. Even though we were not supposed to play with Bucky, Samantha and I did whenever Brian and Mamma were not looking. Brian was very cruel to Bucky and kicked him when he did not obey or when he followed Brian around. I hated to see Bucky sad, so I gave him lots of extra hugs and told him to just let Brian get eaten by a bear, even though I knew that Brian was so mean the bear would not even want to eat him.

When the cold set in, Bucky was all Samantha and I cared about. Brian believed that Bucky should hunt for his own food so we would not have to feed him much. This became impossible though since Brian was constantly kicking him and poor Bucky limped around much of the time. Samantha and I began soaking some cracked grain in the fresh warm goat's milk so Bucky would have a little extra food to keep him warm. Brian began remarking at how Bucky was gaining weight and Samantha and I just shrugged as if we did not care, but we smiled at each other behind his back. It truly is amazing how resourceful children are, and how they are seriously underestimated by many adults.

TEAR DROPS IN THE SNOW

"I wish I could tell you how lonely I am. How cold and harsh it is here. Everywhere there is conflict and unkindness. I think God has forsaken this place. I believe I have seen hell and it's white, it's snow-white."

—Elizabeth Gaskell

The last week of October brought snow flurries and a cold northeasterly wind that whistled through the ravine and up the mountains as if it were a herald announcing the arrival of old man winter. I looked forlornly at the snow flurries and wrapped my thin black blazer more tightly around my shoulders.

Even though it was only the end of October, the thermometer dropped to the mid-twenties in the early morning hours, and a thin layer of ice could be seen on any standing water. My teeth chattered constantly since we had to stay outside most of the day while Brian and Mamma stayed inside, shouting instructions out the door. It did not matter if there was rain or shine, we still had to do our work and would walk around in freezing rain-soaked clothes.

I had low blood pressure and poor circulation, and that made me very sensitive to the cold. I began developing first-degree frostbite on my hands and feet. The tops of my feet and hands itched terribly, and I scratched them until the skin came off. My feet hurt badly, so I put cotton balls on top of each bloody toe before I put on my thin socks and then my thin black canvas shoes. Thankfully, Samantha was not so sensitive to cold and did not have to suffer the ridicule from Brian for being a weakling.

Finally one day, Brian and Mamma came back with coats and boots that they had bought at the Army surplus store in town. Samantha and I were very happy with the long, dark green trench coats that were the same length as our long dresses, and although they were not very thick, we improvised by wearing our blazers underneath. The thick, heavy leather boots were great too because we could wear four pairs of socks inside them, and our feet were no longer numb all the time. I laughed when we all put on our coats and boots, and when Brian asked me why I was laughing, I told him that we looked like the Third Reich that I had read about in one of grandpa's books (secretly I was thinking that Brian was Hitler and Mamma was his general). Brian actually smiled at this comment and said that there were worse things to look like.

Even with the new winter clothes, I could never seem to get warm, and the winds that blew across my cheeks and up my long dress still made my teeth chatter as I went about my daily chores. By nightfall I was often running a low grade temperature that would peak at around 100 degrees in the middle of the night and then ebb in the early morning hours, only to flare up again the next evening. Up until the snow started falling Mamma was unyielding in her rule that Samantha and I must take cold baths outside. We begged Mamma to not make us take baths outside in the cold, but she was obsessed with the idea that we were dirty girls and needed to bathe in large amounts of water. Twice a week, Samantha and I filled the goat's watering trough with water from the creek and Mamma would force us into its icy depths.

I would cry as the wind whipped around us and told Mamma I was afraid we would get sick; our teeth chattered like incoming telegrams. But Mamma just pushed our heads under the water and watched us with a flyswatter in hand as we scrubbed ourselves according to her instructions. Samantha and I did not feel well afterward; we did not have hair dryers, and sometimes it took two days for our hair to dry.

For their baths, Mamma and Brian heated the tea kettle on the stove and bathed from a bowl in the kitchen. When I asked Mamma if Samantha and I could do the same, she said we were too filthy and would not get clean that way. Finally when the snow started to fall Mamma started letting Samantha and I bathe inside. But the little house was not much warmer than outside and as the winter grew colder and colder even Mamma forgot about bathing for awhile. It was just too cold.

AS WINTER SET in, Brian frantically began buying hay in the valley for our herd of twenty goats. We stacked it in piles behind a small fenced-in area that Samantha and I had built next to the shack. After stacking the hay as high as we could, Samantha and I covered it with tarps to keep the rain and snow off. Once, when I was on my menstrual cycle, I was stacking hay bales as high as I could. I was very weak so I just stood on the top bale and dragged the rest of the bales on top of each other. Suddenly I felt something pop in my lower abdomen. I felt very sick and climbed down the hay bale. I staggered into the shack to get some water because I was suddenly very thirsty. I poured some water from the water bottle on the table and drank it. I felt very strange and was still thirsty after I drank the water. I sat down on the bench and suddenly, I felt a gushing feeling and looked down and saw that the bench was covered in blood. I tried to move but collapsed on the floor. After a few seconds, I sat up and put my head between my legs. I felt nauseous and weak, and my stomach was hurting badly. For a moment, Brian and Mamma just stared at me, but then Brian came over and yanked me to my feet.

"What the f... is wrong with you!" he yelled. "You are staining the bench."

"I'm sorry," I whispered. I got up and tried to keep my balance, but I fell back down on the bench despite my efforts.

"Stand up!" he shrieked at me angrily as he slapped me across the face and yanked me to my feet again.

I was weak and shaky and could not maintain my balance or fight back. Brian slammed me against the stove. I stared back at him as I held my stomach. Brian got very upset when I just stood there holding my stomach instead of trying to run like I usually did. His face was horrible and leering. I don't know why but Mamma and Brain always made us feel ashamed of our menstrual cycles and would make so much fun of us. He yelled that if I was going to act like a squaw, he would treat me like one.

"Okay," Brian said. "Squaws don't live inside houses, so go sit outside next to the generator and think about what you did."

As I staggered outside, a gust of wind blew at me and rain drops began to fall. I felt so feverish and I could hear Brian still making fun of me from inside the shack, but I was too sick and cold to care. I sat down in the mud next to the generator while the rain fell on my head. Fever wracked my body. The rain that ran down my cheeks was mixed with my tears. My life was so utterly miserable and pointless. I hated to see Samantha suffer, but there was little I could do to protect her and now as I sat there in the mud, sick and bleeding, I was scared and terrified, there seemed to no limit to the humiliation or torment that Mamma and Brian were willing to inflict on us. There was definitely something very wrong with Mamma, later in life I would learn how most mothers would help their daughters through these times and not just make fun of them or make them work even harder when they knew they were sick. But that was not the case for me. I would get terribly sick and loose way to much blood. The pain was beyond excruciating, and yet there I sat in the rain. A lonely sad girl who did not know when her next beating was coming but that it could definitely be any second of any day.

Even as I sat there, a feeling of certainty came over me. My life cannot be like this forever, I told myself; I have something to accomplish in life. However, even this comforting thought did not make my predicament any less painful, and while I tried hard to listen to the small voice inside me, it was very hard to believe that I would ever be anything other than Brian's pawn for the rest of my life.

As I sat there in pain, it was saddening for me to know that if I died here on the mountain no one would ever know. I would occupy an unmarked grave on a hillside somewhere, one that would only be visited by Samantha; and with the changing of the seasons, would probably be forgotten altogether. With these thoughts, I tried to rally myself. No, I told myself. I shook my head, trying to clear it from the fog that was starting to cloud my thinking. This is not going to happen to me, I thought. God had bigger plans for me; I knew it deep down in my soul. I tried to pray to God to help me. I told him how sorry I was for whatever I had done to make him angry at me. Finally, I was so sleepy and I lay my rain-soaked head down on the generator for just a moment of rest...

𝒥 WOKE UP a couple of hours later, judging by the setting sun. Samantha was shaking me, her face looked worried and I was soaking wet.

"Brian said you can come in now." Her freckles were all the more prominent on her white face.

I put my arm around Samantha's shoulders, and she helped me into the house.

"You looked so sick. I can't believe they sent you out there to sit in the rain, it is going to make you even sicker now." Samantha whispered. "I was so worried and I begged Brian to let me come out and get you."

"Thanks," I whispered weakly.

When we entered the shack, I stood by the door while Samantha wrapped me in a dry towel and then pulled me up the stairs. Mamma and Brian sat at the table and pretended they did not see me.

Samantha helped me up to the loft, where I stayed for the next three days, wracked with a horrible fever. I used a bucket that Samantha had brought me as my toilet and drank the soup she practically forced down my throat. Finally I felt stronger and the fever had subsided so I timidly climbed down the ladder to the kitchen. It was breakfast time, and everyone was at the table. I sat down at the table and helped myself to a biscuit. No one acknowledged that I had just come down, and Brian pretended I had been sitting there the whole time as he began laying out the work for the day. I was still extremely weak and became afraid that I would not be able to keep up with my share of the work. Samantha and I took turns on what we called "inside duties" and "outside duties." That day I was assigned to outside duties, and although outside duties were harder, I was anxious to see all my animal friends.

As I stepped outside, I was pleasantly surprised to find that we were in the middle of a slight warming spell. The old rancher had told us that this usually happened before the really cold weather set in, but no matter; I welcomed it just the same. Bucky ran up to me and frolicked around my feet; I gave him a great big hug but reminded him I was on a timer and that I had no time to play. The goats were as happy to see me as I was to see them, and they nuzzled at my coat pockets where I always kept a couple of handfuls of sugar for them to lick out of my hands.

ᴛWO DAYS LATER, it was time for Mamma to pick up her monthly checks in Wenatchee. Brian had bought two big cans of thick, gray oil paint and told me that while everyone else went to Wenatchee to purchase supplies and sell crafts, I would stay home and paint the floor in order to cover the blood stains that were caused from butchering the goats. It was an awful sight but Brian said that if we covered the floor in oil paint we could just mop up the blood after every butchering and then it would not look so bad.

I also had to sand and oil the bench that was stained with my blood. Every time I went in the shack and saw the stain on the bench, it made me shiver and feel a little nauseous. I think it bothered Mamma and Brian too because I heard Mamma say that if anyone happened to come inside our shack they would think someone had been murdered in there. There was bloodstains everywhere, it was really an awful sight. Brian had just laughed, but he agreed that they had to get it covered up. For some reason that incident really made me quiver inside. It was eerie, the way Brian had laughed at the idea of someone being murdered in that shack.

Early that morning, before they left, I helped Brian move the stove, the table, and the groceries out of the shack. It was cold that day, but the sun was out, so I tied the door open to let in the air. For a moment, I just sat there and watched them drive away. It was my twelfth birthday, and as the sun began smiling at me over the mountain range, I smiled back. Although no one had acknowledged that it was my birthday, I could not imagine a better birthday gift than having a day without Mamma and Brian there to beat me and yell at me. I had the entire day to get my work done, play with the animals and eat whatever I wanted from the food box. I could even eat lunch, and no one would know.

I played with Bucky for awhile and then set to work painting the floor. It turned out to be a harder job than I had thought it would be as the paint was very dense and sticky. I painted one coat and then did my other chores and sanded down the bloody bench. It of course did not look quite right, even after oiling it. There were still some stains on it, that would never come out. Over time they faded but would continue to haunt me for years into the future. That wood picnic table set was the only really nice thing that we owned. I am not sure why but Brian prized it and would scream if it even got slightly damaged. The day I had bled all over the bench I had made a huge mistake.

Four hours later, I gave the floor another coat. I did my best, but the weather was not warm enough for painting, and the sticky paint left little paint balls all over the floor. When I was done with the floor, I did the rest of my chores and then sat outside with Bucky and the goats, hoping Brian and Mamma would not be mad at me because of the terrible paint job and the stains that were still on the bench. At least, the majority blood stains on the floor were covered and would not stare up at us all the time.

That night, after they got home, Samantha whispered to tell me all that had happened—there was not much to tell, really, she said, except she had to sit out on the road with Brian, which was no fun at all and that they had not sold much of anything. Brian and Mamma did not say anything about the paint job or the bench as we climbed the ladder to the loft. Our financial situation was not good and a cruel and unforgiving winter was fairly upon us. We lived in a tiny shack with no heat and everyone was constantly freezing and miserable.

That night as I lay awake, I smiled to myself. I was twelve years old now—in another year, I would be a teenager and then eventually I would be an adult. In only six more years I could rid myself of Mamma and Brian. I lay awake, wondering what would happen to us when we reached adulthood. *Where would we go...would they even let us go? Of course,* I told myself, *they had to, right? But would they really?* I fell asleep to the sounds of coyotes howling in the distance and the wind rustling in the bare branches of the cottonwoods; I dreamed my favorite dream where I was a doctor saving many lives.

It was true that Mamma and Brian could take away my human rights and humiliate me into the ground, but they could never have my dreams. My dreams were the only things that were truly mine, and I cherished them. I hoped that one day they would come true. Out there on that vast mountain range, there were many stars to wish upon, and every night I wished upon a different one, hoping that one would turn out to be my lucky star. It was, at least, worth a try, I told myself.

*W*HEN THANKSGIVING came around, it was a cold, snowy day in the northwest. A couple of days prior, Brian had come home with a large turkey and some other groceries for baking. He had also bought a great big pumpkin. He had said he wanted a giant Thanksgiving dinner like his mother used to make.

Samantha and I eagerly set to work early Thanksgiving morning to prepare the delicious meal. I laughed as Samantha made fun of our clothes and said how funny it was to be making dinner dressed just like the pilgrims themselves. Mamma and Brian sat reading books as usual, and Mamma even smiled a little at us as we got flour and sugar everywhere. This was an example of how they acted a lot. They would seem to be nice, in a good mood and then out of nowhere one of them would explode and it would be worse than if they had just stayed in a bad mood the whole time. The screaming and beatings were so much more violent. It almost seemed as if they were making up for lost time. And so whenever the tension would let up for awhile we knew that a storm was brewing and we would only pretend to be at ease and brace for the worst. It is so hard to explain but I could never let my guard down, I could never let myself be truly happy, even if it was just for a moment. Around every corner was danger, real serious danger. It was better to stay on alert, then I would not miss the brief moment of happiness as it fluttered away.

On that snowy day the cozy cabin atmosphere was an unusual but welcomed relief; however, I could not help but think that something was not quite right, and I timidly avoided Brian's stares—surely he would not make me go to the loft and massage him on Thanksgiving Day.

That afternoon, Samantha and I displayed all of the goodies we had made. I sat down in my designated spot next to Brian, and Samantha sat down next to Mamma. And then I made a big mistake: I smiled at Brian. His mood suddenly changed; he put his book down and looked across the table at the beautiful dinner we had made. Then he looked at Samantha and me; by this time, we were no longer smiling.

"What were you smiling about?" he barked at me.

His eyes were wild, and his stare looked like it was made of steel and ice; it made my blood run cold. These looks he got were utterly crazy and cold; I cannot explain exactly what he looked like, but he definitely did not look human to me. It seemed as if there were a wall of ice behind his eyes, and when he looked like this, I had no doubt that he could do whatever he wanted to a person without feeling even a shred of remorse.

For a moment, everything in the house was still. I just sat there in my chair feeling scared and at the same time I felt slightly numb.

"I asked you a question," Brian barked as he slammed his fist on the table. The water sloshed out of the glasses, and I jumped.

"Well," I stammered, "I was just happy to eat a good dinner, I guess." I looked down at the table as my lower lip began to tremble. Samantha had tears in her eyes, and we just looked at each other. Brian reached across the table, yanked off a piece of turkey and began sniffing it.

"You are trying to poison me, aren't you?" he yelled at me.

59

I looked back at him, perplexed. I did not know how to poison someone, even if I wanted to. He turned to Samantha and asked her which dish had the poison in it.

"We did not put poison in anything," Samantha cried. "Why would we do that?"

"You might not, but *she* certainly would," Brian turned back to me.

He grabbed me by the back of the head and shoved the turkey in my mouth. I began coughing, and he told me to swallow it all, or he would give me something to cough about. I choked down the turkey and looked back at him, not sure what he was expecting to happen. He just shook his head and said that witches were able to stay off the curse of their own poison, so the fact that I was not getting sick did not mean anything. I watched with dismay as he grabbed all the food from the table and threw it out the door into the snow.

Not knowing what was going to happen next in that small room, Samantha and I ducked out the door as soon as Brian had thrown the last dish. Bucky ran up to us, oblivious of what was happening, and wagged his tail playfully. Samantha and I just looked at each other for a moment. We were very hungry since we had not eaten all day; our stomachs were growling noisily, and the smell of good food was wafting up to us from the snow. A couple of minutes passed, but Brian did not come out after us. I looked at the food in the snow and then back at Samantha. We both shrugged simultaneously and then quietly sat in the snow with Bucky to eat our Thanksgiving dinner. We could hear Mamma and Brian yelling at each other inside the shack.

"She wants to kill me!" Brian was screaming. "She wants to kill me."

"That is ridiculous!" Mamma screamed back. "Why would she want to kill you?"

"Because I have been ignoring her advances all day," Brian yelled.

They argued on and on as Samantha, Bucky and I ate all we could of the creamy potatoes, mashed pumpkin, cherry pie, pumpkin pie and turkey. We skimmed off the tops of everything that had landed face down in the snow and ate the parts that were still warm. We could not help but smile since Bucky's stomach seemed to get visibly larger as he devoured huge amounts of turkey.

After about fifteen minutes, Mamma came storming out of the shack with a few of her things, yelling that she was never coming back. I felt the knot in my stomach grow as I watched her stomp over to the truck. She did this sort of thing a lot, at least, three times a week, but the worst part of it was that she always stormed off without Samantha and me. She did not seem to care if she left us with crazy Brian. Even though Mamma was very cold and cruel, she seemed stable and calculating, whereas Brian, although also very calculating, would suddenly snap and rave about things that made no sense at all. When this happened, he was very scary, and it was impossible to reason with him.

That evening when it came time to do the chores, Samantha suggested that we not do them because we would have to go inside to get the milk pail, but I shook my head and said that we had better not give Brian any excuse to fly off the handle at us. I crept quietly into the house to get the milking pail. My hands were shaking, and I was scared that I would drop everything and startle Brian. As I entered the room, I saw him sitting in a corner at the end of the table. As I walked over to the box that held the dishes, he did not even acknowledge that I was there as he kept staring straight ahead into nothingness. After I grabbed the milk pails, I walked hurriedly to the door and gave it a little kick, which was Samantha's signal to open the door for me since my arms were full. I ran out of the house into the frosty winter air. I was quite literally shaking from head to toe. The presence of pure evil and hatred that I felt in that room was so unsettling it left me shaken for days.

Samantha and I quietly did our chores, and after we were done we sat next to the goat herd for a while trying to stay warm. The dark November night was getting very cold, and a few snow flurries could be seen dancing their way down to the quiet mountaintops. Samantha and I were too scared to go inside the shack, not that it was that much warmer inside, but at least, we could have snuggled in our blankets.

"I'm cold," Samantha whimpered as we snuggled against the goats for warmth.

"I know," I said, my teeth chattering. I got up and dusted the snow from my long, brown dress. "Come on. We can't spend the night out here. We might freeze." I went up to the thermometer that was on the door. It read twenty degrees, and it was not even the coldest part of the night yet.

"We will sleep in the basement tonight," I said as I yanked the heavy wooden door open. "At least, we won't freeze because it is underground."

I picked up Bucky and we crowded into the small cellar that was full of canned food and storage boxes. We made a bed for the three of us by moving some boxes out of the way. I took one of the spare comforters out of a box and put it on the dirt floor. Instantly we felt much warmer. Bucky snuggled his warm little body in between us, and with that, we fell asleep.

During the night, I heard the truck pull up. Mamma was back, and I breathed a sigh of relief as I heard the door slam overhead. I wondered if they even knew where Samantha and I were. Did they even care that we were terribly frightened or that we could quite possibly be freezing somewhere? Probably not, I thought with a sad sigh. I lay back down and drifted to sleep with my arm around Bucky while Samantha snuggled next to me.

SEASONS OF SORROW

"The heart has no tears to give,—it drops only blood, bleeding itself away in silence."

— *Harriet Beecher Stowe, Uncle Tom's Cabin*

That winter proved to be extremely difficult in our shack that stood out in the open clearing. The wind whipped around its sides as if it wanted to carry the shack away with it down the hill and into the valley below. The snow got so deep it was almost impossible to walk through and made it necessary that we scrape little paths going to the hay pile, the outhouse, and the truck. Driving the six miles out of town up a mountainside was even more challenging and dangerous than usual. The truck would slip and slide from side to side, and I was always afraid that one day we would end up in one of the deep canyons below. When we got to our road which turned off the dirt county road, we would put on the chains, and after several attempts would finally make it up into our driveway.

On top of all this, we had no form of heat at home, and everyone was always freezing. The water that we brought back from town froze, and before doing dishes we would have to heat up an ice block on the gas stove. This always cut into our timer time, and often a very cold and miserable Mamma would beat us. She always said it made her feel warmer, which it probably did.

Getting water to the animals proved to be a challenge as well, and we would water them one by one in the morning and at night. We would give each one only a little water since we had to thaw it from the barrels we filled up in town or haul it from the icy creek that was now embanked with deep snow.

We were very low on money that winter since it was very hard to sell things on the side of the road when the thermometer read minus twenty degrees Fahrenheit. Mamma and Brian argued constantly while Samantha and I went about our routines. Doing the laundry proved to be particularly challenging. Mamma put wash tubs inside the shack, and Samantha and I would wash the clothes and hang them around the propane stove. They would usually take a couple of days to dry and took up most of the room. Eventually, Mamma started doing the wash at the Laundromat, which was a sigh of relief.

Mamma often blamed Brian for bringing us up on a mountain to freeze to death, and Brian would tell her she should quit being a sissy and learn to deal with real life. But despite the front he put on, I don't think Brian had expected it to be as bad as it was turning out to be. When darkness fell around 4:30 pm, we would all huddle in the shack. Samantha and I would make dinner, and after we ate would do the dishes and then crochet, make dolls or sew clothes. Mamma would read her romance novels, and Brian would sit and brood while he read his Bible. Often when he read the Bible, he would take notes that he thought were relevant to how the government and women were evil.

By midwinter, Mamma managed to find a couple of consignment stores that were willing to sell our Amish dolls, and we were able to sell a few every month, making just enough to scrape by with the help of the government checks.

I also began develop large sores on the top of each of my toes. At first we did not know what it was. My feet were extremely itchy and every step I took was painful. Eventual the sores were so large and bleeding that I just could not walk. Surprisingly Mamma took me to the doctor in Wenatchee and we found out that I had frostbite. It may seem strange that Mamma would take me to the doctor but she loved to go the doctor. Every time she went to Wenatchee she would make a random appointment for herself. When she ran out of reasons to go herself she started taking me sometimes. It was free and therefore we did not have to pay anything. I would always sit with my all my clothes on and never really say anything as the doctors would ask me about my upset stomach, headaches etc. We never followed through with any of the treatment but I could tell Mamma loved the attention.

I am still amazed that none of the doctors and nurses tried to get me alone and question me about my odd behavior, but then they could not see the bruises because I was clothed from head to foot.

That winter however, all ten of my toes were bloody. I am so surprised that Mamma was not worried about getting in trouble for such awful neglect. But she wasn't, the Amish act and the Amish clothes served her well and no one seemed to even question that I might be an abused child.

$\mathcal{T}$HAT WINTER, Brian declared that Sunday was a day of no work. He had finally been convinced by the bishop that we should do no work on Sundays except what was absolutely necessary. So our Sundays, even though there was now the no-work rule, were horrid because we were freezing and we had to sit and listen to Brian as he read chapter after chapter from the Bible, and then listen even more as he interpreted it from his own understanding, which would sometimes go on for hours.

Like always Brian and Mamma continued to do small things that were supposed to be nice. It left us confused and almost thinking we might be able to be happy. At night Brian would read stories aloud to us. We would sit and listen as he read various old books Mamma brought home from the library. We were never allowed to touch these books ourselves, only Brian was allowed to read them to us. Brian would do this reading ritual through out most of my time at home.

Even though we loved stories, we would always listen with mixed fear. The slightest thing would set Brian off, and when he switched from one his *supposed* nice moods to a mad one it was the worst. His eyes would become crazy and I often felt I would pass out just from looking at him. These were the most eerie and crazy times, it was without logic, void of any understanding. One minute he would be reading about the Oregon trail and laughing about something in the book. His laugh was strange and never really sounded like a laugh even though it was supposed to be one. Samantha and I would laugh nervously, hoping he would keep reading. Then out of nowhere he would see a fork on the table, or he just plain did not like the looks on our faces and he would erupt into a madman. Samantha and I would jump up to defend ourselves. We knew if we tried to run, we would get a worse beating once we were caught.

"See what ungrateful horrible creature you are." He would shout at us as he beat us with a belt or a stick, or made us bend over and touch our toes.

"I am being a nice guy and this how you repay me. I am just going to beat the devil right out of you. You lazy, stupid, worthless, ungrateful girls." I would tremble and try not to look in his face. His face was to scary and to evil, how could anyone be so utterly awful.

It was an endless cycle, Never could we relax, never could we let out guard down. Once in awhile in the winter they would let us stop working and take us sledding on inner tubes. Brian would tell us a few stories of his young childhood in Pennsylvania, it seemed to make him really happy.

January brought with it a schnook. The ice melted and the temperature rose into the forties. It was so nice and warm, and the goats happily warmed themselves in the sun's rays. Across the road, we could hear the creek running again, and then as suddenly as it had become warm, everything froze over again in a blanket of slippery ice. We were back on the frozen mountain, and it seemed to taunt us with its icy grip. Eventually March swung around, and with it the first telltale signs that spring was near. The days became warmer, and while the nights were still terribly cold, it was easy to tell that old man winter was on his way out. Every living creature on the mountain breathed a sigh of relief and dreamed of the warm summer days that would restore life and health once more.

The beginning of March brought with it many responsibilities. The goats were giving birth, and Mamma and Brian were busy getting ready to expand the farm. Brian realized we would need a better shelter for the next winter and set out to find a cheap way of building a small house. Of course, with the small amount of money Mamma received from her SSI and the money she got for us, there was not a lot left for building a house.

One day when we were passing one of the local orchards, Brian saw some men tearing down one of the many shacks that were lined up in a row behind one of the orchards. Brian decided to ask the owner of the orchard if they had any other shacks they wanted to get rid of. After a couple of weeks, he was able to find an old one that was going to be torn down. It was twelve feet wide by twenty-four feet long, and it had a loft in it as well, it looked like a mansion compared to what we were living in.

After a few weeks of research, Brian hired a local mobile home company to haul it up the mountain in the middle of the night. It was quite a job and almost too big for the truck. The house swayed back and forth as the truck struggled up the private road and into our driveway, but finally it arrived. Samantha and I were so happy; finally we would have a house that we could put a wood burning stove in. The truck driver backed our new house to the leveled spot we had made about fifty feet to the side of the shack and lowered it to the ground. The house made a thundering noise as it was lowered, and then it sat there and seemed to be staring at us in the moonlight. It would need a lot of work, but it was worth it, and it was definitely cheaper than building from scratch.

In order to get it across town, Brian had had to remove the roof, so we would need to repair that before the house would be livable. When he removed the roof, Brian decided to make the loft bigger so there would be standing room, and then we would have what he called a double-story house.

It took about two weeks to repair the new house and scrub and paint the walls. The house had not been lived in for many years and had fallen prey to vandalism. There was graffiti all over the walls. We also discovered that the floor and the walls had no insulation whatsoever; this was a grim discovery, since without any insulation there would be no way to keep in the heat in the winter time, but the house was more spacious than our shack, and for that at least we were grateful.

As we moved our belongings in the new house, I felt a little uneasy. This meant we would be staying on the mountain for good. Samantha and I had been secretly hoping that we would move and go back to Arizona or somewhere that was closer to civilization, but it did not look like that would be happening any time soon.

We set up the wood burning stove, the picnic table and the wood table on which we put two large stainless steel bowls to use as a sink. We set the two treadle sewing machines along the wall, and as I looked around I thought it looked more like a factory than a home. Upstairs we put two matresses, with Mamma and Brian on one side of the room and Samantha and I on the other side. I always hated these arrangements because Brian stared at us while we undressed, and he would dress and undress in the middle of the room so there was no chance we could miss it.

SPRING BEGAN with much work to be done. Brian and Mamma wanted to make our place into a real farm, and in order to achieve this, we would need to buy more animals and build corrals, as well as get ready for the coming winter by hauling hay, chopping wood and preserving foods.

Needless to say, Mamma and Brian did not plan on doing their share of the work, and Samantha and I were saddled with more work than ever. Besides all these new tasks, we had to make dolls and music boxes in order to make the money to keep things running, since the government checks only went so far. Brian began laying out the work plans the very next morning after we moved into the house. He made a change to our rule of one girl doing chores inside the house one day and then switching off to do chores outside the next day. We would now take one week turns instead. Samantha and I stared at each other. Being the outside girl was extremely hard work, and one day of it was almost more than either of us could stand.

Brian also said that we would start getting up at five am, and while the inside girl made breakfast, the outside girl would take care of the morning chores. Then we would wake Brian and Mamma, eat our breakfast and start the day's work. He also said there was still to be no talking between us whatsoever, unless we were given a message to give to the other. After breakfast, the girl who was outside was not permitted to reenter the house until the end of the day, when we would eat our dinner and go to bed. The inside girl would be in charge of making the bread, making meals, doing laundry, cleaning, canning, gardening and so on, as well as making that week's merchandise to sell in town. In addition to this, she would also need to assist the outside girl with heavy jobs such as fence making, stacking hay and chopping wood for the upcoming winter.

That spring, Brian and Mamma bought many animals, including pigs, chickens, rabbits and calves. The work was endless, and Samantha and I could hardly crawl out of bed each morning when the alarm rang at 5 am. As if this was not enough, the more animals and responsibilities that came with the farm, the less money we had. Samantha and I were constantly blamed for not being fast enough, and the beatings were more brutal than ever. At least three times a day, we were made to bend over and have our dresses pulled up and underwear pulled down as Brian and Mamma took out their lives' frustrations on us. It was unbearable at times, and the pain that filled my heart was absolutely inexpressible. I was always kind and gentle to everyone around me, and I could not understand what was wrong with Mamma and Brian.

I was only twelve years old, and Samantha was only ten. Brian had started molesting Samantha as well, we both knew it was wrong of Brian to molest us but we never talked about it. We just pretended it didn't happen. What else could we do? We lived in a world that did not care, a world that had forgotten us, we knew we did not matter.

SLOWLY, YEARS began to pass as one season blurred into another. My life revolved around getting up at 5 am to work. If I was the inside girl that week, I got to stay indoors with Mamma constantly breathing over my shoulder. If I was outside, I had to work the whole day without a break, frostbitten, bleeding feet and all.

Gradually our farm grew, and we started a farmers' market route. On the weekends, Samantha and I took turns going with Mamma to sell our crafts and produce from the farm. This was the one part of the week we looked forward to. However, when it was Samantha's turn to go to the market with Mamma, my day at home was spent mostly upstairs in bed with Brian. Many times when Samantha would wave goodbye, I seriously considered ending my life. That is how bad it was.

As the farm grew, we started an egg route as well. In time, we had five hundred laying hens at once, and every night before the outside girl was allowed in the house, she had to collect and clean the eggs and put them in cartons to sell in town. We also had numerous pigs, cows, goats and sheep that we sold every fall. In the summer, we gardened, chopped wood, made haystacks and so on.

As the years passed and I became older, I also became less compliant with Mamma and Brian. Occasionally I would stand up to them and refuse to take a beating for some trivial matter, or I would stand in front of Samantha and yell at them. Of course, this always got me a worse beating, one I would hardly be able to stand, but I didn't care. To me, it was worth it.

During this time, Brian was communicating with the Amish bishop on a weekly basis, and he told the Bishop that I held grudges against him for mistakes he made. Brian knew about the Amish policy of forgiveness no matter what, and the Amish belief that if you refused to forgive a person, you were worse than the person who committed the crime. You had to forgive and forget, no matter what they did or continued to do to you, because every man has his cross to bear and it is our place to forgive. When I read the letter that told us this, I pursed my lips and looked at Mamma and Brian.

"Well," I said, "then you have to forgive Samantha and I and stop beating us."

"Nope, not going to happen," Brian said in authoritative voice. "It is our job to mold you into chaste, submissive young women, and we have full authority to do this however we see fit."

I jumped as his hand slammed down on the corner of the table. Out of the corner of my eye, I saw Samantha recoil.

"And you will believe whatever I tell you to believe and do whatever I tell you to do, and you will dress however I tell you to dress or suffer the consequences." Brian was out of breath and his eyes were crazy, as if he were waiting for me to say something smart in return. I was not stupid, however, and knew when a battle had already been lost.

THINGS CONTINUED in the same manner until the summer I turned fifteen. Every day was like the one before it, and time seemed to drag on without end. Occasionally a neighbor would stop by and visit with Mamma and Brian, but Samantha and I were usually sent outside or somewhere we could not be seen. The neighbors were friendly and seemed interested in Samantha and I, but we were not allowed to talk to them.

The only occasions where Samantha and I ever came off the mountain were to help sell things along side the road or occasionally (maybe once or twice a year) we would be invited to one of the Mennonites house for dinner. There was a small community in the valley below the mountain and they had noticed us right away when we had moved in. Brian would usually lecture us for hours on why the Mennonites were going to hell. They wore flowers on their dresses and were just plain *worldly*. On these very rare occasions Samantha and I would stand in the kitchen of the Mennonite house and not really say anything. We would usually quietly help put the dinner on the table and then do the dishes afterwords.

Sometimes we would go upstairs with some of the Mennonite girls but we always knew to never say anything about our home life and we never stayed very long. Brian would watch us from the side of the room where he would be arguing with some of the Mennonite men. I think the only reason he ever agreed to these visits were so the Mennonites would think we were half way normal plain people. We never stayed long, but these visits left Samantha and I feeling more bewildered and sadder than ever. We could glimpse a world beyond our grasp. We did not belong to that world though, it seemed we did not belong anywhere but on the mountain. How many times had there been a chance for someone to help us. Our quiet withdrawn behavior and lack of conversation skills were beyond abnormal.

ONE DAY A neighbor who lived on the county road in a nice cottage asked me if I liked to read. I think she felt sorry for me. I was a teenage girl in a dirty gray dress, a long black apron and a white cap on my head. I was exhausted and sad and wished she could have seen the green and purple bruises that covered my frame beneath all my clothes. I smiled at her, though, and told her I loved the feeling of traveling away when I read books. Mamma frowned at me, but I shrugged, not caring what she thought.

"Well, that is great," The neighbor lady smiled at me. "I have a lot of National Geographics and history books. When I was a school teacher, I used to read to my students all the time."

Brian walked up just in time to hear the conversation, and he got upset that I was talking to a neighbor and told me to get back to work. As I walked away, I could hear him telling the neighbor that he did not want us exposed to outside culture through her books and magazines. I turned around in time to see an angry look on her face.

The next day when I was out feeding the geese, I saw her pull up the road and wave to me, then she backed back down the road out of sight. I looked around to make sure no one was watching and casually made my way down to the road. When I got there, she pointed to a banana box hidden under a bush.

"I put everything in there. I know your dad does not want you to have this stuff, but I find it so unfair to you," she had a sad look on her face. "When I leave it here, just take it back and hide it somewhere." She waved at me and drove off.

I liked her so much; just the fact that she cared that I liked to read was amazing, I thought. Eagerly, I ran over to the banana box and looked inside—it was stuffed with National Geographics, newspapers, Westerns and more. Hurriedly, I put the bushes back in place so the box was well hidden, and then at night when I did my chores, I moved the books and magazines one by one from under the bush to under the house where no one would ever look. Samantha and I took the magazines and books and read them any time Mamma and Brian were gone, or in the moonlight when we were supposed to be sleeping. Afterward, we burned them in the trash barrel or buried them on the mountainside so Brian would not find them. Sometimes she came and gave them to us openly but it made Brian angry and he would order us to burn them after she left. Of course we only pretended to, and usually burned ones that we had already read instead.

Tortured

"As a child I felt myself to be alone, and I am still, because I know things and must hint at things which others apparently know nothing of, and for the most part do not want to know."

— *C.G. Jung, Memories, Dreams, Reflections*

My fifteenth summer was a turning point in my life and in Samantha's as well. One morning, Mamma announced that she had a half-sister that we didn't know about. As her story unfolded, it sounded strangely familiar. Our grandmother had had a child at the age of fifteen, and the child was taken away from her and raised by the mother of the child's biological father, who lived out the rest of his days in a psychiatric facility in Mississippi. Mamma said she had always known about her older sister, but that they had only met once when she was a teenager.

Mamma said the only memory she had of Aunt Fanny was that she was very short with a sort of smashed-looking face, and that she did not say a word the entire day they were together. She went on to say that she had been contacted by a government agency in Prescott, Arizona, informing her that Aunt Fanny was at a facility there that housed people with special needs. Aunt Fanny was in Prescott at that time because her grandmother had died, and she had been brought to Arizona to live with our grandmother, who was actually Fanny's biological mother.

Our grandmother had been unable to care for our aunt due to the severity of her mental impairment (Aunt Fanny had been diagnosed as a schizophrenic, stemming from the fact that at the age of nine she had been raped by a relative and as a result gave birth to a child nine months later).

It was reported that Aunt Fanny constantly walked along the road believing it would take her home to Mississippi and to her grandmother. The facility where she was currently residing had decided they would not be able to care for her any longer because she was constantly finding ways to escape; but the directors were unwilling to turn her over to a psych ward due to her sweet and childlike personality. Thus they contacted Mamma since she was Fanny's last known kin and asked if she would be willing to care for her older sister.

Samantha and I had no idea what schizophrenia was, and neither did Mamma or Brian. When Mamma told us that our forty-year-old Aunt Fanny was coming to live with us, Samantha and I were so excited we could hardly contain ourselves. We imagined that Mamma and Brian would have to watch their behavior and be nicer to us with another adult in the house. We thought this was the best news we had had in many years.

Mamma told us that she would have to fly to Prescott, Arizona in two weeks to pick up Aunt Fanny. I wondered at the time why Mamma cared about her sister's living arrangements when she was constantly cracking jokes about how dumb her sister had seemed the one time she had met her. Eventually I learned the truth when I heard Mamma and Brian discussing how to spend the extra $550 a month they would receive for her care.

I overheard Mamma say, "It will be pure profit. All we have to do is give her some food, a couple of dresses and head coverings, and have one of the girls watch her at all times."

My heart sank all the way to my toes, and I felt more disappointed than I had in years. I broke the news to Samantha that night by passing her a note to read in the moonlight. She shook her head violently, and I could tell that she was even more disappointed than I was. The next morning before Mamma and Brian were awake, Samantha and I held our usual conference by the wood pile; this was one of the few times during the day that we could to talk to each other.

"They can't do that to a grown woman," Samantha exclaimed. "They just can't."

I shrugged, also confused. "I think they are planning on treating her just the same as us," I said sadly.

"But you cannot just force someone to dress like us and make them do what you want. I mean, she is older than Mamma for goodness sake," Samantha cried with disappointment.

I just nodded and shrugged again.

Two weeks later, Mamma boarded a plane in Wenatchee for the three-hour flight to Prescott. Brian waited until she flew back a few hours later, and then they drove the three-and-a-half hours back to the mountain.

It was dark outside when Samantha and I ran to the truck. When Aunt Fanny got out I went to her and she hugged me, but her face was vacant and she did not say a word. I remember feeling very surprised at her appearance. She seemed so innocent and looked like a five-year-old child. She was about four-foot nine and weighed approximately 210 pounds. She had bright blue eyes and porcelain white skin. Her face drooped a little but it was chubby and sweet. Her brown hair was cut very short, and she was wearing a pretty, flowing green summer dress. As I looked at her I could tell that she was very confused, as she just stared vacantly into the empty night sky.

Mamma and Brian were arguing as usual, and Aunt Fanny grabbed my hand. Samantha took her other hand, and we walked into the house. Earlier that day, Samantha and I had fixed a bed for Aunt Fanny next to ours and we had made a divider that enclosed our sleeping area, because we had been told that Aunt Fanny often tried to run in the middle of the night. I had taken two of the cowbells from the shed and tied them on the makeshift doors that we had made so there would be no chance of her escaping without us hearing her.

Samantha and I took her upstairs and showed her the bed. Aunt Fanny stared vacantly at the room while squeezing my hand tightly. Looking back now, I realize the kind of world she was accustomed to, I can only imagine the shock she felt on arriving at a farm in the middle of nowhere with a bunch of people that were dressed strangely. There was no electricity, no bathroom, no television...not even a couch for her to sit on. She must have been truly terrified.

As the three of us stood upstairs, we heard Mamma scream at us to come down. We all ran back down the stairs together. Mamma yanked Aunt Fanny's hand out of mine.

"She is not a baby, you know," she said with a look of disgust.

Mamma pushed Aunt Fanny into a chair and told her to stay put, and then she ordered me to make sandwiches. I made bologna sandwiches and put them on the table. I sat next to Aunt Fanny and pushed a sandwich closer to her, but she continued to stare into space. Mamma looked at her angrily, and Brian just shook his head.

"I cannot believe how retarded she is," Mamma scoffed. "She has been like this since we got on the plane; she hasn't said one word to me since I met her."

Samantha met my eyes across the table. I gave a little smirk as she rolled her eyes and mouthed, "I wonder why?"

"Well," Brian said authoritatively. "Tomorrow I want her in Amish clothes. Misty, that is your job, and I do not want her out of this house until she is properly clothed."

I winced as I looked at Aunt Fanny's short, round figure. Like all Amish, we only had one dress pattern which was made smaller or larger depending on the size of the person that would wear it. The shorter and rounder the person was, the harder it was to get the cut right.

It was late, and Brian ordered everyone upstairs to bed. I took Aunt Fanny outside to show her the outhouse and told her that if she needed to use it to just let me know and I would go with her. I waited outside the door for her, and then we all climbed the stairs to the sleeping quarters. Samantha secured the doors with the latch and the bells while I tried to get Aunt Fanny to change her clothes and lay down; she vehemently refused. Mamma yelled up to see if Fanny was in bed yet. Samantha yelled back that we were all in bed, and I blew out the candle. Aunt Fanny sat on the bed in the chilly room, still wearing her green summer dress and staring off into space with a blank expression on her face.

I awoke in the middle of the night to the loud ringing of cowbells and a crashing sound, followed by a loud thud. I immediately lit the candle, and saw Brian catching Aunt Fanny by the back of the dress as she was starting down the stairs. The makeshift doors Samantha and I had made out of thin plywood were crushed. It looked like Aunty had pushed on them, and when they did not move, she fell over on them. I gasped as I saw Mamma reach for the metal fly swatter next to her bed, and I jumped over the broken doors to stand by Aunt Fanny, who had lost her blank stare and now looked truly terrified. I grabbed her hand and she grabbed mine tightly as Brian pulled her over to Mamma, who was sitting on the edge of the bed.

I stepped in front of Aunt Fanny and screamed, "Don't do this, Mamma!"

Samantha tried to pull me away. "Come on, Misty," she whispered. "You are just going to get hurt, and they will hurt her anyway."

But I did not move. I knew the feeling of the metal fly swatter all too well—I much preferred a branch with thorns than the stinging of that metal. Mamma was both angry and shocked by my actions, and she began beating me all over with the metal flyswatter. Brian grabbed me and threw me against the wall, where I sank to my knees and covered my ears as Aunt Fanny screamed in terror and pain. When Mamma had finished beating Fanny, she dragged her by the ear and slammed her down onto her matress.

"Now don't you move from here or you will get more of this," Mamma said as she waved the fly swatter in Fanny's face.

Everyone went back to bed, and Samantha and I piled the wood with the bells attached in the middle of the room. Before getting back in bed, I started to go over to Aunt Fanny, who was crying in pain. As I reached for her, I heard Mamma's icy voice coming across the room.

"Don't touch her or I will beat her again."

Immediately I retracted my hand and cringed at the iciness of Mamma's voice. I lay down, my body was stinging from the welts that were popping up all over, but I was crying on the inside for the pain my aunt must be going through what with her new surroundings and being beaten in the middle of the night. Although I did not understand what was wrong with her, it was apparent that she was unable to comprehend or understand what was going on.

The next morning Samantha and I got up as usual when the alarm rang. Aunt Fanny was curled up on the end of her matress.

"I think she is supposed to go with us," I told Samantha. "We better wake her and get her downstairs and keep her with us so Mamma does not have a chance to beat her again."

Samantha nodded. We tried to wake Aunty Fanny quietly, but she seemed groggy and dizzy, and when Samantha and I helped her off the bed, she seemed like she was going to pass out. We both took an arm and slowly helped Fanny down the stairs, and then we sat her in a chair next to the stove.

"What do you think is wrong with her?" I asked Samantha.

Samantha shrugged and said she was probably just tired. I shook my head and felt her forehead. She was cold and sweaty. The early April morning was chilly, but Aunt Fanny refused any kind of sweater or blanket. She just sat, eyes closed, leaning back in the chair. After staring at her for a couple of minutes, I went over to the overnight bag Mamma had brought with her. Two small overnight bags were all Fanny had, since Brian had thrown her suitcases away at the airport. In the outside pocket of the bag, I found three pill bottles and some glucose tablets. I tried to read the names of the prescriptions, but I had no idea what they were. The only thing I recognized were the glucose tablets, since I had read about low glucose when I was studying my home remedies and because Samantha had mild episodes of low glucose a few times a week. I realized it had been twenty hours since Aunt Fanny had eaten anything.

"I think I better give her one of these," I told Samantha. "I think she is really sick."

Samantha shook her head and pointed to both of our welts. "No, you don't know how to lie, and if it ticks Mamma off, you are both going to catch a beating."

I pursed my lips. "Well, I don't think they want their new paycheck dying on the first day," I said sarcastically.

I tried to give Fanny a piece of bread, but she did not wake up enough to eat it. It was my turn to work in the house, so while I did my chores, I kept an eye on Aunt Fanny. Before Samantha went outside, she helped me move Aunt Fanny from the chair to the floor, because I was afraid she would fall on the stove if she passed out. When we woke Brian and Mamma about an hour later, they came down the stairs sleepily and sat next to the stove, ignoring a very pale and sleeping Fanny.

"I think Aunt Fanny has something wrong with her," I told Mamma nervously. "I found these in her bag." I held up the glucose tablets.

"Of course she isn't feeling good," Mamma snapped at me. "She is a stupid idiot who did not eat anything all day yesterday."

"No, I mean she is really sick," I said, trying to show Mamma the remedies book with the list of symptoms, but she knocked it out of my hands and shoved me back toward the stove and the burning potatoes. I put breakfast on the table and tried to wake Aunt Fanny again, but there was no response. Samantha and I looked at each other frantically. I turned to Mamma and asked her what the people had told her about Aunt Fanny when she had picked her up. Mamma just shrugged and said she didn't pay attention to that c*** and that all she could remember was that Fanny was schizophrenic and had low blood sugar and some other junk.

I looked through the overnight bag, looking for a glucose monitor. I had read about it in my book and hoped it had not been in the suitcases Brian had thrown away. Thankfully, I found it, and I carefully read the directions. I took Fanny's blood sugar three times since I was not sure I was doing it right, and each time it came back with a very low reading.

I did not know what to do except get glucose into her somehow. Aunt Fanny appeared to be sleeping, but I knew she wasn't really sleeping.

"Samantha," I yelled in a panic. "Come over here and help me."

Finally Mamma and Brian realized there was something seriously wrong with Fanny and came over to assist me. I ordered Brian to pry open Aunt Fanny's mouth, which he did. There was only a small opening, but I crushed four tablets and funneled the powder into her mouth. I was not sure what I was doing, but I massaged her throat to help her swallow the powder. The glucose must have worked its way down, because after a few minutes, she started moaning and moving around. I brought her some potatoes; she only ate a few, but she did drink some milk.

Mamma started yelling, telling Fanny that the next time she put food in front of her, she had better eat it, and that she had better not to pull a stunt like that again.

Right after breakfast, I measured Fanny for her clothes—a task that proved to be especially difficult due to her wide girth and small shoulders. While I was measuring her, I started to notice some very strange behavior from her. At first I thought she was talking to me, and I happily asked her what she had said since she had not said a word since her arrival. But much to my confusion, she was talking to something in the corner of the room. I looked in the corner but saw no one, and then I looked back at her with wide eyes, for the first time truly realizing what her diagnosis entailed. When I saw Samantha outside, I informed her of the situation, but she only shrugged and stated, "I knew she had to be a loony to end up here, Misty. Why else do you think she would be here?"

That was our full understanding of the situation since we had no means of gaining any real knowledge about Fanny's condition. That day, Fanny switched between vacant stares and talking to an unseen person while she danced around the room. It was hard to measure her for the long dress and apron since she was either getting tangled in the fabric, or standing like a statue refusing to help in any way. A couple of times I accidentally stuck Fanny with the sewing pins and I felt awful about it. I immediately applied pressure and told her how sorry I was, only to realize that she had not even noticed and was intent on talking to someone over my shoulder.

Mamma was reading a book as usual. I tried to make light of the situation and pretended that Fanny was just being funny, but much later in the afternoon Mamma began screaming at me because I had been so busy that I had forgotten to make bread. After beating me with the metal fly swatter, she turned to Fanny and said,

"I am tired of your bull****. You don't have schizophrenia or whatever it is, and you are not getting any of those damned pills so you can pretend you are sick or something. You better just snap out of it right now, you hear me?" She started beating Aunt Fanny all over her body and laughing. "That's right; we'll get the devil beat out of you."

At first Fanny kept dancing around and jabbering to the unknown person, and then it seemed to dawn on her what was happening, and she began running with Mamma chasing after her. I ran after both of them, but I am ashamed to say that I then just stood there, not knowing if I would help or harm if I tried to intervene.

Mamma threw Fanny against the side of the house, and in a threatening voice told her that every time she did not do what she was told, she could expect more of the same. After that, she dragged Fanny into the house and told her to stand still while I put her new clothes on her. She was sobbing like a little child, and I gave Mamma the angriest looks I could muster.

"What are you looking at?" Mamma barked at me. "She is standing still, isn't she?"

I didn't answer; I just continued tying the white cap on Fanny's head. As I looked down into her giant blue eyes, I saw a sense of clarity, as if she had suddenly reappeared after having been absent from her body. Our eyes met, and I smiled at her. She just looked at me, as if begging for my help. My eyes were full of tears and I felt so helpless. I really did not know what to do.

After I dressed Aunt Fanny, I hugged her and told her she looked pretty in her new clothes. She shook her head and began pulling them off.

"No, no," I said, trying to stop her for fear of what would happen. Mamma slapped her a few times with the fly swatter, and she finally stopped undressing, although I could tell she was still confused at the strange clothes we had put on her.

And so life began for Aunt Fanny on the mountain. It took Mamma many days of beatings to get Aunt Fanny to keep her Amish clothes on, but eventually Fanny seemed to understand that if she did not wear them, pain would follow. Mamma finally realized that the ugly welts that now covered Fanny's body could cause them trouble if anyone saw them, so she began beating Fanny under her dress, often targeting her large breasts. Mamma would make cruel remarks saying that she did not need her breasts anyway. Fanny would cry and scream, and Mamma and Brian would merely laugh. I would stand shaking and covering my ears with my hands. To this this day, the sounds of Aunt Fanny's high-pitched screams haunt me and cause me to start shaking.

The work on the farm that summer proved to be especially difficult. We now had five hundred chickens, the cows and the pigs. Mamma and Brian loved the idea of having a large farm, but they were not very knowledgeable about how to make a profit from it. Fanny traded off work every day, one day she was with Samantha and the next day she spent with me. She was ordered to help, and although Samantha and I both tried to shield her from punishment, if Fanny was caught dancing around or not working, she was punished, as were we, for not obeying.

When we ate, Mamma placed the fly swatter on the table. I always sat next to Fanny or directly across from her, and whenever she started drifting off, I would nudge her under the table. Sometimes I even pinched her quite hard to get her to eat, because if I did not, the fly swatter would fly across the room, aimed directly at her already sore breasts. My efforts

79

to protect her rarely worked, but at least I tried.

One morning after Fanny had been with us for about a month, Mamma started beating her as usual when suddenly Fanny yelled, "Stop it, Sue."

We all stared in disbelief. We had no idea that she could talk directly to another person, since she was always talking to people who were not there and never said anything directly to any of us. I had suspected from the beginning that this was because she had been taken off her medication after Brian and Mamma had forbidden us to give it to her. We all looked at Fanny in astonishment, and Samantha and I were overcome with happiness—someone who could talk was harder to abuse.

"Oh yeah?" Brian yelled. "Is that how you talk to your sister who took you in after no else wanted you? You stupid crazy b***h!"

"You people are awful," Fanny said defiantly, her chubby face puckering in a pout. And then, just as suddenly as that clear and rational Aunt Fanny had appeared, she was gone.

"All right, nothing for you to eat until tomorrow morning," Mamma threw the fly swatter down. "And if I catch either one of you feeding her even a bite of anything, I will make you and her wish you had never been born." Mamma was so angry that her green eyes were closed like slits, and I could feel her hot breath and spit on my face.

I believe that in that moment pure evil was standing there in front of me. All of the pain and suffering I had endured at the hands of this crazy woman was no match for the pain I felt for my Aunt Fanny, and I glared at Mamma with all the anger I could muster. Brian was standing behind her, and he looked at me and gritted his teeth. Brian was mad at me because I was starting to push him away when he groped me, telling him that it was wrong and against God. He was constantly trying to find a reason to shame me and make me bend over in the middle of the house and touch my toes. Sometimes he'd wait for fifteen minutes before he beat me. When I refused to bend over, he would grab me by the shoulders and bang my head against the wall.

On this particular day, he just smirked at me, daring me to defy Mamma by feeding Fanny. I looked back at him with defiance. I don't know why, but sometimes, based on my level of defiance, they would not beat me. This was one of those times when I felt like drawing a bulls-eye on my heart and yelling, "Come on, give it your best shot, buddy, I dare you. Let's see what you think you are made of." Brian and Mamma seemed to be able to read this message in my flashing green eyes and they usually backed down. I believe it was because they knew that deep down I would always stand up to them when I was convinced that I was standing up for what I believed was right. I had even heard Brian remark once,

"Her eyes are like those of an angel. Are you sure you didn't pick up the wrong baby at the hospital?"

Mamma had just laughed and said, "Yes, I got the right one, but it would be a comfort to think that I got the wrong one, she is such an embarrassment. Unfortunately, she is the spitting image of her great-grandmother."

I had met my great-grandmother once when I was nine, and I remember people exclaiming at the likeness that we shared. This, however, had shattered all hopes I had ever entertained that I might be adopted.

Later in the day, Fanny and I hauled wheelbarrows of soiled chicken bedding from the chicken house to the enormous compost pile around back. Fanny had been dancing around the whole morning, yelling and waving her finger at unseen people in the loft of the chicken house. While I did my day-to-day work, I was usually lost in a dramatic story or off somewhere exploring an unknown land, but on the days I was with Fanny, I was entertained by her.

Much of what she said was just mumbling, but sometimes she seemed to be acting out a play where she took multiple roles. It reminded me of how Samantha had loved acting as a child, and how sometimes when I walked up on her, unannounced, she would still be living her fantasy. Fanny often seemed to fall into the role of Snow White or Cinderella. Sometimes I would stand watching her, trying to figure out the story line, but it switched around so often, that I couldn't make much sense out of it.

That morning, Mamma and Brian had gone to town for supplies, and Samantha was left working in the garden while Fanny and I cleaned the chicken coop. I was worried about Fanny and made her wheelbarrow much lighter than mine. Although it had crossed my mind to give her some of the old bread that we fed the chickens I was too afraid of getting caught. Oftentimes Mamma and Brian would pretend to go to town but instead they would park around the bend in the road, and then would sneak back up the hill to spy on us while we thought they were gone.

Many times they would walk up behind us and catch us when we were talking. For our disobedience we were dragged into the house and beaten. Now we never knew if they were really gone or just watching us from the top of the hill. If Samantha and I caught a glimpse of them in the bushes, we would pretend not to see them but would walk around singing either "Johnny Comes Marching Home," "Mine Eyes Hath Seen the Glory," or "I'll Fly Away." I don't think they ever caught on to our signals, much to our relief.

On this day, as Fanny and I pushed the wheelbarrows to the compost pile, Fanny suddenly stopped and looked at me with a smile and in her sweet southern voice asked me if she could have a couple of sandwiches. My stomach knotted and I looked at her with tears in my eyes. I felt we were being watched, but I could not be certain since it had been nearly two hours since Brian and Mamma left.

"I am so sorry, Fanny," I swallowed hard to try to keep from crying. "I don't want you to get in trouble, though." I reached out and gave her a big hug, hoping she could feel how much I wanted to give her something to eat. Aunt Fanny hugged me back and in her childlike voice said matter-of-factly,

"You are very nice, but Sue is a b***h."

I smiled and nodded. Aunt Fanny looked at the ground for a minute and then looked at me and in a shy voice said, "Brian is mean too, and Samantha is not as nice as you. Why are you nice to me?"

I was shocked at the conversation we were having. I just looked at her for a minute and then smiled and shrugged my shoulders. "Well, I always try to be nice. Besides, you are family and I love you," I reached out again and hugged her tightly, barely able to get my arms around her waist.

I sighed and was just about to give her a piece of the day old bread when I suddenly heard "When Johnny Comes Marching Home" coming from the garden. I jumped and put the bread down and hurried Fanny to the compost pile. We worked as fast as we could for the rest of the day. By late afternoon, I saw that Fanny was getting dizzy and had her just follow me. After I finished cleaning the eggs, Fanny and I sat on the back steps, exhausted from the day's work, but not allowed to enter the house until Mamma and Brian came home. Fanny laid her head on my shoulder, and I could tell she was sick. Samantha flashed hand signals at me from the window asking if Fanny was okay, or if I had seen Mamma and Brian. I shrugged my shoulders to say I did not know if Fanny was okay or not, and I made the secret sign for "no" while pretending to rub my head since I was not sure if Mamma and Brian were hiding close by.

Finally, we heard the truck coming up the drive, and I went out to open the gate for them as always. I unloaded the grain, and then took Fanny inside. That evening, we sat down to eat dinner with a scowling Mamma and Brian.

"Well," I said, trying to break the eerie silence, "Fanny has to eat something or she is going to pass out again." I put some stew in a bowl in front of her, and she began eating like a starved animal. Poor little Fanny, she did not understand why she had been starved. Punishing her was like punishing a new born baby, she didn't understand and never would.

A NEW VICTIM

The tears I feel today

I'll wait to shed tomorrow.

Though I'll not sleep this night

Nor find surcease from sorrow.

My eyes must keep their sight:

I dare not be tear-blinded.

I must be free to talk

Not choked with grief, clear-minded.

My mouth cannot betray

The anguish that I know.

Yes, I'll keep my tears til later:

But my grief will never go."

- Anne McCaffrey, Dragonsinger

The last time Brian had seen his father, he had let slip the name of the town we were moving to. He had made Grandpa promise not tell anyone, but that summer the police showed up at the house with a letter from Aunty Laura. The letter told of how Brian's father had died of colon cancer and how he had begged to see his son before he left this earth. After so many years of not seeing or hearing from Brian, Grandpa had finally broken his silence and told Aunty Laura where we were living. But it was too late, and by the time she was able to locate the local police, Grandpa had slipped beyond our realm and was gone.

Aunty Laura was very angry in the letter and told Brian that he had abandoned his loving family, she said that they had not even known if he was alive or dead all these years. The letter went on to say that their mother had fallen ill in her nursing home in Tallahassee, Florida. Laura included the phone number of the home and underlined and highlighted where she wrote that Brian should call her. The letter ended with Aunty Laura stating that the bike shop and all the rest of Grandpa's possessions had been left to her since they could not be sure if Brian was ever coming back.

Samantha and I were sad to hear that Grandpa had died. Of course, he had been 88 years old, but it hurt that the world had lost a kind man. Brian did not even shed a single tear; he was just angry that he had been pushed out of Grandpa's will.

"I will fix her wagon," he ranted. "She thinks she will get everything. Well, Mom has more than Dad ever had, and I am going to collect."

Samantha, Mamma and I all just looked at him. "What the h*** are you talking about?" Mamma asked emphatically. "You can't collect anything if she is still alive."

"Well she is old and just broke her hip, and it was always easy for me to get what I wanted from her," Brian mumbled as he seemed to calculate something in his head. "I am going to convince her to come live with us."

Aunty Laura, of course, had no idea the axis of evil she had accidentally set into motion. Brian was out for revenge, and revenge he would get no matter what the cost. Later that day, Brian and Mamma went into town and contacted Grandma via a pay phone. She had just moved from the hospital to a senior retirement home. She had suffered a stroke after breaking her hip.

The next week Brian flew to Florida to put his plans into action. He stayed there for a week and then flew back. Brian was actually in a good mood when he got back, because Grandma, whom Samantha and I had never met and Brian had not seen or contacted in more than twelve years, had agreed to come live with us. She was old and frail at the age of 82, and had no idea what was in store for her.

The doctor had stated that Grandma would be unable to make such a long trip for at least three weeks, but Brian was still ecstatic and rambled on and on about how his mom had recently sold her condominium and had $60,000 in the bank. She also got a $1,000 pension check every month from her late husband's estate.

"Well, that is certainly good news," Mamma's eyes lit up at the news. "But you know your nosey sister is going to be here all the time if your mother is here. All she has to do is ask the police where we live now."

Brian nodded. "We have to tell her and invite her here. I want her to know Mom is living with me," His face creased into an evil grin.

A few days before leaving for Florida again, Brian announced that as soon as Grandma arrived, we would be building an addition to the orchard shack we were living in. Samantha and I were excited about having Grandma around, plus, Aunty Laura would most likely come to visit now. Just maybe, life would get better. I lay awake at night dreaming of Aunty Laura asking me to stay with her for a while. At the same time, I knew Brian and Mamma would never allow it...but a girl could dream.

*F*INALLY IN August, Mamma and Brian set out on the long trip to Florida. They were to be gone a week. Brian said that Grandma owned a twenty-foot travel trailer and that she could live in that until we had better living arrangements. I was worried about an elderly woman with health problems coming to live with us. The icy winters we experienced often blocked all roads to the hospital, and it could be hours before any emergency medical treatment could be provided.

That week Samantha and I were left with many tasks to complete, but it was an unusually relaxing week. We knew for a fact that we were not being watched, and there was no one to force us to take baths in the spring water. Fanny seemed happier, too, as she drifted in and out of reality and started talking to us more.

I made up a schedule for the week that, if strictly followed, would give me and Samantha every afternoon to read, and give Aunt Fanny a much-deserved rest while she sat next to us. So Samantha and I scurried around all morning; then we would make our lunch, which was a real treat, and afterward, we would curl up on our mattresses upstairs and bury our faces in the books left by our kind neighbor. I had so much fun as I lost myself in the history of the Civil War, and how the West was won, and the Anne of Green Gables series. My favorite book was Uncle Tom's Cabin. I felt I could identify with Uncle Tom and cried tears of deep sorrow for him when he was sold downriver to the wide-open cotton fields of the South.

It was a very hot week that mid-August and there was not much breeze. Of course, there was no relief from air conditioning or fans since we had no electricity, but we were used to the heat, and sprawled out on our matresses with our heavy skirts pulled up around our waists and our feet kicking in the air. Fanny had bolder ideas, and she stripped down to her underwear. At first Samantha tried to make her put her clothes back on, but I just laughed and Aunt Fanny started to laugh, and finally Samantha joined in our merriment. This led to us rolling around and tickling each other. It was great fun, but in the back of my mind I was sad, thinking that I could not remember a time when Samantha and I had ever laughed like this.

At fifteen years old, I was coming into womanhood, and Samantha, who was turning thirteen in a couple of weeks, would soon follow suit. What would happen to us? I did not know.

ON ONE of these blessed days, Fanny started squirming around and talking. Finally, Samantha got irritated and pushed her and told her to stop. Out of curiosity, I asked Fanny who she was talking to, and to our utter surprise, she began talking and pointing.

"See them black angels over there," she said in a hushed voice. "They are telling me to come over to them, and there's white angels over here that keep telling me 'no, don't go'.

Samantha and I stared at her with our mouths open and looked in the direction she was pointing.

Fanny's voice was just a whisper. "The black angels say if I follow them they will take me back to my old home, but the white angels tell me not to go."

"Do you always see these angels?" I asked.

"No," Fanny shook her head. "But there is a lady, who visits me a lot, and she says mean things to me and we argue a lot."

Samantha and I looked at each other, spooked because we had no real understanding of her condition.

"Well, Fanny," I struggled for the right words, "next time they visit you, just tell them to go away, okay? Tell them you don't want to talk to them."

By this time, Fanny was gone in her own world again, but I was happy that she had allowed us a glimpse into her lonely little world.

Our week alone sped by too fast. On the last day, Samantha, Fanny and I did not take our afternoon break but scurried about, trying to get everything done. We were planting a large patch of garlic for winter, chopping wood, canning vegetables and so on. We could not be sure what kind of mood Mamma and Brian would be in when they returned, but we were planning for the worst.

86

Years later, I would ask myself why I did not take Fanny and Samantha and run away during this time. The only plausible explanation I could come up with was that we were completely brainwashed by the rules (such as: if you did not wear plain clothing and cover your head you would go straight to hell). We were taught that the outside world was worldly and ungodly, and that if you became one of them, you were lost forever. The thought of going to the police never even occurred to us, since Brian and Mamma told us if we talked to the police, the police would just give us back to them as there was no room for us in the crowded foster system. Then we might just disappear for good when we returned home, and no would ever know or care where we were. It is hard to believe that I was so brainwashed at the time, but I was, and Mamma and Brian knew that.

ON A blistering hot day in August, a week after Mamma and Brian had left, we heard the truck driving up the private road to the house. Samantha and I had long ago learned to differentiate the sound of our truck from the sound of any other. As soon as I heard it, I felt my heart sink; the happy week was over. For a split second I stood frozen to the ground, and then I raced over to Fanny to make sure she was properly dressed. I tied her head covering and shook out her dress and apron as Samantha ran over to open the gate.

The truck struggled a little more than usual as it crawled up the steep hill into the driveway, and my heart sank a little—as it always did—when the sun glinted off the hood and the truck rolled up to the gate. As they came to a stop, we peered in the windows, trying to determine what mood Mamma and Brian were in. Brian opened his door and motioned for us to come to the back door. An older woman's voice floated over to us and I heard her say, "Are we home, honey?"

"Yeah, Mom, let's get you out of here," Brian said in a nicer voice than I had ever heard him use. He opened the back door and I helped him ease Grandma to the ground.

Grandma looked at me and smiled. "Hi sweetheart," she said in a frail voice. "I sure am tired. We have been on the road for a long time."

Mamma got out of the car. I heard the door slam, and the truck shook a little. Grandma shrugged and looked at me.

"She has been pissed at me the whole way," Her thin white face puckered in a frown. "All I did, was ask her where she got her dress. Oh, look, you are wearing the same thing."

"Um..." I stammered, not sure what to say. I just smiled at her instead of answering, and she smiled back.

"That's okay, honey," she said as she struggled to walk toward the house. "Brian told me you guys are Amish now. I guess I just didn't put it all together."

I helped Grandma up the stairs into the house, and she sat down at the table. She asked for a glass of water and Samantha got it for her. Then Samantha, Fanny and I stood in front of her just looking at her. She was 82 years old. Her hair was a soft, silvery color and she had had a recent perm. She had on a red polyester dress, pearl earrings and bright red lipstick. Samantha whispered in my ear, asking if I thought she would be allowed to dress like this every day. I shrugged and tried to listen to Mamma and Brian, who were arguing behind the door.

"I can't stand it with her constant 'honeys' and 'sweethearts,'" Mamma said sarcastically.

"Just until I get everything signed, dammit," I heard Brian say with clenched teeth. "Quit acting like a child, Sue, or you will ruin the plan."

Samantha nudged me, and I realized Grandma was talking to me.

"So how old are you, honey?" she asked me while she rolled her false teeth around in her mouth and pushed them back into place.

"I am fifteen," I fidgeted with my apron and painfully realized how poor my communication skills were.

"You girls got any boyfriends?" Grandma asked with interest.

"Boy, this lady doesn't have a clue where she is, does she?" Samantha said under her breath. I gave Samantha a warning look, and she rolled her eyes.

"No, not right now," I answered with a shrug.

"Well," Grandma fanned herself with a potholder she had found on the table. "It sure is hot here. What do you guys do for fun?"

We looked at her and smiled without saying anything. Grandma looked tired, and although she seemed very sweet, I could tell she did not really understand what was going on, and I knew that our living arrangements were nothing like she expected.

Grandma turned to Aunt Fanny and asked her name. To my surprise, Fanny answered and stepped forward to take Grandma's hand. Suddenly it dawned on me why Fanny was staring at Grandma and standing so close to her. Fanny had been raised by her own grandmother whom she had loved very much; it was her grandmother she was constantly trying to get back to when she tried to run away. Fanny seemed unable to comprehend the finality of death.

Grandma smiled and shook Fanny's hand. "You must be Sue's sister, huh?" Grandma said. "My Brian told me about you."

"Yeah," Fanny frowned. "That's what they tell me, but I don't know if she is really my sister."

Grandma seemed confused. "You don't know your own sister?"

Fanny just smiled, and I put my arm around her, thanking her for being nice to Grandma.

Just then, Brian opened the door and told us to come outside. He told Grandma that we would be right back and closed the door behind us.

"Okay," Brian looked at us sternly, "this is the deal. It is going to take about a month to get the papers signed, and my sister is coming out in two weeks." He paused and looked at us threateningly. "I want you girls to be happy around my mom so she does not complain to Laura when she gets here. You will be watched, so I better not see any funny business going on." He pointed a finger at us. "She will be sleeping in the trailer till the house is fixed, so Misty, you will sleep in the trailer with her and help her go to the bathroom because she cannot walk on her own. She is on a lot of medication and eye drops, so you will be in charge of seeing to that, as well as helping her dress."

I stood there listening to my instructions with raised eyebrows. Brian was standing in front of me, looking into my non compliant face. I nervously straightened my small frame. At only five feet tall and a hundred and twenty pounds, I was certainly not a physical threat to him, but I knew he felt threatened by my new found attitude of indifference to him. He reached for me and grabbed me by the front of the dress, twisting it so the neck of the dress tightened, making it hard for me to breathe.

"Don't think you can spend this time dallying around, either," His voice threatening. I winced at the smell of his hot breath in my face. "I will expect your usual work to be done and I don't want anything cute going on here, because if I hear so much as a peep from my mom about anything..." He twisted the dress tighter and I began coughing.

Brian let go and gave me a shove, I fell backward onto the dusty ground. I got up and dusted myself off, scowling at Mamma and Brian as I did so. I looked over at Fanny and Samantha and I could see that they both got the message loud and clear. Mamma was standing there with a pout on her face.

"I can't stand the b****," she said vehemently.

I breathed a sigh of relief, though. Brian's orders were to treat Grandma nicely, at least for now.

We backed the trailer under the tree and got Grandma situated. She constantly complained of the heat, but Brian laughed at her and told her to remember the 40s and 50s when there was no air conditioning. Grandma laughed back and said that was when she was a young chick and could handle it.

That night, I got Grandma ready for bed. She was very stiff and could only stand if she had her walker or someone to hold on to. I dressed her in her nightgown, and Brian sat on the bed to talk to her. I could not believe it—he seemed so normal and charming. I had never seen him act so nice before. Grandma laughed and called him her baby boy as she stroked his cheek. I could have been happy with this scene, had I not known that it was all a charade to get Grandma to sign everything she owned over to Brian. I felt very sad, as I did not know how Grandma was going to be treated once she signed her life over to her evil son.

That night, I woke several times to help Grandma go on the pot next to her bed. I was happy to do so, as I pretended that I was working in a hospital and that I was the nurse and she was my patient. It sounds a little childish now, but when you are in a hopeless situation, you have to find ways to cope mentally. I still had to get up at 5:00 am, and I jumped when the alarm went off. I looked at Grandma, who was sound asleep, and I pulled on my dark blue dress and black apron, then twisted my knee-length, brownish-red hair into a bun and slid on my white head covering. All of this took less than two minutes, and then I was off and running. I met Samantha in the house, where she was standing in front of the wood-burning stove with Fanny.

"How was it?" Samantha whispered as I put an arm around Fanny's shoulders.

"It was okay," I mumbled as I tried to stifle a yawn. "I had to get up four times to help her on the pot, which is not easy when you are half asleep and she is too." I yawned again and rubbed my eyes as I tried to wake up.

That morning, as I did my chores outside, I kept checking in on Grandma, who was sleeping soundly. At eight o'clock, Brian called me into the trailer to dress Grandma. I was not used to any clothes other than the things we wore, so when I opened the closet at the back of the trailer I looked with interest at the clothes Brian would call "worldly." There were bright pant suits with elastic waists, colorful dresses and pretty shoes. After rummaging about for a few minutes, I helped Grandma into a flowered T-shirt and pink pants that she had picked from the clothes I held up. Dressing her was difficult because her left side was stiff from the stroke and the broken hip. After I helped her dress, Grandma had me help her with her makeup. I could not remember ever seeing someone put makeup on before, and I watched her frail, shaking hands as she applied her lipstick.

"Do you want to borrow anything, dear?" she asked me.

I shook my head.

She looked at me and smiled. "You should put some mascara on those lashes; it would make your bright, green eyes really stand out."

I did not know if Brian was listening at the window, so I just smiled and closed the makeup kit. When I opened the door to call for Samantha's help, I was not surprised to see Brian sitting in a folding chair under the window with a Bible in his hands. He looked at me with steely eyes from under his black Amish hat, and I stared back at him with raised eyebrows.

WITHIN A few days of Grandma's arrival, construction started on the new addition to our house. It was going to be a twenty-four by thirty-six foot addition to our twelve by twenty-four foot orchard shack. There was going be an upstairs and downstairs with two new bedrooms upstairs and two downstairs; it would also have a living room. The old part of the house would be converted into a sewing area, and the back of the house would become the kitchen.

Mamma announced that she and Brian were going to try to get foster children as soon as construction was done on the house. Samantha and I were dumbfounded at the news, and I could only pray that would never happen.

The construction workers told Brian the whole thing was going to cost a lot because they were going to get it done in six weeks time. It was very important that it be done by the end of September for Grandma's sake; otherwise, there was no telling what problems the cruel winter winds would cause for her.

While the construction workers were busy, Samantha and I cared for Grandma and Fanny all the while continuing to do the work around the house and farm. Caring for Grandma, while enjoyable, turned out to be a big responsibility. She had to have her blood pressure taken twice daily, eye drops for glaucoma put in three times a day, and she was on at least six different medications. Then there was dressing her, bathing her, and helping her to the toilet. I enjoyed this work, but it was difficult to keep up, especially when it was my week to be outside. After a week, Brian created a new rule that the inside girl would care for Grandma and the outside girl would care for Fanny.

During this time, Brian and Mamma were constantly taking Grandma back and forth to lawyers and to the bank so she could sign over her late husband's post office check, her bank account and the trailer. Brian was so sweet to her it made me sick. I could see he'd had a lifetime of practice manipulating people. He even convinced his mother to give him power of attorney and told her he would manage things for her. She agreed with little protest, only too happy to have her baby boy doting over her.

Grandma was bored much of the time, and she spent a lot of time sleeping in her wheelchair. The stroke had left her the ability to speak, but I could see she frequently struggled for words and became tired easily.

THE HOUSE began to take shape, and Mamma and Brian spent most of their time watching its progress or going to town. This was a nice time for Samantha, Fanny and me, since Brian and Mamma could not hurt us while others were around. The construction guys thought Samantha and I were cute, and a couple of the young guys kept trying to talk to us. Samantha and I were not used to young men looking at us so we only smiled at them. It was enjoyable, until one day a couple of weeks into the construction when Brian came around the back of the house where I was picking up firewood and found nineteen-year-old Jonathan leaning against the back of the house frame, asking me questions. Brian got very angry at him. He went to the foreman and told him that we were Amish and he did not want the men talking to anyone other than him or Mamma, and if they did not like it, they could leave and he would get another contractor.

Jonathan never spoke to me again, and I was sad because he seemed nice. The next day when I was passing him, my eyes on the ground, I heard him mumble,

"Your old man is a real prick."

I smiled—exactly my own thoughts, just in different words.

BRIAN HAD MANAGED to stave off Aunty Laura's visit until construction was over and the last papers were signed by Grandma. He was constantly coming into the house and saying, "Okay, Mom, sign here," and she would sign, no questions asked. Grandma could not see very well and would just ask,

"Where, honey?"

"Right here, Mom," Brian would say as he pretended to be patient and loving.

"Okay, sweetheart, is that it?" Grandma would ask in her shaking voice.

"For now," he would say with an evil grin.

When the house was done, it was very nice. The living room and two downstairs bedrooms had been painted and sheet rocked. The kitchen and upstairs were just walls with insulation stapled in them, but the fact that

92

there was insulation at all was a comforting thought. The October wind was already howling and the temperature was dipping below thirty degrees; Grandma was constantly cold. Brian had installed a large barrel heater in the corner of the living room, and this is where we started parking Grandma's wheelchair every morning.

It was during this time Samantha and I both noticed that Grandma was starting to sleep all the time instead of just taking frequent naps throughout the day and she only woke up when we shook her. I was worried, and when we checked her blood pressure, as we did every day, it was always higher than it was supposed to be.

IT WAS AN exciting day when Aunty Laura showed up. It seemed like it had been a lifetime since we had seen her, but she looked the same. Although she was now in her late fifties, she still had soft, curly blonde hair, porcelain white skin and kind, sparkling, blue eyes that always seemed brighter when paired with her usual red lipstick. She was always dressed sharply, even for an excursion to our farm which was in the middle of nowhere.

Her black pencil skirt and button-up pink blouse seemed out of place to us, but that was Aunty Laura. Her husband, although quiet, always had a smile that stretched from ear to ear, and although he lived in the city, he fancied himself an outdoors-man and had dressed as such for this exciting trip to the middle of nowhere. Samantha and I giggled when we saw Uncle Bill dressed in camouflage pants and a bright orange hunting sweater.

"They look funny together," I laughed.

Samantha just shook her head and rolled her eyes in amusement.

Before their arrival, Brian had given Samantha, Fanny and me explicit instructions on how to act around Aunty Laura. We would take turns doing chores that day, and one of us would always be with Grandma, taking care of her and reading to her. He had bought some storybooks just for this occasion.

As Aunty Laura got out of the car, she removed her sunglasses and walked toward us with a smile, but there was a bit of disapproval in her eyes as well.

"Hey, Brian," she said, giving her little brother a hug. "How in the h*** did you get Mom to agree to live up here in the middle of nowhere?"

Brian was taken aback and said defensively that Grandma had asked to live with us. Aunty Laura did not seem to buy his story, but she looked over at me and Samantha and smiled.

"Wow, you girls are all grown up," she said, hugging us. She looked at me and asked how old I was now.

"I will be sixteen next month," I said with little enthusiasm.

She raised her eyebrows and looked at me in my long, dark dress, cape apron and covering.

"So, did you finish school already?" she asked with raised eyebrows.

Mamma popped over and put an arm around my shoulders. "Our Misty is really smart," she said. "She just finished the tenth grade but has decided to stop now."

"Well, she still has those giant, green eyes. I am sure some boys are going to come knocking your door down any day. Better have your shotgun ready, Brian," she laughed and winked at her younger brother.

I smiled as I was supposed to, thinking how much I wished it were true but knowing all too well it was not.

Aunty Laura hugged Samantha as well and exclaimed at how Samantha, who had always been short and chubby as a little girl, was now several inches taller than I was. When she asked Samantha what grade she was in, Mamma butted in and said she was in the eighth grade. It was obvious that Mamma and Aunty Laura still had no intentions to like each other even a little bit.

In stark contrast to Aunty Laura's trim figure and confident manner, Mamma, who was nearing two hundred and seventy-five pounds, had a sullen and defensive-looking face and a brow that was constantly furrowed and angry. Her green eyes were penetrating and miserable, and her blackish-brown hair was always combed severely back away from her face. I had always wondered what Brian saw in her, besides himself, of course.

"Well, where is Mom?" Aunty Laura asked, trying to lighten the mood that had suddenly become ignited with hostility.

We went into the house, and Aunty Laura looked around with interest as she went over to Grandma. Grandma was sleeping again with her head slouching into her lap.

"Hi, Mom," Aunty Laura and Uncle Bill each lightly jiggled one of grandma's shoulder. Grandma woke up and looked around blankly.

"Oh, Laura, honey," she smiled and extended one of her pale, thin hands.

Uncle Bill took her hand in his giant one and patted it gently.

"How are you, Mom?" Aunty Laura asked from the wood chair in which she was sitting.

"I am fine," Grandma said in a shaky voice.

"Hmm..." Aunty Laura mused, not convinced. "How often has she been to the doctor since she has been here?"

"Don't worry about that, Laura," Mamma said in her annoying, it's-none-of-your-business tone.

"Yeah, I know just how you handle things, Sue," Aunty Laura snapped back. "However it suits you."

"Now listen here, Laura," Brian piped up. "We got this handled. She is going to the doctor next week." He frowned. "She is my mom too, you know."

"Unfortunately," Aunty Laura snapped, she looked very worried.

"Besides," Brian said, standing a little taller and pasting a smug look on his face, "I have power of attorney over her, so legally you have absolutely no say."

"Oh yeah, Brian? You really want to go down this road with me?" Aunty Laura got out of her chair.

"I don't know what you mean." Brian feigned ignorance.

"Okay, cut the c****, Brian. We all know what this is. You don't give a d**** if Mom is happy or not. You are just trying to get back at me for some reason," Aunty Laura clenched her fist and got right up in Brian's face.

Samantha and I were quietly cheering, and as much as I liked Grandma, I sincerely hoped for her sake that Aunty Laura would take Grandma with her.

"It's okay, honey," Grandma said in her small voice. "I like living here with my little boy. He takes good care of me."

Brian bent over into Grandma's hug and looked at Aunty Laura tauntingly.

"Oh, God, you are an evil ba**ard," Aunty Laura tapped her foot in annoyance.

"About time someone noticed," I said under my breath. Out of the corner of my eye, I saw Fanny and Samantha smile and could not help but smile too. Brian noticed this and glowered. Instantly, we changed our expressions to ones of concern.

"All right, everybody," Uncle Bill clapped his hands together. "We came here for a visit, not a brawl. Come on girls, take your Aunty Laura and show her your pets. I will go with Brian to see his wood shop, and Sue, I am guessing you will be making lunch?"

Mamma did not answer, but went angrily to the back of the house where the kitchen was.

We each took one of Aunty Laura's hands and went outside with her. We showed her our chicken coop with its five hundred laying hens, but she seemed unimpressed and asked me if we had any friends up here. We were scared to say anything and just smiled at her.

"I know you guys are Amish now, but are you girls happy?" she asked.

I desperately wanted to talk to Aunty Laura, but I did not know what would happen if I did. If she did decide to help us, I was scared we would not live until help arrived. Now I kick myself, wishing I had slipped her a note or something, but I was so scared I couldn't bring myself to do it.

We took her to see the pig pen where we had about ten sows. We visited the six cows that we milked every morning; we made butter and cheese from some of the milk and cream, and the rest went to make dog food as well as pig food and chicken mash. Next were the twenty goats and thirty sheep whose babies we raised and sold every fall. We also had five Great Pyrenees dogs that we had trained to follow the animals while they grazed. Since we had free range grazing in the area, our animals were allowed to roam the hillsides, but we also had many bobcats, bears and coyotes that were looking for an easy dinner.

Sadly, Bucky was gone. Brian had shot him in a fit of rage one day because Bucky had dragged a chicken that we had skinned down from a tree branch. I was heartbroken when I saw his lifeless body on the ground, but even more so when Brian made me help bury him. Brian was also cruel to the dogs, and when they barked at night to protect the animals, he would grab a belt and beat them while they yelped in pain. Sometimes he even wired their mouths shut. I would run out of the house in the middle of the night and scream at him to stop. Then he started making me beat them. He would tell me, "Go beat that dog" as he dragged me out of bed. At first I refused, only to regret it when I heard one of the dogs screaming in agony. Eventually I complied and would beat the dogs just enough so they would barely whimper while the tears ran down my cheeks. Then I would hug the dog and tell it how sorry I was. Many nights when I didn't have to care for Grandma, I would make sure Fanny was asleep and then spend the night out in the cow pen or goat pen so the dogs would not bark. They would curl up around me and go to sleep, thinking it was now my turn to guard the animals.

Of course, I did not tell any of this to Aunty Laura as she petted the big, fluffy white dogs, but I wanted to.

After the tour of the farm, we went back into the house where Mamma had made sandwiches. Everyone played nice as we ate, and all too soon Aunty Laura and Uncle Bill were saying goodbye and preparing for the five-hour drive home. Aunty Laura gave Grandma a goodbye hug and then she gave Brian instructions to send her the results of next week's doctor's visit or she would be back.

"Well, when the snow sets in you won't be able to get over Stevens Pass in your car, and you definitely won't be able to get up here," Brian said with a smile.

"So, what of it?" Aunty Laura asked with raised eyebrows. "You got more tricks up your sleeve or what?"

In response Brian just kept smiling that same irritating smile

Aunty Laura gave us a long hug goodbye and told us to write her. Grandma fell back to sleep as Aunty Laura and Uncle Bill disappeared around the bend in the road. I felt a tear roll down my cheek as I watched them go. It is easier for an abuse victim to deal with the everyday torturous life because it is always the same, but when a breath of hope comes and goes, it feels worse than ever.

THE NEXT week, we took Grandma to the doctor. It turned out to be a family affair because Brian and Mamma did not want to have to handle Grandma by themselves. We had to bring Fanny as well, since we could not leave her at home alone.

So we all piled in the backseat of the truck. It was the first time Samantha and I had been out together in a few years, and it was odd for people to see so many of us walking on the sidewalk at the same time. Now that I was nearing sixteen, I was becoming more and more self-conscious of my looks and wondering where I stood in the world of women. Of course, this was very hard to determine since everyone else dressed so differently from me. As we walked down the sidewalk, someone tried to take our picture. I always hated this, but it seemed to make Brian and Mamma feel good.

At the doctor's office, I looked at everything with great interest. The nurses and doctors seemed so smart and kind. I pretended I, too, was a nurse and in my mind I copied everything the nurse was doing. After Grandma's examination, we learned that Grandma's blood pressure was out of control and that she needed to be on heavy blood thinners because of her recent stroke. After the doctor looked at Grandma's medical history, he asked us if there had been any progression in her Alzheimer's.

"We did not know she had 'old timers'," Mamma said in her

97

uneducated manner of speaking.

The doctor looked at Mamma for a minute as if he thought she might be mentally challenged, and then looked back at Brian.

"Well," he glanced back at the chart, "since you are her caregiver I am authorized to give you full disclosure. She really needs to keep her blood pressure down, keep her on her blood thinners, watch out for urinary infections, and be careful because she might start forgetting where she is or where she puts things."

I realized that she was doing all of this already, but I had thought it was because of the stroke. I felt a little sick. This was bad news for Grandma. If she had no memory she wouldn't be able to tell Aunty Laura anything when she came to visit and no telling what Mamma could get away with doing to her then.

After the visit to the medical doctor, we took Grandma to the eye doctor; he gave us more eye drops and told us we had to be sure to give them to her if we did not want her to go blind. Grandma was very sweet with the doctors and told them how they reminded her of someone she used to know. They just laughed and accused her of flirting with them. Samantha and I laughed too. It was funny to be in the outside world where everyone was friendly and polite to us. One of the young doctors seemed to like asking me questions, and when Brian told him I was Grandma's nurse, he told me that I should go to school and become an RN. He said I seemed intelligent and had a kind face, and that was what they needed in nurses. I smiled and informed him that that was just what I planned to do.

Brian frowned as the doctor raised his eyebrows in surprise and said, "Well, that's awesome. I really hope you do it."

Samantha snickered. "He thinks you are pretty," she whispered.

I nudged her lightly with my elbow.

"You are going to be a nurse?" she continued. "I am sure Brian will love that."

"Hey," I hissed between my teeth. "I am going to be eighteen in two years...they can't keep us up there forever."

"Oh yeah, and how are we going to get out alive?" Samantha whispered back.

"I don't know, Samantha, but I am going to get us out somehow," I clenched my fist with determination. "God did not put me on this earth to die on a lonely mountain somewhere, I know it; I can feel it in my soul."

"Well, let me know when he sends you the exit plan," Samantha whispered back sarcastically.

Samantha sometimes made me so mad with her attitude, but how could I blame her? I was small and slim and was no physical match for the much heavier and taller Mamma and Brian.

Despite this, I had a firm belief in God and believed that someday he would deliver me from this evil. In the meantime, I told myself not to give in to the constant evil around me, and to continue to try to intervene for anyone who was being harmed when the opportunity presented itself.

Near Death

"Honoring all ways we survived our childhood abuse is healing. We were amazing and courageous."

— *Jeanne McElvaney, Spirit Unbroken: Abby's Story*

That week, the weather became intensely cold, and I knew snow would soon follow. The cows and goats began huddling closer together, and in the mornings when I went to feed them there was a thick layer of ice in their watering troughs. How I hated winter; it was nothing but cold and cold and more cold, raging fevers and a crazy mother who made us take icy baths and then go about our work with wet hair. The fevers that had been plaguing me for years were persistent even in the summer; whenever I was tired and a cool breeze blew over me, I would start shaking with cold and my temperature would spike. During August, I was always careful to collect wild yarrow, which was supposed to be good for fevers. I would make a tea out of the bitter-tasting flower and drink it almost daily. It helped a little and made it possible for me to go about my daily chores.

But now we also had poor Grandma to look after. She was old and frail, and I was afraid I would find her dead in her bed each morning when I went to her room to wake her. We had been ordered by the doctor to give Grandma baths several times a week to help prevent the urinary tract infections to which she was predisposed. This proved to be challenging, since the house was very cold despite the large barrel heater in the living room. The tub in the bathroom had no running water, so Samantha and I had to heat water on the stove to make the bath as warm as possible for Grandma.

Still, Grandma cried and tried to cling to her sweater as we took her clothes off and lowered her into the tub. I felt sad for her but did not know what else to do. The doctor was adamant about reducing the risk of UTIs. He had put Grandma on antibiotics for ten days, but he warned that the more she took, the less they would work. Brian got on to me about letting her get an infection and told both of us to keep her clean because he was not going to lose her paycheck now. While Grandma cried from the cold, we could hear Mamma's voice coming from the living room, telling her to shut up and quit being a baby.

Grandma's happy days were over. With snow coming soon, Mamma and Brian knew Aunty Laura would not be coming back until the spring thaw, and by then they figured Grandma's Alzheimer's would be in full swing, so there was no need to pretend any longer. Mamma and Brian took Grandma's trailer and sold it with all of her things in it; I was instructed to make dresses, aprons and head coverings for her. Samantha and I were also told to not give her any eye drops.

"The sooner she goes blind the better," Mamma said. "And the more she sleeps in her room, the happier I will be. I don't want some Chatty Cathy sitting around here all day."

To my surprise, Grandma made little protest to the new clothes; she only wanted to put on her coat and did not care what else she was wearing. I told her the head covering was to keep her ears warm, and she put it on herself. Once, on a really cold day, she asked me if I could make her ear warmer out of wool instead of the thin white material. I laughed, but put a scarf around her head under her covering instead. Grandma always liked to sit next to me when I sewed, and once when she was lucid, she told me that the sound of the treadle sewing machine reminded her of her mother, who had been a seamstress many years ago during the Depression era.

My sixteenth birthday came and went without much fuss. I shed a couple of tears that morning when I awoke. To me it seemed that years were passing, wasted and lost in the dark abyss that was my existence. Every teenage year that passed could never be regained, and the loss felt like a knife in the heart.

Samantha and I had recently gone to the eye doctor to get our prescriptions renewed, and while we were in town, I looked around at other girls my age. They were so different from me, and as I stood off to the side and watched them with their families or friends, I could not understand why my life had to be so vastly different from theirs.

ON DECEMBER, when Mamma and Brian came back from Wenatchee, they were both yelling and upset. They called me into the house and showed me a letter from the government. I looked at it, not knowing what to expect. The letter stated that because I was now sixteen, Mamma would no longer be able to collect a check for me unless I came into the office to talk about a work program.

"So you think it's cute that you are sixteen now?" Mamma shouted angrily. "I had to go into the office and meet with a social worker and tell them you had run off with your boyfriend to Canada."

"They believed that?" I asked with surprise.

"Of course they did," Brian scoffed. "You think they really care about you?" He laughed. "Now it is documented that you don't even live with us anymore. No one would even come looking for you here."

"You mean here or your fake address?" I asked angrily as I threw the letter in his face. I was very upset that even the government did not care. Brian and Mamma could have said I had died in an accident and no one would have even investigated my death.

Brian grabbed me and slammed me into the wall. "Now listen here, little missy," he hissed. "You are the only one here who is not bringing in a check. You better watch yourself and get your work done."

I was angry and snapped back, "So if I die, are you going to do all my work, Brian?"

He hated when I called him Brian since he had ordered us to call him Dad. He slapped me so hard I fell over the chair behind me, and as I sat up I could hardly breathe. My back hurt so badly I could not stand up, so I just sat there wiping the blood from the corner of my mouth and glaring at both of them.

After a few minutes, their attention shifted from me to Fanny, who had also gotten a letter. Mamma was being ordered by the state to take Fanny in for a psychological evaluation. Mamma and Brian were very worried about this and decided that I would go along with Mamma to keep Fanny calm. Mamma had orders from the government to comply by the end of January, and I could not help but hope that Fanny would be taken away from Mamma at that interview.

Christmas came and went without anyone even announcing that it was Christmas. Brian had forbidden us to mention Christmas that year, fearing Grandma would remember her favorite holiday. From the stories Brian sometimes told us, we had learned that Grandma loved Christmas, and just about every other holiday, for that matter. Brian said his mother had always used holidays as an excuse to invite family and friends over for a giant meal which she would spend hours preparing.

On Christmas Eve, a chilling and blinding blizzard had blown in, and on Christmas Day everything was covered in a blanket of white and there were deep snow drifts everywhere. Samantha, Fanny and I spent Christmas Day shoveling snow away from the gates, the barn and the house. As I shoveled, I sang a few Christmas carols under my breath. I loved the Christmas holidays, and whenever I was in town around that time of year, my eyes would look hungrily at all the beautiful decorations. I especially loved Christmas lights and would sometimes stand frozen in place, gazing at their beautiful colors. At times I would even wish that I was a beautiful light on a Christmas tree; maybe then everyone would love me and no one would scream at me and beat me, I thought.

That morning as I knelt behind the hay pile, pulling out hay for the cows, I started sobbing—an explosion of tears and emotion so violent that I was left shaking. My life consisted of one dreary day after another and there was no hope for any changes, never a hug or a smile from anyone except Fanny and Grandma, and they were even more helpless than I was. The pain I felt was like someone had stabbed me in the heart with a jagged blade and that anonymous person was now slowly turning it as it lay buried inside me.

"Dear Lord," I prayed as I had prayed every day since I was nine years old, "please get me out of here. I don't belong here. I try so hard to abide by your example of kindness, so why am I here? I want to do so much in life. I want to travel the world helping people, but every day that passes is another day wasted, and it looks like I will never get out of here." Here I paused, feeling guilty for not having faith. "I know I will get out of here, though," I continued to whisper. "I can feel it; this can't be my destiny." I yanked the hay harder. "It just can't be," I thought, "I can't die up here. It is not going to happen; this is not my destiny."

I repeated this prayer every day, and while it gave me hope, it also made me more and more aware of how desperate my situation was. Especially now that I was not bringing in a paycheck, I was afraid Brian would snap one day and either beat me to death or shoot me. It was a truly frightening existence, and I could see this same fear mirrored in Samantha's face whenever Brian got mad at me.

AS THE weeks passed, Brian grew tired of Grandma and gave Mamma full rein to do whatever she wanted to her. Mamma gleefully started tormenting Grandma whenever she felt like it. She would purposely serve Grandma the food she did not like, and when Grandma refused to eat it, she shoved the food in her mouth. The first time Mamma did this, Samantha stopped her—much to my great surprise and happiness. I walked through the door just in time to see Samantha grabbing the food away from Mamma and telling her to stop. Samantha was five foot five by this time and the same height as Mamma, which gave her an advantage. Mamma slapped Samantha across the face and told her to get out of the way.

"No," Samantha said. "You can't hurt a poor, defenseless old lady like this."

I looked at Grandma; she was trying to get out of her motorized wheelchair and was calling Mamma an "ugly b****."

I sat Grandma back down since she had almost lost all ability to walk. As I was doing so, Mamma picked up a large chunk of wood from the pile next to the stove and started beating Samantha on the back with it. Samantha screamed in pain, and I was scared that Mamma would seriously injure Samantha. I started to yell,

"Grandma, Grandma! Are you okay?"

I was standing in front of Grandma, so Mamma could only see her if she stopped beating Samantha and came around to the other side of me. To my relief, it worked. After all, Grandma was a big paycheck, so she was an easy way to get Mamma's attention.

"What is wrong?" Mamma asked as she shook Grandma, who was trying to wipe the oatmeal from her face.

"Get your filthy hands off of me," Grandma said as she slapped at Mamma's hand.

Mamma turned to me. "Why were you yelling?"

I feigned a look of grave concern. "Well, she was gasping for breath," I said as I pretended to listen to Grandma's breathing.

"What is wrong with your breathing, Mom?" Mamma asked impatiently.

Grandma seemed quite aware of her surroundings that morning and spat back, "Oh, what do you care? And don't call me that; you are no daughter of mine."

Out of the corner of my eye, I saw Samantha crying in the corner. I left Grandma and went to her.

"Samantha, is anything broken?" I asked, putting my hand on her cheek.

"I don't know," Samantha tried to stand up but the pain was to great. "My shoulder hurts really bad, though."

I unzipped the back of her dress and examined her back. I had learned in my outdoors emergency medical book how to feel for broken bones. Gently I palpated over the small bones, listening for a crunching sound that would indicate a break. Thankfully, I did not find anything broken, but she did have several cuts that were bleeding from contact with the jagged wood, and several dark bruises were starting to form.

As I was zipping up Samantha's dress, I heard Mamma's angry voice.

"Take Barbara to her room—now," she barked at me.

I turned around, glowering at Mamma.

"What the h*** is your problem?" Mamma asked, as if daring me to speak.

"You hurt my sister," I said with all the authority I could muster.

Mamma seemed surprised at my response and walked toward me menacingly. "Well, it just so happens that your sister is my daughter, miss smarty pants."

"She is?" I asked as if I were shocked at that information.

Mamma became so enraged now that she did not know what to do. She walked back to the wood pile and threw two large chunks of firewood at me. Thankfully, they missed and caught the wheel of Grandma's motor chair instead. I raised my eyebrows and pushed Grandma to her room. As I lay her in bed for her nap, I felt a little scared. I knew that there was going to be hell to pay for my little theatrical performance once Brian found out about it.

As I put Grandma into bed, I put antibiotic ointment on the sores that were starting to form around her buttocks. I was no nurse, but I did the best I could under the circumstances. Despite my efforts, however, I was afraid Grandma would not last long under these conditions.

That evening when Brian got home, Mamma told him what had happened. I suppose they figured Samantha had been beaten enough, since she had been crying in pain as she put the food on the table. I swallowed hard. I was so scared of what Brian would do to me. Of late, I had been wrestling away from him, and since I had either Fanny or Grandma with me at all times, he would have to pull me around a corner to rub on me or masturbate. His favorite thing now was to come up behind me when I was doing the dishes and rub on me. It was gross, and I found it even more disgusting than the times when he pulled me into bed with him.

The last time it had happened, I had told him he was disgusting as I glanced over at his mother, who was sleeping only a few feet away. Mamma, Fanny and Samantha had gone into town to get supplies, and Brian wanted me to go upstairs with him for his daily message. I had a fever that day and did not feel like dealing with him. Brian kept whispering that I was beautiful, and it made me sick to my stomach just to hear his words. I knew that he really did believe me beautiful now that my scars were hardly visible, and I hated giving him that satisfaction.

Remembering all that on this night as I stood there trying not to shake, I knew that my punishment was going to be severe, not only because I had made him angry when I pushed him off me and because I didn't want to undress, but also because I had called him disgusting.

After Mamma told him what had happened, he walked over to Samantha and smacked her on the back of the head. Then he came over and grabbed me by the hand. I thought I would pass out and blinked my eyes several times.

"Come on, Sue," he said. "Let's teach this girl a lesson."

Brian dragged me out the door while I instinctively dug my heels into the floor. When we got to the door, I fought to get away from him, but he managed to push me through the open doorway and off the steps. As I landed on the hard ground, I felt my ankle twist underneath me. I screamed in pain and tried to pull away from Brian, who was grabbing me by the hair.

"I think I sprained my ankle," I cried out in pain.

"That's the least of your worries," Brian said with a menacing grin.

As Brian yanked me to my feet, I choked back a tear from the searing pain that shot up my leg. I completely panicked, when I saw Mamma's leering face as she stood by the steps with a lantern and a coiled rope in her hands. For some reason, Mamma loved to hear people scream. Even now, when I think of it, I shudder at how much she enjoyed the misery of others. Frantically, I looked around into the dark night as if looking for help, but there was no one nearby, and the night was pitch black, save for the lantern light.

I remembered what Brian had said about me not bringing in a paycheck anymore and I wondered if this was the night my life would end. I felt, in my soul, that Mamma and Brian both toyed with the thought of murder. Why would they mention it all the time if they were not thinking about it?

I began screaming into the darkness. "Somebody help me! Somebody help me!" I screamed in desperation.

"Who do you think is going to hear you?" Brian's laugh was haunting.

I listened into the night, but all that returned was a faint echo as my cry for help bounced from hilltop to mountaintop, as if in search of the help that would never come.

Brian dragged me to the shed where we kept the small animals and shoved me inside. I tumbled over, and Mamma grabbed me by the shoulders and stood me back up. Brian came at me with the thin rope, which was wound into about eight lengths.

He said with an authoritative tone, "You believe you are growing up, huh?" and with that, he shoved me into the wall. "Let's see how tough you are," he ground out between clenched teeth, his face an inch from mine.

106

I was starting to lose my fear as I realized there was nothing I could do to stop them from whatever it was they were planning. I pushed Brian out of my face. Even if I could not stop them, I thought, I could at least show them how much I despised them.

"That's all you got?" Brian leered at me as he recovered his balance. "Who do you think you are, telling your mother what is right and wrong? And yesterday, instead of doing your work, you were putting another blanket on your grandmother and putting her feet up, and then you brought the laundry downstairs so you could fold it next to her. What, do you think you are running the show here?"

"I was just trying to make her comfortable," I said defensively.

"Nobody asked you to make her comfortable," Mamma gave me a hard slap. "You do not make any decisions around here, girl."

"And you can't tell me not to be a nice person," I screamed at her. I was still scared, but I was too angry to remember my fear.

"Yes, we can," Brian grabbed me and shook me by the shoulders. "We own you, and you will do and be what we tell you! I don't want to see any more of this soft character...just trying to save Grandma cr**, you hear me?"

"No, that would make me like you and I will never be like you!" I screamed. "Never! Never! Never!"

Mamma was so angry she was grinding her teeth. She grabbed the rope from Brian and began beating me all over with it. I screamed as the rope cut into my arms and legs and back. My ankle was throbbing, but when she stopped beating me, I glared at her with as much contempt as I could muster.

"What, you got something to say to me?" she hissed, standing over me with the rope in her hands.

"Yes," I shouted. "I can't wait till I'm eighteen and can leave this hell hole forever." I stood up and stamped my good foot to mark my defiance.

Mamma's green eyes sparked as she snapped, "Who says you will make it to eighteen?"

I shrugged and with even more defiance. "I have a strong faith that God will deliver me from this evil one day."

Mamma flew into a fit of frenzy then, she grabbed one of the cows' lead ropes from the gate and started beating me with that. The metal clasp sank into my flesh, and I screamed and screamed. Finally she stopped, and Brian dragged me into the house by my hair and shoved me up the stairs.

Sobbing from the horrific pain, I pulled off my dress. The moon had come out from where it had been hiding behind a cloud and was now streaming in through the window. With a hand mirror, I began examining my wounds. There were marks all over my body from the ropes, and my ankle was swollen to more than twice its normal size.

I lay on my mattress and sobbed softly. The light that had guided me and given me hope for so long seemed distant, and the pain and desperation I felt is hard to describe. I thought how evil my mother's face had looked, and I shuddered. I wondered why she hated me and Samantha so much, and why we did not deserve anything in life except shame and beatings and a hopeless existence. I could hear Samantha putting Grandma to bed downstairs while Mamma screamed at her. I heard the door close and lock, and Samantha and Fanny came up the stairs. Mamma and Brian slept downstairs now next to Grandma's room, at least that is one thing to be thankful for, I thought with a sigh.

I got up slowly and tiptoed over to Fanny to hand her a night dress. I pulled the blanket over her when she lay down. Samantha sat down on the mattress, rubbing her shoulder and shaking her head as she looked at my ankle.

"These sons of bit**** are really going to kill us," she said angrily as we sat there, both of us all beat up. "We have to stop fighting them, Misty." She continued trying to rotate her shoulder. "They are going to fly off the handle one day and pick up the rifle by the door and shoot one of us."

I nodded. This was a fear I had, as well. There was always a loaded rifle leaning against the wall by the front door, and I have to admit I was scared of it. Brian said it was there in case robbers came, but I had watched many times as he grabbed the rifle and shot one of our geese because it was making too much noise. Sometimes he even shot in the air at the barking dogs or just to get our attention if we were down at the pigs pen. This always left me shaking and sometimes I would burst into tears realizing just how much I feared that rifle.

The moonlight had come out of hiding and was shining brightly through the window, I looked at Fanny, who was not sleeping but talking to an imaginary being next to her bed. It was not only ourselves we had to think about now, but also Grandma and Fanny. I wanted save them all, but I did not know how. I was convinced that I must dress Amish and abstain from all worldly conveniences and devices in order to go to heaven. I know it does not make any sense that I would believe the doctrine of two crazy people, but I did, and my wish is for you, the reader, to connect with this young sixteen-year-old girl and try to understand the utter hopelessness of her situation, so that you may appreciate what happens later on.

The fact that Samantha and I had practically zero knowledge about the justice system and other things that could potentially have helped us did not help matters. Brian and Mamma loved to tell us stories where kids were taken from their parents and then locked in closets or killed by their foster parents. Also, there was no surety that we would be taken from them, and even if we wanted to get help, it was too risky, so we did not know what to do except live one day of terror after another.

Samantha and I crawled under the blanket, our teeth chattering with the bitter December cold. I picked up the mirror again and looked at an angry red welt that was forming under my armpit. It was very painful, as were all the others. I stared into the mirror for a moment, and my pale white face stared back at me; my green eyes were swimming with tears, and I brushed them away with a callused hand.

As I looked in the mirror, I could that see the scars that had once defined my face, had now faded and were barely noticeable. I looked intently at myself. Knowing that I had a somewhat pretty face made me cry even more, although I thought, who cares? No one even sees my face. My teenage years were passing me by, and I longed for friends. I wanted to be recognized as a budding young woman, but the closest I would get to my wish was the feel of Brian's groping hands and the stench of his bad breath.

⟨*T*HE DAY of Fanny's psychologist appointment finally came around. I got up early that morning to give her a bath and dress her in a new green dress that I had made for the occasion. Brian had lectured me all day the day before the appointment on how the psychologist was an idiot that thought he was smart because he had a degree, and he would just try to play with our minds like all the other government employees.

It took three hours to get to Wenatchee, and we drove the entire way in silence. I stared out at the bleak, winter countryside and dreamed about being anywhere other than where I really was.

When we arrived at the doctor's office, we had to sit in the waiting room. Fanny seemed agitated, and when I tried to keep her seated so she wouldn't dance around, Mamma said to just let her be, because the less orientated she was, the less likely she would be to answer the psychologist's questions coherently. The psychologist came out for Fanny, and when we started to follow him, he told us he would like to see Fanny alone.

I could see this did not sit well with Mamma, and she stammered, "Um... We don't allow our women to be in a room with a man by themselves." She tried to fake a German accent as she said it.

"What do you mean?" the psychologist frowned as he motioned Fanny to follow him, but she did not. "Well," he seemed a little surprised at Fanny's behavior, "I suppose you can come in if you are quiet and don't say anything."

We all sat down, and the psychologist began questioning Fanny about her age, her name and so on. Fanny did not respond but kept twitching her fingers and talking to someone over the psychologist's shoulder. The doctor pulled out some blocks and began asking her to do things with the blocks. Fanny haphazardly arranged them as she continued to twitch her fingers.

"So how do you like where you are living, Fanny?" he asked in a soothing voice.

"I don't like it much," Fanny said as she went back to twitching her fingers.

"What don't you like about it, Fanny?" he asked, trying to draw her attention.

"I don't know," Fanny answered distractedly.

"She doesn't like anyone or anything," Mamma said abruptly with a worried look on her face.

The psychologist put a finger to his lips and shook his head at Mamma. Although he was trying to connect with Fanny, it was futile, and after about twenty minutes of getting nowhere, he took off his glasses and turned to Mamma. With a solemn look, he said matter-of-factly, "She is not taking her meds, is she?"

Mamma looked at Fanny and raised her hands in a helpless gesture. "We have tried, but she knocks them out of our hands and runs from us. It is impossible, but I guess we can try again if you think it is that serious."

The psychologist nodded thoughtfully. "If she is to have any quality of life, she must be on her meds." He put his glasses back on and looked at some papers.

"So you have had Fanny about eight months?"

Mamma nodded.

"And how is that working out for your family?"

Mamma shrugged. "She is adjusting to our customs and our ways of dressing, but most of the time she is so absent minded she doesn't even seem to care."

"Uh huh, I see," the psychologist studied Mamma's face. "And how often do you engage Fanny in conversation and activities?"

Mamma shrugged again, she was obviously nervous now. "We live on a farm, so there are countless chores and lots of animals...that is just about all the stimulus one could hope for."

"And does Fanny have a lot of chores?" he asked with interest.

Mamma's face turned red, and she nodded vigorously. In my mind's eye, I was envisioning the many bruises up and down Fanny's body, as well as my own. If only the good doctor could see them, I thought, but that was impossible, as our long dresses and aprons covered everything. There was no reason for him to suspect anything, and there was no way for him to see the numerous bruises on Fanny's breasts and arms and legs.

The doctor thought for a moment and then matter-of-factly stated, "I am just not sure that your home is the best environment for Fanny."

My heart skipped a beat and I silently prayed that this was Fanny's ticket out of hell.

Mamma seemed to panic for a moment, but then she leaned forward with a deceptively shocked face. "Why would you say that?" she asked, as if she really cared about Fanny. "I don't understand; this is my sister and I love her. It would make my whole family sad if she left us."

The psychologist looked at Mamma curiously, and I wondered if we were the first *Plain people* he had ever seen. "Well," he looked back at the papers in front of him. "She is off her meds, and the progress notes from her last visit in Arizona clearly show that she has relapsed and any kind of progress she was making there has been lost."

He studied Fanny for a moment, and then looked back at Mamma. "Clearly, she is completely in another world now, unlike when she was last seen in Prescott. These documents show that she was far more advanced than she is here in this moment."

"Yes, that may be true," Mamma leaned forward again. "But they were also ready to ship her off to an asylum where they could keep her locked up, since she has the tendency to run off whenever she gets the chance."

"And how do you prevent these episodes?" the psychologist asked with raised eyebrows.

"One of my daughters or I are with her at all times," Mamma said in a defensive tone. "And besides," she added, "you have to admit the fresh open air and good farm food are way better for her than the stale, closed-in environment at one of those homes."

Although I could see the psychologist did not like Mamma, her words seemed to convince him, and he nodded slowly.

"All right," he said after a moment of thought. "I will write you a prescription, and we will see how it goes from here."

He stood up from his desk and walked us to the door. He smiled at me, and I smiled back. For a split second, I toyed with the idea of grabbing his arm and begging for help, but then I remembered he was also a worldly outsider who was going to hell because he did not practice a plain lifestyle. It was a catch twenty-two situation, and I walked past him and let yet another opportunity for freedom slip through my fingers.

"Wow, that was close," Mamma said as we got back in the truck. "I don't think he is going to do anything. There is no one else who wants her, so we are home free."

"Unfortunately," I thought to myself.

Mamma seemed relieved and wanted to celebrate, so she stopped at Burger King and got us all hamburgers. It felt creepy when Mamma was in a good mood. It made me kind of sick that she was trying to be nice to us now when she was usually so mean. I shuddered as she put a hand on my shoulder and squeezed it while she gloated about her ability to fool the government and how easy it was to do so.

I ate my hamburger and pretended to listen, although her ravings made me feel ill. I was disgusted by my own mother, but at the same time, I felt sorry for her. I watched her mouth flapping as we drove north, not really listening to what she was saying anymore, but rather trying to figure her out and how it was possible for her to live like this, surrounding herself with misery and hurting the very people who could have loved her and made her happy if given half a chance.

Mamma was coarse and uneducated, and she seemed to like that fact. She got angry at people when she felt they thought they were smarter than she was. Her chubby face was constantly frowning and angry, and I wondered if she had ever smiled as a girl, or if she had ever been normal. Although it seemed unlikely, I thought she must have been at one time or another. But then, maybe not; even now as she was gloating about pulling the wool over the shrink's eyes, her face had an expression that said, "Don't mess with me, or you will get what's coming to you."

I lay my head on the car seat and closed my eyes as words Brian had once said echoed in my ears:

"Children always turn into their parents. If you don't like us, just watch out. You will be us in a few years, and then you can come back and apologize for your uppity 'what would Jesus do' cr*p."

I looked anxiously at my face in the side mirror to see if there was any resemblance to Mamma there. Although we both had bright green eyes, their shapes were different; Mamma's eyes were small and squinty, while mine were large and almond-shaped. I was also smaller and thinner than she was. I sighed thankfully. There was not that much resemblance between us. I knew this was not what Brian meant, but it did make it easier not to have to see Mamma's face staring back at me in the mirror every day.

Samantha, on the other hand, was the spitting image of Mamma—a much younger and prettier version, of course. I sighed as we kept driving. I was so tired of life, but despite this tiredness, I still had the feeling things were going to change for me someday. I had a destiny far beyond this bleak place I was in. But with every passing year, every beating and degrading act, that feeling got fainter and sometimes it would disappear completely for a while, leaving me sobbing in desperation. But thankfully, it always returned and gave me renewed hope. Like a lighthouse in a storm, I reached out to it and held it deep in my heart, and as I knelt in the straw behind the barn I would pray every day for help for the four of us who were entrapped in this evil web.

WINTER SLID into spring, and I was happy to finally hear the birds singing and to see the green grass and wildflowers again. The winter had been bitterly cold, and despite the large wood burning stove, the house was still freezing—so much so that Grandma and Fanny cried from the cold. Samantha had become sick in the early spring when Mamma lined Fanny, Samantha and me up for our weekly bath outside. She made us strip off our clothes as the icy wind blew past us. I already had a low grade fever, and I shivered, my teeth chattering uncontrollably. Mamma had started to let us bathe inside, but still occasionally lined us up outside for baths. On this particular day, Samantha and I were feeling especially sick, and I begged Mamma to let us take a cold bath inside the house. She refused, telling us that we were too dirty and would not get clean. I was worried since Samantha also had a fever and was having trouble breathing from a cold that had been plaguing her.

As Mamma dumped the icy water over my head, I felt a surge of warmth go through me, and I saw Samantha begin coughing as Mamma dumped the water on her hair. Finally I could not take it anymore, and I crawled out of the watering trough the three of us were standing in and grabbed Fanny and Samantha by the hand. Naked, the three of us ran through the freezing wind and into the house while Mamma screamed at us to get back in the water. I could feel my fever spiking, and I saw tears on Fanny's chubby cheeks as I wrapped her in a blanket. My main concern, however, was Samantha, who seemed unable to breathe and kept holding her chest as she coughed and struggled for air.

Samantha always seemed to get really bad colds, but I knew this was different. Samantha just sat there as Mamma stormed into the house and ordered us back outside. I glared at Mamma from where I was standing with a blanket wrapped around me, Samantha and Fanny sat on the floor as close as they could get to the stove, and Brian was sitting in a rocking chair nearby, grinning at our half-naked bodies.

When no one obeyed her orders, Mamma got angry and stormed over to grab Samantha, who was hunched over and weakly gasping for breath.

Mamma grabbed her by the chin and looked at her for a moment, then ordered me to put her to bed.

Fanny and I helped Samantha upstairs, and I piled all the blankets I could find on her. After that, I got out my herbal remedy book and painstakingly followed the instructions for making a mustard plaster. While Mamma shouted at me. I think she realized she may have finally pushed the envelope a little to far. I don't know why she was obsessed with those icy baths, or why she never cared that we were freezing, but she had to have known that we could sick and die being exposed to such unforgiving elements. Anyone would know that, right? Even the very idea that we had to wash our hair and were not allowed to leave it down while it dried was so crazy. It would not dry for days sometimes and quite frankly I just do not know how we survived.

My hands shook as I mixed the mustard plaster. It was supposed to loosen the mucus in the lungs and allow the person to cough it out, thus making breathing easier. I spent a while pounding the mustard with a mortar and then mixed it as directed. Then Mamma and I went upstairs to Samantha's bedside and applied the poultice to her chest. I worried we were too late as I listened to the sharp, ragged sounds that escaped from Samantha's mouth with every breath. After a few hours, Samantha whispered to me, asking if I thought she was going to die. I shook my head and smiled at her reassuringly, but when I went downstairs, I could not see for the tears that were streaming down my face. My little Samantha was very ill, and I was not sure if I was doing the right thing for her. Mamma seemed even a little worried. I think she knew it was a possibility that Samantha could die. I stood by the stove shaking inside. I tried not to think of it. Frankly I was surprised Mamma looked so worried.

All through the night I stayed with Samantha, frantically praying for a change for the better. The room upstairs was freezing, and it seemed that winter was fighting spring to the death. We boiled water and put it in a bunch of canning jars and then Fanny helped me carry them up the stairs where I packed them into the bed with Samantha. We did this every half hour until the bed had warmed.

Every two hours, Mamma and I changed the mustard plaster, hoping the frequency would somehow help. Samantha whimpered at the blisters that were forming on her chest from the mustard, and I told her I was sorry, but I was more worried about saving her life. She knew I was trying to help her, so she graciously suffered through the pain.

The next morning I was also overjoyed to see the warm sunshine that came streaming through the window. Samantha was breathing easier, and although she was still struggling for breath, she no longer exhaled the sharp, jagged sounds every time she breathed. Samantha lay in bed for several days, and I kept monitoring her and putting Vaseline on her blisters. A week later, Samantha was still weak but she was breathing well again. I was the outside girl for the next month and Samantha stayed indoors taking care of the house. It was still hard work but at least she was not exposed to icy winds that blew down from the frozen mountain tops.

Brian gleefully made this month as awful as he could for me, but it was worth it to see the color coming back to Samantha's face, and it made my heart warm when she mouthed "Thank you" out the window to me. I thought of how sad I would have been if she had died. My heart would have died with her. Where would she have been buried? It was all too terrible to even think of, and I was still determined to figure out a way to get us out of there, but how? I just did not know.

FACE OF EVIL

"I have seen the dark universe yawning

Where the black planets roll without aim,

Where they roll in their horror unheeded,

Without knowledge, or lustre, or name."

— H.P. Lovecraft, Nemesis

In May, we received another letter from the government regarding Fanny. The results from the psychologist had come in, and he had evaluated Fanny as having the IQ of a three-year-old. He recommended that a social worker come to our house and check the living conditions to be sure they were suitable for a person with special needs such as Fanny's. However, his review came through too late. Mamma had already finished the paperwork that would give her full custody of Fanny. Because of the psychologist's suggestion, the social worker said she would still like to visit the house.

Mamma went to see her and told her our church did not like having government people in our homes, and that the church could punish her for disobedience if she allowed the visit. The social worker bought Mamma's story and told her to just send some family photos for her file, and they would call it done. This was just one of the many close calls Mamma and Brian were having with the law of late.

Mamma bought a disposable camera, and one sunny day we all lined up with fake smiles to have our pictures taken. We were all pretending to have fun while Mamma screamed at us to put bigger smiles on our faces. There were pictures of Mamma hugging Fanny, Fanny sitting on the hay while Samantha and I worked and so on. Then Brian took a picture of all of

116

us women standing together. I pointed out to Mamma that I was supposed to be in Canada when she told me to smile in a picture. I think she had forgotten about that but did not seem worried that anyone would remember.

After we were done taking the pictures I went back to raking the pig pen. Those pictures were so bogus; how could a government employee not realize she needed to come out here and check up on us? Weren't they trained to know that abusive people are some of the best liars in the world? I felt we were "falling through the cracks;" society's anonymous victims who would live and die in unacknowledged misery...

THE SUMMER passed filled with hard work, misery and scalding heat. Aunty Laura came to visit twice and was very sad when Grandma was unable to recognize her due to the extent of her Alzheimer's. While Aunty Laura was there, Mamma had Samantha and I pretend to be putting drops in her eyes. On their last visit Aunty Laura and Uncle Bill stayed for a few hours but then left and said they would be back before the summer was over. Samantha and I looked forward to their next visit, but they did not come back again that summer. I figured Aunty Laura was discouraged when her mother did not recognize her anymore and she did not feel like making the five-hour trip just to watch Grandma sleep in her wheelchair.

Winter came again, and as always, Mamma was up to her evil tricks. Grandma had just been released from the hospital after battling a severe urinary tract infection that had led to a kidney infection. A few days after her release, I was outside chopping wood when I heard Grandma screaming. I raced into the house to see what was wrong. To my horror, I saw Samantha standing with her hands over her ears.

"What is wrong?" I asked in a panic as I heard Mamma's evil laugh coming from the small room where the bathtub was.

"Mamma's giving poor Grandma a cold bath," Samantha's voice was shaking.

"Oh no!" I said with great concern. "She is going to kill her."

Samantha nodded but grabbed my arm as I started to run toward the bathroom. "Don't go in there, Misty. You will make it worse, and she will leave Grandma in there longer just to spite you."

I nodded as I bit back tears. It made me so angry, but what could I do? I always felt guilty, as if there were something I should be doing to save us, but I did not know what.

And so it was then at the tender age of seventeen that I began slipping into a depression such as I had never experienced before. The weight on my heart was so great and my existence felt so unnecessary that I began thinking of suicide every hour of every day.

Samantha saw the change in me and figured I was sad, but she did not know just how sad I was. We were two extremely troubled and scared teenage girls, so alone and unloved that I figured there was no reason to live any longer. Although I still believed in God, my faith was dormant; I felt only pain and helplessness. I sunk to the depths of despair and didn't have any fight left in me. I stopped fighting for others—it was no use, and besides, it only made their torture last longer.

I was beaten often for being slow and not meeting time limits. I don't know why, but as I was bent over and my underwear was pulled down in front of everyone, I no longer felt the shame or even the pain. I willed myself away...I went somewhere else in my mind, and would return only when Mamma and Brian were finished. It was better that way, I told myself. Why fight? It got me nowhere.

THAT WHOLE winter, Grandma was in and out of the hospital with kidney infections. Once they made her stay at the hospital for a week to stabilize her. As winter gave way to spring, she went to the hospital vomiting blood. It turned out that she had a perforated ulcer and was very near death. The doctor who performed her surgery only gave her a slim chance of survival, but somehow she pulled through. Brian answered Aunty Laura's letters telling her that everything was alright; and since she was having some trouble with her granddaughter, Aunty Laura decided not to visit. Samantha and I were worried that Grandma would die on us one day when Brian and Mamma were not home.

"What should we do with Grandma if she dies?" Samantha asked one day in early spring.

Brian shrugged. "Just put a sheet over her till we get home. Then we will take her and get her cremated and send the ashes to Laura," his laugh was menacing.

I raised my eyebrows. This seemed a rather callous way to treat his mother, even for Brian.

As the summer progressed, Grandma did not get better, and after doing extensive tests the doctor decided that Grandma needed to have her left kidney removed in order to save her life. It had shut down completely, and was causing one infection after another. The doctor told Brian to take her to the Spokane hospital three-hours east by ambulance. Brian and Mamma took me with them.

We arrived late in the evening and Grandma was already in surgery. Because she had already had stomach surgery in the early spring, the doctor thought that her chances of survival were slim. Brian decided he had better call Aunty Laura in case Grandma died. He said he did not want her to get angry with him if Grandma died at the hospital. Aunty Laura was furious that she had not been notified of Grandma's illness. It was going to be a seven-hour drive to get from Seattle to Spokane, but she said that she and Uncle Bill were already in the car.

I actually enjoyed staying in the hospital waiting room. I tried to watch the news that was on TV, but Brian made me sit on the opposite side of the room. I shrugged and picked up a magazine instead. It was still exciting enough I thought as I listened with interest to the nurses and the doctors talking as they walked by. I secretly pretended I was one of them. Grandma was out of surgery after a few hours and was transferred to the ICU. Her condition was listed as unstable.

Aunty Laura and Uncle Bill got to the hospital in the wee hours of the morning. I was asleep in the waiting room when I heard Aunty Laura's voice and felt her hugging me.

"Hi honey, how are you?" Aunty Laura felt warm and she always smelled of perfume.

I smiled sleepily and hugged her back. I looked at the clock on the wall to see that it was three in the morning. It was chilly, and I wrapped my black shawl tighter around my shoulders.

"How is Grandma?" I asked, rubbing my eyes.

"I don't know yet," Aunty Laura put a hand on her hip and made an annoyed face. "You are the only person we saw sitting here at this hour."

I looked around and did not see Mamma and Brian anywhere. "Where are they?" I asked.

"Probably halfway to Mexico by now," Uncle Bill scoffed as he took off his hat.

Just then, Mamma and Brian rounded the corner coming from the direction of the nurses' station.

"Hi, Laura," Brian said casually.

"Don't 'Hi' me, Brian," Aunty Laura marched up to him. "What the h**l is wrong with you? You were lying to me in those letters, weren't you?"

"Hey, don't get all mad at us," Mamma piped up, her arms folded in front of her. "It isn't our fault she is sick; she is such an ornery old woman she probably got sick on purpose."

"You stay out of this, Susan, or I swear to God I will do something I

119

won't be proud of," Aunty Laura shook her finger at Mamma and her pale face had a hint of red in it.

Uncle Bill sat down next to me as they argued back and forth. "How are you doing, honey?" he asked, putting an arm around my shoulders. He looked at me strangely when I jumped at his touch and pulled away.

I just smiled at him. I was painfully shy and could not talk to others without getting very red in the face.

"You sure don't talk very much, do you?" he said, smiling. "You have a big birthday coming up in a few months, huh?"

I nodded again and tried to listen to what Brian and Aunty Laura were saying. I could tell that despite Uncle Bill's efforts, he had trouble relating to me because of my odd clothes and demeanor, and I to him for the same reason.

"I want Mom to come home with me," I heard Aunty Laura say in a matter-of-fact voice.

"Oh, no, you don't." Brian stepped forward. "I have custody and power of attorney, and you can't do squat."

"Just watch me," Aunty Laura spat back. "I know you just want her money. It's no secret, Brian."

"Hey," Mamma looked around the waiting room. "You watch your mouth. I work my butt off taking care of this woman."

"Doesn't look like it," Aunty Laura shot back, looking at Mamma's ample rear end.

Uncle Bill got up and took Aunty Laura by the hand. "Come on, honey," He gently pulled her in the direction of the exit. "Let's go check into our room and we will come back in the morning to see how Mom is doing."

They left and I went back to sleep, covering myself with my long black shawl. I had a bad headache, and due to the severe depression, I was tired all the time. I would often fall asleep wherever I was, and I had little interest in anything. Even now, in the exciting surroundings of the hospital, I was only about half as happy as I would have been a couple of years previously.

The next day, we were able to see Grandma, but she was very confused and even more disoriented than normal. When Aunty Laura bent over to hug her, she had no idea who she was, and this made Aunty Laura very upset. It was sickening to watch Mamma go up and hug Grandma as if she really cared. Brian sat by the bedside, holding Grandma's hand and stroking it.

120

Since Brian and Mamma were preoccupied with Grandma and Aunty Laura, I let myself wander off around the hospital. I walked by the nurses' station, where I saw a doctor writing on a chart. She took off her glasses and smiled at me. I could see she was trying not to stare at my long dress, black shoes and stockings topped with a black apron and white head covering. She saw me watching her and asked if I was interested in studying medicine. I smiled and hugged the counter at the nurses' station.

"Yes," I nodded. "I want to be a doctor."

"Oh," she smiled with surprise. "That's great. How old are you?"

"Seventeen," I answered, stretching my five-foot and one inch frame to its fullest potential.

"Wow, so you are graduating soon. Have you applied to any colleges?"

I did not really know what a college was and just shook my head.

"What grade are you in?" the doctor asked after she studied my face for a second.

My face turned red and I felt a tear of frustration well up in my eye. I just looked down at the counter.

The doctor came over and squeezed my shoulder. "It's okay, honey," her voice was gentle. "I know you can do it. You seem like a very smart and sweet girl. We need people like you in medicine."

I looked up at her. She thought I was smart? Really? I was so used to being called retarded and dumb by Brian and Mamma that it was a surprise to hear that someone thought I was smart.

Just then, I heard Mamma's voice coming around the corner. "Misty! What are you doing over here? I told you to stay in the room."

"It's okay, ma'am," the doctor turned and looked at Mamma with dislike. "We were just having a chat."

Mamma's eyes darted at me anxiously. "About what?" she demanded.

"About college," the doctor tilted her head and smiled at me.

Mamma snorted and grabbed me by the sleeve of my dress and pulled me back to Grandma's room. I turned and smiled a goodbye at the doctor, who smiled and waved at me. I so much wanted to be like her, standing there in her white coat, sharp shoes and pant suit. She was someone who helped others, something I seemed incapable of.

Brian glared at me when I came back in, but it seemed he did not want to break the facade of being the caring and worried son. Aunty Laura and Uncle Bill left to go home that evening, as did we. The doctor was insistent

121

that Grandma stay in the hospital at least a week longer.

GRANDMA WAS released from the Spokane hospital a week later and transferred to the hospital nearest to us so we could take her home. She was very weak, and we kept her in bed most of the time. Aunty Laura came to visit a week later. She did not seem to like the living arrangements we had for Grandma, and it dawned on me that she had no idea how Grandma was being treated, or she would have removed her immediately. But how could she know? I had come to realize that Brian and Mamma were fantastic at acting and making people believe they were nice people in order to protect themselves.

The summer passed like all the other summers before it, filled with endless work and blisteringly hot sun and lots of screaming from Brian and Mamma. I took to writing poetry to try to relieve the anguish I felt. As I concentrated on rhyming things, it seemed to dull the monotonous everyday struggles and the echoing screams that resounded as Mamma or Brian beat one of us.

One day, when Fanny was supposed to be mopping the front porch, she accidentally broke the mop head off the handle. I saw her holding the two pieces in the air as I walked to the house from the pig pen. I felt a knot grow in my stomach as if some impending doom was descending on us. Just then, I saw Mamma come out the front door and look at Fanny.

"What the h**l did you do?" Mamma yelled.

Fanny began to cry as Mamma grabbed the metal pole and began to beat her with it. The screams were awful, and I knew Fanny could be seriously injured, but I was afraid of making it worse if I intervened. I could only stand by the porch, looking at Mamma with all the disgust I could possibly manage. She finally stopped and went back in the house, slamming the door. Fanny sat down on the porch, wailing as loud as she could.

"Let me look, Fanny," I pulled her arms open. I was thankful for the little rolls of fat that covered her body, as they seemed to have saved her from any broken bones. I took her to the watering trough and applied cold water to the giant bruises that were forming. I let her sit while I worked the rest of the day. I felt like hitting Mamma upside the head with a shovel; I fantasized about doing just that, but of course I never went through with it. I did not understand Mamma or how she could possibly get enjoyment from the pain of others. I was affected deeply if I saw any living thing hurting, and I would immediately rush over and try to make it better. It puzzled me that Mamma was so much the opposite. How this woman could possibly be my mother, I did not know.

122

The next day, I started my week's rotation as the inside girl. I was doing the dishes and feeling badly for what had happened to Fanny; I just could not get her screams out of my head. As I washed the sharp butcher knives, I suddenly grabbed one and put it to my wrist. I took a deep breath and closed my eyes as I tried to force myself to slice through my skin. I only made a light scratch, just enough so that there was a light trickle of blood. "Come on," I told myself, "just do it. I can't stand these screams of pain anymore, I just can't." It pained me too much to constantly see tears streaming down the faces of Fanny, Samantha and Grandma, and all just so Brian and Mamma could relieve themselves of some stress.

I was turning eighteen in a few months but I could see no way to escape. My life was drudgery that meant nothing to anyone. I tried to cut again, but I couldn't. As I stood there in the kitchen, I suddenly felt alive again, as if I had awakened from an eight-month sleep. I realized that I could not kill myself because I wanted to live; I wanted to change the world somehow, and I could not leave Samantha, Fanny and Grandma by themselves. They depended on me too much.

I applied pressure to the small scratch I had made and wrapped a towel around it as I finished my work. A new fire was burning in me, and my focus now was, "I've got to get the hell out of here, somehow. Oh God, please get me out of here. I don't belong here, please God...please God." I must have repeated this prayer at least two hundred times that day, and I had a renewed surge of hope and unwillingness to bend to the evil hands of the people who were supposed to be my parents.

THAT AUGUST Samantha turned sixteen, and just as I had, she also got a letter from the government stating she had to come in and meet with them to set up a few hours of volunteer work in order to keep receiving her check. I am not sure what kind of excuse Mamma gave them for her, but since Samantha did not go in, her check was cut, too. Samantha and I began trying to figure what I could do when I turned eighteen to change our lives. We had no knowledge of the outside world or how it worked, so we did not know where to start.

"Well," I thought aloud, "I know when I turn eighteen they cannot beat me anymore. I will be an adult and able to make my own choices."

These dreams, however, were smashed by Brian as he was beating me for not meeting one of my time limits one day.

"So you think because you are almost eighteen you can start slacking off?" he asked with a frustrated look. "You better pick up the slack. I swear to God I will be beating you when you are fifty. You are never going to get away from me, never!"

"No," I yelled back. "You can't do that!"

"Oh yeah? And who is going to stop me?" he hissed, putting his face up to mine. "What are you going to do, run away and prostitute yourself? Oh yeah, maybe you should." He threw me to the ground. "You would make a good little whore."

I was crying as I stood up and ran into the house. He was right; how would I stop them? I did not know how. I was scared, so scared he would kill me, and yet determined to shake the dust from this horrible place off my feet as soon as I got the chance.

AS FALL started to settle in I noticed Brian was more insistent in molesting Samantha, she had filled out well and I had noticed Brian looking at her for quite some time. I had known Brian was molesting her for a few years already but we never talked about it. We just did not want to acknowledge it.

Although I was sure that Mamma knew what Brian was doing to us, she never mentioned it, and the times she had walked in on Brian while he was rubbing against me or fondling me she had merely yelled that I was "being to slow and I had better speed it up".

When Mamma wasn't in the house Brian would sometimes pin Samantha down and dry hump her in the middle of the floor. She would laugh as she tried to pretend it was a joke and I would pace back and forth next to them, wanting with all my heart to kick Brian in the gut as hard as I could. I knew Samantha was terrified when he did this but by laughing she was trying to pretend she did not know what he was doing and therefore did not pose any threat.

Sometimes he would get off of her and grab me, but I had started to wriggle away from him and now as I was nearing eighteen he seemed less insistent on molesting me. In my soul I quivered and wondered if Samantha had taken my place. I tried not to think about it, even though I knew she had.

THE MONTH of November proved to be quite cold that year, and along with the cold came a sense of entrapment. I would be turning eighteen in a week, but what could I do to save us when we were trapped on a frozen mountain in the middle of nowhere? Samantha was constantly telling me that it was my job to save the both of us, since I was the oldest.

"You've got to get us out of here, Misty," she kept saying over and over. I nodded in agreement, but I did not know where to start.

Early in November, I came into the kitchen to get some hot water. As I came through the door, I heard the crying that always seemed to be present in the house. Samantha was in the middle of the room, bending over with her underwear down and Mamma and Brian were standing behind her. Mamma came around to face her with a plate in hand.

"Does this look clean to you?" she asked, pointing at a spot on the plate.

"No," Samantha whimpered.

I stood in the middle of the room, glaring at Mamma and Brian, my disgust for them was so strong that it is hard to describe.

"What are you looking at?" Brian sneered, challenging me to react.

I took the bait and stepped toward him. "I am looking at you punishing someone for something stupid, just like you always do," I said in a cool, even tone.

"Oh, you think it is stupid, do you?" Brian walked up to me menacingly.

"Yes I do," I was trembling with a sudden surge of anger. "If I gave you all of those dishes to wash, Brian, and gave you a ridiculous time limit to meet, I bet I would find way more dirty dishes than just one plate."

Brian grabbed me by the front of my coat and tried to throw me against the wall, but I braced my five-foot one inch frame, and much to his astonishment, I did not go flying into the air like I normally did.

"Oh, you think you are all grown up, huh?" Brian shrieked. He grabbed hold of me again and yanked me to my tip toes.

"I know," Mamma chimed in. "We will have Misty punish her." She handed me the stick she was using to beat Samantha.

"Oh yeah, that is a great idea," Brian laughed as he released me.

I shook my head. "I won't do it," I said, backing up.

"Oh, so you are going to tell us what you are and aren't going to do?" Brian reached out and grabbed me again.

"I will not beat my sister," I yelled in his face. "Never, no matter what she does. I will not beat my sister!" I was screaming as loud as I could. "It is wrong, and you guys are wrong in how you treat us. You should be ashamed of yourselves!"

"Listen to me," Brian hissed as he twisted the coat tighter around my neck. "You will do exactly what we tell you, or I will not be responsible for what happens to you." His teeth were clenched and he was in a dangerous mood, but under no circumstances was I going to beat my sister just to give them enjoyment.

"Take the stick," Mamma said, jabbing me with it.

"No," I choked out as the coat twisted tighter around my neck. I looked into Brian's eyes and hissed at him with all the disdain I could manage. "You will just have to kill me because I will never be like you guys! NEVER!"

He released me but he managed to slam my head into the wall as he let go. I stood there stunned for a minute as the room spun. Out of the corner of my eye, I saw Samantha stand up and go back to doing the dishes. I took a deep breath and walked out the door, trying to pretend my head was not spinning. No one followed me, and I could hear the sound of Fanny grinding grain to feed the cows that evening.

I sat in the snow for a moment. The sound of the chickens clucking and the goats milling about traveled to me on the brisk November wind. I looked around with a sense of satisfaction. Brian always told me I would grow up to be like them and there was nothing I could do it about it, but I had just proven him wrong. I would be turning eighteen soon, and I was nothing like them, not even remotely. I was proud of that, and I believed it was the only tool I had to fight them. Of course, they had to know deep down that I was right; how could they not? I told myself that as long as I stood on good, honest principle, maybe I would find a way out of this mess.

MY EIGHTEENTH birthday came and went with little fuss, as my birthdays always did. Samantha, who was the inside girl that week, secretly made a cake just to draw attention to the fact I was turning eighteen. Mamma looked at the cake with disinterest, and Brian told me I would have to start pulling my weight around the place more if I was planning on eating.

Samantha looked at me over Mamma's and Brian's heads from where she was standing by the wood burning stove, and motioned for me to make the speech we had been rehearsing at night. I was supposed to tell Mamma and Brian that now that I was eighteen, there would need to be a few changes made, starting with me making my own decisions. I cleared my throat a couple of times, trying to muster the courage to speak, but I could not do it. Samantha threw her hands in the air and shook her head.

Something I had noticed about myself was that I was only courageous and willing to stand my ground when it was to protect others. If I saw someone else being picked on, it enraged me and gave me the strength to stand up to the devil himself and tell him to go back to the hell from whence he came. But when it came to me, it was always harder because despite the fact that I prided myself on always trying to do the right thing, I had very low self-esteem and always believed I must be doing something terribly wrong to have such a miserable existence.

"What is wrong with you?" Samantha whispered as I put Fanny's coat on her to go back outside to work.

I shrugged. "What do you want me to do, Samantha? You know they are never going to agree to anything I ask, and they could very well really hurt me. I don't know what to do." I shook my head. "I really don't. They will never let any of us leave here, you know that."

So I bided my time. I tried to figure out the perfect time to confront Mamma and Brian, and to plan the perfect things to say, but I was just too scared, so I kept quiet.

THAT DECEMBER, Brian announced he was going to have to get a hip replacement. He had been having trouble with his right hip for a long time, and the doctor had told him he needed to replace it. He was in the hospital for a few days before he came home. He was taking morphine and seemed to be in a lot of pain. Mamma and I tended to him, but he was a foul-tempered patient and was constantly hitting us and throwing things at us if we caused him more pain. He was constantly asking for things and would throw his walker at us if we did not respond quickly enough.

Once I slammed a glass of water down next to him, and said in a sweet voice, "It's really awful to be in pain, huh?" He just glared at me and drank his water.

Mamma's mood seemed to get worse while having to care for Brian, and she was especially mean to Grandma, who in her full-blown Alzheimer's was refusing to eat anything except pudding. Grandma would throw dishes around and more than once I ended up with oatmeal in my hair after trying to coax Grandma into eating something more nutritious. Mamma announced one day that Grandma's diapers were getting too expensive and she could only wear them during the day, and that if she wet the bed, she would have to wash her own sheets outside. The next morning when Mamma found poor Grandma's bed wet, she dragged her outside in the cold January air and set her up with a bucket and a plunger to wash her sheets.

Grandma cried from the cold, but Mamma would not let her back in the house until I came in and told Mamma her thousand-dollar monthly check was about to die. I think she saw how dumb she had been and did not try anything like that again; however, every day she constantly made fun of Grandma for wetting herself. I actually found comfort in a saying that kept running through my head, "Karma is a bi**h." Aunty Laura had said that to Brian once in her self-confident way. If that were true, I thought to myself, Mamma did not have a very comforting future.

THAT JANUARY, Mamma took me to Wenatchee with her and told me she was going to try to get me on SSI.

"I have to have some kind of disability for that, don't I?" I asked, not wanting to bring in another check for them.

"Yeah," Mamma said. "But you can fake it. Besides, you have back problems. You just need to play it up a little for the doctor, and he will sign the papers."

It was true—I did have back problems, mostly from Brian kicking me in the back, but also from trying to lift things that were nearly as heavy as I was and getting beat if I did not do it fast enough.

Mamma took me into the doctor, and he examined me. Mamma motioned for me to pretend I was in pain, and I tried to play along because I did not know what else to do. After the doctor visit, we drove over to the welfare office and Mamma pulled out some forms.

"I need you to sign these as if you were the doctor," she handed me a pen.

I looked at her, shocked, and shook my head. "I can't do that; it's forgery and it's illegal. We could go to jail."

"Look here," Mamma's voice was angry. "I work my butt off getting money for this family, and all you do is come at me with your high and mighty ways."

Finally, I took the pen and forged the doctor's signature as best I could. It did not really resemble his signature very much, but Mamma said they would just throw it in the back of the file and never look at it again. I hoped she was right as I waited out in the truck, shivering in the January cold. Fortunately, despite Mamma's shenanigans, I did not qualify for SSI, and for this I was very happy.

THINGS WERE quiet the rest of that winter while Brian was recuperating. I had promised Samantha that as soon as Brian was better, I was going to stand up to both him and Mamma and demand they treat me like an adult, or I would go to the police station. I knew that as an adult it was against the law for them to beat me, and the only way I could think of getting help for us was to go to the police and ask for it. My only problem was that the police were not Plain people, and I did not know how they could help me get away. I would not be able to live like them because I did not think they were following the Bible, and I wanted to be a good Christian. It never occurred to me to go to an Amish community. I did not know how to join one or if they would even accept me, since they were pretty much closed off to outsiders.

We had a lot of books on the Amish that we were forced to study so we could mimic how they lived, and although I was fully brainwashed into believing it was the only way to get to heaven, there were a lot of things I did not agree with, one being the "forgive and forget" policy. Brian, over the course of the summer, had written the Bishop that his eldest daughter was holding some things against him. Of course, the Bishop did not know the whole story, but what he wrote back was a little troubling:

Although you did not exactly specify the transgression against your daughter, I, being human, can assume. In the Amish church, we are very firm that the one who has transgressed must confess to the church and be placed in six weeks of punishment if deemed necessary, and then the matter is forgiven and never brought up again. If the individual refuses to forgive and continues to talk of the matter they are then punished as well, since we believe firmly in the power of forgiveness and abhor those who are not willing to forgive. Although you do not have a church present there, you still must instill in your daughter humility and forgiveness or she will never see the face of God.

I was angry when Brian read me the letter. How dare that bishop insinuate that I should forgive Brian for all he had done to me and my sister? Brian was even bold enough to read it at the table after the morning Bible reading.

"See, whatever things you girls think you have the right to be mad at us about, you don't," he jabbed his finger in our direction. "You have to forgive us as Jesus would, or you are worse than murderers and will go to hell."

I shook my head. "No, Jesus said, 'repent and be forgiven.' He did not merely say, 'come and be forgiven.'"

Brian's gaze flicked dangerously in my direction. "Oh, he did? And what do you think makes you an expert on the Bible?"

I cocked one eyebrow. Over the years, I had memorized a lot of the Bible. I could tell you who had written which parts just by listening to a few words. One thing you did not want to do with me in those days was start quoting scripture and telling me that things were in the Bible which were not, because I would most certainly know if you were lying. Brian knew this, and I think he was jealous that he could not quote as much scripture as I could. I, on the other hand, was quite pleased seeing him squirm.

"Well," Brian shouted angrily. "Does it not also say women are to listen in silence?"

That shut me up, although I knew my bit about repentance had stolen his thunder.

BRIAN'S HIP was healing fast now, and I was starting to chafe at the injustice of being an eighteen-year-old going on nineteen who was still beaten and yelled at, and with no rights whatsoever. If I did not do something, my life would be the same when I was thirty years old. "No," I told myself, "it can't happen this way; life has got to change. I have had enough. I am going to change things or die trying."

Finally, one sunny April morning, I got up the courage to do something that would completely change our lives forever and send me spiraling headlong on a crazy and dangerous quest for truth and justice.

T HE COMMUNITY

"By this time I was no longer very much terrified or very miserable. I had, as it were, passed the limit of terror and despair. I felt now that my life was practically lost, and that persuasion made me capable of daring anything."

— H.G. Wells, The Island of Dr. Moreau

On a sunny mid-April day, I was outside with Fanny, thawing out a water faucet that had frozen overnight. When I finished, I went into the house to get a hammer so I could nail the wood and insulation back around the faucet. As I went back to the house to return the hammer, I saw Mamma and Brian walking around and watching me. I shrugged. They were really annoying me lately as they searched for things to yell at me about or reasons to beat me. They had started something new with me—instead of telling me to bend over as they once had, now they would just take the flyswatter or the big leather belt and start beating me with it—as if my compliance were not necessary. They would just strike me whenever they felt like it.

When I reached the house, I saw Samantha was mopping and not wanting to track mud all over her floor, I set the hammer inside the door and took Fanny with me to finish our morning work. About ten minutes later, I felt Samantha tap me on the back. I jumped and then looked at her, perplexed.

"What?" I asked, a little anxiously.

Samantha shrugged. "I have no idea. Brian said to come and get you."

I motioned for Fanny to follow us, and we all went into the house. The three of us stood in the middle of the living room, looking from Brian to Mamma inquisitively. As we all stood there, I was again reminded that I was the smallest of the bunch—not a comforting thought when you are faced with a hostile audience.

"What do you want, Dad?" I asked Brian impatiently. I was tired and still had a lot of work to do.

Brian pointed to the door. "Did you put that hammer there?"

I looked at the hammer and nodded. "Uh, yeah," I answered, confused. "I was going to put it away at dinner time."

"Why did you not put it away when you were done like you were supposed to?" Brian's teeth were clenched.

"Well," I stammered, "I didn't want to track up Samantha's floor while she was mopping, and I did not think it would hurt anything."

"Why did you not come and ask our permission?" Mamma asked with a hand on her hip.

"What?" I queried with a look of astonishment. "It seemed kind of unimportant, I guess."

"Oh, asking our permission is unimportant to you?" Mamma fumed.

I lifted my hands in exasperation. "It's just a hammer. I don't understand what the big deal is."

"The big deal is that you think just because you are eighteen, you can do whatever you want without running it past us first. And at the same time you assume we should feed you and clothe you with your arrogant and evil attitude," Mamma shot back at me.

I felt hurt. They had called me evil—these people who were the very epitome of evil. How dare they call me evil? I felt a surge of anger toward them because I knew they were just looking for a reason to attack me.

"Now, to teach you a lesson," Brian walked toward me. "You will bend over and touch your toes like a good little girl while I beat the h**l out of your bare butt."

Out of the corner of my eye, I saw Samantha shaking her head and mouthing, "Don't do it, don't do it."

I was trembling and very scared. Despite the fact that Brian had had surgery four months earlier, he was stronger and much bigger than I was.

"I told you to bend over," Brian snapped as he pointed to the floor.

Suddenly I straightened my small frame and clenched my fists at my side while whispering, "Please, Lord, help me. Please, Lord."

"Excuse me?" Mamma asked sarcastically.

"No, I will not do it," I said emphatically. "I am a grown woman, and you have no right to tell me what to do or to beat me." I took a deep breath to keep my voice from shaking. "That much I know about the law. And if I go to the police station right now, they are going to haul you both off to jail where you belong." I stamped my foot for good measure and for a split second enjoyed the looks of shock on their faces.

"You are going to do none of those things," Brian barked at me. "And you know why? Because we did not give you permission, that's why."

"No," I shook my head. "I don't need your permission. I am an adult now, and I will do what I think is right."

"Bend over and touch your toes—NOW!" Brian growled, pushing me.

"No," I protested.

"NOW!" he repeated

"NO!" I shouted back.

"I said touch your toes, da**it." He grabbed me and tried to make me bend over.

I pushed back at him, yelling, "No! And you can't make me."

Suddenly Brian snapped and he began twisting my head as if trying to snap my neck. I felt the pressure growing in my head, and I thought for a moment I was going to die. "No," I cried inwardly, just as I was on the verge of blacking out. "This is not how it was supposed to end." As if in slow motion, I felt my neck twisting farther and farther, and I was waiting, wondering if I would be able to hear the crunching sound or if I would die first. I was unable to move, although I was resisting as much as possible with my neck. I figured if Brian was going to kill me I would make it as hard as possible for him complete the task.

Suddenly I heard Samantha scream, "You are killing her, no! No!" Her voice came to me as if through a tunnel.

I heard Mamma's voice, "Samantha, don't; leave him alone. She deserves it."

Samantha, however, ran at Brian and jumped on his back, wrapping her arms around his throat and trying to choke him. The sheer force of her weight threw him off balance enough that he lost his grip on my neck just seconds before everything went black. As I fell to the floor I saw Brian throw Samantha across the room and over the table; there were some canning jars on the table, and I heard Samantha hit the floor with a tinkling of broken glass. I saw Brian run over to her angrily calling her a "meddling little bi*ch."

I could not believe Mamma could stand calmly by as her daughters were being treated this way, but she had never been a mother to us, so why should I be surprised? I heard Samantha screaming as I struggled to my feet. I was dizzy and could not believe I was still alive; I had been so sure I was dying, and in the split seconds before Samantha had jumped on Brian's back, I had even felt at peace. At least I was dying with dignity, I had thought. I had stood up to the lion and lost, but at least I had tried.

But now, I was suddenly alive again, and Samantha's screams were ear-shattering. I was terrified of what Brian might do to her. In a panic, trying to divert Brian's attention away from Samantha, I raced up the stairs and yelled down, "I am leaving now. I am going to the police, and they are going to enjoy all the evidence you guys are leaving for them."

I knew I had trapped myself upstairs, but I did not know how else to get them off of Samantha. I was very afraid we both were going to end up dead that day. Samantha's screams suddenly stopped and I heard running. The whole house seemed to shake as Mamma and Brian both ran up the stairs. I looked around frantically, as if for a way to escape, but of course there was none, so I jumped up on my bed and backed into the corner hoping that somehow I was out of their reach. I balled myself up, putting my head between my legs in an attempt to protect myself. But it was to no avail, as Brian grabbed me by the feet and pulled me to the edge of the bed. I kicked at him catching him in the fore head; it stunned him for half a second and I took advantage of the situation and scrambled back into my corner. Brian reached for me again and this time managed to yank me off the bed. I was terrified of what Brian might be planning to do to me. Brian shoved me into the wall, and I saw Mamma standing there again with her arms folded. "Mamma," I screamed. "Help me get this j**k off of me."

"Why should I protect you when you want to betray us?" Mamma shot back as if I were a traitor.

"I am your daughter," I shouted as I fell to the floor, trying to shield myself from Brian's open-handed slaps.

Suddenly I saw a way to escape. I quickly rolled onto my stomach and slithered my small frame past Mamma's and Brian's legs and made a dash for the stairs. I fairly flew down the stairs. Mamma tried to grab me, but I slipped past her. When I got to the bottom of the stairs, I heard Samantha yelling for me to run. I raced out the door and down the drive. As I ran, I remember thinking, "I cannot believe I am actually doing this." I heard Mamma screaming behind me. Brian, due to his hip surgery, was not able to run long distances. I heard Mamma yell at Brian to get the truck, but I just kept running as fast as I could. I was scared; and I did not know if there was a rifle pointed at my back or not.

I did not get far when I heard the truck barreling down the road. I did not know how I was going to get past them to get into town; it was six and a half miles to the pavement in the back of the orchards, and another mile to the tiny police station. How was I going to get into town without them spotting me and taking me back? As the truck came up behind me, I dove off the road and into the sagebrush and continued walking toward town. I heard Brian's voice floating to me on the spring air.

"Get in the truck right now."

I did not answer and just kept walking.

"Misty, get your a*s up here and get in the truck before I come down there and make you!"

I still did not answer and continued to fight my way through the bushes, which was not an easy fight. All the while I was thinking they must be crazy to think I would actually go anywhere with them.

"You know," Brian said in a casual voice, "the police are not going to believe anything you say. They don't even know who you are. And because we are strict Christians, they will believe we are good parents, and all I have to tell them is that you are a rebellious teenager who is trying to get her parents in trouble because we do not let you date whoever you want."

"That's ridiculous," I finally yelled back, "of course they will believe me; it's the truth."

"Oh, no." Brian laughed. "I am a good Amish father trying to keep his daughter from a life of sin. They will believe me over you. Besides, because we are Amish they won't want to get involved; they will just call it a religious dispute."

I began losing my drive to try to get into town. My head was pounding so badly I could not think. I felt nauseous and could not go another step. I decided I would go back with them and try to make a run for it in the night or sometime when I could get a head start.

I climbed up the embankment and into the truck. Although I am sure it is hard for you, the reader, to believe any girl would return to the home of people who harmed her so badly, you must understand that I was not a normal teenager. I was clothed from head to foot in plain clothing, and I did not have any knowledge of or experience with carrying on a conversation with outside people. I did not understand anything except our daily life on the mountain. What was I supposed to do? Besides, I needed to get back to check on Samantha.

When I got out of the truck, Samantha seemed disappointed that I had come back with them. Brian told everyone to get in the house, and as we walked in that direction my neck was aching and my head was pounding loudly in my ears.

Samantha whispered, "You know he was for real trying to kill you, right? He was just about ready to snap your neck when I jumped him."

"Yeah, thanks for that, Sam," I rubbed my now swollen neck.

I scanned Samantha from head to toe. My heart sank as I saw a dark bruise on her cheekbone and the many tiny cuts on her arms from where she had fallen on the glass. I felt so sick from the headache I could not think clearly. I kept blinking my eyes, trying to clear my head—this was not the time to have a foggy brain, I told myself. But my thoughts didn't help, and with every step the pain got worse. I ended up vomiting next to the steps.

"All right, sit down," Brian ordered as we walked through the door.

Mamma was standing there, arms crossed again, with a frown on her face. I looked her directly in the eyes, and she looked back at me for a moment, and then looked away, her frown getting deeper, if that were possible.

"All right," Brian said again. "I knew this day was coming, so I have been writing to the Bishop. A few weeks ago he sent me the address of one of their Amish communities in Minnesota, which is closer to us than Pennsylvania would be. He knows the bishop there and has written that the community would be willing to take you girls in so you can join the church. They are in desperate need of new bloodlines, so you would be an asset to them," Brian stated as if we were livestock.

Samantha and I looked at each other in shock. This was the first we had heard of this. Mamma snorted in contempt and Brian stared at us as if we were bad little girls whom he was shipping off to boarding school.

"Believe you me," Brian said through his clenched teeth, "they know all about rebellious teens and girls that do not want to conform to the church, so whatever cockamamie stories you try to tell them about me or your mother, they are not going to care. They already know that you are unruly, but they have agreed to give you a trial period since you have pretty much been raised Amish. But the Bishop said you will be watched closely, so you had better behave or you will be in trouble with them."

I looked at Samantha. Could this be true? I wasn't sure that I agreed with everything the Amish did, but we had to agree because there was no other way to get to heaven. We had to join the Amish, this I knew; we could not even join the Mennonites, I thought, because they were too worldly and were not going to heaven. The Mennonite women wore flowers on their dresses and their head coverings were too small. I know this must sound crazy to the reader, but this is what I was taught to believe, and I *did* believe it with all my heart.

136

The news was amazing to Samantha and I; we could not believe we were actually going to get out of this horrible place that had been our reality for so long. Even more shocking was the fact that Brian was thinking of letting us go. I have always wondered why Brian agreed to give us to the Amish community. I thanked God for this, but I did not understand what could tempt Brian and Mamma to give away their two slaves.

The only explanation I could come up with at that time was that they were really afraid that I would make good on my promise to turn them into the police, and that if I did not, Samantha would. By removing us from the farm, I think Brian believed he was punishing us, as we would have to follow the very strict Amish church laws for the rest of our lives. We would be entrapped and would not be able to bring any harm to Mamma and Brian, since the Amish did not allow their people to contact the police. Also, I believe it gave Brian a feeling of power over us, as if he were responsible for how our futures turned out, thus taking any freedom to which we thought we were entitled away from us. It was all about power with Brian.

Mamma and Brian would still have all their government checks coming in, so they would be fine. To me, it looked like their evil empire was crumbling around them, and now they were scrambling to rebuild. I would later learn that Brian and Mamma expected Samantha and I to fail at joining the Amish, that in itself was the main reason they let us go, they expected us to fail and realize we had no way to survive without them.

A FEW days later, it was decided that Brian would drive us to the Amish community. The plan Brian had made with the Bishop was that Brian would bring Samantha and I to attend church once every two months. Then in September I would move to the community and get situated there and Samantha would follow a few months later. I was nervous about leaving Samantha on the mountain by herself with them and at first did not want to go, but Samantha scolded me, saying,

"If we don't go along with the plan, we are not going to get out of here alive, ever."

"All right," I finally agreed. "But if you don't show up when you are supposed to, rest assured this time I *will* go to the police and report a possible homicide."

Samantha agreed that this was good idea, and I believe Mamma and Brian were already thinking I might do such a thing; at least I hoped so.

Although it was a long drive, Brian did not trust us enough to get on a bus, so Samantha and I sat in the back of his truck on what seemed to be an endless drive as we watched hundreds of farms and fields roll by. Brian sat in the front, driving and lecturing us on everything he could think of, but we were not listening. I was lost in my own thoughts. Now, at eighteen and a half years old, I was finally going to meet girls my age. Girls that dressed like me and understood, to some extent, who I was; I would be part of an actual group of people that were like me. But the best part of all was that I would not have to see Brian or Mamma ever again, since they were divorced and not allowed to join the Amish church. The Bishop had offered them the opportunity to move close by so they could attend church and be a part of the community, but Brian and Mamma had declined, much to my relief. They were way too antisocial to ever want to be that close to a community.

After driving for more than twenty-four hours, we finally approached the Amish community. I heard the clip-clop, clip-clop of a horse pulling a buggy as we approached it from behind. Samantha grabbed my hand.

"That's going to be us; can you believe it, Misty?" she whispered ecstatically.

I smiled at her, wondering if she had ever been this happy in her lifetime. I was not as excited as Samantha, my life's dream was still to be a medical missionary and travel the world, helping the sick and impoverished. To be educated in the field of medicine was only a dream, though. There were no Amish doctors. I would never be a nurse or a doctor or anything other than a farmer's wife with a large brood of children. As I saw the Amish farm houses through the window of the truck, I whispered to the glass, "Lord, if it is so wrong to want an education and to travel the world taking care of the sick, why do I want it so badly? I only want to do what you want me to do, and it is never going to happen. It's virtually impossible." I leaned my head against the glass as the truck rumbled to a stop. *This is it*, as Samantha had said earlier during our stop for a bathroom break,

"This is our only ticket out of hell; let's not blow it," she had said, more to herself than to me, as she nervously squeezed a roll of toilet paper between her sweaty palms. "There won't be another chance for us. We are just nobodies, you know, we really are. If Brian had killed us last week, no one would have known, and if the Amish don't want us here, Brian is going to keep on hurting us."

I nodded in agreement. I knew this to be true, but I wondered what was making Samantha so nervous. I felt very calm about the whole thing, but Samantha was having difficulties concentrating and sitting still. Maybe it was the fact that I had thought I was dying just a few days before and that made me want to sit back and contemplate life and just observe the behavior of others. Yet, I still wondered why life was the way that it was, and if it really mattered at all when you took into account the enormity of the universe. Did our petty "You must do this" and "You must do that" really matter in the slightest?

We pulled into the drive, and Brian turned off the truck and twisted around to look at us.

"Pull your head coverings forward," he barked at us. "These Amish are very strict and don't want no 'hoochie mammas' running around the place."

Samantha and I pulled our caps forward so hardly a hair was showing and straightened the new, dark blue dresses and black aprons that I had made for the occasion. By this time I was starting to feel a little excitement, and I knew we were both wondering if we would be prettier or uglier than the other girls. How would we look compared to the rest of the people here? We had no clue.

I opened the door of the truck, and Samantha and I hopped out. We stood there for a second as if frozen. A man with a long beard streaked with brown and gray and wearing a large black hat came through the front door, waving at us to come inside.

"Come in, come in. You must be Brian," he said with a thick Pennsylvania Dutch accent.

"Yes, and you must be the Bishop," Brian replied, pulling his hat down further as if to appear more Amish.

"Oh, no..." The man shook his head and smiled. "I am Uriah Hostetler, the minister, but we thought it best if you came here since our family has daughters close to the age of your daughters. The Bishop is a younger man and only has small children, so we thought you would all be more comfortable staying here for the night."

I thought he seemed like a nice person as he guided us into the main area of the large farm house. I looked around and smiled. This house had centuries of tradition screaming from every beam. There were light blue walls and plain, dark blue curtains at the windows. In front of one of the windows was a large quilt frame, and not far from the quilting frame were two treadle sewing machines with small, unfinished clothes hanging from them.

As we stood in the middle of the room, the man yelled, "Alma, children, come here!"

Out of the kitchen and through the side door tumbled twelve children, ranging from nineteen to one-and-a-half years old. Samantha and I were in shock as they stood there looking at us. The mother seemed to be a kind lady with gray hair popping out from under her stiff white kapp.

"Nice to meet you! Nice to meet you!" she said in the same heavy accent as her husband.

Samantha and I just stood there. We had been exposed to so few social interactions we did not know what to do or say.

"Okay," the mother turned to two of her teenage daughters, "Matty and Laura, you can help the girls take their things upstairs and then come back down to help with dinner. Uriah, you can take Brian to finish choring, Ja?" she turned back to her husband.

As Brian and the Hostetler menfolk went out choring, Samantha and I followed Matty and Laura upstairs, where there seemed to be an ocean of bedrooms.

"Hey, they are really nice, huh?" Samantha whispered in my ear.

I nodded, pleasantly surprised by the family's welcoming manner.

Matty, who was nineteen, stopped at one of the doors. "This is my room. You will be sleeping with me," she said pointing at me.

I smiled. They seemed a little awkward too, I thought. That was a relief.

"Matty and Edward are the only ones who have their own rooms," Laura said, walking down the hall. "I share this room with Eliza, and Samantha can sleep with us in here."

I smiled at Laura, who was intently studying my face whenever she thought I was not looking at her.

"Oh yes," seventeen-year-old Laura continued, "you will be wearing some of our extra clothes to church so you blend in and look more like us." She looked at our dresses and aprons.

I had noticed that, although to any outsider we would all look Amish, our clothes were very different. Among the Amish there are many subgroups, and among the subgroups are even more subgroups, all with their own strictly enforced dress codes. The girl's' clothes were much neater than ours, I thought, and instead of zippers, the girls over eleven years old wore straight pins all the way from their high collars to the apron belts at the waist. They did not have black aprons, either, but matching aprons.

I was very excited to wear clothes just like theirs and be matching— finally I would belong to something, I thought. My musings on the way to the community about wanting to be a doctor were long forgotten. I was here with people who resembled me and were of the same faith. It was such a great feeling, one I had never experienced before, and I felt alive and as if I mattered just a little bit.

140

"Let's see," Matty pulled me out of my thoughts. She looked us over, trying to determine what family members' clothes would fit us best. Cocking her head sideways, she looked at my short stature.

"You are just a couple of inches shorter than Eliza, so you should fit into her extra church dress and apron," Matty walked to the closet in Laura and Eliza's room. She pulled out a dark gray dress and held it up to me. It nearly hit the floor, but they seemed to think it looked fine. She rummaged around, looking for Eliza's old white organdy church apron that was saved for emergencies. Laura went to her side of the closet and pulled out one of her church dresses for Samantha. It was a nice teal color and seemed like it would fit Samantha quite well. Amish dresses are made with long belts and a lot of material in the front that you just pin under, so that if you gain weight you can simply unpin some extra folds of the material, rather than making a whole new dress, since that is quite expensive for an Amish family.

"We just need to starch these before morning," Matty gathered the white church capes and aprons.

As we made our way downstairs, I heard chattering and small children laughing in the kitchen. Dishes were clanging as two small girls who could barely reach the table slammed metal plates and spoons on the table. Wow, I thought to myself, there was no Mamma or Brian beating anyone; these children looked comfortable as they raced around the kitchen. They were obviously not deathly afraid of their mother as she playfully swatted their behinds, hurrying them to get the dinner on the table.

We sat at the table in the order of our ages. There were so many customs we had to learn, I thought, but one thing I did notice was that Samantha and I would probably pass on the behavior issue with flying colors. We were both quite rigid and used to do doing what we were told immediately. I had noticed that the mother had to yell several times for everyone else to get to the table, whereas Samantha and I sat down as soon as the words came out of her mouth. Oddly, she did not seem at all put out as the children sat down, one by one. The girls sat on the right next to their mother, and the boys on the left of their father. The line tapered down until the oldest boy and oldest girl were sitting at the opposite end of the table, and then there was Brian.

"Let us bow our heads for a moment of silent prayer," Uriah said, and we all bowed our heads. I opened my eyes and peeked around the room. The kerosene lamp in the middle of the table was casting a soft glow as it flickered in the late spring air. I could hear the horses nickering to each other in the barn, and as I looked around the table, I saw one of the little boys staring at me. I smiled at him and he grinned back at me; the grin was missing a few teeth, but he was very cute. *I can do this*, I told myself; *these are nice people, and I have no other options. This is the only way to avoid going to hell.*

Despite our upbringing, we did not have that deeply ingrained love for Amish tradition stamped in our brains, which was something I was sure they would be looking for and something we would have to learn quickly.

The family ate in silence, as is typical in Amish culture. Two of the small boys quarreled over which one was hogging the bench, but the mother put a quick end to it by making one of the boys sit next to her. Among the Amish, for a boy to sit with his mother is to be shamed, especially with company around, and he bowed his head, red faced, refusing to eat anything after that.

After dinner, Samantha and I helped clean the kitchen while the men and boys sat on the long benches that were used at the table. The boys played a game of checkers while Brian and Uriah talked and stroked their long beards. I rolled my eyes as I watched Brian. He was simply copying the actions of Uriah. Brian was actually a pretty good actor and could appear kind and sincere on a whim. It was only if you knew him and could look into his evil, dark brown eyes that you could tell it was all merely an act and that he was laughing inside at the person who was dumb enough to believe it.

After the dishes were finished, Uriah clapped his hands. "All off to bed; tomorrow is church Sunday and we must get up early." By church Sunday, he was referring to the fact that Amish have church every other week rather than every week.

We all hurried off to our beds. The parents slept downstairs while the children slept upstairs. Brian slept in eighteen-year-old Edward's room while Edward bunked with his younger brothers. Matty and I put on our night dresses, and as I was slipping out of my dress and into the night dress I heard Matty gasp behind me. Startled, I turned around to look at her.

"What?" I queried.

"How did you get that giant bruise?" she asked with wide eyes as she touched the purple-green mark on my back that was, not surprisingly, the same size as Brian's shoe.

I cringed. I had forgotten about it. I held my dress in front of me, I wondered if anyone had noticed the bruise on Samantha's cheek.

"I got kicked by a cow," I stammered. My gaze met Matty's, and I saw in her eyes that she did not believe me, but she did not say anything else. I was relieved, but could not help noticing it did not seem like the first time she had seen such things. Still, I felt more at ease, as if I had let her in on a secret that was bothering me.

142

"I don't know what time you stand up at home," she said in her Amish-accented English, "but we stand up at 4:30 a.m. here."

I looked at the alarm clock that was ticking on the dresser. It read 9:30 p.m..

"That's about what time we get up too," I nodded, "but we usually go to bed much later."

"Oh, really?" Matty cocked a brow. "Well, when it gets high summer we do too, but not now, it is not necessary."

I snuggled down into the lumpy cotton mattress and fell asleep. Tomorrow I would finally go to church. No one would beat me or try to hurt me tomorrow. Maybe this was how life was supposed to be, I thought.

THE NEXT morning, Matty and I bounced out of bed with the sound of the alarm. The quiet, dark house seemed to bounce to life as Mom Hostetler's voice floated upstairs:

"Children, time to stand up!"

When that did not work, I heard the deep, resonating voice of Uriah telling the children they had better get up because it was church Sunday. Samantha and I went with the four oldest girls to milk the family's five cows. This was nothing new for us, and I think the girls were impressed with our milking skills.

"If you could speak our language, I would never know you were not born Amish," Laura bubbled.

"Do you think it is going to be hard for us to learn German?" I asked, a little worried at having to learn a new language and knowing that my status would depend on how quickly I picked it up.

"I don't know," Matty shrugged. "We usually learn English when we start school; we are only allowed to speak English in school so we can learn it. I went through eight grades and my English is still broken, so I really do not know how you are going to learn German."

"Yeah, it's going to be tough," Laura chimed in. "But also, it is against church rules to be speaking English amongst ourselves, so until you learn it you will feel like you are outsiders."

Samantha and I looked at each other and shrugged; we would do our best.

After the breakfast dishes were washed and put away, all the children clattered up the stairs to start dressing for church. I stepped into the gray dress Matty handed me and tried to start pinning the front like Matty was doing. It took her less than a minute to pin down the front of her dress. She saw me struggling and smiled as she took the pins out of my hand.

"It takes all the girls about a week to learn how to do this so the pins don't poke you when you are moving. See," she pointed to her mouth where she was clenching pins between her lips, "just hold these in your mouth like this and then move your pin in and out of the dress front until you reach the end, like that." She let go of the top pin.

I followed her advice and finished pinning the dress. Next came the stiff white cape that went around my shoulders and pinned in the front and to the dress belt in the back, and finally the stiff white apron that was only an inch shorter than the dress itself. I combed my long hair back and twisted it in a bun, then slid on the black Sunday kapp. It is tradition among the Amish that unmarried girls wear black kapps to church so the boys and men can easily tell who is unmarried. As I tied a neat bow under my chin, I looked in the tiny mirror on the dresser.

"I really look different," I mused.

"Yep, you look like one of us," Matty smiled as she placed the towel back over the mirror.

It felt good to actually belong to something. This was the most amazing day of my life. It really was, if you consider what my life had been. Little did I realize then that I was starting a voyage through dark and murky waters filled with secrets and hundred-year-old customs. Worst of all, most of the people with me on this voyage were mere sheep that did not care about right or wrong, only about tradition and the church rules. One of the most common phrases I would hear on this voyage was "Be silenced." But, of course, I could not know this on that first Sunday as I smoothed down the gathers ironed into the dress and apron. I deserved a moment of bliss, didn't I? And even if I had known what was to come, how could I have changed the course of events that were about to transpire?

Excitedly, I walked down the steps with Matty. As the teenage girls came down the stairs, I noticed that one by one they had to stop in front of their father for inspection, and he gave a little nod or a criticism. When he gave an order to Eliza, I asked Matty what he had said.

"Oh, he just told her to pull her kapp further up on her head," Matty answered. "We are only allowed to have two finger widths of hair showing, and it is better if Dad looks than the Bishop or other church members. There is nothing people love more around here than to wag their tongues. Just wait; you will find out soon enough."

"Oh," I nodded, not fully understanding the implications that could follow a tongue wagging. I had never had the privilege of gossiping, since there had never been anyone to gossip about on the farm, unless you counted Mamma and Brian.

"Okay, let's go, let's go," Laura called from the door that she was holding open. "We have to hurry; it's a mile's walk over to Jacob C's, and if we are going to make it by 8:30, we better move it."

We set out walking as the buggy clip-clopped by with the parents inside. Brian and the four youngest children were all cramped inside as well. More buggies passed us as we walked along the side of the road, and in front of and behind us I saw other groups of young people in their church clothes walking in the direction of Jakey C's farm.

"Must be a big church, huh?" I asked Matty.

"Not really," Matty looked around at the small groups of young people. "Only about fifteen families, but a lot have eight to twelve children, so it adds up. You know, our church is held in a house so we have to cut ourselves into districts. When one church gets too big, we just keep cutting more districts, but we are allowed to go to a different district's church if we want to occasionally, and all of our churches and districts interact with each other on a daily basis."

As we neared the house where church was being held, we saw many buggies out front. The men let the women and children off on their way to park the buggies near the barn. Samantha and I followed the unmarried girls, aged thirteen and over, into the wash house where we waited for our cue to enter the main room.

"We go in order of our ages," Matty whispered to me. "Since you are going to be nineteen in a few months, you can just follow me, and Samantha can go ahead and follow Laura."

I nodded, and we all stood there in silence. *Hmm...*, I thought, not as bad as I had feared. *These girls are not very talkative.* In fact, in the Amish, women are taught that silence is a virtue, and if too much chatter is heard, the Amish father or mother will look at the girl and shake their heads. And besides, I thought, they don't want to start any 'tongues wagging'.

"Okay," Matty looked at Samantha and I. "Get ready, and pull your kapps forward. I know you probably don't realize it, but everyone is going to be looking at you two." She motioned for Samantha to come over. "Just act like you know what you are doing and keep a straight and humble face. We sit directly in front of the minister's bench, so be warned."

I felt butterflies in my stomach as the girls started lining up to enter the main area where church would be held. It was my first time at an Amish church, and I could not help staring as we filed in. The married women sat first, with the oldest sitting closest to the back and the younger sitting more toward the front. Next came the unmarried girls, with the oldest going first. We all filed solemnly past the married women, and one by one sat on a long bench—in front of the married women and about eight feet away from the minister's bench. The men also entered in order of age; they sat facing the women. I sat stiffly for a moment as the eyes of the men, ministers, the Bishop and the Deacon all looked me over from head to foot, just as they did the other girls.

Now I knew what Matty had meant when she said it was better for the father to find fault with your appearance rather than have it be done by the church members. It was not hard to see that the unmarried girls were the main topic of any 'tongue wagging'.

A couple of minutes after we sat down, the unmarried boys filed in. I did not think it fair when I saw them clattering onto a bench behind the older men. I wondered why they got sit in the back where no one could see them. But I knew, since it had been ingrained in me from an early age, that Eve had eaten the fruit first, causing man to sin; therefore, women were a source of evil and temptation, and needed to be closely watched until marriage and even after that, until they were no longer in their attractive, youthful state.

As I sat there frozen in place, Matty nudged me. She picked up one of the thick, black church hymnals when one of the men started singing. I looked at the German writing; I was unable to read it, but I pretended I could all the same.

As the slow Gregorian chant reached its second verse, the ministers got up and went upstairs to a room prepared for them, where they would discuss the sermon for the day, church matters that must be handled between church members only and so on. We had just finished our third song approximately thirty minutes later, when we heard the ministers coming back down the stairs. The Deacon stood up, and we all turned around and knelt with our heads touching the benches as he read from the Prayer Book. Then the Bishop and ministers took turns reading scripture and preaching.

After three hours of sitting on the hard wooden bench, I could hardly keep my eyes open, and my head was nodding. I peeked around and saw that several people were sleeping, the boys in the back were sneaking looks at the girls sitting in the front and small children were playing behind me. I realized that, like me, the church did not really understand much of the sermon because it was in High German rather than in the Pennsylvania Dutch dialect that the Amish spoke.

I was relieved when we finally closed with the final hymn and the girls filed out first, going upstairs to the girls' rooms to wait for the women to call us down for lunch. Here, we split into two different groups: the younger girls who were thirteen to sixteen, and not yet eligible to date; seventeen and older was dating age.

I sat on the bed and looked at the girls as they quietly giggled and teased each other about that night's singing and who would be taking whom home. They were nice to me, and I could sense they had all been ordered not to ask me questions, which was a relief. About an hour later, the house mother called the girls to come down and eat. The married women, small children and men had eaten first, and now it was the young people's turn. A few of the church benches had been placed in the middle for a table, with the other benches available to sit on. The lunch consisted of the standard Amish church lunch everywhere. There were stacks of homemade breads staggered along the bench-tables with little dishes of butter, homemade spread cheese, peanut butter, jam and pickles. There was also coffee and mint tea to drink. This was a very unique lunch, I thought, but it was good and definitely a good way to feed so many people quickly. I winced and Matty laughed at me as I watched her put the spread cheese, jam and pickles all on one piece of bread.

"Get ready for a culture shock just from our eating habits," she laughed, licking her fingers. "You want a bite?" she asked, offering her bread to me.

I shook my head and smiled as I tried to replicate the sandwich, just to see what it tasted like.

"Hey, that's actually good," I grinned as I crunched down on a pickle.

Samantha looked like she would be sick as she glanced at my sandwich, and the other girls and I laughed at her; she just shook her head and smiled. I kept smiling as I looked down the long line of girls. This was a lot of fun, and the girls were nice. It was true that if we had spoken German others would have hardly been able to tell that we had not lived amongst them our entire lives. It was an awesome feeling, and I could hardly believe my good fortune. This is happening to me, I thought, who would have believed it could happen to little old me? The 'nobody' that would not have been missed had I died was now going to belong to a group of people that would actually think she mattered just a little bit. It was truly amazing, and I blinked back a tear as I whispered "Thank you Lord" under my breath.

Uniformity: *The Loss of Identity*

"To be given dominion over another is a hard thing; to wrest dominion over another is a wrong thing; to give dominion of yourself to another is a wicked thing."

— *Toni Morrison, A Mercy*

After Samantha and I helped the girls do the dishes, the Bishop's wife beckoned for Samantha and I to follow her. We walked to the stairwell where the ministers' wives, the deacon's wife and the Bishop's wife were all standing. Samantha and I stood there as they looked at us solemnly.

"Okay," Alma, Matty's mother began. "So this is Samantha, and this is Misty. Misty is eighteen and Samantha is sixteen." She pointed to each of us.

The women nodded solemnly, and then the Bishop's wife, who was surprisingly young and very pretty, spoke. "Well, I guess I will start. Our husbands are upstairs talking to your father and we will join them soon, but first we wanted to tell you girls a few things." She paused and peered at us with eyes that seemed to be searching our very souls.

"First of all, your dad told us that you girls have been sheltered from most worldly things, which is a good thing. However, since your parents were raised amongst the '*Englisch*' there is no way for you to know some of things we expect, and there are a few things you probably *do* know about that you should not, and you don't know not to talk about them."

"Okay, first of all," she pointed to her stomach. "So you know I am pregnant, right?" she asked.

Samantha and I nodded blankly. Her pregnancy was very obvious.

Alma, the minister's wife, nodded. "Just as I thought," she continued.

"You see, unmarried girls do not acknowledge pregnancies. It is not discussed with them until the night of their weddings. I won't say that the older teens do not figure it out, but they never comment or stare or anything of the sort. We do not want our unmarried girls to know how babies come about, and we never speak of sex...ever. You girls do know what that is, right?" she asked, looking at us sternly.

"Yeah, of course," I shrugged. I thought everyone over the age of twelve knew about these things, or had at least figured them out.

The deacon's wife nodded. "This is a great concern to us. We do not even let our unmarried people read the German Bible as it speaks of these things." The women looked at us earnestly and shook their heads, as if trying to evaluate how much of a threat our knowledge was.

"You have now been told of these things," Alma admonished. "You will be watched, and we will punish you if we hear you speak of any of these things, especially around the boys; the boys are already more knowledgeable about these things since they help breed the animals on the farms." All of the women nodded in agreement, and I swallowed. I felt I was on trial for a crime not yet committed and was determined to be sure I did not transgress any of these orders.

"That is another thing," the Bishop's wife held up one of her thin, frail hands. "I have noticed that when I go to English farms the whole family talks about breeding this horse to that horse or whatever. Women here are never involved in such conversation...ever. My husband does not even discuss such matters with me. We never mention if a dog is in heat or anything like that. Do you girls understand what we are telling you?"

Samantha and I nodded, not sure how we were supposed to react.

"Okay," Alma seemed satisfied. "Just so you know, this first year is a probation time. Then, once you are members of the community, you can be placed in the Bann for breaking any of these rules. We take them extremely seriously. All parents, if they feel their unmarried children have acquired such knowledge, will talk to them just as we have talked to you, but for the most part our young people just know not to speak of such things, even the older ones if they are unmarried. It is only for married people to talk of such things."

Samantha and I just smiled and nodded politely. That was fine, I thought. I did not really care, although I did realize I would need to be sure never to ask a pregnant woman when her baby was due or look at her swollen stomach. I now knew why Matty had averted her eyes to look past the Bishop's wife when she had come over to us. *There was no way Matty did not know that it was a baby that was causing that swollen stomach*, I thought to myself. But tradition was what we were here to learn, and we had to learn it well.

"Okay," the Bishop's wife motioned to us. "Let us join the menfolk upstairs. We need to go over a few more things."

Samantha and I followed the women upstairs and sat down on the bench the Bishop pointed out, which was in front of where the men were sitting. I sat down and looked at Brian, who was seated with the ministers. They all looked so grave; I felt I had committed some sort of crime.

"Well, I guess I will start," the Bishop stroked his long, red beard. "This is a very serious matter for our church, as you well know." He paused for a moment, and the ministers nodded in agreement.

"The biggest hurdle we face is the fact that you do not speak our language or know how to read the hymns during church; and, as we have never known anyone to join our church before, we do not know how to teach you the language, so that will be totally on you. But," he continued, "you must know our common language before you are baptized, as the instructions for baptism are in our language. Also, the twice yearly reading of the church Ordnung [rules] is also in our language."

Samantha and I nodded to show that we understood the depth of what was expected of us.

"And, of course, there is the fact that you, Misty, are nearing nineteen. Our young people enter their instruction for baptism the fall after they turn seventeen, so you are much older than any of our unbaptized people. This could prove to be awkward, as the girls your age must remember not to discuss church matters with you, since church matters are for baptized members only."

"Okay," he turned to the other ministers. "Anything you want to add?"

The Deacon nodded. "I just want you to know we expect you to pick up on all of our traditions and practices as soon as possible. We do not want to feel like we have outsiders among us." He paused as he put special emphasis on the word "outsiders." "We need to feel you are a part of this church and willing to follow all rules, or it is going to be very difficult for everyone. We will not baptize you until we feel you have become a part of the church, and you may not marry until you have been baptized, so it is all up to you."

I nodded and sighed. I had a lot to learn and quickly, before I was too old for marriage. There was one thing I knew—if you were an old maid in the Amish, you were looked down upon and had no more status than a teenage girl. Even if you were in your fifties, you were still considered on the same level as a teenager. If you were still unmarried at the age of twenty-five or so, your chances of marrying were extremely slim. It was also a custom that if a girl was from a family that was looked down on by the church, the parents of the community might order their sons not to date any of the daughters from the family. I was not sure how Samantha and I measured up in the line of girls, but I supposed we would see soon enough.

"So," the Bishop continued, "it has been decided that Misty will live with my neighbor, Jacob, and his family. They were only able to have four children, so you will make five. They will be your new dad and mom, and you will use their last name as well. Samantha will live with the Deacon and his family and take their last name. This way you have someone accountable for you at all times."

I squirmed on the bench. I did not want a new mother and father. I had not had good luck with the first set and was not anxious to have new ones.

"Also," the Bishop's wife added from her seat behind the men, "we will need to change your names to more Amish names. We do not have any Misty's or Samantha's in our church. They sound like very prideful names, and we cannot have that."

Samantha and I looked at each other. We had to change our first names, too? *It was like entering the witness protection program*, I thought to myself; our entire identity had to be changed.

"What are we going to call ourselves?" I asked, feeling as if I were losing a part of what made me who I was.

"You can name yourselves," the Bishop's wife answered. "But you will need to pick an Amish name. As you have probably noticed, a lot of us have the same names. The difference between us is set when we use the first initial of our father's name as our middle initial; middle names are prideful. For example, I am Phyllis E," she pointed to herself. "Just think about it and pick a name and then you can ask me if it is okay, all right?" She smiled at us, probably realizing that this was a real shock to us.

The Bishop stood up. "We better all get home and get our choring done before the evening singing," he stifled a yawn.

I rolled my eyes as I saw Brian nod with the same solemn face as the other men. The entire time the ministers were talking, Brian sat there, smugly listening to all the rules we would have to follow. I could tell he was enjoying the shock on our faces. But, I thought to myself, he had no idea how much I was enjoying the idea of never having to see him again.

Samantha and I stayed seated on the bench until the others went downstairs.

"What the heck," Samantha looked at me. "Are we joining the Amish or the Marines?"

151

I shook my head in disbelief. "I don't think the Marines make you change your name, Samantha. This is going to be really hard," I said as I rubbed my swollen neck.

"I know." Samantha nodded. "But we have to do it; we can't stay on the mountain, and this is the only way to go to heaven. There is no other church that is strict enough or plain; this is it."

We stood up and pushed the bench to the wall. "I don't know," I mused. "I hope we will blend in and not just be in trouble all the time. You know that we have zero social skills, and we don't know how to act in groups. When we were in the wash house, I wanted to crawl in one of the wash tubs and hide. I don't know how I am going to make it with everyone staring at me all the time."

"We can do it," Samantha vowed as we went down the stairs. "We just have to."

We went outside to find Matty and Laura waiting for us to start the walk home. They did not ask us any questions, as if there were some unspoken ban on questioning us.

"Well..." I ventured after we had walked in silence for a few minutes, "Samantha and I have to pick new names."

"Yeah, I thought you probably would," Matty nodded. "There was a younger couple in the east district a couple years ago who tried to name their baby girl Iris. It was the wife's favorite flower, but she did not get to keep the name, because there was no one in her family with that name, and we always must name our children after people in our family. Since we are related, we kind of all have the same names."

"Tell us some common names so we can pick one," I had no idea what names might be appropriate for us.

"Okay," Laura was enthusiastic. "Of course you can use Laura and Matty, or you can choose Ida, Alma, Eliza, Miriam, Beth, Ella, Ruby, Alice, Phoebe, Emma, Edna..."

"Beth, I love that name," Samantha breathed, and I smiled. Beth would be a nice name for Samantha, although I liked the name Samantha better.

"Beth? That really suits you," I nodded in approval. "What do you think, Laura?"

"Yeah, I think it's great," Laura clapped her hands. "Which do you like?" she asked, turning to me.

I shook my head, not really knowing what to pick. I liked my own name; everyone always remarked on the uniqueness of it.

"Misty is a really a strange name," Laura commented. "I have never heard of any English with that name."

"I know," I said, "my mom doesn't even know how I got the name. She said one of her friends named me or something like that."

By the time we got to the farm, I had decided on the name Emma. I thought it was a nice name, but really, what did it matter, as long as it was not a prideful name.

With the names decided, we hurried upstairs to put our choring clothes on. We lay our church clothes over the beds and when it was choring time we ran out to the barn to milk and collect the eggs while Alma and the younger girls prepared a quick supper.

"We have to hurry," Matty told me. "Since you are over seventeen, you will go into the singing with me, Edward and Laura. Samantha...I mean Beth...is not old enough to sit at the table with the young people, so she will sit in the back with the families."

We all ate the cracker soup Alma had prepared and washed the dishes, then hurried back into our church clothes.

"Here," Matty handed me a stiffly ironed white kapp. "We are allowed to wear white kapps to the singings."

I smiled happily as I put on the white kapp. It was so much neater and nicer looking than the ones I had made for us at home. As I slid the large black bonnet on over my white kapp, Matty commented that I would need to put a larger brim on my own bonnet when I made it, because she could see my nose sticking out whenever I turned sideways.

"We are not allowed to have our noses sticking out," Mary informed me. "You have a long, slender nose." I felt my nose and laughed. It was definitely my dad's nose, I thought.

We walked back to the house where the church services had been held. The girls waited in the washhouse again until it was time to go in. It was a little different than it had been in the morning, I noticed. The light scent of perfume was in the air and all of the girls seemed to be wearing Chapstick, the only makeup they could get away with wearing. Quietly they teased each other, while I just smiled, wishing I could understand what they were saying.

Unlike the well-known, more liberal Amish churches that have what is called Rumspringa (literally, "running around", this is the time when the young people go out into the world to see what is out there) the Schwarzentruber Amish and other strict divisions of the Amish do not have any such thing. Actually, these stricter Amish churches are somewhat in the majority, unlike what the public is led to believe. Most of the more liberal Amish are scattered across Pennsylvania and Ohio; they overlap with the districts of much stricter divisions, although to outsiders it would be hard to tell them apart. To an Amish, however, it takes a mere glance to decide what division one is from.

"Okay," Matty said in English as she nudged me. "Let's go."

We did not have to go in order of age this time. Instead, we went in with friends or cousins or however we wanted. We filed in past the parents, and one by one sat down on benches next to a long table in front of the unmarried men. The guys stared at us, grinning. Boyfriends grinned at their girlfriends, and I felt my cheeks growing warm as nearly all the boys stared at me. They were curious because I was different, I told myself, and like the other girls, I bowed my head slightly in a show of humility. Even though we were not allowed to look directly at the men, I could still feel them staring and was very uncomfortable. I was not used to attention, and I was certain the ministers would not be happy if they noticed.

The young people's' songbook was not nearly as thick as the church hymnal, but it was still in German. The melodies for the songs had been lost and over the last hundred or so years the young people had used English tunes when the words fit. I smiled as we sang a German hymn to the tune of "You are my sunshine" or "I am so lonesome I could cry." This was as worldly as these young people would ever get, and I could see they were enjoying their evening of daring worldliness.

We sang for about two hours. After each song, we paused for a couple of minutes until someone in the group—a boy or a girl—started a song they liked. If too much time elapsed, a sympathetic parent would start a song and get the young people back on track.

After the singing, the girls filed back out to the washhouse. The girls with boyfriends waited for their boyfriends to drive up to the door so they could climb into his buggy for the ride home. Girls without boyfriends waited, hoping a friend of one of the boys would come in and ask if so-and-so could take her home.

I was very sleepy and climbed into the buggy with Matty's brother, Edward. Neither Matty nor Edward had anyone they were seeing. I noticed Matty looking at the door, waiting for someone to ask her, but no one did. She was already nineteen and had not had a date yet, she told me with a sad look. This was not a good sign. Although Matty was a very sweet girl, she had a severe acne problem that made her thin cheeks and forehead red. I felt sorry for her. This was bad for an Amish girl. Since we were not allowed any type of jewelry or makeup, there was no way to make yourself look better, especially if you were dressed exactly the same as every other girl. I was thankful, for once in my life, to know that I would not be considered ugly, at least. In the past I had wished I were ugly, thinking this would keep Brian away from me, but not now. Here amongst the Amish, it was either get married or become an old maid and live out your life caring for other women's families. A rather bleak outlook, and such a waste, I thought.

*T*HE NEXT morning before breakfast, we left for the long drive home. When we got home, I hugged Fanny, who came running up to me, obviously very happy that I was back. Mamma had done the minimum work necessary to keep things going while we were gone. She did not even say "Hi" as we walked in the door, but just sat in her chair, reading her romance novel.

I peeked in on Grandma and was repulsed by the smell of urine. I felt very sad as I looked at Fanny and Grandma. How could I leave them here to be tortured? What was I going to do? I felt a knife go through my heart. My probation had already started, and I would soon be Emma Schrock. I felt nauseous and guilty as I shook my head, trying to think of something I could do.

When I met Samantha at the woodshed that night, I told her my dilemma. "We can't leave them here, Samantha," I frowned and bit back tears. "It's not right that we get out and they don't."

Samantha frowned. "Your only concern should be to make sure I get out of here. I am your sister."

I sighed. It was true—if I tried anything, I was not only jeopardizing myself, but Samantha, too. I could never forgive myself if I failed my sister, but the knife in my heart dug deeper every time Fanny hugged me, and the pain was so great I thought I would lose my mind. I could not eat and lost several over the course of the summer.

*W*E VISITED the community twice more that summer, and it was decided that I would move there for good the second week of September. It was the week Amish school started, and Matty had the idea that I could accompany the children to school on Fridays, as that was when the children grades three and up learned to read the German hymn book. It seemed like a fantastic idea—at least it was a start. The fact that we had no education was of no concern to the community. It is better than having too much, the Bishop had commented.

Brian and Mamma had sold many of our animals over the summer, they seemed resigned to the fact that they would caring for Grandma and Fanny. Samantha and I spent most of the summer staining the hardwood floors in the upstairs bedrooms and sheet rocking the rooms that had not yet been finished. Mamma announced that they need to sell some of the animals and fix everything up, because they were going to apply to be foster parents. I had gasped in horror when she told us this. Oh no! I thought, more children to torture. This was an unending nightmare.

"What?" Mamma asked with an evil smirk when she saw my reaction. "You want to stay instead?"

I did not reply. What good would it do?

Samantha and I did not argue with Mamma and Brian all that summer. We were living in petrified fear that something would happen and we would not get safely moved. Brian had written a list of rules we were supposed to follow and liked nothing more than to catch us with our kapps too far back or wearing dresses that were too short. They still beat us, but just with the belt...catching us wherever it landed. Fanny, however, was subject to many beatings, and my hands were tied. There was nothing I could do to help her without jeopardizing Samantha's chances of getting out of there. I got thinner and thinner and was happy when September finally came around. I would soon be leaving this house of horrors for good.

IT WAS early afternoon one day in September, just a few days before I was to leave. I was standing in the kitchen, canning pickles and daydreaming about my new life, when I heard the truck racing around the bend in the road. Mamma and Brian had gone into town earlier to sell some chickens. Samantha opened the gate, and they raced in and parked violently. They both jumped out and started looking around as if someone was chasing them.

"What's wrong?" Samantha asked in a panic.

"There has been a terrorist attack," Mamma gasped. "America is under attack! We are under attack!"

"What?" I queried, not knowing what I was supposed to do in such a situation. I did know that Mamma and Brian were anti government and believed the end of the world would occur any day.

"Are you exaggerating?" I asked, looking at Brian and trying to figure out what was going on.

"Nope, nope," Brian shook his head. "The Twin Towers in New York fell; the Pentagon has been hit, and who knows what is next."

"Yeah," Mamma chimed in. "You might not be going anywhere, Misty; they might declare martial law or something."

"That's ridiculous," I said, seeing Samantha's panicked face from where she stood behind Brian.

"This is God's punishment on the harlot, the United States," Brian ranted, holding his hands in the air. "Yes, Lord, bring your judgment, bring your judgment; destroy her, the fat harlot!"

"Oh my God," Samantha came over to where I was. "They are both so crazy I can't believe God does not bring the terrorist here to blow *them* up."

I turned around so the frantic Mamma and Brian could not see me gasping with laughter. "Oh, I can't believe it; they really are gone in the head," I laughed, trying to catch my breath.

Samantha and I went back to the woodshed, where we laughed uncontrollably at Brian with his hands still in the air, and Mamma who was looking for smoke from other possible terrorist attacks. I knew this was not a laughing matter, and I felt bad afterwards, but I think it really hit us in that moment how utterly insane they both were.

After about ten minutes, Mamma and Brian announced they were going back into town to find out more details. That night when they returned, we heard the sobering news of all the people who had lost their lives, and although I did not know what the Twin Towers were, I knew they were something important and that the country would sleep in the grip of fear that night.

The next day, Brian went into town and brought back a newspaper. As I looked at the pictures, I remember being stunned that such a thing could happen in the United States. It truly was a tragedy. One thing I was happy about though, there was no martial law in effect, and Brian still seemed on track to drop me off at the community.

THE ORDNUNG

"Leaders who do not act dialogically, but insist on imposing their decisions, do not organize the people--they manipulate them. They do not liberate, nor are they liberated: they oppress."

— Paulo Freire, Pedagogy of the Oppressed

A couple of days later I put a few belongings in the truck. There was really nothing to take with me. I did not own anything, and the clothes I had were not according to the Ordnung, so I just took my few pairs of underwear and a couple dresses and kapps to wear until my new clothes were made. Samantha was going with me to attend church, and then she would return home with Brian. She would visit a couple more times during the winter, if possible, and then in March she would join me for good.

I hugged Grandma and Fanny goodbye, trying not to cry. Mamma looked at me coldly as I waved goodbye to her and she made no move to hug me. *Why would she?* I asked myself with a shrug. I don't know why I wanted her to. I thought maybe at the last minute she might feel a little remorse for how she had treated me all those years, but she did not, and I felt deep sadness as I got in the truck.

Fanny's face was the one that was difficult for me to look at, so I looked straight ahead as we pulled out of the drive. A lot of kids would have felt a twinge of sorrow if they knew they were leaving home for good, but I only felt extreme sorrow that people like Mamma and Brian existed in the world. They were horrible people that brought sorrow and fear to those around them. The tears streamed down my cheeks as I thought, if only Brian and Mamma had been nice to us, it would not have mattered that we did not have friends or an education or anything. All we had ever wanted

158

was to be loved by them, but they weren't capable of that. Instead of giving us hugs, they gave us emotional wounds so deep they were gaping, open wounds that refused to heal. The trauma was just too deep.

WE STAYED at Matty's house again that week, and early Monday morning, I hugged Samantha goodbye. She was crying and saying she did not want to go back.

"I know," I tried to soothe her. "But just think...when you move here it will be easier for you because I will be able to tell you what to do." I wiped the tears from her face. "I am the one who has to break the ice," I tried to make it sound worse than it was so she might feel better. "That is not going to be easy. It's going to be really hard."

Samantha nodded. "I know," she said. "I know."

"Don't worry," I went on. "If you are not here in March, I am going to send the police there. I swear to God, Samantha, I don't care if they kick me out of here, I will go to a neighbor's house and call the police."

Brian came over to me before he left, and in his cocky voice he remarked, "I told them you were a troublemaker. They are going to be watching you like a hawk."

Realizing that Brian had no more control over me, I snapped back at him, "Anything is better than being around you, Brian."

He glared at me as he stepped up into the truck, and I cocked an eyebrow back at him as I waved goodbye to Samantha. I quickly changed my demeanor as Matty walked up to me with the milk buckets. This was exactly the kind of attitude that could land me in a lot of trouble. Instead, I clenched my fists at my side and glared at Brian until he pulled out of the drive. He held my gaze for a while and smirked. He thought he had won, just as I thought I had.

"Well," Matty turned towards the barn. "I wish you could stay here with us, but after breakfast I have to hitch up the horse and take you over to your new home with Jacob C."

I nodded, only half listening. My thoughts were far away, and I wished Samantha did not have to go back to the mountain. But I had to be strong, I was the oldest and I had to do this, if not for me, then for her. Samantha was my little sister. I had to protect her, and the only way I knew to do that was to become Amish so she could follow in the springtime.

Matty and I finished the morning work, and by 7:30, I was learning how to hitch a buggy. On the three-mile ride to my new home, Matty filled me in on the basics about my new family. Because Jacob was the name of the father, my middle initial would be J. My name was now Emma. J. Schrock. I repeated it to myself, trying to get used to the sound. Matty told me that Jacob C only had four children and from what she had heard, they were probably not going to have any more. She went on to explain that they had a butchering business where the *Englisch* brought their chickens and other animals for slaughter. Jacob also had a machine repair business on the side, and their house was on top of the machine shop.

As we clip-clopped off the paved road and down a dirt drive, I saw Phyllis, the Bishop's wife, wave at me. I waved back and smiled. Jacob C's place was the next farm over from the Bishop's, and upon arrival I was greeted by the entire Shrock family. Jacob was the father. He was average height and build with dark, reddish-brown hair shot with a few flecks of gray. His wife Lillian was a quiet, somber woman of medium build, and when she smiled I was surprised to see a tooth missing in the middle of her bottom row of teeth. Then there were the children. Elam was the oldest and had just turned seventeen, after him was thirteen-year-old Ella, followed by ten-year-old Moses and seven-year-old Ida.

I smiled at them as I stepped off the buggy. I was nervous, to say the least, and was not very comforted when Jacob just nodded to me and they all turned and walked into the machine shop. On the way up the stairs, the two youngest came up on either side of me, smiling as if they would burst. I smiled back, happy that there would be some younger children in the house.

"I can speak English like you," Ida whispered as she grabbed my arm.

"Me too," chubby little Moses grabbed the other arm.

"We will teach you how to speak Amish," Ida said with a little skip. "Mom said we could, and that you would be our new sister."

I looked down at their excited faces and nodded enthusiastically.

"That sounds great, I need all the help I can get."

When we got upstairs, I saw a large, open room with three small bedrooms lined up against the south wall. The curtains were the usual dark blue and went nicely with the light blue walls. On the north end of the large room was the kitchen. There was a large wood burning stove, a small sink with a drain and there was a red pump next to it. There was a dinner table and a counter-top against the wall and around the corner was the pantry where the food was stored. I stood there for a moment looking around, too petrified to move. I did not want a new family, but I was very grateful for this opportunity and vowed to myself to do my absolute best.

"This way," Lillian motioned me back to one of the small bedrooms. "This is the girls' bedroom, and we squeezed in a small bed for you at the end of their bed. Here is a drawer and part of the closet where you can put your stuff."

I smiled at her. "Thank you. I appreciate it."

She looked at me, nodded and walked out of the room.

I stood for a moment looking out the bedroom window that overlooked the farm, I could see all the way over to the Bishop's house from my vantage point. It certainly was beautiful and serene. No one was screaming in pain here. But for some reason, I could not shake off a strange premonition that I should run. *Run from what?* I thought. This was my golden ticket out of hell. I moved my shoulders up and down, trying to shake the feeling, and finally just shrugged it off as nerves. I knew the family must also be very nervous taking in a strange girl, and I was determined they wouldn't regret it. I came out of the bedroom, and they were all staring at me.

"Well, all right," Jacob stroked his beard. "We have a lot of work to do today. They dropped off one hundred chickens already; we better get butchering. After that we have to get back to the fields and pick up the hay we already cut." He turned to me. "You will follow Ella, but first you need to change," he looked at my clothes. "Lillian has an old dress you can wear. She hemmed it up a little so it will be short enough."

I looked at Lillian, who came out of the middle bedroom with an old-looking, dark blue dress. I smiled happily as I took it from her. This was great. I would look just like everyone else. She followed me into the bedroom and stood there while I started to undress. She snorted in disgust as I pulled my dress over my head and she saw my half-slip and bra.

"No." She shook her head. "We do not wear half under dresses, and we don't wear these at all," she pointed to my bra.

I had noticed this but was half-hoping I would be able to keep mine.

"I will get an underdress." she opened the door, "Put those things in the incinerator after you are done changing."

As she went out to get the underdress, I opened the drawer where my things were and took out my other bra so I could do as she said.

When Lillian returned, I slid the underdress on and then the long, worn blue dress. Lastly, I pinned the matching apron around my waist. Even after I had put on so many clothes, I felt naked and self-conscious without my bra. Well, I thought, just something else I will have to get used to. As I walked out, Ella and Ida clapped when they saw my new outfit.

"Mom says we will make your new clothes in the evenings," Ella handed me a scarf to put on my head.

I followed the women out to the slaughter house to help with the day's work. Work was something I could do with no problem. Due to my training with the timers on the farm, I was faster at working than the Amish girls. I am sure I probably looked a little strange as I dove frantically from one task to the other.

Alma had noticed this about Samantha and me, and I heard her tell the other women this in English as they nodded their heads in approval at our strong work ethic. Amish men might get away with being a slacker, but no Amish woman was worth her weight in salt if she could not multitask and get things done quickly—and if she could not do so, she would certainly not be sought after as a potential wife.

The slaughter house was about twenty-five feet square. There were five large, stainless steel sinks with drains and a garden hose was filling one of the sinks as we entered.

"Elam chops off the chickens' heads," Ella pointed to the chopping block on the side of the slaughter house. "In the back room, Mom and Dad pull off the feathers and throw them in one of the sinks, and then after the menfolk leave, Mom and Ida and I scrape them, gut them and cut them up if that's what the *Englisch* ordered."

"Okay," I smiled. This was something I already knew how to do—not on such a large scale, but I could learn.

The first chickens came flying in from the back, and Ella and I each grabbed one and with our paring knives began scraping the pin feathers out of the skin. This might take anywhere from three to eight minutes, depending on how many feathers were stuck and how badly.

"Be careful not to break the skin," Ella motioned with her knife. "The customers want their chickens to look like they are from the town supermarkets, even if they bring them here when they are molting. The *Englisch* are really dumb sometimes," she grinned and shook of her head.

After the plucking, which only took about forty-five minutes, Lillian joined us.

"We have to hurry, girls, we got a late start and they want to pick these up by 4:00 pm." She looked at the clock that was about to strike ten and mumbled something in German I could not understand.

We worked in silence much of the time, and I was happy the Schrock children had been allowed to stay home from school that day in order to meet me. Ida and Ella kept smiling at me as we worked, and I smiled back. They would make nice little sisters, I thought. My only wish was that Samantha could be here as well, but I blinked the thought away. I had to focus on my new life or I might mess everything up for her. Now was not the time to break down, even though I felt tired and overwhelmed.

Around eleven-thirty, Lillian went into the house to heat up lunch. At twelve precisely, I heard the menfolk talking as they came in from the field, and we girls quickly ran to set the table. For lunch we had canned sausages and mashed potatoes. It was very good and satisfying after a long morning of work. Eating lunch was something new for me, and I tried not to eat too much. After lunch, the family talked in German, as I smiled and tried to figure out what they were saying.

After a few minutes, Jacob turned to me. "I am sorry, but we must speak Amish. We must not get the children used to speaking English in the home. It is against our church rules, and we will get in trouble if anyone hears us speaking too much English. You will have to learn Amish."

I smiled and pulled a small writing tablet from the pocket in the front of my dress. "I am going to learn ten words a day," I pointed to the ten words I had already written down.

Jacob shrugged. "It's your responsibility. Honestly, I would not know how to learn another language," his eyes widened as he scratched his chest-length beard. "Learning English was easy because it was used every day at school for eight years, but I know I would not be able to learn another."

I thought it was funny that their main concern was the language, and they were not even optimistic I would learn it well. But they did not know me or my determination, I thought.

THE NEXT day the younger children went to school after breakfast, and Elam and I stayed at home to help with the work. We only had twenty-five chickens that morning, and Lillian was glad as we had too much other work to do. Fall is one of the busiest times of the year for the Amish, and the days were never long enough.

Lillian and I worked in silence as we cleaned and gutted the twenty-five old laying hens. After about an hour, Lillian spoke in her low, mopey voice.

"I took you in because my husband insisted, you know," she looked at me sadly. "I am unable to give him more children, so it is my duty to take in a child if he requests. But while you are here, I will expect you to mind yourself around my older boy and my husband."

I looked at her, feeling a little nauseous as I felt her jealousy coming at me full force. I wished I could have stayed at Matty's house, but of course I could never have asked such a thing. As soon as I had met Lillian, I could sense she was not happy at having a teenage girl living with them, especially not one who was a novelty for the time being. I had noticed in the short time that I had been at the house that Lillian seemed depressed and Jacob was indifferent to her. I frowned. The last thing I wanted at this point in my life was to get caught up in their marital problems.

She looked back at the chicken she was cleaning. "I am of no use to my husband now," she said after a few more seconds. "Even when I was younger, I was sick a lot, and we had to have young girls from the community live with us to help out. His eyes always wandered, and there was nothing I could do to stop it." She put her knife down and looked at me, the frown on her face growing deeper. "You are required to call us Mom and Dad. My husband and children are thrilled to have you, but I am not, and rest assured I will be watching you and will personally report any bad behavior, do you understand me?"

I nodded and held up my hands pleadingly. "I don't know why you are telling me this," I said in a hurt tone. "I did not do anything to you, and if you want me to leave, I will. I don't want to be where I am not wanted." I tried to keep the tears from my eyes. *This can't be happening*, I thought. *What is wrong with this lady?*

"No," Lillian barked. "If you say anything about this to anyone, I will be in trouble with the church, as it was my husband who volunteered first. There were many young families who wanted you to help out on their farms, but we were chosen out of pity, since I am now barren." Her green eyes were sad, but at the same time, threatening. "I will not bring shame to my family and have the church members discussing these things, but I have warned you to mind yourself."

"Oh, I will," I nodded, I had most definitely not planned otherwise. "It will take me a while to get used to calling you Mom and Dad though."

"No, you will call us Mem and Datt. That is the Amish pronunciation, and you will start now," she was furiously scraping at her chicken.

I sighed and looked down at my chicken. I could not help pouting. The last thing on my mind was Lillian's husband. Why she felt the need to come at me with all of this, I did not know, but at that time there was no way for me to know the deep sadness that was compelling her to act this way.

As I worked, lost in thought, I was not worried about bodily harm, but I worried about what people would say about me, and how Lillian, an Amish mother, would portray me. Reputation was everything, especially to me and Samantha, because we had no real family to back us up.

Lillian seemed sorry for what she had said when she noted a tear that streamed down my cheek and plopped into the sink.

"You are a good worker," her voice had taken a softer note. "And if you are humble and obey all the rules and do not do anything to bring attention to yourself, you will eventually marry and have children of your own." She looked at me and smiled a small smile.

Well, lady, I thought to myself, *you don't know anything about me or what I want out of life.* But I knew I had to be careful. If my reputation was ruined here, I would grow old and become a maid to young mothers, while others shook their heads at me in pity. It was a dreadful thought, and I vowed to obey everything so I would be allowed to marry.

That evening after supper I practiced my ten words with Moses, Ida and Ella. I loved it when the children were home because they were so nonjudgmental and full of life. Haltingly, I sounded out the words. I repeated them over and over while the children laughed at my pronunciations.

The lantern light flickered in the cool September breeze. Jacob was reading the *Die Blatt* newspaper. He commented that rain would be coming soon and he needed all non-school people in the field the next day. Lillian, who was reading the family newsletter, said that we had to get the soap made, but Jacob shook his head, stating that the hay was more important. A half-an-hour later we all retired for the night only to arise six-and-a-half hours later when the alarm clock jarred us awake at four-thirty.

We scurried about all week, trying to get all the work done. Every night I practiced my ten words with the children and throughout the day I pulled the tablet from my pocket and repeated each one several times. It was a great method, and by the end of the week I could already say several words.

That Friday I accompanied the children to the one-room school house for German day. We had fun as we skipped through the woods over to the Hostetler farm where the school was located. The teacher this year was a married woman in her mid-thirties. Although school was normally taught by a teenage girl, the church had agreed to let Mary King teach this year. I had heard that Mary King had been married for ten years but had no children. It was very sad, and her husband, feeling her sadness, had persuaded the church members to allow his wife to teach as her household duties were light, and the hundred dollars a month the teacher earned would help them greatly.

I found her to be a very kind person, perhaps due to the fact that the community considered her almost on the same level of an unmarried girl, since she had no children. She seemed to have compassion for me and immediately got me situated.

Amish children start learning to read, write and spell German in the third grade, so I sat with them. The third graders laughed happily and told everyone that I was theirs. When one of the first graders protested, the teacher laughed and tapped her ruler on the desk.

"Okay, how about we all share Emma, huh?"

Everyone nodded, and I so much wanted to hug them all, but it was not the Amish way to give hugs, so I just smiled at their bright faces.

In the beginning, I struggled with the third graders as I tried to properly pronounce the German words. The children tended to try to say things using the Amish dialect, while my pronunciation was decidedly English. Mary was very patient as she helped each child, but when she rang the bell, I was just as happy as the children to run out into the cool September air.

"Come on," Ida ran up to me. "We will teach you to play baseball. It is what we always play at recess."

I gave it my best, but I was not very good. The children laughed when I hit the ball and it bounced sideways and almost hit me in the face.

"It's okay." Mary laughed. "It's just for the exercise. We don't keep score as we don't want the children to be proud."

After recess we had a half-hour lunch. The oldest child in each family lined up at the wood stove in the back of the schoolhouse to heat up the lunches. The children sat at the desks with their families—the oldest helping the youngest. As I sat there with Ella, Moses and Ida, I wished that Samantha and I had grown up like this. How different our lives would have been, and as young adults we would have had a better, more secure future than what lay before us now.

THE NEXT day was Saturday, and was the day set aside to get ready for the following Sunday. This Sunday was what the Amish called 'in-between Sunday'. This would be a Sunday used for relaxing and reviving after a long week's work. Ella and I scurried about as Lillian jumped from one task to another. We had to make the bread and clean all the lamps and fill them with kerosene. Ida helped as well, though she mostly got in the way.

After lunch Lillian braided Ida's hair in tight braids that she then tied up into a bun on the back of her head using pieces of yarn. This was something Amish mothers or older sisters did every Saturday until a girl was twelve and able to twist and roll her hair back, like a woman. Before Lillian braided Ida's hair, she gave me the task of unraveling the braids from the previous week. As I loosened the braids in Ida's long, blonde hair,

166

I was shocked to see yellow scale under the braids and orange spots where iodine had dried.

"What is this?" I asked, nudging Ella, who was standing behind me.

"Oh, that is from braids that are too tight. The head gets infected so we put iodine on it like we use for the cows."

"You should let her hair down to get some air flowing through it," I fluffed Ida's hair around her head.

Ella shook her head. "Against Ordnung," she said matter-of-factly.

"Well, maybe when we wash it she will feel better," I mused as I watched little Ida scratching her head furiously.

"We only wash our hair on Saturdays before church," Lillian said with a slight eye roll as she walked toward us with a glass of water and a comb.

"Oh," I nodded. "I did not know that."

"Hm..." Lilian grunted as she vigorously yanked at Ida's hair, slicking it back and braiding as tightly as she could.

Ella shivered. "I am so glad I am thirteen. Getting braided is sheer torture." She shuddered again. "But if you have hair in your face, the Deacon will pay a visit, so Mom has to do it this way."

I shrugged. "That's how it is, I guess."

That afternoon, Lillian started teaching me how to sew my dress for church the next week. She had me choose between black or blue poplin. These were the two most prominent colors for church dresses, but black was the most practical since it was worn to funerals, weddings and baptisms. I picked the black because I wanted to prove myself a sensible girl.

I was not unfamiliar with sewing, but I had to learn to sew according to our district's Ordnung. The sleeves of the dress had to be very wide so as to not show the shape of the arm. The measurements for all hems were precise: sleeves had to be one-half inch wide; belts had to be one-and-a-half inches wide; dresses had to be four inches wide; apron belts had to be one-and-a-half inches wide; apron side hems had to be half-an-inch; apron hems an inch and a half. While I had followed a pattern at home, I never thought about tearing out a seam because it was off half-an-inch this way or that, but Lillian constantly hovered with a measuring stick and made me tear out a seam if it was off by more than a quarter-of-an-inch

"What happens if it is a little off?" I asked feeling too tired to rip the seam of my dress belt.

Lillian squinted as she read the measuring stick to see if I had folded the material properly. "Well, if you are a church member, you will be paid a visit by the Deacon, and if you do not correct your behavior you will be placed in the Bann. If you are not a member, the person responsible for you could be put in the Bann."

"Oh, okay," I apologized. "I am sorry I am so frustrated."

"It takes time to learn how to eye these things," Lilian encouraged, and I detected a softening in her voice. "My mother did the same with me. Also, you have to stop saying sorry all the time. It's not the Amish way." She shook her head for emphasis. "We also do not say please and thank you. It makes you seem English," she shook her head as she walked back to where she had been wiping down the men's Sunday suits.

I nodded and caught myself before I said sorry again. Although Lillian was constantly criticizing me, I felt that deep down she was really a kind woman. It was obvious when she was with her children that she really loved them, and she hardly ever yelled at them. I felt at times that she really did want to take me in and mentor me, but there was something keeping her from it, something that seemed to make her chronically depressed and made her resent her husband. This was the conclusion I came to as I sat at the sewing machine; I told myself that no matter how she treated me, I must be nice to her because, compared to Mamma, Lillian was practically a saint.

That evening Lillian had Ella and I bring the bathtub that was hanging on the side of the house into the side pantry. It was a short watering trough, but long enough for a person to sit down. At least I don't have to freeze taking a bath outdoors, I thought as I helped Ella pour two tea kettles of hot water into the tub followed by two teakettles of cold water and a piece of soap.

"Is this enough soap?" I asked Ella, remembering how Brian and Mamma would make me put almost an entire bar's worth of soap lather on my face and body and even then would call me dirty.

"Oh yes," Ella took it from me and set it on the overturned bucket. "We only use soap if we are very dirty, like for our feet. Soap is expensive to make and prideful, so we don't use it very much."

"Oh," I shrugged my shoulders again in a sign of no contest.

As Ella exited the pantry and went into the kitchen, I put a hand to my forehead. Would I ever stop sounding like a dummy? I wondered. Having grown up with a solitary lifestyle like I had, you would not think there would be that much for me to learn in the Amish community, but it seemed there was truly a rule for everything and I had to learn them all... and quickly.

Baths went in order of age and gender, first the prepubescent girls and boys and then the unmarried girls and the mother, and then the teenage boys and father went last, all bathing in the same water.

After the bath, everyone put on clean workday clothes—all clothes, including undergarments, were changed once a week after the bath. Each Amish person owned two sets of workday clothes. To change more often would be prideful and against the Ordnung.

Since I did not have new workday clothes yet, I wore the same dress. Jacob grumbled at Lillian that she needed to be faster with the work next week and get my clothes made. Lillian bowed her head in obedience but sent a pouting look my way. I pretended not to notice, but I did feel sorry for Lillian. Jacob was very unkind to her and made fun of her all the time. *Oh well,* I thought hopefully, *I will try to help as much as I can and maybe she will like me more.*

THE NEXT day we were permitted to get up whenever we awoke, since it was 'in-between Sunday' and a day of rest and play. I awoke around seven o'clock, the latest I had stayed in bed in years. As I rubbed my eyes, I heard soft giggling and felt something small and warm crawling in bed beside me. I laughed as I looked down and saw Ida's big blue eyes peeking playfully at me from under the covers.

"Ella won't get up yet, and I want to go outside," she threw off the covers.

"Okay," I whispered quietly, sitting up. "Let's go get the milking done and surprise everyone."

Ella nodded eagerly as she jumped up and grabbed my dress for me. Quietly we opened the door and tiptoed out into the main room so we would not wake anyone. I heard a door creak and smiled as I saw Moses tiptoeing out of the boys' room, being careful not to wake his often foul-tempered older brother.

"I heard Ida giggling and thought she probably got you up," he whispered, coming over to join us as we crept down the stairs. "Ida and I are always up first on 'in-between Sundays'."

We picked up the milk buckets and headed out to the barn where the four cows were already complaining about our lateness.

"Let's hurry and surprise everyone by getting all the chores done," I proposed as I sat down to start milking.

"Yeah, that will be a fun surprise," Moses clapped his hands. "Elam hates choring, so maybe it will make him happy."

As Moses and Ida scampered off to feed the calves, chickens, pigs and horses, I sat milking and thinking about Samantha. I was so worried about her all alone on that mountain with two of the world's craziest people. *And poor Fanny*, I thought as two tears ran down my cheeks. I blinked, as I was in the habit of doing when a terrible memory popped into my head. It was so quiet here. There were no screams, but the screams that lived in my head and the sorrow that dwelt in my heart would leave me shaking at times, and I would gasp for breath to try to clear my head before anyone saw.

"Okay, we're done, Emma," Ida called from the other end of the barn as she and Moses ran toward me, out of breath.

"I am on my last cow," I called back, trying to match the merry mood of the children as I quickly wiped the tears from my face.

Ida looked into my face with all the innocence of a seven-year-old and asked sweetly, "What is wrong, Emma? Are you okay?"

"Oh, yeah," I said with a quick smile, pretending to rub my eyes. "Betsy here just swatted me in the eye with her tail and it burns really bad."

"Oh, I hate that," Moses playfully swatted Betsy on the rump.

Ida and Moses helped each other carry one of the large milk buckets to the back of the machine shop where the wash house and cellar were located. Here we strained the milk and put it in large stainless steel pots so the cream would rise to the top for skimming. We skimmed the cream from the previous night and put it in gallon jars, which we stored in the ice house that was located on the north end of the house. The milk from the previous day was then dumped into buckets to be given to the chickens and pigs at the evening choring.

We were just creeping back up the stairs when we heard the other family members getting up.

"We did all the chores," Moses and Ida shouted, jumping up and down and clapping their hands in sheer happiness.

Everyone smiled and nodded happily. Ella wagged her finger playfully at Ida. "I told you not to wake Emma up so early," she pretended to frown as she tried to grab Ida. Ida squealed and ducked behind me, wrapping herself in my wide skirt and then losing her balance, causing us both to tumble over onto the floor.

Moses came over to help us up and ended up joining us in laughter on the floor. Suddenly the room grew quiet as Jacob came over, yanked Moses off the floor and swatted him on the seat.

"No laughing before twelve," he pointed to the clock.

"Girls, get off the floor," Lillian's voice was stern. "You know girls are not permitted on the floor."

I stood up quickly, my face turning red. Of course, nothing like this would have been permitted at home, but I did not realize that was the case here.

Ida's face looked scared and she seemed afraid Jacob would spank her for laughing, but he did not. He merely sat down at the head of the table to wait for breakfast.

"I'm sorry," I whispered in Ida's ear. "I did not know that rule."

"I knew," Ida pouted. "I just forgot for a minute."

Ella and I quietly helped Lillian put breakfast on the table while the men sleepily sat and watched. Before breakfast, we all knelt and put our faces in our hands on the bench top as Jacob read the Sunday prayer from the Prayer Book. There was a prayer for every day of the week which was read morning and night on that day. After breakfast we did the dishes and then sat in the open living room. Lillian read from the Prayer Book, Jacob napped and we children just sat at the table, waiting for noon.

"After noon we can play games and go for walks and do whatever we want," Moses said happily as he checked the time again. "Oh, it's only eleven-thirty," he groaned, slamming his face into the table.

The clock finally struck twelve, and Moses and Ida began chasing each other around the house. I got out my pen and paper and wrote a letter to Samantha. Ella sat beside me, also writing to one of her friends in another district. Elam, whom I did not know very well yet, announced that he was going for a walk. Jacob told him he must be back in an hour-and-a-half.

In my letter, I included all the words I had learned and spelled them out as best I could so Samantha would be able to get the pronunciation right. I also included all the dos and don'ts I could think of. I stressed to Samantha that she should make a book out of these things and study them so it would be an easier transition for her in the spring.

In the mid afternoon, we were visited by Katie, the oldest child of the Bishop. She was a dark-haired, rosy-cheeked ten-year-old girl. She smiled a big smile as she ran through the house and handed a note to Lillian.

"Oh, how nice," Lillian smiled as she read the note. "Phyllis is inviting us over for supper."

"Okay," Jacob said as Katie dashed back out the door. "We will get the choring done early, then."

I was glad when it was time to milk. I found 'in-between Sunday' to be boring and long. I had wanted to visit Matty but knew it was not Amish custom for young people to visit each other except at church or at the singings.

After chores, we all changed into nicer clothes and walked to the Bishop's house for the evening meal. Ida and Moses quickly scampered off to play with the bishops six children, and Ella and I sat quietly with the women as they chatted. Phyllis asked if I had made the new black dress I was wearing, and I nodded. She nodded with approval, telling me I had done a nice job.

After a while, the men came in and we all sat down to eat. The meal was a simple Amish dinner that consisted mostly of coffee cake and milk. Phyllis had made two large pans, and we all put big chunks of the cinnamon cake on our plates and then dumped liberal amounts of milk over the top. Although I always found it an odd dinner, I liked it and was not about to complain, given the many times I had gone hungry as a child.

After the dishes were cleared, we all gathered and sang a few German hymns before walking home in the moonlight. As we walked home, I could not help remembering how I had longed to go to medical school and be a missionary, to do something that would change the world and make it a better place. I looked up at the twinkling stars and sighed. I had to release this desire; it brought me nothing but pain. I walked to my new home with my black, wool shawl hugging my shoulders. *I have to let my dreams go,* I thought; *they will only get me in trouble,* and amongst the Amish that was definitely not a desirable place to be.

"Be Silenced!"

"The moment we begin to fear the opinions of others and hesitate to tell the truth that is in us, and from motives of policy are silent when we should speak, the divine floods of light and life no longer flow into our souls."

— Elizabeth Cady Stanton

The next week was much like the week before. Lillian and I worked until the children got home from school, and then Ella helped Lillian while I sewed my new clothes. In the middle of the week, I got a letter from Samantha, which I hurriedly ripped open. To my disappointment, there was not much in the letter. It just said that everyone was well and they would make the trip to see me the first of November if the weather did not get too bad. I shrugged. What did I expect? The letter was censored by Mamma and Brian.

On Sunday we left for church early since it was the day the Ordnung was read and communion given to the members. Lillian told me I would come home with the children after one o'clock because only members could stay for the Ordnung reading, breaking of the bread and foot washing. This sometimes did not end until six o'clock. There would also be no singing that night, as the day was just too long.

Church started at eight o'clock and went on without stop until one o'clock. It was a long day for me since I only understood a little of what was being said, and I was not as used to the long service as the others. I saw quite a few people sleeping and kept battling the urge to nod off myself. Instead, I wrote a poem in my head. It was something I enjoyed doing when I was bored; rhyming words was fun, I thought.

At noon we went to the basement in small groups for a bite to eat and then returned to our seats. After everyone had been to the basement the Bishop said something in Amish, and all the non-baptized members stood up and filed out of the house. Some of the fathers came out to help the smaller children hitch up the buggies. Only very small babies were allowed to stay. All the other children had to go home with older siblings or cousins. Elam, Ella and I were responsible for the Bishop's six children, as well as Moses and Ida.

We decided to stay at the Bishop's house with the children since it was bigger, and we happily spent the afternoon playing board games and hide and go seek. As I played with the children, I wondered how the members could sit in church for three-four more hours—not a fun thought in the least.

That night, Lillian and Jacob talked in low tones while we were milking, and afterward they sent us all to bed early.

"I wonder what is wrong." I whispered to Ella, who was sitting by the door trying to listen to what was being said. I crept over to her to listen, too, even though I could not understand the language. Ella gave me a guilty grin.

"I am not supposed to listen. You won't tell on me, will you?"

"Of course not," I gave her a quick hug. "We are sisters, and sisters don't tattle on each other."

Ella smiled and nodded in agreement. "They are always like this when the members have to stay in after church," she whispered. "It usually means that someone confessed to something bad and is being punished."

"Who was bad?" I asked with heightened curiosity.

Ida shrugged and shook her head. "Alma M told me her dad was going to get in trouble today, and I was trying to hear why. A neighbor saw him doing something against the Ordnung, so he had to confess."

"I wonder what it was," I put my ear even closer to the door.

Ella shrugged again. "I can't hear anything," she stood up. "We better get back in bed before Mom comes to see if we are sleeping. She would be really mad at me for disobeying her."

Softly, we crept back into bed, making sure the old springs did not creak too loudly. As I snuggled under the covers I could still hear low tones coming from the kitchen and I could see the flickering light from the kerosene lamp on the table. I wondered what Alma's dad had done to receive punishment, but since I was not a member I would not find out until the gossip began circulating.

WEEKS TURNED into months and soon snow flurries heralded the upcoming icy winter. By the first of November, I had already learned a lot of German words and was starting to piece together sentences. I was not quite such outsider anymore and was beginning to feel like one of the community. Samantha wrote that they would not be able to make it before spring due to the winter snow in the Dakotas that would make driving impossible.

She wrote again in mid-November, and I was excited to find that she had managed to slip in a secret note, undetected by Brian. Our plan was that she would give Brian the letter to read as he would insist, then after Brian sealed it and put it in the truck to take into town the next day she would unseal it and put it in an identical envelope and stamp with the real letter tucked inside the fake one. I quickly realized she had finally succeeded when I saw the letter was not paper thin. When I opened the letter, I quickly pulled out the middle sheet of paper and stuck it in my pocket. It was Amish custom that if an unmarried person received a letter from anyone other than a boyfriend or girlfriend, they must leave the letter on the kitchen table for the whole family to read.

I scanned the letter, pretending to be happily reading, and then gave it to Ella, who was trying to read over my shoulder. I excused myself to go to the outhouse, and there I sat reading the real letter I had been anticipating for two months. Tears rolled down my cheeks as I pictured Samantha's face while I read.

Mamma and Brian are not beating me that much, only once or twice a day, and that is usually with a belt or stick as I run away from them. I spend most of the day taking care of the few animals we have left, as well as taking care of Grandma and Fanny. Mamma and Brian are still terrible to them. They don't time me anymore and at times they act like I am already gone.

Brian has a lot of books on how to adopt foster children, and he and Mamma spend a lot of time away looking into how to bring the house up to the minimum code while still remaining Amish. They said they plan to have just a hobby farm—they'll adopt two children and then foster about four children for the income. They will be forced to take them to the school in town every day, so it won't be as bad as we had it, but it won't be good either. They tell me these children will be more grateful than we were. Brian says we are ungrateful little bi**hes and he should have chopped our heads off when he had the chance.

All in all it is not that bad, and I am trying to learn everything you send. Mamma seems especially excited about getting new foster children to torture. I hope they get caught and thrown in prison for the rest of their lives.

Aunty Laura stopped by in October and asked where you were. Brian proudly told her you were in instruction for baptism and that I would be joining you in the spring. She did not seem too thrilled, but said maybe you would at least be able to hook a cute Amish guy... Sounds like Aunty Laura, huh?

I better go and make the switch. They are both reading and I am supposed to unload the truck. I am in the chicken coop collecting eggs with Fanny right now. I really hope I don't get caught. This is the only letter I will send, Misty, as it is just too risky. Brian is really weird lately and I am afraid to set him off. I am just a shadow here awaiting escape.

Samantha (Beth)

I tore the letter in little bits and threw it in the incinerator because I did not want anyone to find it and possibly send a letter to Brian. It was the Amish way that you must obey your father and mother no matter what they did. The Amish community held respect for Brian as our father figure. It was also the custom of Amish mothers to search the belongings of their unmarried children every so often to make sure they were not hiding anything forbidden by the Ordnung. Lillian had already been through my few belongings twice. I had gone into the girl's' room to find my things in a pile on the bed. When I asked Ella what had happened, she pointed to her things on her bed.

"Moms do this after you turn thirteen," she said as she put her things away.

I frowned as I put my stuff back. I was now nineteen and felt it was not nice that Lillian had nosily gone through my things. I could see she had read my poem book, something that was private to me, and I did not like it.

"When you are a maid for someone, the house mother does it too," Ella went on. "It's just our way, I guess."

"I guess," I pretended to smile as I closed the heavy wooden drawer.

I continued to go to school on Fridays until the winter break in the middle of December. I learned how to read and spell in German very quickly, and Mary said I was functioning at the highest level, so there was no need to waste my time on Friday lessons anymore if I did not want to. I received nods of approval from the older women as they asked me to read from the hymnal one day after church.

"Just for fun," they said and they all leaned in to listen as I read Das Lob Leid in my low voice. As I read without even a stutter, they smiled and said I was better than many of their own people that had been reading in German all of their lives.

176

It was nice to be in church and be able to read like everyone else. It made me feel less like a *nobody* and just a little bit like a *somebody*.

CHRISTMAS MORNING was spent fasting, as is the Amish custom on all holidays. In the evening, we gathered at the house of Jacob's parents. Jacob was the oldest of ten children, three of whom were still at home and unmarried. As the siblings gathered for the evening meal, I could see Lillian's face grow even sadder than usual as she saw her sisters-in-law with their large families. These women seemed to have more favor with their mother-in-law, I noticed.

We had 'haystack supper' for dinner, an Amish favorite during special occasions. You start by putting crumbled tortilla chips in your plate, followed by peas, tomatoes, lettuce, green beans, hamburger or whatever else someone had thought to put out, and you topped it off with a thin cheese sauce. It was delicious, and Ella and I laughed when we saw little Moses holding his stomach after eating three heaping plates of the tasty treat.

After dinner, we played board games and trivia while the younger children scampered about, playing their favorite game of hide and go seek. The day was a lot of fun, but in the back of my mind, I couldn't help thinking of Samantha and wishing her a silent Merry Christmas. As I sat there on the wooden bench in my dark brown dress, apron and stiff white kapp with children running about and laughing, I blinked back tears and quite successfully put on a happy face. I reflected on how Brian and Mamma were always at their worst around the holidays, and I could only imagine how Samantha's Christmas was being spent.

When the holidays were over, things were very quiet. Elam and Jacob worked in the machine shop whenever jobs came along. Lillian and I sewed clothes for the family and quilted for one of the Yoder women, who owned a quilt shop. We were paid fifty cents for each yard of thread we sewed into a quilt. The average quilt held anywhere from three hundred to five hundred and fifty yards of thread, and the average Amish woman could quilt between twenty to fifty yards a day, depending on her speed. The average was twenty-five yards a day, and that was if she started early in the morning, stopped only at lunch and continued till chore time. As it turned out, I really enjoyed quilting. Quilting is similar to handwriting, and while some are able to make small, neat stitches, others are not and often make very large, uneven stitches. Lillian prided herself on being able to quilt with neat stitches and was amazed when my stitches were smaller and more even than her own. She did seem happy about this, though, since it meant that Sarah Yoder was more likely to give us quilting jobs. Jacob nodded as he measured how many stitches I was able to do per inch.

"Hmm..." he said. "Ten per inch and Lillian's are eight per inch. Very good," he nodded. "This will bring us a little extra money."

I was happy, as was Sarah Yoder, the shop owner. "The neater the stitch, the faster they sell," she smiled when we dropped off the quilt we had spent a month making.

She paid Lillian two hundred dollars for our work and gave us another quilt to put in frame for the month of February. "I am very happy to be able to contribute this money which we are so badly in need of," Lillian said as we trotted home in the buggy with the freezing Minnesota air whipping at our faces. I smiled and nodded. We sat mostly in silence for the rest of the two-mile buggy ride, but then Lillian abruptly turned to me and said in a rather flat tone,

"I have been meaning to say something to you but have not been able to find the right time."

I swallowed a little, beginning to feel uncomfortable. Even though I was calling her Mom now, there was still a lot of tension between us.

"Uh, what is it?" I asked bowing my head and staring at my hands as they lay folded in my lap.

"You are pinning your dresses too tight," Lillian looked at me sternly as she guided the horse off the pavement and onto the dirt lane.

I looked at her with a frown and a bit of confusion. "What do you mean?" I asked, pulling at my loose-fitting bodice.

She looked at me with a serious, no-nonsense face. "Erma Wagner and I both noticed when the girls filed into church last Sunday. You don't have a figure like most of our girls, and you need to disguise it better."

I sat up straighter, feeling my face get hot with embarrassment and anger. "But it is just my shape," I said in a hurt tone. "It is not my fault God made me like this." I was very sad, because it was Brian who made me aware of my thin but curvy shape. I had always hated it, as I knew it brought me a lot of pain, but there was not much I could do about it. Most of the Amish girls seemed to be either straight all the way down or chubby. I had noticed this, but did not realize others had.

Lillian was angered by my response. "That is Hochmut [pride]," she snapped at me. "And I will not tolerate it from any girl in my house. I saw my Jacob looking at you last night when you were doing the dishes. You will pin your dress very loose and wear your kapp farther forward like you are supposed to, or I will report you for disobedience to the Ordnung and you will not be in the placement for baptism next fall."

I choked back tears as I helped unhitch the horse and put her in the stable. I dawdled for a few moments and let Lillian walk back into the house alone. After Lillian walked away, I jumped up on the stable railing and sat there feeling very sad for a moment. Girls were not supposed to be in the barn when it was not choring time, as this was the men's hangout spot. I knew this, but I always felt comforted around animals, and I smiled when our horse, Lucky, nibbled at the back of my cape.

I sat thinking in the cold winter air. I, too, had noticed a change in Jacob—one that was making me uneasy. I could now speak a lot of German, and this seemed to surprise him and make him extremely happy at the same time. During the last few weeks, he seemed to just appear in places where he knew I would be alone: carrying in the milk buckets, skimming the cream and so on. He never said anything, rather he pretended to be doing something else, but I could see him watching me from the corner of my eye. I shrugged it off. After all, he was a male and I was a new and interesting female, but I was also nineteen and in search of a father figure. He was, on the other hand, a married man in his mid-forties.

I did not want to cause any trouble, but it already seemed too late. I wondered what had happened between Lillian and Jacob to make them so icy toward each other. While it was not Amish custom for husbands and wives to show outward displays of affection toward each other, it was still easy to see which couples had warmth for each other and which ones did not. Divorce is never allowed under any circumstance among the Amish, so even when couples hate each other they must live together until one of them dies. In doing so, they must also pretend nothing is wrong; otherwise, they will be visited by the ministers and possibly be punished.

As I sat there on the fence, I suddenly heard rustling behind me and turned to see seventeen-year-old Elam approaching.

"What are you doing out here?" he asked in English.

I smiled at him. The awkwardness we had shared at first had since melted, and Elam now liked nothing better than to tease me and play pranks on me whenever possible. Elam had bright red hair and blue eyes. At times he was very bad tempered, but at other times he was quite the jokester.

I shrugged. "I better get back to the house," I jumped down from the railing.

"Mom going at you again?" Elam asked as he slapped a twig on the railing.

"How did you know?" I tried to smile.

Elam laughed. "Mom used to be sick all the time, and we had teenage girls from the community who lived with us. Mom would always scold them. When I asked Mom why she was mean to them, she told me they were too nice to Dad. "Don't worry," he shrugged. "You are way nicer than the other girls. You smile a lot." He grinned at me. "You will win her over eventually."

I smiled at him and playfully threw a handful of hay in his direction as I walked toward the house. In the stairwell, I took off the cape I had over my work dress. It is Amish custom to wear a cape over your shoulders when you leave the house and go out in public. The cape comes over your shoulders and pins in the front under your apron belt. This is made to disguise the woman's shape even more, but in my case it was not very successful. After unpinning my cape, I unpinned the front of my dress, let out some of the material and then pinned it again. It looked a little strange, but it was better than getting reprimanded. I pulled my kapp farther forward and walked into the main area to help Lillian put the quilt in the frame.

We worked in silence, something that was quite common amongst Amish women, but this silence was filled with unspoken tension. I tried not to feel angry at Lillian, although I was. I was smart enough to know that in reality she was more worried about Jacob's behavior than mine, and I felt deep down that she had not wanted to talk to me as she had, but it was much easier to tell me what to do rather than her husband. I told myself maybe she was protecting me from gossip. I was not so naive, however, that I did not notice that Lillian was truly jealous of me—jealous, yes, but at the same time she did have motherly instincts toward me, and this made her a truly miserable woman—something I was sad about. At the same time it made me angry that she did not trust me and even sadder when I realized she had no idea about the terrible things I had been through in my life.

A lot of the time I struggled with the past memories and the present imposable situation I was in. I often wished that I had been placed with another family. There were other, much nicer families in the community. Ones where I could have blended in with the other teenage daughters, and would not have been quite so noticeable, but that was not my lot. Thinking back I know that things would have turned out very different in my life had I been placed with a less dysfunctional family.

SLOWLY THE winter months passed. In February, I was asked to be a maid for the Bishop's family. Phyllis had suffered a lifelong battle with seizures and had a shoulder that was constantly coming out of place. Usually her seizures came about once a week, but sometimes she had them twice a week. Their newest baby was only a month old, so she needed a lot of help. Matty, who was my best friend, had been working for them for a month but said she did not want to work there any longer. A month was a substantial amount of time to work for someone as a maid, and it was not unusual to have another girl take over. Taking care of seven children under the age of nine was a considerable amount of work for a teenage girl, but it was looked at as a great opportunity to prepare them to be mothers themselves one day.

I was happy to help out as the Bishop said it would probably only be during the week and for only a couple of weeks. Normally an Amish girl gets three dollars a day for working as a maid. This money goes to her parents until she is twenty-one; after that, the parents save the money she earns until she is married. However, since it was the Bishop, Jacob volunteered me because they were in sore need of help and had little funds available.

I enjoyed working for Phyllis. She was pleasant and very beautiful; she had red hair and the clearest blue eyes I had ever seen. She was thin and delicately built, and her smile was kind, though often very weak. The children all knew me, and we got along great. Although they did not listen to me very well, we still managed to get the work done. The Bishop, whose name was Peter, would tinker around the barn and then sit and read the German Bible.

Amish preachers and bishops are not allowed to read their sermons, so they have to memorize it or make it up as they go along. It was rumored that the Bishop was lazy and used reading the Bible as an excuse to get out of other work, but who could say?

I spent a lot of the time doing chores around the house, getting the three oldest children off to school, taking care of the baby and quilting so as to earn some much-needed income for the family. I really enjoyed being away from Lillian and was always careful to avoid meeting Peter alone in a room.

When Matty heard that I was the new maid for the Bishop, she seemed distressed.

"What is wrong?" I whispered as we stood in the milk house, waiting to go into church services.

Matty shrugged and stomped her feet to warm them up. "Do you like being there?" she asked as she traced some invisible wrinkle on her white church apron.

"Yeah," I nodded. "I love taking care of the baby and the children. I am so busy that when the alarm goes off at four-thirty, it feels like I just went to sleep. Peter usually takes care of the baby at night so I can rest."

"Is Phyllis up most of the time?" Matty asked.

"Oh yes," I frowned, perplexed . "She usually sits and sews or quilts on the days she does not have seizures."

Matty looked at the floor for a moment, and I was concerned. Matty was my best friend and was usually in a good mood.

"Matty, what is wrong?" I asked impatiently, giving her a push.

The other girls stopped their whispering and looked at us for a moment. Matty laughed a fake laugh and pushed me back.

When the other girls looked away, Matty motioned for me to lean over to her.

"It's just that Peter tried to grab me sometimes," she whispered in my ear. "That's why I said I didn't want to work there anymore. If I passed by him and Phyllis was not in the room, he put his hand on my behind, or he would come up behind me and push his body next to mine. And we both know it was not because I am beautiful." She pointed sadly to her blotched red face. "There is something wrong with him, and you better look out, because you are way more attractive than I am," Matty pushed a strand of hair out of my face and tucked it into my kapp.

I gasped and stared at her. "Did you tell your dad?" I asked, trying to soak in what I had just heard about the leader of our church.

Matty shook her head. "No, and you are not to tell a soul," she grabbed my arm. "If it were any other girl I would not have said anything, but I had to warn you because you are sort of pretty and I am sure the Bishop has noticed, and I just knew you would keep a promise."

"But you have to say something, Matty," I said, remembering my horrific childhood with Brian. "You just have to."

"Shh..." Matty whispered as the other girls kept glancing our way. She nodded at me and we went outside, pretending to use the outhouse before church.

When we got outside, Matty turned to me with a grave look on her thin face. "Good thing I brought this up before you get into a lot of trouble."

"I don't understand what you are talking about, Matty," I shivered in the cold. "Your parents seem really nice. I don't understand why you don't tell them."

Matty shook her head. "I could never bring shame on my family like that." She kicked the snow. "We already had one problem with my sister Laura.

"What happened to Laura?" I asked.

Matty looked at me and then past me. "We had an *Englisch* man who wanted to be Amish, but he could not join the church because he was divorced. He knew German, though, and picked up our dialect very easily. He used to visit, and then he moved into a shed on our farm. He was fifty-something, and the English neighbors did not like him because they said he had spent time in prison for keeping some women from a different country locked in his house." Matty paused and shook her head, as if unable to believe what she was telling me.

"But," she continued, "the church decided that since he dressed like us, he could live among us as a friend and come to social gatherings. He lived on our property for about four months. I did not like him," Matty shivered. "Then one morning I heard Dad yelling at him to get off the property. I was milking at the time, and I ran out of the barn and into the house to ask Mom what had happened. I heard voices coming from upstairs, and when I got to the top of the stairwell, I could see Laura looked frightened, Larry was there standing in the room looking at the floor, Dad looked furious. Mom saw me and motioned for me to leave, so I went back to milking.

Laura had been sick the night before, so she had stayed in bed when we went out to chore. That day, while we were quilting, Laura kept talking about how scared she had been. She made sure Mom was out of hearing distance, then told me that Larry had done something bad to her, but that Mom and Dad told her she was never allowed to tell anyone and I was not allowed to tell anyone either."

She was only fourteen," Matty continued. "I wondered exactly what he did to her, but all she would say was that it was bad.

Matty wiped at the tears and went on. "When Mom knew that I had found out she admonished me and said it is our job to forgive... that Larry just had a weakness, and that Laura had to forgive him.

I pursed my lips and stared at Matty wide eyed.

Matty nodded. "Larry had to have been waiting for Mom and Dad to leave for choring before going upstairs. Anyway," she continued, "they said that they expected the same punishment for Larry that they would for one of our own members and that Laura must forgive him.

I frowned. "Why didn't they not just turn him into the police or something?"

"Oh, we would never do that," Matty shook her head as she rubbed her hands to warm them. "He was not one of us but he almost was, and Dad says many men have this weakness and we must forgive as we would want to be forgiven, like it says in the Lord's Prayer."

I shook my head. "But these men do these things over and over again if someone does not stop them," I was remembering Brian and his so-called weaknesses.

Matty shrugged and shook her head. "I don't know why. It is just our way. I only know what happened because Laura told me when she was not supposed to, but Mom said that no one should know except the married church members, unless someone confesses in the church. If they confess, they are put in Bann for six weeks. Then no one is to ever speak of it again, and if they do they can be put in the Bann for refusal to forgive."

"That seems so harsh," I felt somewhat hopeless at hearing what I had already guessed.

"Yeah," Matty looked off into the distance. "But that is how it is. Some people say Laura must have done something to attract the attention of Larry and it was mostly her fault, so she needed to be quiet and search within herself to find the pride that had attracted him in the first place."

"But it wasn't her fault," I was growing angry at the injustice of the matter.

Matty shrugged again. "That's why Laura wears her kapp so far forward on her head. It looks a little funny, but she is afraid of attracting another man like Larry."

"Oh," I nodded my head. I had wondered why Laura wore a bigger kapp than everyone else and why it was pulled so far forward you could not even see a strand of hair. That explained a lot, I thought.

"Matty gazed absently up into the overcast Minnesota sky.

"What happened to Larry?" I asked, wondering why I had not seen him around.

"Oh, I don't know," Matty shrugged. "He left a couple of weeks later and we haven't seen him since."

"Well, that is good for Laura," I thought aloud. "At least he is not still here."

"Yeah," Matty nodded.

Just then, Lizzie Burkholder stuck her head out the door. "Come on, you two," she said in English. "Get in here before one of the women comes out here to get us."

Matty and I hurried to our place in line and filed into the house. As we took our seats on the long wooden benches, I stole a glance at Laura. I knew Matty was not supposed to talk of such things with me but I was grateful, still at the same time, I wished I did not know. As far as I was concerned, my life in the community had been rather nice up to now.

Despite the strict rules and Lillian's jealousy, I felt like a person that actually belonged to something. I believe most people in the community were good people. They were very strict and sometimes harsh, but I know they really believed that what they were doing was what right and I was grateful to finally be in a better place.

But still I wondered and fretted abut these ancient traditions that allowed crimes of violence and sexual abuse to go virtually unpunished. I felt like I had been drowning in dark, murky waters for many years and then had been rescued for a few brief moments, only to find myself slowly submerging again.

I looked down at my black shoes. Sometimes I could see my reflection in the shiny black leather. It was a trick a lot of teenage girls used, since if you got caught looking in a mirror too often, you were considered prideful. Windows and shiny shoe tops did the trick. As I looked at my pinched face I let my wander to what Matty had said about the bishop, her words had only been confirmation to something that I had already felt in my soul, something I had tried to ignore.

I was suddenly jolted out of my thoughts as I felt a poke from behind. I turned to see one of the women handing me a baby. I had become rather well known for my skills at quieting babies. No one—not even I—could figure out why, when I held a baby who had been crying nonstop for hours, it would suddenly fall asleep when I held it. Although it was not usual for mothers to pass babies to the front girls, in some cases when the crying was extreme, one of the older women would motion for the mother to hand me the baby, and I would be allowed to go into the kitchen to quiet it and then pass it back to its mother.

I loved these times. Holding a baby was like holding a priceless gift from heaven. I always felt the closeness with these babies that I had longed to feel my whole life with the people around me but couldn't due to strict rules, bad tempers and just plain evil.

That day, as I held the small baby and marveled at its tiny fingers, I prayed fervently that it would never suffer the crushing pain so many of us felt. It fell asleep against my chest, and I put my cheek against its soft skin and choked back tears. I always felt I had to save everyone; I thought it was my job, but how was I going to do that? There was no way to save anyone here. Everyone, including myself, was afraid of not following the Ordnung. If I could not even save myself, then there was nothing to do but comply. I lived in a word where sexual abuse was considered to be either a weakness or mostly the fault of the victim. If someone was sexually assaulted it was best to never tell anyone, because it would somehow be their fault; it would bring shame to their name or their family's name if the man confessed to his weakness in church. It was better to be silent.

THE NEXT week at the Bishop's house was pleasant enough. I enjoyed myself as much as possible. Matty's cautions were tucked in the back of my consciousness, and while I tried not to think of it, I made very sure I was never in a room alone with Peter. I noticed him watching me, but I figured he was scared to do anything to me because he was not quite sure how I would react. At least this is what I was banking on as I enjoyed my week away from Lillian.

That Thursday, as I gathered a few of my things to return home, Phyllis grabbed my arm as I opened the door. She smiled at me with her beautiful smile and then in a weak voice said.

"Don't take it to heart when Lillian is harsh with you. She has had some very sorrowful times in her life." She paused and glanced around, then in a low tone she continued, "I know you know about pregnancies and such, and I also know I am not supposed to talk to you about it." She paused a second time as if trying to decide whether she should tell me or not, and then she hesitantly continued.

"I feel that in order to understand, you must know that Lillian has had over thirteen miscarriages. It causes her great sorrow, and after the last a few years ago, the doctors did a hysterectomy to save her life."

As the words slipped out, Phyllis put her hand to her mouth in remorse. "I should not have told you; it was not my place," she shook her head. "I just could not stand for her to treat you like she does without you knowing why. You are a young woman of childbearing years, and she feels threatened by you."

I was stunned by what I had heard but was also hurt that I was seen as a threat. "That is ridiculous," I gasped. "Why would I be a threat?"

Phyllis just shook her head. "There is more to the story, but it is not my place. I should not have told you what I did. I must tell Lillian I told you," she bit her lip as she closed the door behind me.

As I trudged home in the snow, I thought about the more than thirteen miscarriages Lillian had had. I did not know it was possible to have so many. *Poor Lillian*, I thought. If all the pregnancies had come to full term, she would have over seventeen children instead of four. Of course, she most likely would not have become pregnant so many times if they had been full term, but it must have made her sad every time she saw large families gathering together. I felt sorry for her and got angry at myself for being sharp with her. It is okay, I told myself; she is grieving and that explains her behavior. Sorrow was something I understood very well, and I could definitely sympathize with Lillian now. I felt bad for some of my past actions. Lillian had never wanted me in her house, that was her right.

I am sure many women would have felt the same way, threatened by a young woman from nowhere suddenly showing up and becoming part of her family. Attention that the children had paid to her in the past was now directed towards me. I was younger and had less responsibilities. She was the one that had to dole out punishments or work assignments or anything that would be unpleasant. I never had to do that and it made me look better in the eyes of the children. It was the impossible situation that made her not like me. If I had been fourteen instead of nineteen I am positive she would have adopted me and loved me as a daughter. But I was not and neither of us could change that even though we both might have wanted to. I am not sure any other woman would have acted differently under similar circumstances. In the future I would sometimes forget her pain and feel only my own when she lashed out at me. I would feel rejected and wish I had never been born. I would grow angry at her, I know I could have acted better towards her at times, but we are all human and tend to feel the unfairness of our own situation first. Unfortunately, that is what we both did.

PERSONAL CONVICTIONS

"The first duty of a man is to think for himself."

- José Martí

To my relief, during the first week of March I got a letter from Samantha saying that Brian would be dropping her off on the next church Sunday. I was so excited that she was finally getting away from the mountain and that she would be safe. She would be living with the Deacon and the Borntrager's' family. The Borntrager's were what would be considered Amish upper class, while I and the Schrocks were from the lower class. Although many people never admit there are class distinctions among the Amish, they most certainty exist.

The Schrocks were more damutt (humbly) clothed than the Borntrager's, who were more Hochmut (proudly) clothed. All this amounted to, of course, was the limit in the length of the dresses, how far down dress pleats were ironed and the width of the pleats on the backs of the kapps. Since the limit from the floor was six inches for dresses, the Schrocks' dresses measured four or five inches from the floor, while the Borntreger women's dresses measured exactly six. Pleats on the dresses and aprons were to be from one quarter of the length to one half the length of the garment, and while the Schrock women always did no more than one quarter, the Borntreger women did exactly one half.

I thought that because of these differences the Borntreger girls were always a little stuck up and hard to like. I did not even bother to try since I always wanted to be friends with everyone and did not like their snickers if a girl showed up at church with a wrinkled apron or had something spilled on it.

"Those girls need to get their pretty, blond hair ripped out of their

188

heads, rolled in the mud and laughed at so they can see what it is like," Matty had whispered to me one Sunday after they snickered at Laura, who had accidentally splashed mud on her white apron when climbing down from the buggy.

I tried not to laugh at the thought, but it was so funny I could not help it. I held my ribs as my body shook with laughter while I pictured Matty ripping their hair out. The Borntreger girls stared at us as we whispered the scenario to a few of the other girls they had teased, and they, in turn, exploded into laughter.

"What's so funny?" Katie Borntreger demanded as she smoothed out her immaculate, neatly ironed white organdy church apron.

"You're funny," Matty answered, pointing and laughing.

"You girls are being mean," Katie's younger sister said defensively.

"Ohh...." Matty laughed even harder.

We must have gotten a little noisy, because one of the women came to the door and asked us if we were okay. All of us erased the laughter, and I nodded to signal that we were fine. When she closed the door, the girls buried their faces in their hands, trying to drown out the sounds of their laughter. It was hard sitting in church that day and trying not laugh as one girl after the other hid giggles behind a coughing fit. It must have appeared that we all had bad colds, and I was so afraid we were all going to burst into laughter while we were kneeling for prayer. The thought of the stern talking-to we would get from our fathers was enough to curb the desire to laugh, however.

On the way home, Ella and I laughed again as we embellished the idea of Matty taking on all six of the beautiful teenage Borntreger girls one-by-one and pulling out their hair and rolling them in the mud.

"We are being mean," I finally said, putting my hand over my mouth to hide the smile.

"Yeah, I know," Ella laughed. "But I bet Matty could pull it off if anyone could. She hates those pretty girls with a passion."

I nodded. Those girls were mean to the other girls but appeared to be the sweetest girls on earth when they were in front of the boys and the married folk.

I sighed. This was the family my sister was going into, and while Samantha was not gorgeous like the Borntreger girls, I knew that in order to fit in she would overcompensate for her looks with the mean girl spirit. Samantha was definitely not an ugly girl. While she was heavier and taller than I was, she did have a similar build and the same bright green eyes;

and while my hair was straight and reddish-brown, hers had brighter red undertones and curled softly around her face.

She will be just fine, I thought, but from now on I would have to try to be friendly with those girls. I gritted my teeth, thinking of how that would make Matty feel. Well, I thought, they are going to have to be friends with me too. I was going to enjoy every minute of watching them give me their fake smiles while they pretended to be my friends.

FOR THE next few days I waited anxiously for Samantha's arrival. Brian would let her off at the Deacon's house the Saturday before church, and while it was not Amish custom to go visiting during the week, I had been given permission to sleep over and go to church with the Borntrager's the following morning.

When Saturday afternoon finally arrived, I hopped in the buggy with Ella, Moses and Ida. All of them had wanted to drop me off and since I could not decide who would take me, they all went. I laughed at them and told them I would drive to spare them fighting over the reins. The horse seemed extra slow that day as we trotted the three miles to the Borntreger farm. When we finally arrived, I hopped out and blew each of the children a kiss and told them to let Ella drive home as she was the most responsible. Moses and Ida pouted a little but quickly bounced back and gave me a wave goodbye.

"Oh, we are not going to see her till tomorrow now," I heard Ida say.

"Yeah, I know," Moses said, as if I were going on a month's journey.

"Come, children," Ella chided. "She has to visit her other sister, you know."

I smiled and felt warmth go through me. These children had readily adopted me as their sister, and they seemed jealous that I had another sister separate from them. It really was very sweet.

As I walked into the Deacon's house, I was greeted by the oldest of his five daughters. She was eleven, and her name was Ella, too. The Deacon and his wife were young—in their early thirties—and had five chubby daughters. They were much nicer than the rest of the Borntreger clan living only a stone's throw away in the big house.

"Is Samantha here?" I asked Ella.

She came skipping up to me. "Who?" she queried, pretending to be confused.

"Okay, smarty," I swatted at her playfully. "I mean, is Beth here?"

"Oh, you mean my new older sister, Beth?" Ella asked with excitement. "Yeah, she is upstairs with Mom. Come on," she grabbed my overnight case, which held my Sunday clothes, and the suitcase that held some clothes for Samantha.

Hesitantly I climbed the stairs, worried about my little sister's state of mind. It had pained me so much to leave her behind on the farm all by herself, but I had had no choice. I felt there would be a divide between us now. It had only been eight months, but it seemed a lifetime already. So much had changed, and I was now part of the community. I was fluent in the language, I knew the rules and brought little attention to myself, I had a good name as a worker and I got the feeling I was well liked by most.

Samantha, on the other hand, as I had heard from Phyllis, was probably going to have a harder time since she had been quickly identified as someone that sought attention and was a little moody. Phyllis told me that if I wanted her to do well, I should talk to her right away and tell her not to bring attention on herself, as this could be detrimental to her baptism. I promised I would, but I was not too worried about her. Samantha had a keen ability to mimic the behavior of those around her; I figured the Borntreger girls would love that. While I did not like them and would not have fit in with them myself, I wanted Samantha to fit in somewhere.

When I got to the top of the stairs, I saw Annie, the house mother, standing next to the bed. Samantha was sitting there staring at the wall. Annie was asking her questions but she was not responding. Annie looked perplexed as I approached them.

"Is she alright?" she asked me in Amish.

I smiled and nodded. "Oh yeah," I said in English as I bounced down on the bed next to Samantha. "She is just tired. That is such a long drive, and Brian does not stop very often." I reached over and slapped Samantha on the leg to try to get her attention.

"Well, okay," Annie looked concerned. "Um... I made some room here for her clothes." She pointed to the girls' closet and smiled at me. "I heard you made her Sunday dress and workday clothes already, so you can hang them here if you want."

"Okay, thanks Annie," I said in English again. Everyone had grown accustomed to speaking to me in Amish, and I was afraid Samantha would feel like an outsider, so I thought I would speak English around her.

Annie went downstairs, and I turned to Samantha, who was still just sitting on the bed. *This was not going to go over well when the others heard,* I thought as I bit my lip trying to decide on the best form of action to take.

191

"Come on, Samantha," I tried to break her out of her thoughts. "Look, I made you three dresses. Black for Sunday, and blue and green for workdays."

Samantha looked at me and just nodded.

"Okay," I was really starting to be concerned. "What happened? Did Mamma and Brian hurt you?"

Samantha looked at the wall and then handed me a letter. "This is for you," her voice was emotionless. "Did you know that Brian and Mamma did not expect you to make it here? They thought you would get in a bunch of trouble with the Church and they would send you back and we would both be stuck there forever."

I looked at Samantha and shrugged. I had suspected as much.

"No, really," Samantha insisted. "When we went home after we left you here, Brian said the Bishop would probably send you back within the month. They never intended to let us go, ever..." Samantha stared at the wall and her eyes got rounder as she repeated it, "...never...they were never going to let us go.... Up until last week, Brian was still waiting for a letter from the Bishop saying you were just not fitting in."

I sat a little straighter knowing that pride was bad but unable to keep it at bay.

"Almost everyone likes me here," I said with a smile.

"Of course they do," Samantha rolled her eyes.

"So what made them bring you here if they weren't going to?" I asked, feeling a little dizzy at the thought of them keeping Samantha on the mountain.

"I told them you were going to the police if you did not see me within one week of the set day," Samantha kept staring blankly at the wall in front of her, it looked very strange and unsettling to me.

"And I would have," I nodded fervently.

"Yeah, I know," Samantha finally looked at me, her eyes were glazed and out of focus. "But Brian said you wouldn't because the Amish do not allow their people to go to the police. And then Mamma said that you never cared what someone else said if you thought you were doing the right thing. She said you were the most stubborn-headed mule she had ever met, and you would do it even if it meant getting kicked out of the Church."

I shrugged. "Well, there was no way I would have let those monsters keep you there," I reached over and hugged her.

Samantha was like a brick in my arms. She was acting so strangely, and I did not know what to do. Although Samantha always put up a big front, I knew she was more scared of things than I was, and I feared my little sister was in shock. I knew I had to reach her quickly before any tongues started wagging about her strange behavior.

"Well, they dropped you off, though; that's great," I said, trying to get her into a happier mood.

"I am only seventeen, though," Samantha pointed out. "What if they come back for me?"

"Oh, don't be silly," I chided, pulling her new Sunday dress out of the suitcase. "Why would they do that? It's only six months till you are eighteen, and if they come for you, you just won't get in the car with them, plain and simple."

"Mamma was very mad at me," Samantha was still staring at the wall. "She called us ungrateful bi***es who deserved to be stoned to death for our disloyalty. She said if we ever had children she was going to call the state and tell them we are Satanists so she can get custody of all of them."

"Oh, fiddlesticks," I spat angrily. "Mamma is nothing but a crazy psycho who deserves to be locked away from society for the rest of her natural life."

I wanted to ask about Fanny and Grandma, but I was too worried about Samantha's mental state.

"Come on," I strained to pull her to her feet. "Try this dress and church apron on."

Samantha stood up slowly, still staring at the wall. I pulled her dress off over her head and slid on the new black dress. As I pinned her up she started shaking her head.

"What?" I asked with a mouth full of pins. "Don't you like it? I ironed it so that you would fit right in with the Borntreger girls."

"No, that's not it," Samantha pouted.

"Then what?"

"I am not going to fit in as easily as you."

"What are you talking about?" I pretended I did not know. "I am way shyer than you are, and you are more confident and able to talk to people." I smiled encouragingly. "You are a way better conversationalist than me."

"No." Samantha shook her head irritably. "You laugh at yourself when you make mistakes, and you are smart. I can't help it, but I get mad easily.

I don't like to be made fun of and I am not smart."

I was getting frustrated with Samantha's pity party. I knew she was in shock, but so was I when I came here all by myself, and I had had no big sister to help me. Besides most of the things she was saying about herself were not true. I realized that right there in that moment the fear of failing was starting to take hold. I had felt it that morning I had arrived at Jacob's for the first time. It was a scary feeling.

I grabbed Samantha by the shoulders. I decided it was time for some tough love.

"Samantha," I raised my voice. "You need to snap out of it. When I came here, I had no one to help me. You have me, and you know I will be there for you whenever I can, but it is sink or swim time, and if you want a good reputation you better shape up and say thank you to Annie and put a smile on your face, even if it is not real."

I paused and studied her face. I was trying to provoke a reaction out of her, but her eyes still seemed glazed over. "Like you said," I continued, "this is our ticket out of hell, and if you don't stop feeling sorry for yourself your ticket is going to be revoked. I am serious, Samantha." I shook her shoulders again and looked deep into her tired, green eyes. "You could ruin your life here before it even starts," I shook my head disapprovingly at her like I had done when she was little. "Once rumors start flying, it is hard to squelch them."

Samantha was a little taken aback by my attitude and I saw a flicker of anger pop into her eyes. Finally there was some show of life, I thought. I was relieved and could not help remembering when we were smaller and she would come running to me for help. I felt I had failed her many times in the past, but now I was determined to get her situated and secure so she would be able to survive on her own. It really was sink or swim time, and I was determined to make sure she was swimming, even if I had to pretend to be angry at her.

Now that Samantha was more coherent, I showed her the secret to pinning her dress and apron so the pins would not poke her when she moved around. Self-consciously, she looked at herself in the mirror and smiled.

"Looks nice," she smoothed down the wide, black dress skirt.

"Yep," I smiled encouragingly. "It's nice to be like everyone else, huh?"

She nodded and looked at herself again. "Yeah, but now I have to learn German, and they are going to expect me to learn it as fast as you did, and you and I both know I am not half as fast at learning things as you, even if you did have your head crushed."

I pursed my lips. This had been a concern of mine. At home, when we were given the school books to teach ourselves, I learned how to add, subtract, use Roman numerals and even multiply single digits; I stopped short of double-digits since they were harder. Samantha, on the other hand, could barely add or subtract. She was a fantastic reader, but even the simplest addition problems took her a while to figure out.

"That's okay, Samantha," I tried to reassure her. "Annie runs a bakery here and she always has that old cash register down there, and they don't mind at all that we didn't have that much schooling."

"But learning German is going to be hard," Samantha whined.

"Haven't you been practicing the words I sent you?" I went through her suitcase looking for the writing tablet.

"Yeah," she sighed. "But I don't know if I am saying them right. I practiced every night for an hour after everyone was in bed, and even worked on them during the day. Mamma and Brian tried to learn them, too, because they said it would help their image, but I thought their German sounded more like French."

We both laughed. I was so grateful to finally hear a laugh from Samantha.

"Well," I pulled a writing tablet out of her suitcase. "I see you copied down all the words and sentences I sent you. No one knows I sent these to you, so they will think you are picking it up super-fast."

"Oh yeah, you think I am dumb," Samantha kicked the bed in frustration.

"Don't do that, Samantha," I said a little sharply. "I don't think you are dumb. You are good at many things that I am not. We all have our strong points, you know, and mine is memorizing things."

"What am I good at?" Samantha asked with a pout.

I thought for a moment. I knew how scared Samantha was and hoped with all my heart I was helping a little. We had been raised to think we were nothing, that we were worth nothing and that we did not matter. It was so sad that Samantha could not think of one thing she was good at when she had so many talents. But that was how we had been raised and what we had both believed for most of our lives.

"Well, you are really good at baking, and Annie has a bakery, so you are in luck. Also, you are great singer and the children seem to love you. You are good at a lot of things and you are going to do great," I hugged her again. "You just need to keep that temper in check."

After Samantha tried on her other dresses, we went downstairs to help with the evening chores. It was very awkward to call Samantha 'Beth', and I could see it was just as awkward for her to call me Emma. We only did this around others, and when we were by ourselves we continued to call each other by our birth names.

Samantha was not very talkative to her new family throughout the evening. The Borntreger girls wanted to play with her, but she did not want to play and just kept glancing around at everyone as if she expected them to burst into laughter at her. I could not blame her, and I am seriously surprised we did not both lose our minds on that mountain, I don't think anyone could of faulted us if we had.

I smiled as if I did not notice her strange behavior and kept trying to draw her into the conversation. I felt a little sick, though. I was worried that the years of terrifying trauma we had lived through might have altered Samantha's perception of reality. The extreme stress she was feeling was obviously affecting her. The only problem was that her new family had no idea what she had been through, and even if they were told, they would expect Samantha to hold her chin up and act as if nothing were wrong.

Twice Ella came over to try to get Samantha to look at the new kittens that were under the house, and twice Samantha shook her head irritably. I saw Ella's face fall in disappointment, and as she walked past me, I put my arm around her shoulders and whispered in Amish, "Just give her some time."

"Oh," Ella looked at me. "She is sad, huh?"

I nodded and smiled at her.

Annie took me aside and asked me if everything was okay with Samantha. I assured her it was and that she just needed some time to adjust. My eyes fell to the floor, however, under the deep scrutiny with which Annie searched my face. Annie was known to be a very nice lady, and I was happy that Samantha had been placed with her family.

"Well," Annie's voice was laced with concern, "she is acting strangely, and there is nothing I can do for her if she acts like this in church tomorrow. You are her sister, so do whatever you can."

I nodded, thankful for Annie's concern and understanding. I saw her husband, the Deacon, quietly observing Samantha and was not sure he had as kind and understanding a heart as his wife. In reality Samantha's behavior was much better than most peoples would have been given the severity of stress she had been under.

We all went to bed after the evening baths, and I snuggled into bed next to my sister and gave a sigh of relief that we were both finally free of Mamma and Brian. It was a dream come true, and despite the disturbing things I was finding out about my new home, it was heaven for two girls who had feared they could die on a mountaintop without anyone knowing or caring what had happened to them.

As I lay there listening to Samantha's even breathing while she slept the sleep of someone who was overly exhausted, I suddenly remembered the letter Samantha had given me from Mamma and Brian. I crept out of bed and pulled it out of my dress pocket. I went over to the window, and in the moonlight I read one of the most horrible letter ever written. They wrote that I was nothing but a Jezebel. Mamma said I was no longer her daughter, but that I was a child of Satan, and when I died she hoped I would be reunited with him. It was so bad and so hateful. There were some scriptures that Brian included which he said proved their point. Rather than being sad, though, I felt angry. How dare these two lunatics quote scripture to me? They were insane. I tore the letter up and put it into the wall where there was a hole in the sheet rock.

"Crazy people," I muttered to myself as I crept back into bed beside Samantha. I fell asleep to the sound of soft wind blowing. Clouds were starting to form and block out the moonlight, the night was peaceful and my sister was safe. What a truly wonderful world.

THE NEXT morning, it was raining softly as Samantha and I jumped out of bed. I was pleased to see that Samantha was in better spirits as we hurried to help with the chores and get breakfast on the table. After the dishes were washed, all seven of us girls raced upstairs to get ready for church. Samantha slipped into her black church dress with some excitement. I had brought my black dress so we would be matching—this was something sisters often did. The Borntreger girls had asked us what color we were wearing the night before, and when I said black, they had all begged Annie to let them wear black too, so they could match their new sister.

Annie had set aside dark blue for church that day but laughingly gave in to the girl's' pleas and agreed that everyone could wear black. Before I left the day before, Ella and Ida had asked me what color I was wearing as well.

"It's the battle of the sisters," I laughed as I pictured the two families of girls all in black. Although it was not unusual, it would be conspicuous with people knowing our connection and seeing that we all matched.

"They are not my sisters," Samantha corrected me.

"Oh, come on, Sam," I grinned. "They are very sweet and love the thought of having a big sister."

197

"They are not my sisters," Samantha repeated again, starting to get flustered with her cape as she tried to fold the top into her neck string.

"Here, let me help you," I untied the string. "You have to tie it tighter for it to work." I tied the string snugly around Samantha's neck and tucked the cape inside. The string was placed right above the collar and tied snugly with the cape tucked in, allowing only a couple inches of neck to show.

"I look like a turtle," Samantha complained, yanking at the string to loosen it.

"Hey, they are going to be watching you, so don't make that too loose," I admonished as I pulled her arm away.

Samantha frowned at me and wiggled her neck around, finally managing to get everything in comfortable condition.

I watched as she looked at herself in the mirror, just as I had done a few months before. I knew it was probably just now sinking in that she was going to be joining the Amish Church and that she would no longer have to go back to the terrifying mountain.

I sighed with relief when I saw her calm down and smile at herself. She seemed to be mellowing, and the prospect of a new life seemed to surge through her as she turned around and tied on her bonnet. She never did talk to me about what had happened those last few days at home, but I believe it was something awful that she was trying to forget. Whenever I brought up the subject, she would immediately pretend she had not heard and would start talking about something else to distract me. But behind her eyes I could see she had heard me and that there was something she was locking away forever.

As we approached the church house, I saw the Borntreger cousins looking at us from the kitchen window. Since we were close by, we had arrived early, and the house family was still getting everything ready. As we walked through the door, we were greeted by the sound of benches banging on the wood floor as two of the young Borntreger brothers finished opening them for the church gathering. Samantha and I followed the girls down to the huge basement, where we waited for the rest of the girls.

We stood in silence as the Borntreger girls looked Samantha over from head to foot. I saw them looking at the slightly fancy way I had ironed her clothes. They did not know I had ironed them, and I was hoping they would think she had done it. To my relief, as the other girls started streaming in, the Borntreger girls closed ranks as usual, but this time with Samantha in the middle. I had explained the situation to Samantha, and while I was afraid Samantha would go too far with the mean girl act, she had to fit in with them somehow. We waved to each other from opposite sides of the room, and Samantha seemed excited as she nodded when asked questions. The girls laughed annoyingly as they talked to Samantha, shutting out the rest of us as they pretended to be important.

Matty and I rolled our eyes. Finally, I could not stand it anymore and walked over to them, pretending to remind Samantha about our Wednesday schedule when I planned to help her learn how to read German. Samantha smiled at me, but noticing the standoffish behavior of the cousins, she turned back to Erma, who was only a year older than herself. I was taken aback, but I shrugged. I knew that whenever we were out somewhere, Samantha would always mimic the behavior of whomever she was around. She was good at it—a little too good, I thought as I walked back over to where Matty and Laura were standing and smirking at me.

That night at the singing, as the boys and girls sat around the young people's table, I smiled at Samantha, who sat down the row from me. She had snapped out of her coma-like state and was happily putting stickers in the new German song book that the Borntreger girls had given her as a welcome-to-the-family gift. These German song books were usually given to young people on their seventeenth birthday by a parent or other relative, and it was theirs to write in, or put stickers next to their favorite songs, or to doodle the names of their boyfriend's or girlfriend's favorite song. Many girls had bright sparkly heart stickers throughout their song books.

While many of the youngies found the old German songs boring, turning the pages in the song book and looking at the stickers gave them the chance to laugh or snicker softly and a reason for a boy across the table to look at a girl as he pretended to make fun of her stickers. Although it was highly discouraged to bring things to the singing in the song books, the boys often passed around inappropriate pictures they had cut out of newspapers. Matty and I laughed into each other's shoulders as one of these pictures was passed to Samantha. I saw her face go beet red, and Erma whispered in her ear as they tried to figure out which boy had started it. It was funny, but we tried to keep everything quiet as the eyes of the elders bored into our backs.

THE NEXT morning, the school-aged children dropped me off at home on their way to school. I waved goodbye and felt very comforted that Samantha was in a good place now. She would be helping Annie with the bakery and would be very busy. I hoped this would draw her more and more out of her shell. Samantha had already learned more of the Amish language than she had thought. All through the day on Sunday, she had asked me if they had said this or that, and I nodded with great relief.

Before I left, she promised me she would have the children help her with ten new words each night, and it looked like everything was going smoothly. Samantha had started talking to her new sisters, and although I chided her not be too bossy, I smiled as she reluctantly assumed the role of older sister. She had been my baby sister her whole life and I could tell she was now realizing the responsibility that came with being the older sister.

Although I felt relieved at how things were turning out, I could not help feeling disturbed at the same time. As I walked up the stairs from the machine shop, I could not rid myself of the gnawing pain in the pit of my stomach. What about Fanny and Grandma and the future foster children? I swallowed hard. Samantha was in too fragile a state to talk about it now, but I knew I had to do something. I had to tell Jacob and Lillian our real home life story. I will wait two weeks, I thought, and then I have to do something. Samantha, who was my primary concern, was safe now, but I could not just leave Fanny and Grandma to suffer. I would never be able to live with myself if I did.

*T*HAT WEEK passed like most others. On Wednesday, Samantha came by for her first German lesson. We sat at the kitchen table, and with a German song book I attempted to teach Samantha how to read the strangely-shaped letters and went through the different ways to pronounce things in German, which was quite different from English. Lillian did some baking in the morning while we practiced, and then after lunch, the three of sat and quilted while we waited for the school children to return home. Samantha was just learning to quilt, and I kept complimenting her on how fast she was learning. It was great to see her buckling down and really trying—she was smarter than she gave herself credit. In fact I believe she was and is extremely smart and had she had half a chance in life she could have proved that to herself.

*S*PRING APROACHED with the promise of warmer weather and the hope of new life. Spring was always my favorite season. Baby animals were born, and the earth seemed to spring to life with green hillsides and early flowers. The men started getting the fields ready for planting, and the women folk quilted and finished up the last of the sewing in preparation for a long summer of hard work outdoors.

I continued teaching Samantha her German, but she was a fast learner, and after only four lessons, coupled with practice at home, she was off and running. Samantha had bounced out of her shell and was settling into her new life with great excitement. I was very happy about this and praised her every chance I got. Prior to her coming to live in the community, I had never realized just how much she looked up to me and how hard she believed it would be to walk in my shadow. But she was catching on fine, and everything seemed to be going smoothly.

By the first of May, life had settled into a normal routine, and Samantha and I led separate lives except for when we met at church every other Sunday or at a house cleaning to get ready for church or some other social event. I, however, was growing increasingly agitated about leaving Fanny and Grandma on the mountain by themselves. It had now been two months, and I was still trying to muster the courage to do something. Every night when I went to sleep, I tossed and turned, seeing Fanny's chubby face with tears streaming down it. I would eventually fall asleep, only to see her in my dreams. Sometimes I would struggle with Mamma, trying to rip the belt out of her hands, or I would try to push her off Fanny's lifeless body. These dreams always ended with the sound of a gun going off, and me clutching my stomach and falling to the floor. I would awaken and sit up in a sweat with tears streaming down my face, and there in the middle of the night I would pray for hours for God to protect Fanny and Grandma from any severe pain and to somehow rescue them.

Sadly, I thought, even death would be a sweet rescue. At least then they would not suffer so much. I started reading the Bible in the middle of the night. I knew I was not supposed to read the English Bible, but what harm could it do? I told Lillian I was using the English Bible only to learn the High German that was read in church. She had had it in her hands, ready to take it away, but given my explanation she shrugged and put it back.

Due to the stress and the nightmares I was having, I was very tired during the day. I started to get dark circles under my eyes, and I could not eat much. I was so distressed that I began losing weight rapidly. One morning at the breakfast table after I ate only a small dipper of oatmeal, Jacob asked me if I was feeling okay. I nodded and smiled at him.

"Oh, yes," I said quickly. "I just am just not hungry."

"You haven't been hungry for weeks," Jacob pushed half an egg into his mouth.

Out of the corner of my eye, I saw Lillian squirming at the attention I was getting. Jacob had been paying a lot of attention to me lately, and I did not know how to get him to stop. If I ignored him, it seemed to make him try harder.

My hands trembled in my lap, and I was afraid I would burst into tears at all the pressure I was feeling. Everyone around the table was staring at me. Elam, noticing my discomfort, decided to help me out.

"Oh, come on, Dad," he grinned mischievously. "You know the girls at the youngie table always have a bet on who can lose the most weight the fastest. You were with the youngies once, too."

"Is that true?" Lillian asked with a frown. "I don't like my girls being proud like that."

I just smiled, not commenting yes or no.

"Well," Jacob pushed his chair back from the table and stood up, "we best be getting on with the rest of the harrowing today. I am going to take Emma again to help." He nodded to me.

"Why Emma?" Lillian asked, standing up with a frown on her face.

"Well, we need help," Jacob answered. "We have to get that motor fixed for the Johnson's by the end of the week, and Emma is good with the horses. You already know that."

I winced. It was getting to be very tense here, and I felt I was the pawn in a marriage that had been long over. There was zero chance of divorce among the Amish, so couples had to stick it out for life. I got up to grab my coat and scarf, happy to be going out to the field. It was true that for some reason I was able to control the horses quite well and they seemed to love me as much as I loved them.

"Yeah, it's like with the babies," Elam scoffed as he grabbed his coat. "She cuddles with everything."

I made a face at Elam. In the reflection of the kitchen window I saw Lillian, and Jacob's stern face looking at her matter-of-factly. He was so unfeeling with Lillian, I thought. Never had I heard him say anything kind or loving toward her. I felt really sorry for her, wondering if he had ever loved her. Amongst the Amish, it is strictly forbidden to show any kind of affection between married couples, not even hand holding, but despite this strict rule, it was still easy to see when a couple was not getting along just from their body language.

I went outside with the men and helped Elam put the harness on Lucky, who was my favorite of the Belgian horses. He was a massive brown and white horse who, despite his gigantic stature, was really quite gentle.

"Okay," Elam patted Lucky on the neck. "You are all set. Better hop to it."

I smiled and took the reins. Just then, Jacob came into the barn and told Elam to take some extra fodder to the sow with the new piglets. Elam raised his eyebrows at me, and I gave him a perplexed look. I started to lead Lucky out of the barn, but Jacob grabbed my arm. I jumped and stared at him, feeling panicked that this man who was not even allowed to hold his wife's hand in public now had me by the arm. I pulled away from him, but he grabbed my arm again.

"Hold on," he said in his softest voice. "I just want to talk to you. You never let me talk to you. You just seem to disappear on me."

"Uh... why would you want to talk to me?" I asked, trying to squirm out of his grip, but to no avail. I was afraid Lillian would think up a reason to come out to the barn, and I was starting to panic.

"Come on. I am supposed to be your dad, and I know something is wrong with you, but you won't tell me. I know how Lillian is with you, and I am sorry," Jacob pulled me closer to him.

Lucky stomped his foot impatiently. Lucky did not like Jacob at all and would even try to bite him sometimes.

"I'm fine," I tried to pull away again.

"No, you are not," Jacob shook his head. He seemed a little angry, I thought.

"You know," he released me and looked away, "my wife is very suicidal. She is constantly telling me she is going to kill herself—she did so even before you came here—so don't take it so hard when she gets on to you. She is not quite right, you know?" He pointed to his head.

Yeah, I thought to myself, of course she wasn't. *After thirteen miscarriages, who would be?*

I looked back at Jacob and saw that he looked sad, to the point of tears. Maybe I had misjudged him, Maybe he really did care, and with all the pressure I was under I felt I could not keep my problems to myself any longer.

"No, wait," I looked up at him nervously. "There is something I need to tell you. I really need help with something, but I have to talk to my sister first." I started to lead Lucky out of the barn.

"Did she do something wrong?" Jacob asked with concern.

"No. It is about our parents, but I can't tell you what it is until I talk to Samantha. I mean, Beth," I corrected myself, it felt good to have told someone. "You won't tell anyone, right?" I asked, looking at him under Lucky's belly.

Jacob laughed and waved at me to get going. "I am going down that way this afternoon," he smiled. "You can come with me and see Beth for a few minutes while I get the rest of the seed from Elam M."

"Okay," I nodded, and I found myself smiling back at him. Something in the back of my head was telling me that this new pact was not a good idea, but I was desperate for help, and, being naturally friendly, what was I supposed to do?

As I walked to the field with Lucky, I mentally kicked myself. I did not remember Jacob laughing like that before, and he was certainly not as accommodating with Lillian. *Oh, no,* I thought with panic; I just opened a flood gate I had been trying to keep closed for the past ten months. No, no, I told myself; this was not happening. I could not go on a buggy ride with Jacob by myself. The rumors would be flying. But I was their adopted daughter, right? And I did need to talk to Samantha right away. I bit my lip as I sat on the furrow going back and forth, up and down the field. I felt trapped and did not know what to do.

AFTER THE noon meal, I helped with the dishes, and as I was throwing the dishwater off the porch, I saw Jacob hitching up the buggy and motioning for me to come down. I hesitated for a moment, and then gave in. He was supposed to know what was in the Ordnung better than me, I thought as I took the dishpan inside.

"Lillian, I am going to see Beth," I announced, walking to the bedroom to put on my green cape.

Lillian looked up from her seed bucket and frowned. "Why are you going to see Beth?"

"Well... Jacob is going down there to get some of the seed he ordered and said I could come along to see Beth," I came out of the bedroom and looked at her nervously as I tucked my cape into my dress belt.

Lillian looked at me and then looked back at her seeds. "Yeah," she bit her lip. "He always liked to take the maids home so they could visit their families for the weekends. He never seemed to mind the heat or cold. He's really nice that way."

I felt a knot grow in my stomach. I needed to get out of this ride somehow. Just then, Moses popped his head through the door.

"Dad asked me to tell you to hurry up," he gasped, out of breath, his chubby face smiling at me mischievously.

I gave one apologetic glance to Lillian and then ran down the stairs to the buggy. We rode in silence for a few minutes, with me wishing every inch of the way that I was not there. I felt I had really put myself in a touchy situation. I hugged my side of the seat, careful not to touch Jacob's wide-spread knees.

"So what do you need to talk to Samantha about?" Jacob asked, turning to me.

"Uh... just something I need to tell her about," I mumbled into my bonnet.

I saw Jacob's eyes looking me over, and I moved even closer to the corner of the seat.

Jacob laughed a little at my uncomfortable posture and bumped my knee with his. "Come on, Misty," he said. "It's okay for you to ride with me to see your sister. No one would have a problem with it."

I looked at him, surprised that he had used my real name. Sensing my surprise, he grinned. "I like your name. It has a nice ring to it," he studied my face as he smoothed down his reddish beard.

We drove in silence the rest of the way, with me trying to reassure myself that I had not made a terrible mistake.

It was with great relief that I jumped down from the buggy and ran into the bake shop, where I was sure I would find Samantha either tending the store or baking. As I pulled open the glass door, the bell rang and I saw Samantha look at me with surprise from where she was putting cookies in the oven.

"What are you doing here in the middle of the week?" she asked as she wiped her hands on her apron.

I looked around to make sure there were no little ears hiding in the corners somewhere.

"I have to talk to you, Samantha," I pulled off my big black bonnet. "We have to do something about Fanny and Grandma. I just can't stand it any longer."

"I thought we said we would let it go once we got the hell out of there," Samantha snapped at me.

"No." I shook my head vigorously. "That is what you said. I would never agree to that and you know it. I can't take it anymore, and I am going to do something with or without you, but I just wanted to tell you first."

Samantha bit her lip and shook her head. "I am not going to get involved. If anyone asks me if what you are saying is true I will tell them yes, but I will not get involved, do you hear me?"

"Okay, if that is what you want," I sniffed the air as the aroma of oatmeal cookies tickled my senses.

"Want a cookie?" Samantha asked, handing me one of the warm, delicious treats.

I smiled and nodded, suddenly feeling hungry again now that I had voiced my plans to help Fanny and Grandma. Samantha and I stood in silence while I ate my cookie and she waited for a new batch to finish baking. As we stood there, I found it amazing that we were both here in the

Amish community. I could not help but remember the little girls who had to sit in the back of the truck for hours while their parents were out shopping. I shook my head to try to get the horrible images out of my head. It seemed a lifetime ago, and yet there were still two people suffering terribly at the hands of those two crazy people. Something had to be done about it. The only problem was I did not know what to do about it, or if the church would even allow me to do anything.

I shook my head again, blinking myself back to the present, and began tying on my bonnet. Samantha seemed agitated and a little scared as she grabbed my arm. "Hey, just be careful... whatever you do," her eyes were frightened. "We are safe now. We have new lives; we can't go back. Not now."

I nodded to reassure her. "Okay, Samantha," I looked out the window and saw the buggy already coming up the lane. "I've got to run." I reached over the counter, gave her a big hug and ran out the door.

As I jumped in the wagon, I saw Samantha waving at me from the bakery window. I waved back and blew her a kiss as we disappeared around the bend in the lane.

"You and your sister figure things out?" Jacob asked.

I looked out at the rolling hillsides covered with pretty wildflowers that were springing up. I loved flowers; they were so beautiful and innocent looking. Their brightness would make me smile, even when I was in the worst of states. I especially loved yellow flowers. That day I tried to lose myself in the beauty of the flowers as I struggled with what to do about Fanny and Grandma. How could I explain such a horror story? I began shaking my head as I wrung my hands in my lap.

I jumped as I felt a hand on mine. I looked down to see Jacob's large, coarse brown hand. His faded blue shirt sleeve was rolled up to his elbow, and I could smell the sweat from his damp skin.

"Your hands are trembling," he said in a soft voice. "I wish you would tell me what is wrong."

I was so confused. I really wanted Jacob to be a father who would love me. I so longed to be loved and accepted as someone's daughter. I think it is every girl's dream to have a father who will love and protect her, no matter what. At least I did, and I really wanted to tell myself that was all Jacob wanted to provide, too. It was against Amish culture for a father to show any kind of affection to his daughter, so this was completely out of the ordinary and only added to my stress.

"What is it?" Jacob asked again, still holding my hand.

I sighed and pulled my hand away. Finally unable to hold it in

206

anymore, I told him the true story of our childhood.

Jacob nodded as I told him how cruel Mamma was and how she loved to torture people, and how Brian would even hit his own mother.

"I want to go to the authorities and have them do something about this," I said as Jacob guided the horse down the lane to the barn. I saw a curtain flutter as we passed the Bishop's house and thought I saw Phyllis quickly walking away from the window.

"We have to talk to the Bishop first," Jacob told me as I jumped down from the buggy. "I really want to help. We will talk more about it tonight with Lillian present." He leaned over to me and whispered quietly, "Just pretend you did not tell me, okay?"

"Okay," I agreed, although it made me feel like I was hiding something, even though I had nothing to hide.

As I came into the house, Lillian would not look at me, but pretended to be busy with her tomato plants. I sighed as I took off my cape and began helping Ella make noodles which we would sell in the Borntreger bakery. I was worried about Lillian. She was really acting strangely, as if I had punched her in the stomach. I had not meant any harm, but I could still feel the sensation of Jacob's hand holding mine. It was not something I had asked for, and I dared not say anything about it. I felt sick to my stomach. *What had just happened?* I thought to myself, not really knowing. Jacob was so nice to *me*, but so rough with his wife. It was tempting to give in to his fun, kind behavior, but I knew it was not right. It was a very uncomfortable situation, and I did not know what to do about it except to ignore him whenever possible.

FREEDOM FROM PROSECUTION

The world is a dangerous place to live; not because of the people who are evil, but because of the people who don't do anything about it.

- Albert Einstein

That evening after the other children went to bed, Jacob asked me to stay up.

"I think you are in trouble," Elam snickered at me as he snapped Moses's suspenders on the way to their bedroom.

"Ow," Moses complained, rubbing his shoulders. I shook my head at Elam as I sat back down on the bench at the table. The light of the kerosene lamp flickered softly off the light blue walls and helped calm my nerves.

"Okay," Lillian looked at me inquisitively after the younger children closed their bedroom doors. "What is this about?"

Jacob nodded toward me. "Emma has something she wants to tell us."

"How do you know?" Lillian asked, not trying to disguise her anger about the events of the day.

I was offended by her accusative tone. "Look," I reached over to her, "I just went with him so I could talk to my sister. I have far greater concerns than your marital squabbles."

Lillian pulled away from my touch like I was poison. "And what was so important that you could not wait till Friday when we go to help clean for church?"

Suddenly I felt so overwhelmed that I burst into tears. I buried my face in my hands and felt myself shaking uncontrollably.

Lillian sniffed impatiently. "So what did you do that you need to confess?" she asked impatiently.

I stood up from the table and shoved my chair back. "You know what, Lillian?" I took a deep breath. "I am very tired of having you accuse me of trying to get attention all the time. Do you know the very real problems I have? No, you don't," I answered for her. "I have an aunt who is literally being tortured every day by my evil mother and stepfather. My grandmother was once made to wash her own sheets in the freezing cold when she wet the bed. They are both starved and given ice-cold baths. And my wonderful parents are soon going to be foster parents. That is why I have lost weight and can't sleep at night."

I sat down and stared at the wall. I felt bad for yelling at Lillian; after all, I was living in her house, but it did feel good to finally tell her what had been bothering me.

I looked at Jacob and Lillian's surprised faces. To my dismay, I saw admiration in Jacob's eyes. I looked away quickly.

"So what are you planning to do?" Lillian asked.

I looked at her, overrun by guilt. "I am sorry, Lillian," I apologized. "I shouldn't have yelled."

"No, you shouldn't have," Lillian's voice was hostile. "You need to work on your sense of entitlement. Do you think you are the only one with problems?"

"No, that is not what I think," I blinked back tears, "but I do think I am the only one who is willing to do anything about them. I have to do something. I can't just let them stay up there and suffer like this. It is wrong, and I cannot live with myself anymore."

"Well, we don't go to the police, so I don't know what you plan to do," Lillian shrugged.

"What?" I snapped, growing angry again. "That is your response when I tell you someone is being tortured?"

"It's not the first case of this I have heard of," Lillian looked at me sternly. "I know many families where the fathers and mothers beat their children. It's just how it is, and we can't stop it."

"No, you can't think like that," I pleaded. "It's wrong, and people like this have to be stopped. We are Christians and are supposed to follow Christ. He would never have condoned such behavior."

"And who put you in charge?" Lillian quipped. "Your job is to do what you are told and make sure you are following the rules."

"No." I shook my head violently. "My job as a fellow human being is to care for the helpless whenever I can. It is inhumane to allow this to continue. It goes against nature itself."

"That is not your concern," Lillian snapped at me. "You are far too proud if you feel you could ever change anything. Just who do you think you are?"

"No," I snapped back. "The question is who do you think you are? Do you honestly believe you are incapable of helping anyone if you try?"

Lillian was seething mad and turned toward Jacob. "It is not our way for our people to interfere like this. Tell her, Jacob."

"No, it's your way to let people suffer, just as long as *you* don't look proud doing it," I muttered angrily.

Jacob, who had been silently watching us argue, held up a hand to silence us. "Hold on, I will talk to the Bishop and elders about this matter. We normally would not do this, but the fact that Brian is beating his own mother and Sue is beating her older sister is a grave matter. This shows disrespect for their elders, and since they are not Amish anyway, it may be acceptable to alert the authorities about this matter."

Lillian shrugged and got up from the table. "You're good about making up rules when they are in your favor, Jacob. I might as well kill myself since I don't matter anyway. You just asked me here tonight so I would not think something was happening between you two." She turned to me. "I know you would be happy if I kill myself. You could have my family then."

I stared in astonishment. "What?" I gasped. "I don't want your family. Why would you say such a thing?"

"Lillian, you will be silent," Jacob stood up and yanked her arm. "Are you trying to ruin us or what?"

I saw tears running down Lillian's cheeks, and I felt a twinge of pity for her. I had no doubt that Lillian would have been a far nicer person if Jacob were better to her. But I needed Jacob to help me sway the Bishop. I looked around the room. Suddenly the kerosene lamp light seemed suffocating, and I felt trapped. I could not understand why helping someone had to be given so much thought. How could it be that saving someone might be against the Ordnung? Where was that written in the Bible? I unpinned my dress collar in frustration and took a few deep breaths. I was confused and hurt but still determined to do whatever I could.

EARLY THE next morning as I was straining the milk, I heard light footsteps behind me and felt a hand gently rest on my shoulder. I looked up to see Jacob standing behind me. I pulled away from him and backed up, glancing around to see if anyone had seen us. I was not scared of Jacob. I knew he would never hurt me. I think that he thought himself to be a charmer and was wondering why I was not responding to him.

To my relief, Ida popped in through the door by the ice house and scampered down the stairs to grab my hand. I looked at Jacob, who just looked back at me, obviously he had been expecting a different reaction. I knew I had to stop this before rumors got started. I did not know how they might get out, but I knew they could definitely be my ruin. I could end up an old maid for the rest of my life over something like this.

A week later, all of the ministers showed up at our house with their wives and Samantha in tow. The men and women stayed downstairs, and Samantha came upstairs where I was ironing church clothes.

"What did you do?" Samantha demanded as she came through the door.

I looked at her quietly as I slid my dress on the ironing board, "We talked about this. I am trying to do what needs to be done."

"Well," Samantha sighed, plopping down in a rocking chair, "they are down there arguing right now. I am not sure what they are going to decide, but I wish you would just let it go."

I shook my head as I guided the iron up and down my dark gray dress. "I will not rest until I have done what I can, Samantha. Twenty years from now, I do not want to be huddled up in a corner somewhere crying because I did not do something."

Samantha took off her kapp and loosened her hair. "Just don't think about it, I don't, and I am fine."

"I wish I could," I squinted at her. "But I am not like you; I can't keep myself from thinking about it. I'm not made that way."

I lifted the dress from the ironing board, and Ella began ironing hers. A few minutes later, Samantha and I were called downstairs and told to stand in front of the ministers. The Bishop asked us many questions about our home life and why we thought it was okay to contact the authorities when such actions were strictly forbidden by the church.

Samantha was quick to say that it was my idea, and that she had told me to just drop it. The ministers nodded and were silent for a moment. I felt a surge of strength as I stood there, watching them try to decide if this

211

was against the Ordnung or not. This was ridiculous, I thought. Someone was suffering every day, and these people were worried about the Ordnung.

I took a deep breath and stood as tall as I could. "Look," I said impatiently, "they are not even Amish and don't live anywhere near an Amish community."

The Bishop nodded, and I heard Phyllis quietly clear her throat. I looked at her pleadingly.

"Well," Phyllis began slowly as she caught my eye, "it is very grave how they are beating their mother. If one of our own did such a thing, we would put them the Bann for dishonoring their mother."

"But then *they* would be dishonoring *their* mother," Alma countered as she pointed to Samantha and me.

"Wait a minute." I frowned. "Is anyone concerned about the people that are suffering, or just about who would be getting whom in trouble?"

The Bishop glared at me, and I grew quiet, but I could not help but feel there was something not right about the way things were preceding. They argued back and forth for a few minutes. Some were in favor, some were not. I translated for Samantha when they said something she did not understand.

Finally the Bishop turned back to us. "I wish this circumstance had never occurred. It is something unusual and we do not take this matter lightly. We do not believe in contacting the police, we handle things amongst ourselves.

I bit my lip, where they going to let me call the police?

The Bishop cleared his throat again. "Since you are not yet a church member, we will let you make these calls, but only because these people that are being harmed are your parents' elder relatives. You are not yet a church member and they are not members at all, so you may pursue this, as long as it does not take more than a few phone calls, and you may not break any rules while doing so. Understood?"

"Oh, yes, and thank you," I clasped my hands to show my gratitude. "I am sure Fanny would thank you, too, if she could."

The Bishop put a finger to his lips. "That is quite enough," he furrowed his brow. "We will not hear more of this, I hope.

"I will make a call at the neighbor's house tomorrow, and hopefully the authorities will handle it from there," I smiled, they did not smile back.

The Bishop and ministers nodded as they filed out of the machine shop. I waved goodbye to Samantha and went upstairs behind Lillian and Jacob.

THE NEXT day I walked over to the Fletcher's house. They were our English neighbors and they let the Amish use their phones and would drive them into town for a fee. As I knocked on the door, I looked around the well-kept residence. There were statues on the lawn and an American flag on a pole next to the driveway—so different from what I was used to.

The door was opened by Mrs. Fletcher—a nice, cheerful lady in her mid-fifties. She smiled at me and asked what she could do for me.

"Uh…" I stammered as she showed me into the house. "I need to make a call to Washington State. I will pay for it," I handed her the five dollars that Jacob had given me.

She took the money and looked at me curiously. "And why do you need to do that, honey?"

"Well, I know of someone who is being hurt there, and I need to call the authorities and tell them."

"Does your family know you are here?" Mrs. Fletcher asked, reaching for the phone.

"Yes, of course. I am staying with Jacob Schrock just down the lane." I pointed in the direction of the farm.

"Oh, okay," she nodded. "I give the men lifts into town sometimes. So do you need me to look up a number for you?"

I nodded. "I guess the police department in…"

Mrs. Fletcher sat down at her computer and put on her reading glasses. "So how do you know about this?" she asked me as she wrote down the phone number.

"I would rather not say," I looked at the floor. I felt shy standing in the middle of the room with carpeted floors and electric lights. I had not been in many *Englisch* homes since I was a small child, and again I was reminded of the stark contrast between my plain life and that of the rest of the world. The modern house made me uncomfortable, and I was keenly aware of the sound of the refrigerator in the kitchen and the low volume of the television. These were foreign sounds, and I found them annoying.

"Okay, here you go, honey," she handed me the phone and a piece of paper with the number on it. I stood there for a moment, realizing I had never dialed a phone number before.

"You do know how to use a phone, right?" Mrs. Fletcher's face was concerned, I am sure I was not like the nineteen year old girls she was used to.

"Oh, yes, of course," I took the strange-looking object and walked to a corner of the room.

I dialed the number. My heart was racing from nerves. I had wanted to do this for so long, and I could not believe I was finally doing it. I knew I was being frowned on in the church for it, but I really did not care, even though it was bad for my reputation to bring so much attention to myself.

After several rings, I finally heard, "Police department; how may I direct your call?"

After explaining the nature of the call, I was transferred to someone else. After about twenty minutes of being transferred from one person to another, I finally talked to an officer who seemed willing to listen to me.

"Okay, and how long have you been out of the house?" he asked.

"About ten months," I answered. "But my sister just got here a few months ago. I was waiting to make sure she got away before I called you."

"I see." He paused. "It still would have been better if you had called right away. Why did you not call sooner?"

I stood quietly for a moment. "Because I am joining an Amish community, and we are not allowed to call the police."

"So how are you calling me now, then?"

I was getting a little flustered with the questioning. I had thought I would just call, and they would go up the mountain and take Grandma and Fanny out of there.

"Look," I gritted my teeth. "There are two people up on that mountain that are suffering every day and need your help. I am going against the rules of my church to call you, so will you just send someone up there to get them out?"

"Okay..." the officer paused for a moment. "We are a small town with limited resources, as you know, but I will send a couple of my guys up there tomorrow. I will contact you at this phone number when I have more information. In the meantime, I want you to write a page or two for me about what your life was like when you lived there and fax it to me."

"Okay," I agreed, hoping this would be the last week Fanny and Grandma would be in such pain.

I walked into the kitchen where Mrs. Fletcher was and handed her the phone.

"How did it go?" Mrs. Fletcher asked, looking at me with her motherly concern..

"I would rather not say," I said again. "I am trying to help someone who really needs it, and this is how I have to do it."

Mrs. Fletcher shrugged, and, seeing tears in my eyes, hugged me.

"You are a very brave girl," she said. "I hope whoever you are trying to help appreciates it."

I nodded, and for a moment I let my weary soul get lost in the comfort of her warm embrace.

"Thank you so much, Mrs. Fletcher," I wiped the tears from my face and pulled my kapp forward. "I wish I could tell you the whole story, but it is very long and confusing."

"No, don't worry, dear," she patted me on the shoulder. "It is enough for me that you are trying to help someone."

I smiled at her. I keenly remember thinking that she was *Englisch*, an *outsider*, a *worldling*, and yet she was so nice and she never even questioned the idea of calling the police if someone was in danger. She did not say she had to call her entire church council to see if it was okay to let me call the authorities. In fact, as soon as I said I was going to help someone else, she seemed ready to help me even though she did not know the entire story.

I rubbed my head in confusion as I walked back down the lane. How could this lady who was not Amish have such a kind soul? In fact, she seemed much kinder than any of the Amish I had met. She had even given me back my five dollars. You would think that in the end kindness was what truly mattered in life, but not according to my church. To them, the most important thing was to follow the church rules. Yet hadn't Jesus preached over and over about being kind and helpful to those in need and not judging your fellow man?

I shrugged as I climbed the stairs to my house. I had already been warned by Phyllis that my habit of analyzing everything was not good and would most likely get me into trouble with the church. And yet, I thought, why did God give me a brain if he did not want me to use it? If I listened to the church leaders, I would do everything they said; I would just turn off my brain and simply walk around with a blank look on my face, as many of the other girls did. That was not me, , and it never would be. I knew I had to be careful or I could very well end up in trouble, and among the Amish that was a very bad place to be, especially for a young, unmarried girl like me.

THE NEXT day I waited anxiously for word from the officer, but none came. I wondered why, but remained hopeful for news. Finally, around one o'clock the next day, I saw Mrs. Fletcher's car coming down the lane. I dropped what I was doing and raced out to meet her.

"Get in." Mrs. Fletcher shouted as she waved me over to the car. "The detective called; I told him to call back in an hour."

When we got back to Mrs. Fletcher's house, I paced anxiously up and down the living room while Mrs. Fletcher sat on the couch, watching television. A couple of times I put my hands over my ears to drown out the noise which bothered me, especially in my agitated state. Finally the phone rang, and Mrs. Fletcher answered.

"Hello. Oh, yes, hold on, Misty is right here." She handed me the phone, and I just stood there, unable to say anything and not sure that I wanted to hear what the officer had to say.

"Hello...Hello," I heard someone saying on the other end of the line.

"Oh, yes. Hello," I finally answered. "It's Misty, "the girl that called you a couple of days ago."

"Hi, Misty," the detective's voice was pleasant. "I just want to update you on the situation here. I sent a couple of my guys up to your parent's house yesterday, and when they got to the farm, they said everything looked fine. Your mother invited them in for coffee, and your step-dad seemed very friendly, too. When they told them that we had a complaint from you about physical abuse, they said your mother got very sad and began to cry. Your step-dad said you had been a troublesome teen and that they had sent you to a special community for help."

I waited for him to pause, a sinking feeling in the pit of my stomach. I had almost forgotten what good actors Brian and Mamma were.

"That's not true," My voice shook. "My step-dad almost killed me. They were just acting for the officers. Did anyone look for bruises on Fanny or Grandma?"

"My officers said they saw a couple bruises, but nothing that could not be explained, especially since they live on a farm."

"Well, did they lift up their dresses and look them over?" I was trying not to cry. "Underneath those dresses they are covered in bruises."

"We can't do that," the detective answered. "They are Amish, and we cannot violate their religion by looking at the women underneath their religious clothing."

"That is ridiculous," I cried. "They know that, and that is why all the bruises are under the clothing. By the way, did you question Fanny and Grandma?"

"Yes; my men asked them if anyone was harming them, and they both shook their heads no. They seemed happy, and your mother was hugging your aunt."

"It was fake!" I insisted.

"Okay, so at this point we have your word against theirs. Given your religion, it is going to be very hard to prove you are not just a rebellious teen trying to get back at your strict parents."

"But I don't understand," I pleaded. "They tortured us for years, and they just get away with it?"

"Do you have any evidence?" the detective asked.

"I don't understand," I repeated. "Why don't you want to help these poor, helpless people?"

"If they were minors, we could remove them," the detective answered. "But given that they are adults and when questioned they did not express any impending threat, we cannot just remove them from the house."

"But they said that because they are scared," I shouted into the phone. "And besides, one has dementia and the other is severely mentally challenged."

"Well.." the detective was thoughtful, "if you are willing to come here and go to Adult Protective Services and explain the situation and then jump through all the hoops that protect religious freedoms, you might be able to accomplish something, but at this point, without more to go on, my hands are tied." He paused for a moment. "Personally," he went on, "I believe your story. Just from your voice tone, I do not believe you are a rebellious teen trying to cause trouble, but my instincts will not hold up in court. And to be honest with you, if it did go to court, I doubt they would be prosecuted. No one will sentence an Amish person to jail without real, hard evidence. They look too innocent, and I don't believe you would be allowed to testify anyway, would you?"

"No," I answered as I tried to choke back tears. I was trying to get Fanny's image out of my head. "I have no way to do any of that" I mumbled. "I just wanted to help them, but I guess I've failed."

"No," the detective answered in a kind voice. "Trying is not failure... failing to try is."

I smiled a little, surprised at how much better that made me feel. It sounded like something I would say to Samantha. I had tried; that was

217

true. I had even argued with my church elders on Grandma's and Fanny's behalf, but somehow it did not seem enough. What was a young Amish girl like me to do, though? I couldn't answer that, so I just stood there, staring at the wall in dazed silence.

"Well, I guess that is it, then," the detective sighed. "Have a nice day, Misty, and thank you for caring. I am sure you will do well in life with your attitude."

"Thank you," I whispered into the phone before I hung up. I felt numb. Once again, Brian and Mamma's 'religion' was protecting them. The protection that was offered to people of strict religions did nothing to protect their victims. How could that be? I walked out of the house without saying anything. I could not speak. I felt so betrayed. I had worked so hard to get this chance to save Fanny, and it had been thrown back in my face like an ice-cold drink. Mrs. Fletcher did not say anything; she just watched me walk out of the house. I think she knew I was hurting, and she was very understanding. Slowly I walked back home, unable to feel any emotion other than total defeat. As I passed the Bishop's house, Phyllis came out and ran to me.

"How did it go?" she whispered, grabbing my dress sleeve.

I just shook my head. "I don't have any hard evidence so they won't do anything because of the freedom of religion thing."

"Oh, I am so sorry," Phyllis searched my face.

I nodded. "Yeah, thanks for swaying the vote for me, Phyllis. At least we tried, huh?"

I left Phyllis standing there as I made my way down the lane. I looked back once and she was still standing there, watching me, her long, blue dress whipping in the wind. She had one frail hand over her mouth and I was surprised to see that she was crying. I was perplexed as to why she was taking such an interest in my case and why she was crying so hard. The sight of her standing there, crying, with her back to her home burned an image into my mind that I will never forget.

THAT FRIDAY, all of the women were headed to the Troyer farm to help with the house cleaning in preparation for church. It is a custom amongst Amish women to gather the Thursday or Friday before church at the member's home where services would be held and to scrub it from top to bottom. Typically, there are ten to fifteen families per church, and anywhere from four to ten churches in one district, depending on the number of Amish settled in the area. If the numbers are large, there will be several districts made up of several churches. Responsibility for hosting church usually comes around to each family's house twice a year. Most Amish women count on the help from fellow mothers and daughters to get much of the heavy cleaning done.

As we trotted out to the lane, we stopped near the mailbox, and Ida jumped down to get the mail. As she hopped back up into the buggy, my heart sank as my eye caught an all-too-familiar address on the corner of an envelope.

"This one is addressed to Misty," Ida said, waving it around in the back seat. "Misty, Misty," she repeated my name over and over.

"Ida, give it to me," I reached for the letter.

She started laughing—not realizing what was in the letter. "Boing," she said, hitting my bonnet with it.

Ella grabbed it from her and handed it to me. Lillian raised her eyebrows and looked away. It was not hard to see that she greatly disapproved of my calling the police, and that I was now was getting letters from my real parents. She thought I was proud and thought too much of myself.

"Read it us. Read it to us," Ida chimed from the back, mischievously yanking my bonnet off my head. I heard the clip clop of a buggy behind us and did not want to be seen in public without my bonnet on; it would start tongues wagging. I turned around in the seat, trying to grab the bonnet from Ida, who was giggling and wearing it over her own, smaller bonnet. Finally Lillian yelled at her to behave, and I put my bonnet back on before the other buggy reached us. I made funny faces at Ida, who was now pouting, and tucked the letter into my dress pocket to read later.

When we got to the Troyer farm, I saw Samantha and a couple other girls taking everything out of the washhouse to give it a good cleaning. I hopped out of the buggy, letting Ella and Ida take it over to the barn. As I neared Samantha, I waved the letter in her direction. She wiped her hands on her green apron and pulled a letter out of her own pocket.

"Oh, you got one, too," I could not help feeling relieved.

"Hmm," Samantha grunted. "I see you did not read yours yet."

"No," I took off my bonnet. "I could not make myself open it."

Samantha grabbed it out of my hands and opened it, shaking her head as she read.

"These people are full of bul***it," she said in English. "I cannot believe how they try to lie to us like we weren't there when they starved us and left us in the back of that stupid truck in the freezing cold and all that other stuff."

219

I sighed and took the letter. "You know I called the police, right?"

"Yeah, I know," Samantha looked away.

"Are you okay with it?" I looked at her trying to gauge her reaction.

"Yeah, I am okay with it I guess," Samantha shrugged and angrily grabbing the wash tub again. "I would be more okay if they had locked them up and thrown away the key, but judging from the letter, they didn't do anything."

I put a finger to my lips as the Borntreger girls walked up. "We will talk later," I motioned with my head in their direction, and then walked to the house to get my work assignment. On the way, I finally brought myself to read my letter. I also read Samantha's letter, which she had given me.

Mine was a devastating letter, calling me a traitor and the devil's child. They said they had sent a letter to the Bishop explaining the real story, and from that point on if I sent them anything, it would go straight into the stove. I was dead to them forever. I had never existed, as far as they were concerned. I felt a tear trickle down my cheek, but then wondered why I cared. I didn't know why, but I knew I cared. After I read my letter, I opened Samantha's. Mamma had drawn hearts on it and told her she was worried about her. She said that if Samantha ever needed anything to just send them a letter and they would be there for her. She ended the letter with "Love, Mom and Dad." I felt my heart constrict. How I had always longed for those words. "Love, Mom." They were such precious words.

I swallowed and stuffed the letters back in their envelopes. It was over. I would never see or hear from them again. This was it, and I had to let it go, or I would never be happy. Just let it go, I breathed. Let it go.

Little Lizzie Troyer toddled out to me with her arms up. I smiled and scooped her up, burying my face in the black curls that popped out from under her kapp. She giggled and put her chubby arms around my neck. *This was my life, and I must look to the future*, I thought as I tickled Lizzie's stomach. I had too much attention on me already. I certainly could not afford anymore.

AS SUMMER approached, thoughts of Fanny and Grandma were pushed farther and farther to the back of my mind. My days were full tending the garden and working in the slaughterhouse as the first waves of the butchering season came. Any spare time that we had was spent in the hay and wheat fields.

Despite all the work we already had to do, Jacob decided to start an organic egg business. The business offered five hundred chickens and an agreement to sell the eggs at the local supermarket. We bought the business, and the men from the community gathered to help build the giant chicken house. These were fun times in the summer sun. Many women came along to help with the noon meals. Of course, Samantha and Matty came to help as well. As the hot July sun shone down on us, we made pitchers of lemonade on a makeshift table we set up outside. When Matty went inside to get more sugar, I turned to Samantha as she was cutting lemons.

"Samantha," I whispered, "what is this I hear about you and Matty's family moving in the fall?"

Samantha nodded. "We are moving to Wisconsin. I wanted to tell you before you heard the rumors, but I see you already heard."

I nodded with a frown. "Why are you guys moving?"

Samantha sighed. "Mom's family is there, and her dad is sick. We are going to take over the farm, and Mom's parents will live in the Doddy house."

"Why is Matty's family going?" I whispered, sad at the news of losing my sister *and* my best friend at the same time.

"Matty's uncle lives there and he has wanted them to come back and work in his furniture shop for years. It will be easier to move together rather than separately, so we will move at the same time. We are having an auction in the fall to pay for the move."

"Oh, Samantha," I whispered, "I am so sad." I put my arms around her.

Samantha nodded. "I know. I will need to make new friends, but I guess it will be an adventure. We will write every week. Mom says it will be better for the two of us to be separated. We will fit in better, she thinks."

I sighed as Matty came back with the sugar. Matty looked at me and cocked her head. "Oh, you heard," she looked relieved, as if she were not supposed to tell.

I nodded. "Yeah," I grinned playfully. "About a week ago already."

"I wanted to tell you," Matty pretended to pout, "but we were trying to keep it a secret until later in the year." She sighed. "I really don't want to go. I will miss you and my cousins. I am not going to make new friends so easily, and the youngie group there is huge."

I smiled and raised my eyebrows mischievously. "Lots of young men, huh, Matty?"

"Yeah," Samantha giggled. "Brand new fresh meat to drool over."

Matty blushed and slapped at us both with her dish towel. "You two are terrible," she said as she poured lemonade into the glasses. I laughed, but I wondered if maybe that was the real reason she was moving. Matty, her brother and her sister, Laura, had never been on dates. The prospect of having three children that would never marry was not good for any family.

As we poured the lemonade, the little children, wanting to help, grabbed the cups from the table and ran around to the men, giving them to anyone that reached for a cup. We laughed as little Edna tripped over her dress, spilling the lemonade she was carrying, and even though the cup was empty, she handed it to Isaiah Troyer. He laughed and tapped her playfully on the head with the empty cup.

"Here, Edna," he said, handing it back to her. "Tell Emma J to put some lemonade in here for me." He glanced at me and grinned.

I felt my face growing warm and heard a slight gasp from Matty.

"I knew it," she whispered in my ear.

I swallowed and frowned at her in frustration and embarrassment. "Knew what?" I asked as innocently as I could.

"Yeah, right," Samantha said in English, smirking. "Play dumb, as if no one knows."

I was only half listening to them as I caught Jacob watching the whole incident from the other side of the wall. I caught his eye, and he stared at me with what looked like anger.

I poured the lemonade into the glass with shaking hands and timidly smiled back at Isaiah. He nodded to me before he drank the lemonade. When I glanced back at Jacob, I saw him furiously ripping nails out of a board. What was wrong with him, I wondered? Why did he care if Isaiah was paying attention to me? *As if I really don't know.*

After lunch, the women gathered to work on a quilt we had put in the frame the night before. I loved quilting, but on that day I could not concentrate. While the other women gossiped around the quilt, I motioned for Samantha to follow me outside. Unable to hold it in, I told her about the uncomfortable situation with Lillian and Jacob and what I had witnessed that day.

Samantha nodded. "It is the same at my house, sometimes, most of the time not, but sometimes. I don't know what to do but ignore it."

"I can't," I put a hand to cheek. "I am going for instruction for baptism soon, and then I know Isaiah and I will most likely start seeing each other. He has been paying attention to me ever since I got here. I am afraid Jacob is going to do something to disrupt my plans because of some crush he has on me."

Samantha nodded again. "Yeah. I did not want to say anything," she looked around, "but I do live in the Deacon's house, and I saw Jacob and the ministers gather outside the other evening. I don't know what they were saying, but I saw them agreeing about something, and I really think it was about us."

I wrung my hands. I did not know what was coming, but I knew it was not good.

I FOUND out what was going on a couple of nights later when Jacob called for me to come out to the barn. As I came downstairs, I saw two buggies parked outside. I felt a knot forming in the pit of my stomach as I walked into the barn and saw Samantha standing there in front of the ministers. They motioned for me to stand beside her, and as I glanced at her, she shook her head to tell me she did not know what was going on.

The Bishop cleared his throat and said, "It has been brought to our attention that Emma has been going out of her way to attract the attention of the men and boys. We do not like to see such behavior in our young women. We have questioned Lillian, and she said Emma has been too familiar with the men of this household."

I gasped and looked over at Lillian. I could not believe it. She had really done it, and Jacob was going along with it. I saw Phyllis in the back with her mouth pursed. I don't think she believed the accusation, but she could not help me. I started to speak, but Samantha grabbed my hand and shook her head, so I stopped. I was so outraged at this behavior. I stared at the Bishop through squinted eyes. How dare this man who grabbed at every maid he could get his hands on tell me I was acting indecently?

Matty's dad nodded in agreement with the Bishop. "It is important for us to protect our young brothers from these advances. We have been made aware of the actions of both of you, such as pushing your kapps back in the presence of men and trying to make eye contact with them. The Bishop nodded. "Because of this and for other reasons we think it is best if you do not date for a year after your baptisms. We will leave it up to the discretion of your Amish parents and the parents of our young men but this is what we are recommending."

I saw Samantha's face crumble. A girl without a boyfriend or future husband was truly a nobody.

"None of these accusations are true," I stepped forward. "I am tired of being caught in the middle of Jacob and Lillian's marital squabbles. That is what this is about and I want it to stop."

"Silence!" the Bishop's voice was angry. I saw Phyllis shaking her head at me in the back row where she sat breastfeeding her baby.

"Why?" I shot back at him. "It is not right that Lillian is constantly accusing me of trying to get attention from Dad. It's not true and it's not right, and I do not want to live in that house anymore. I want to live by myself," I clenched my fists at my side.

"I told you to be quiet!" the Bishop shouted angrily.

I realized I was not helping my case, but I could not back down. I wanted answers as to why they were able to do this to me or anyone else.

Matty's dad looked at me and shook his head. "These are wicked thoughts you have," he looked genuinely sad. "You know we do not allow unmarried girls to live alone unless they are in their fifties. Even then it is greatly discouraged."

"But why?" I insisted, trying to choke back angry tears.

"It makes access too easy for young men," the Bishop answered, looking at me with all the authority of a king.

"How dare you talk to me like that?" I exploded. "Is that what you think of me, or what you wish I was?" I shrieked at him. I was so angry. I was being falsely accused and implicated as a whore who would open her door to any man who walked by.

"I will not tell you to be silent again!" the Bishop shouted at me.

I saw looks of shock on everyone's faces. They could not believe I was talking back to the Bishop. But I was not sorry. They all had to have known what kind of man he was, and yet he was standing here, passing moral judgment on me, and I had not even done anything wrong.

I heard Samantha whisper for me to shut up. I looked at everyone, turned on my heel and walked into the house.

Once in my room, I sat on my bed and cried. There was no way Isaiah would wait nearly two years for me and I knew his mother would definitely not let him date me until a year after I had been baptized. He was already in his mid-twenties and ready for a serious relationship. He was tall with curly brown hair. He was very nice, and I really liked him. I had noticed he was nicer to his horse than a lot of the other boys, who merely treated their horses like objects. Ever since I had arrived at the community he had been smiling at me and passing me things under the youngie table. I felt Isaiah could tell when I was sad, and he could always make me smile, even when I did not want to.

I wondered if someone was going to talk to him about me, and I wondered if he would believe them. I could not believe this was happening to me. It was so embarrassing. I had not tried to seduce anyone, so why was it okay to falsely accuse me? I cried, heartbroken, into my pillow. Who knew if, after the Bann was lifted, I would find anyone? I can't just be an old maid, I thought. I have too much to share to simply be a nobody my whole life. And there was no way I would ever be Jacob's mistress. I sat there feeling numb as the tears rolled unchecked down my cheeks.

I did not come out of my room for the rest of the evening. I did not help with the chores or eat supper. I just sat on my bed, looking out the window. Once, Ida popped her head in the room and asked me what was wrong. I told her I was feeling sick and just wanted to lie down. She came over to me and felt my forehead.

"You don't have a fever," she looked into my eyes. She noticed my tear streaked face and hugged me, and then went back out to eat supper.

As I sat there, I finally came to the conclusion that there was no way to fight this. I would just have to prove to them that they were wrong about me. No matter what they did to me, it could never be as bad as what I had experienced with my mother. I knew that I had called too much attention to myself by calling the police, and some people were whispering that I thought myself smarter than everyone else. *Oh well,* I thought, *there is nothing to do but stick it out and show them that none of this will break my spirit.* That was what they wanted, I knew, but I vowed to myself that it would not happen.

ON THE days following I threw myself into my work. I loved working, and accomplishing things always gave me a sense of worth. My plan was to work as fast as I could. I found myself acting like Matty's sister, Laura. I kept pulling my kapp forward, trying to cover every strand of hair. This was difficult since my hair was fine and slippery.

Whenever I came in contact with Jacob, I did not even look at him and quickly walked in the other direction whenever possible. I could tell it was making him angry, but I did not care. I was angry, angrier than he could imagine. I carried on like this for a week without having to say a word to him, but one day he finally he cornered me in the barn. I tried to get out when I saw him coming, but Lucky was being difficult; Jacob walked toward me and grabbed Lucky's reins.

"We can't keep doing this," Jacob grabbed my dress sleeve. "The children are noticing, and children talk."

"You should have thought of that before you let your wife lie to the ministers," I tried to pull away. "And stay away from me," I shouted. "You are the real reason I got in trouble."

"No." Jacob shook his head. "You don't know the whole story. It was Isaiah's mother and Lillian who got you in trouble."

"But Samantha saw you at the Deacon's house," I was not sure whether or not to believe him.

Jacob nodded. "I was trying to help you and your sister out of this. It appears that Isaiah's mother noticed him looking at you in church, and she was not happy about it, so she told her husband that she saw you push your kapp back when you knew Isaiah was watching."

"No, that's not true," I bit my lip in agitation. "I never did that."

"Let me finish," Jacob held up his hand. "After that, Isaiah's mother talked to Lillian, and she did not stop to think if it was true or not. Eventually, the whole church got into a gossiping frenzy about you and your sister; I was just trying to help you is all."

"Well," I scraped the barn floor with my shoe, "this is all ridiculous and unfair. If you want to help me, stay away from me." I clicked at Lucky to follow and started out of the barn. I looked back at Jacob and saw him watching me. I was glad that he had tried to help, but now, how could I get him to leave me alone?

Ancient Traditions

"Facts do not cease to exist because they are ignored."

—Aldous Huxley, Complete Essays 2, 1926-29

After that incident I tried to ignore Jacob whenever I could, and Lillian noticed and rewarded me by calling me her daughter—something she had not previously done. I realized that any contact with males inside the church was going to get me in trouble somehow and so I decided to try and ignore them all, except for the ones who were under seventeen.

Jacob was angered by this turn of events, and I could tell the honeymoon stage of his attraction to me was over. Be that as it may, he tried even harder to get me alone, but I always kept one of the children close to me in order to prevent his advances.

I was starting to realize that Jacob's treatment of Lillian was worse than I had previously thought and that made me sad for her and angry at Jacob. He took every chance he had to ridicule her and often made her cry. She in turn was generally very submissive and I could tell she tried hard to please him but she couldn't. Sometimes I would walk up on her when she was just staring out the window with tears streaming down her cheeks, other times when I would walk out to the outhouse I would hear her sobbing and quietly retrace my steps.

She sometimes referred to herself as a "worn out shoe that was no longer wanted" in front of Jacob and the children, but even then Jacob showed her no sympathy and continued to ridicule her for being to heavy (which she was not) or to slow and so on. It was no wonder that she had not taken nicely to me and was sometimes hostile. I was getting what she so much longed for from her husband, attention and emotional affection. I

227

had not asked for it but it was there and poor Lillian was beside herself with sorrow and jealousy.

    *A*S FALL approached, I began going to the Borntreger's to help them get ready for the auction. I was sad at not seeing Isaiah at the singings anymore, but the whole ordeal was fading into the back of my mind as I prepared to say farewell to my sister and my best friend.

    Despite my home life, I was happy again, and although Samantha was leaving, I was excited for her to start a new adventure. We did not hear anything from Mamma and Brian, which was a good way to let our problems with them fade into the background. My new connection with Lillian made me happy, and finally I was able to breathe and even thrive in my new home.

    The day of the auction was exciting. It was mid-September. The week before the auction, the women of the community gathered to help the Borntreger's make baked goods to sell in order to help pay for their move. We made over two hundred loaves of bread and five hundred pies. It was so much fun as the women made an assembly line formation. One woman put the bottom crust on, another put in the filling, another put on the top crust and so on. There were many food fights and much bread flour in our hair as the youngie girls played practical jokes on each other. The married women looked at our antics and tried not to laugh, but were not always successful.

    Samantha's family and Matty's family each rented a semi-truck that would haul their most precious items to the Wisconsin farm. The rest of the things would be sold at the auction where Amish and *Englisch* alike would bid for things standing side by side. The young men had the task of grooming the horses and cleaning the farm equipment. They also hung signs that advertised the auction in the local town. I really loved the sense of community we had. It was so rewarding to pitch in and get your hands dirty while helping a fellow family in their time of need.

    On the day of the auction, I was with Samantha, helping sell baked goods to the *Englisch* that showed up. Some tried to take our pictures, which was extremely annoying. We had to turn our faces from the camera because it is against Amish rules to have your picture taken.

    We sold all of the baked goods by noon and then we were free to watch the auction. It was fun, especially when the quilts came up. Several women had donated or made quilts for the auction, including Lillian and myself.

    "There's mine," I pointed to the sunshine and shadow quilt I had designed myself.

"Yeah, thanks for that," Samantha smiled. "It is gorgeous, and I think it will fetch a pretty penny."

I smiled. I had had a lot of fun picking out the colors for it. I lost myself in the deep blues and pinks and greens. I loved making quilts so much. It was like creating a flower, I thought.

"Do I hear seven hundred? Now eight?" I heard the auctioneer calling in his sing-song voice. "Now eight and a half?" he droned on. "Sold!" he called out. Eight hundred dollars. That was a great price for an auction, I thought. Hmm.... maybe I did have a real eye for colors.

That night after the auction, Samantha, Annie and the rest of the children climbed into the back of the semi. "It will save on bus fare," Samantha told me, clapping her hands. "It's going to be so much fun."

I waved goodbye as the semi pulled away. Samantha and I both tried not to cry; we tried to tell each other we were embarking on a great journey, and that the future was going to be bright and exciting for us. As the semi pulled away, however, I could not help the tears that rolled down my cheeks. I quickly wiped them away and told myself this would be better for Samantha, as there would be less gossip about the two of us now.

That winter, I started instruction for baptism with the rest of the youngie. Normally, instruction for baptism would be in the spring, but the church had decided to have one that winter since they did not want to wait until the next Fall to have me baptized. The same had been agreed for the church Samantha would now attend. This was an exciting time for me, as it was a rite of passage all youngies must pass through. After the first song was sung, the ministers went upstairs and the youngies that were to be baptized followed and sat in front of the ministers, who then spoke to us about our forefathers and the rules of the church. After half-an-hour, we came downstairs again, and the ministers followed a few minutes later. It was a very exciting day for me when we started instruction for baptism. I would finally, truly belong, I thought.

THAT NOVEMBER brought with it my twentieth birthday. I sighed as I looked in the mirror that morning. Wow, I thought. I am twenty years old. The last two years had flown by in a whirlwind of life-changing events. As I looked into the mirror, I remembered being on the mountain, and the sheer loneliness and terror that had enveloped every day of my life. I stepped closer to the mirror and inspected my face, looking for any traces of scars that might be left from the dog bite so long ago. There was only a faint scar on my left cheek and one under my right eye. *I am lucky,* I thought. Those scars could have been much worse. As I put the towel back over the mirror, I rubbed the top of my head, trying to relieve one of the awful headaches that still plagued me at times.

That day, Lillian told me we had to start collecting things for my hope chest. Phyllis had her brother-in-law make one for my birthday. Usually the hope chest is given to a girl on her sixteenth or seventeenth birthday, but better late than never, I thought. I could not help remembering how uneventful and scary most of my birthdays had been. This was such a nice change, I thought. How sweet of Phyllis.

I was excited as I breathed in the smell of the cedar wood. A hope chest was used to store gifts that were given to a girl for her birthday or Christmas, as well as presents from her boyfriend. These presents were usually dishes, clocks, salt and pepper shakers or anything that would be useful when she became a married woman and set up housekeeping herself. It was every girl's hope to have a brimming chest full of colorful dishes and whatever else she might need by the time she was married. Each girl also made three quilts for herself, which the family or women from the community helped quilt. Happily, I opened my new chest and saw there was already a small set of pretty, light blue plates inside. They were a birthday present from Lillian and Jacob.

"Oh, thank you," I squealed, and Lillian smiled at me.

"It is very empty, so the girls in the community are going to donate one item from their hope chests to yours. I am not supposed to tell you, but I thought it was a great idea. Phyllis asked the girls if they would like to do this, and they all thought it would be fun."

"That is so sweet," I hugged the chest with both arms.

Ella came up to examine my hope chest. "Oh," she stroked the top. "I am going to get one pretty soon too, right, Mom?"

Lillian laughed at her fourteen-year-old daughter. "Getting a little ahead of yourself there, aren't you?" she asked playfully.

I smiled at Lillian. She seemed a tiny bit happier lately, I thought. It was like I was her ally now.

That winter—in between the daily household duties and the long nights spent getting eggs ready for market—I started piecing my first quilt for my hope chest. I chose a North Star pattern that combined many shades of blue. I had wanted to use white, but since white was not allowed in quilts that were to remain in an Amish household, I picked the lightest shade of blue I could find in Lillian's fabric closet. Lillian explained to Ella and me that white was not allowed in Amish quilts because that was the color the *Englisch* most commonly used for their bedspreads, and we did not want to be like the *Englisch*. Ella and I nodded in agreement.

One day in December as Jacob sat reading the Die Blatt, the Amish newspaper, he abruptly asked me if I wanted to write for the paper. I saw Lillian frown, so I just shrugged, but secretly I was tingling at the idea. Writing for the Amish newspaper meant there would be a piece with your town or district name at the top followed by the events that happened in the community, such as births, deaths, baptisms and funny tidbits of news.

"Yeah," Jacob nodded. "She is always walking around on Sundays with that poetry book she writes in. She would probably be a good writer. And no one else in our community will do it. It would be nice to see us represented in this paper, too."

"Well," Lillian looked at me and nodded approvingly at the way I was ignoring Jacob, "I guess if she wants to. Do you want to?" she asked, turning to me.

I clapped my hands together with excitement. "I would love to," I smiled happily.

That day, I started writing for the Amish newspaper. I had never written anything before, but found it fairly easy. I tried to put in a lot of comical happenings in addition to covering the serious topics. The next month, I eagerly grabbed the copy of the Die Blatt out of Ella's hands.

"Let me see. Let me see," Ida and Ella both clamored as they tried to read the page where I found my piece. At the bottom of my article, I saw an editor's note. Eagerly, I read what he had written. I smiled as I read the sentence.

"This is the entertaining writing we are looking for from our writers. We need less yawns and more fun in the writing, guys."

"Wow, they really like your writing," Ella smiled at me with pride. "You could be famous. Everyone who gets the paper is going to read this."

Lillian frowned at Ella, and Ella quickly bowed her head with humility.

"The owners of that newspaper are of a more liberal Ordnung than we are. Be careful what you send in. I saw once where two different Amish communities carried on a long debate through that paper," Lillian admonished, looking at me sternly.

I smiled. This was exciting for me, and even though I had to be careful not to become proud, it truly was an exciting feeling, especially given the fact that I had very little education.

The next church Sunday, I saw people grinning at me, and I knew it was because of the funny rhymes I had made in my article—I decided to rhyme half of the happenings in my next piece.

THAT WINTER was very cold, and the entire community came down with terrible colds that turned into pneumonia. All the old home remedies were pulled out as croupy babies and children with swollen tonsils cried endlessly. As a result of this epidemic, a boy in a neighboring community died from pneumonia. It was a very sad affair. The boy was a very sweet, nine-year-old, and his death was unusual since it was usually babies that died. The boy's family believed in the old ways and refused to take him to the hospital, despite the fact that he was obviously dying.

His father staunchly held to the old tradition of waiting three days before taking a sick person to the doctor. If they survived the three days, they were going to live; if they did not, they would have died anyway. People in my community did not go to the doctor often. Broken bones and wide cuts could be taken care of by any Amish person in the area with a talent for these things, but each family had the right to take someone to the hospital if they believed the family member was going to die. On the other hand, they also had the right to not take them if that was what they wanted.

"That's outrageous...they just let their son die," I commented between coughs one day. "They just wrapped him up in a blanket and put him by the stove for three days while he got worse and worse."

Jacob shook his head at me to be quiet. "It is not our place to judge," he said solemnly. "It is the practice of their family, and we must respect it."

"Well, I agree with Emma" Elam announced as he shook hay out of his hair. "Just because family traditions allow you to kill someone doesn't mean it is okay."

I saw Jacob grow angry, and he told us both to be silent.

"It is outrageous," I mumbled under my breath as I hooked up my coat in preparation to go out and help Phyllis. Snow was swirling outside, and a cold, northeasterly wind was blowing across the flat area where our farm was located. It nearly blew me off my feet as I made my way across the field to the Bishop's house. As I blew in through the door, I was met by the sound of crying children. School had been canceled due to the severity of the storm, and Phyllis looked ready to collapse as she tried to soothe the six feverish children that were all reaching for her. Peter sat in the rocking chair—*was he reading the Bible, or just staring into space?* I wondered as I shivered with a light fever.

"Oh," Phyllis sighed as I came through the door. "I am so glad to see you." She handed me the youngest child, who was screaming at the top of his lungs.

"Are sure you are okay, Phyllis?" I asked. I tried not to notice her stomach, which was beginning to show the signs of early pregnancy.

232

Phyllis nodded. "Yes, I just need a break. The story of the Byler boy has me freaked out. I hope my children are not sicker than they look."

"I will make everyone tea," I looked at the miserable children. "It will make everyone feel better."

I mixed peppermint, chamomile and yarrow together to make a tea I hoped everyone would like. Amish children usually liked tea, as it was a sweet drink. It was a little more difficult to get down them when they were sick, but I managed. I winced when I looked at their tonsils and saw inflamed, bright red goblets on them.

"My throat hurts so bad" Danny cried.

"Mine too," Katie whimpered.

I sighed as I felt my own temperature skyrocketing.

"We have to swab their tonsils with turpentine," Phyllis was agitated that her children were suffering so much. "They are in too much pain."

I nodded and went to the basement to get the turpentine. Using a Q-tip, I painted the smelly turpentine on the children's tonsils and backs of their throats. This was also an old remedy, used for the numbing properties the turpentine provided. I was not sure how safe it was, but it seemed to work for tonsillitis and strep throat.

After administering the turpentine, I wrapped the children in quilts and sat them by the wood stove while I made supper. I rummaged through Phyllis's basement and pantry where I found mostly crackers, flour and potatoes. There were not many canned goods either, I shook my head. Despite all of Lillian's help and the fact that she sent me and the other girls to help out often, Phyllis was having a very hard time, and her creepy husband wasn't much interested in helping.

After the supper dishes were done I staggered back across the field in the freezing snow. As I pushed the machine shop door open, I collapsed on the cement floor, only half conscious; I felt Jacob pick me up and heard him yell for Elam to help him carry me upstairs. I awoke a few hours later to the sound of Grandma Schrock's voice mumbling over me. I put a hand on my feverish forehead and then opened my eyes to see Ella standing next to me, holding the palm of my hand open as Grandma Schrock mumbled and twirled a fingernail clipper over some capsules that were on my palm. I tried to pull my hand away, but Ella held it firmly and I was too weak to resist.

"She doesn't like this sort of stuff, Grandma," Ella whispered.

Grandma Shrock nodded. "I know," she concentrated on the fingernail clipper. "But she is very sick and might not last till morning if we don't get some medicine in her."

I felt a burning sensation on my chest, and the strong smell of ground mustard made my eyes water. My chest felt tight, and every breath I took was a struggle. Grandma Shrock told Ella to keep me sitting upright while she went for more supplies.

"I told Grandma you didn't like the fingernail clipper thing," Ella patted me on the head. "But you are so very sick and we did not know what else to do. You should never have gone to help Phyllis."

I nodded weakly and smiled at her. The fingernail clipper and arts like it were highly controversial, but they were old traditions amongst the Amish. There were certain families that practiced it, while others considered it a form of witchcraft. However, among the Amish, families were allowed to practice their own handed-down traditions. I personally did not like the use of the fingernail clipper. I thought it too creepy, although it seemed to be accurate at times.

One of the Troyer women, who was now an advocate against its use, claimed that when she was with the youngie, all the girls got in a group and asked the fingernail clipper how many children they would have. She said that it had told her she would have seven boys and three girls. At the present she had six boys and two girls—hardly a coincidence, she thought. She said the idea of knowing the future was playing with her mind.

The fingernail clipper was used to tell the sex of unborn babies as well, and almost always seemed to be accurate. Although these practices and others like them were old superstitions, I found them to be rather odd, and when Matty and Samantha tried to get me to use the fingernail clipper to see if I would ever marry, I threw it as far as I could into the nearby pond. They laughed at me. The fingernail clipper told them they would both marry, so they were in good moods.

I was awakened half-an-hour later when Grandma Schrock returned, and Lillian and Jacob followed her into the bedroom.

"She is very sick," Grandma Schrock shook her head as she held her palm over mine. "I am not feeling any electricity from her."

"What should I do?" Lillian wrapped her hands in her light blue apron.

Grandma Schrock shook her head and dumped some more capsules into my hand. This time the fingernail clipper began swirling in a fast clockwise motion, meaning this was the medicine that I needed. My throat was so swollen I could not swallow the capsules, though, so Grandma Schrock put them in water and I choked them down.

I lay in bed for three days, and every day Grandma, who was the Amish medicine woman for our church, visited me, mumbling as she tried to feel my body's strength through my palm. She put different herbs and capsules in my hand, and my chest was blistered from the strong mustard plasters, but to everyone's great relief, I was getting better. Although I still did not like the fingernail clipper routine, I had to admit I had been very ill and now I was better. It might have just been the mustard plaster, but who could tell for sure?

I sat in the rocking chair, knitting, for the next week. I was irritated at being sick and tried to get up and help around the house, but Ella, who was enjoying the role of my nursemaid, made me sit back in the rocking chair and stuffed quilts around me to keep me warm. Grandma Schrock checked on me every other day. She told me she thought that I had caught strep throat, bronchitis and pneumonia all at once. I smiled and told her I really appreciated her help in saving me.

She smiled at me. "You know, I will be honest. I did not really like you much in the beginning, but since I have been around you, I feel an energy coming from you. Here, take my clipper."

I shook my head. "No, I don't want to."

"But you admit you got better. Why are you so afraid of it?" Grandma frowned.

"I don't know, I just don't want it."

"I think you could be the next medicine person in our family," Grandma Schrock closed my fingertips around the string attached to the fingernail clipper. "Not everyone possesses enough energy for it, but when I saw you with the babies and the horses, I knew you had it."

I felt squeamish as she held her hand under the fingernail clipper to test the amount of energy that ran between my hand and hers. After about a second, she yanked her hand back, rubbing it.

"You have very strong energy," she said matter-of-factly. "I want you to start stopping by every so often, and I will show you many things from my medicine closet."

I shook my head no, but she just nodded at me and left.

"That's exciting," Ella came over and rocked the rocking chair for me. "She has tested all of the children and grandchildren, but so far she has not found anyone with the right energy. Aren't you excited?"

"No," I answered, picking up a book. "I don't believe in that stuff."

"But it made you better," Ella frowned at me in confusion.

"The reason for that is unknown," I shrugged. "Besides, I don't mind if other people use it. *I* just don't want to."

"I think you are being ungrateful and selfish," Ella gave the rocking chair a hard push.

I smiled. "Maybe, and maybe not, Who knows?"

After a week of being sick, Grandma Schrock told Lillian and Jacob that I was still unable to go to church that Sunday. The thermometer was dipping below minus twenty degrees, and the icy wind that came into the buggy was a danger for my lungs. I was disappointed, feeling I had been a prisoner in the house for too long, but I knew Grandma Schrock was right, and I could not afford to get sick again. When the rest of the children heard I would be staying home, they begged to stay home as well, and Lillian and Jacob decided that the Bishop's children would stay with all of us and only the adults would go to church.

I spent most of the day rocking little Henry, who was still not feeling well. The rest of the children grabbed the checker games and coloring books and camped out on the floor.

"Hey," Elam complained when he saw the children everywhere. "It's not noon yet; they can't play."

All the children looked at me since I was the oldest. I smiled at their pleading faces and shrugged.

"Oh, come on, Elam," I frowned playfully. "Everyone is sick. I think it is okay."

Elam thought for a moment. "Okay," he agreed. "As long as you don't tell if I read this book in here." He grinned as he flashed the cover at me.

I was taken aback to see it was a romance novel with a nearly naked woman on the front.

"Where did you get that?" I walked over to him and picked up the book.

"Oh, it was easy," he smiled. "Whenever we go to the Fletcher place to help out, I just take them. Mrs. Fletcher has boxes of them in her garage, and all the guys just take them. She saw Leroy M take one last week, and she just laughed at us. I don't think she cares."

I raised my eyebrows, trying not to blush at the erotic picture on the front cover. "Okay," I tapped him playfully on the head with the book. He would read it anyway, I thought.

After a couple of hours with children playing and shouting through the house, I decided I was ready for a time out and made them sit quietly with books so the littlest ones could take a nap. The snow swirled outside the window. As I sat back down and rocked the baby I almost felt happy, here I was surrounded by sweet small children, it was so much better than my life had been with Mamma and Brian. And yet something nagged in the back of my mind. I could not quite put my finger on it. It seemed that something in the distance was looming out in front of me, something dark and foreboding. I don't know why or how I could have known that but I did. I just did not know what it was.

Forced to Forgive

"Goodness is something chosen. When a man cannot choose, he ceases to be a man."

—Anthony Burgess, A Clockwork Orange

Slowly everyone got over the terrible colds and pneumonia that had spread through the community and March brought with it warmer weather and the hope of brighter days. I started going to visit Grandma Schrock when I could and I enjoyed drawing on her knowledge of herbs and procedures. The medical part I enjoyed and was eager to learn, but every time she referred to the fingernail clipper or her ritual chants, I shied away. Grandma Schock told me that during the summer, she was going to take me to a chiropractor who specialized in buried feelings that cause illnesses. I furrowed my brow when she told me how this chiropractor would ask a question and then pull on a raised arm to get the answer. If the arm remained upright, it was the truth. If it went limp, then it was false.

"That sounds a little weird," I looked at her skeptically, not wanting to hurt her feelings but at the same time not wanting someone asking me questions I might not want to answer.

"No, it's not weird. A lot of our people do this. From these questions you create a script that you then chant every night, and it will make you feel better," she told me with a nod of her head.

I raised my eyebrows, still skeptical. This was definitely something I wanted no part of but I was not sure I had any choice.

As the end of March approached, I started to get nervous about my upcoming baptism. Our communities had decided to delay baptisms until the first of April and then start over again the next spring to get on track again. A letter from Samantha told me she was feeling the same way about her baptism, but that she was also excited because a young man in the community was paying special attention to her; she hoped he would wait another year for her. Samantha and I wrote letters to each other every other week and kept each other updated on what was happening; Matty and I wrote each other once a month. I was glad to hear that Matty had finally gone on a date. Even if it was only a one-time thing, at least that was an improvement.

The instruction for baptism classes had proved to be long and boring; the ministers went over the rules of the church, how to act and so on. I didn't understand all these rules. I had once remarked at the dinner table,

"If we really have to dress plain and simple like the apostles say, then why do we dress like they did in the 1500s during the Reformation? We are we wearing the style of that time when the church was formed. That means that the church forefathers actually dressed like the people of their time, and no differently."

Jacob frowned at me. "You should not say such things, It is not your place."

"But I don't understand," I went on, truly confused and wanting a concrete answer for once. "If Jesus said to do away with oppressing traditions of men, then why do we have to follow every little detail of the rules if we want to get into heaven?"

"We must follow these rules or we most certainly will not go to heaven," Jacob admonished sternly.

Ella frowned. "But Jesus was not Amish. Did he go to heaven?"

Elam burst into laughter. "Yeah, Dad, did Jesus go to heaven?"

Jacob frowned, and Lillian in her low voice said, "Of course he went to heaven, silly."

"But," I continued, "Jesus wore sandals and a robe. Why can't we wear sandals?"

"Enough," Jacob slammed his fist onto the table. "I cannot believe you are talking like this. This is ridiculous."

I knew better than to continue, but even though I was being a little smart-mouthed, I could not help but wonder why Jesus could wear sandals and a robe and I could not. If we really had to be different from the world, then why did we not dress like they had in Jesus' time rather than the 1500s? Why did it matter so much which century we picked, anyway? And why would wearing sandals send me to hell?

That afternoon, I got a little uneasy as I saw Jacob walk over to the Bishop's farm. I puckered my lips as I always did when I was disappointed. Why did he have to tell the Bishop what I had said? I was merely asking questions. It did not mean I was going to publish them in Die Blatt.

That night as the children and I candled the eggs in order to get them ready for market, I heard Lillian's voice travel up the stairwell, calling for me to come out to the barn.

"You're in trouble," Elam chanted, pointing at me.

I walked slowly into the barn. I was a little nervous since my baptism was so close at hand. I wondered if I was going to be punished or just reprimanded. As I approached the barn, I could see the yellow flicker of lamp light and hear the low mumble of men's voices. When I entered, the ministers all turned and looked at me with grave, solemn faces. I knew that look and did not like it. Quietly I stood in front of them and glanced over at Lillian, who was standing off to the side. Her face was blank, and she looked back at me with no expression.

The Bishop cleared his throat as he always did before he spoke. "It has been brought to our attention," his voice was low, "that you have been questioning the rules of the church and have been doing so in front of children who in turn started asking questions of their own." He paused and looked at me before continuing.

"You know that you should not be talking so in front of the children, or anyone for that matter. I do not understand why we must constantly reprimand you, and why you cannot simply obey the rules and live quietly like the other girls. This behavior is what we usually see in young men, not young women, and it is very disturbing."

I stood there, frowning, waiting for the opportunity to defend myself. When the Bishop nodded at me to speak, I straightened to my full height, almost standing on my tip toes. The Bishop and ministers were very intimidating as they stood in a group with their wide-brimmed, black hats and solemn expressions, staring at the accused.

"Well," I tried to keep my voice from shaking, "I was just asking some questions. I meant no harm."

"What did you mean by saying we should wear robes and sandals like Jesus?" Minster Troyer asked me pointedly. "You know full well that is against our Ordnung."

I furrowed my brow. "If we are really going to follow the Bible and shun the world and follow everything that the apostles wrote in their letters to the churches, then why don't we dress like them and live in communes like they did? It does not make any sense to say we are shunning the world and living like the Bible tells us to when we merely dress like the first Amish people did when they split from the Catholic Church? And why do we speak the same language they did when they came here. It seems that if you hold all of the church rules under that light, we are merely living like the people of that time, who in turn lived like the people of their time. They did not dress differently, so why should we?" I paused and looked at the minister's, wondering if they really knew the Bible as well as they thought they did. "Doesn't the Bible also say not to make a show of your religion?"

I saw looks of confusion on everyone's faces. I could see they never thought of things like I did and had never given thought as to why we did the things that we did.

When no one responded, I continued. "Also, when I ask people things like why we wear the bonnet or the head covering and what it symbolizes, no one knows the answer. The women here do not know why we cover our heads. They have no idea that it is written in Apostle Paul's letter to the Corinthians."

"How do you know that?" The Bishop asked with a startled look on his face.

Because I read the Bible every day and nowhere have I found these rules. On the contrary, it says to do away with the traditions of men and to not make a show of your religion."

"Silence," the Bishop barked angrily at me. "You are in no position to preach at me. Is this Bible in English or German?"

"English, of course," I said defiantly.

The Bishop looked at Jacob and Lillian. "Why is she, an unmarried girl, allowed to read the Bible in your house, and an English one at that?"

Lillian was wringing her hands. "She told me she was learning German with it, so I let her keep it," she looked at me with a frown.

"Oh, I was," I said honestly, wondering what kind of trouble I was in now.

The Bishop shook his head. "This was very bad judgment on the part of the people that are now your parents. I was ready to keep you from baptism, but now I see it is not your fault and you were merely led astray by bad parenting." He looked at me for a long moment. "You do realize that if you were to practice any other religion, you would go to hell...that all of these questions you have are from the devil, right?"

I nodded my head, but I was so confused. I knew if I were not Amish I would go to hell, and even though I did not agree with everything the

Bishop was saying, there was no reason to embarrass Jacob and Lillian by postponing my baptism. I flinched as he continued.

"These were thoughts put in your head by the devil. They were temptations of the flesh. Talk of wearing any clothes outside the Ordnung is a sin of the flesh. It is vanity and pride and something to be greatly ashamed of."

He paused and spoke briefly to the other ministers, some of whom lived nearby but were from neighboring districts. (We were short on ministers since Matty and Samantha's fathers had moved away.)

After a moment, he turned back to me. "Are you sorry for what you said, and do you confess that these were merely thoughts of vanity and worldliness?"

I thought for a moment. I really believed that I would go to hell if I was not Amish; I don't know why, but I did. At a loss for any other solution, I nodded and whispered, "Yes."

The ministers nodded and told Lillian to take the English Bible from me, and they told her they did not want to hear any more about this. As they continued to talk to Jacob and Lillian, I walked back into the house. My legs were trembling as I realized that they had almost taken me out of line for baptism. What a shame for me that would have been. I would have been mortified at being made to sit with the rest of the church while the youngie were baptized. All eyes would have been on me, and the tongue wagging would have been unbearable.

I went upstairs to my bedroom, where I took my orange King James Version Bible from the drawer. I did not like the fact that I was not allowed to read the Bible. I loved reading it and I was good at memorizing its passages. *This is like Nazi Germany*, I thought.

I took the Bible and placed it where Lillian sat at the table, as a sign of good faith and obedience. I wanted it to appear that I was in total compliance, even though I was confused and felt as though I had been hushed rather than given answers. Whatever the circumstances, however, I was convinced that I would most certainly go to hell if I was not Amish, so once again I pretended to give in, while in the back of my mind I could not help but think my arguments had been at least worthy of debate.

THE NEXT week, I sewed my baptism dress. It was black and would be the new black dress that I would wear at many social functions throughout my womanhood. I also made my new white church apron and black kapp. Among the Amish, baptism clothes must be new to signify the starting of a new life and a commitment to following all rules without question.

Fourteen-year-old Ella happily took my old dress, kapp and apron as her own. She had been waiting for them since hers were starting to get too small. She would soon be finished with the eighth grade and would be staying at home, so she was learning to sew, and altering my clothes to fit her made her feel grown up and useful. I finished ironing my new clothes and hung them on the window so I could inspect my work. Ella came in to see them.

"Wow," she breathed. "Are you excited?"

I frowned for a second and then nodded. "Oh, yes," I tried to hide the gnawing uncertainty that was clawing at my mind.

"In three years that will be me," Ella clasped her hands. "I can't wait. Then I will be all grown up and be able to sit with the members after church is dismissed. It will be great."

I smiled at her childish excitement and put my arm around her. "It will come soon enough, Ella dear..." I whispered "...soon enough."

*T*HAT FRIDAY before church, Lillian sent me over to help Phyllis clean house. Her parents and brother's family were coming on the bus from Wisconsin on Saturday and would be staying with her for the next two weeks. Phyllis's dad was a minister and had volunteered to give counsel during the upcoming baptisms and communion. Samantha had written that she had discovered one of the ministers in their community was Phyllis's dad, and since they were coming out to visit Samantha and Matty were sending presents for me as a remembrance of my baptism. I told her I would send one back with Phyllis's family for her as well.

As I walked into the house, I was greeted by the smell of fresh bread and plum pie. Phyllis came over to me with her hands out-stretched in gratitude.

"I am so glad you are here," she exclaimed as she grimaced and rubbed her swollen stomach. "I have so much to do in less than twenty-four hours. My brother's wife is such a gossip and does not like me much. Everything must be perfect for them."

I squeezed her shoulder and smiled at her. "It's okay, Phyllis," I said, trying to soothe her. "Don't worry. I will stay here till midnight if I have to."

She smiled at me and sat down with a sigh. "I am so glad you moved in with Jacob and Lillian, I don't know what I would do without you."

"I know," I grinned playfully as I gazed around the house, which looked like a tornado had gone through it.

We dug into the work right away. The two oldest girls shook jars of cream to make butter, while the younger children and I went upstairs to start mopping and dusting the bedrooms. I laughed as the little children ran around, moving stuff out of my way as I swept and mopped. I was one of their favorite people, and they had playfully started calling me Aunty Emma. I liked to hear them shouting "Aunty Emma's coming" as I walked up to the house. Phyllis would laugh and tell them they were silly, but she never told them to stop, so the nickname had stuck.

After we finished cleaning the upstairs, we started on the downstairs, and after three hours, we all plopped on the floor, exhausted.

"Well," Phyllis looked around with satisfaction at the clean house, "I am so glad that is done."

"Yeah, me too," I yawned as I stood up. "But we better get the kitchen cleaned and the rest of the baking done."

Phyllis nodded. "I want to braid the girls today, too, so I won't have to do it tomorrow."

We finished the housework by early evening and then, while the children played in front of the house, I helped Phyllis with the ironing for Sunday.

"So your baptismal clothes are ready, huh?" Phyllis asked smiling at me as we both stood by the wood burning stove, ironing church clothes.

I smiled and nodded as I placed my iron back on the stove to heat and took another.

"Everything okay?" Phyllis looked into my face with a frown.

I nodded again and stared out the window.

"Okay, what's wrong?" Phyllis asked me as she put down her iron.

"I just wish I had a real mom and dad to be here when I am baptized. I would like someone to be really happy, you know." I bit my lip, trying not to cry. "All of the other youngie have real family around them, and I feel like I don't really have anyone."

"Well," Phyllis touched my arm, "we are all happy for you, you know. You are one of us and everyone seems to like you."

I smiled at her gratefully. "But I really think it would be easier if I had real family around, like you have. Your mom and dad are coming. I wish my parents were nice and could visit. It would be so nice to feel a real family connection like that."

Phyllis looked down at her ironing for a moment and then suddenly burst into tears. I looked at her in shock. Crying was something you did not see much among the Amish, and I just stood there for a moment. After I got over my shock, I put my arms around Phyllis and hugged her. She put her head on my shoulder and cried for a couple of minutes. I did not say anything, but waited to see if she would tell me what was wrong.

I had long suspected that Phyllis was hiding a dark secret that was haunting her, and that this was why she had helped me when I was fighting for the right to call the police about Brian and Mamma. After a moment, she straightened and dried her eyes with a handkerchief she took from her dress pocket. She sat down in a nearby chair and watched me iron for a moment.

"You know," she said finally, "I am terrified that my parents are coming here. I do not want them here. I was very happy when I married Peter and moved out here to be near his family."

"Why?" I asked curiously.

"My father is an evil man, he molested all ten of us girls," she said in a low voice, "He went after every last one of us when we were between the ages of twelve and fifteen. Those were the ages he liked, and it meant three years of hell for each of us." Phyllis pulled her handkerchief from her pocket again. "I can't help but think that my Katie will be twelve in a little over a year,"she blew her nose and wiped the tears from her cheeks.

"I don't understand," I shook my head and pursed my lips with anger. "Why didn't anyone do something to him? How could he just get away with it?"

Phyllis shook her head and crumpled her handkerchief into a ball. "Oh, Mom would report him to the Church every couple of years, and he would confess to his so-called weakness. When I became a church member, I had to sit there and hear his confessions in church. It was such a joke, and it made me sick. All he confessed to was having a weakness of the flesh. While he cried and begged for forgiveness from the church members, no one was even remotely concerned about the well-being of his children. No one asked if we were okay or anything. One night, when I was eighteen, I walked into the furniture shop for something I had forgotten. I saw him there on the floor with my sister who was about to be married, they were both moaning in the dark. I don't think they saw me, but there has been gossip that her first born child is my father's. Those two still have a strange relationship to this day, it is so gross.

A few more tears trickled down her cheeks "I think at first my sister was a victim of my father and then something happened to her, we were never close and most people think she is really odd, but it is not her fault. I think something snapped inside her and she is not really quite all there.

Even though she was beyond my father's preferred age she became easy prey." Phyllis shook her head and held the handkerchief to her trembling mouth.

"There was no one who would stop him. Even if a man is put in the Bann, he still has full access to his victims. Our dad continued to molest us even while he was in the Bann. It did nothing. And to think our entire church knew about it. How could they just leave us there in that house? But they did....and we were not the only family that was like that. I was so glad to marry Peter and get out of that house," Phyllis looked out the window. "It is good to know that he no longer has any children at home." She paused as if in a daze.....So"But the grandchildren..."

"I don't understand how our church can put up with this evil," I spat out. "It is an outrage and a crime against humanity." Angrily, I slammed the iron down on the stove.

Phyllis nodded in agreement. "There is nothing we can do, though. If anyone knows I have told you this, *I* will be placed in the Bann for bringing up church matters that have been resolved and for not forgiving my father. I am supposed to forgive and forget, but I can't. I just can't. He hurt me and my sisters so badly, so very badly, and then a few years ago, he was elected minister. Why would God let that happen?" she turned and looked at me for an answer.

I shook my head and looked at her with her same bewilderment.

"I am very afraid to have him here," Phyllis stood up. "A couple of years ago when we went to Wisconsin for my brother's wedding, I saw him looking at my older sister's thirteen-year-old daughter. I could tell by the way the girl cowered when he looked at her that he had done something. I was sitting next to one of my younger sisters at the dinner table, and I sort of lost my mind for a minute. I grabbed one of the forks next to me and was ready to lunge and stab my father in the eye when my sister, figuring out what I was about to do, grabbed the fork and pulled me outside."

"You should have done it," I muttered to my ironing board.

Phyllis looked at me with her clear blue eyes and matter-of-factly said, "I wish I had." She shook her head as tears streamed down her face. "When I was nineteen, I rebelled against my father and started screaming at him in the buggy one Sunday afternoon as we were leaving church. I had caught him with one of my siblings again, and I told him I would not go home with him."

She smiled as she remembered her bravery. "Anyway," she continued, "everyone was looking as my father slapped me and pushed me out of the buggy. Eventually I did go home, but the ministers had a meeting, and my father told them I was proud and refused to forgive him like Jesus taught us. Eventually I said that I forgave him and began to pretend nothing had happened."

"Did you really forgive him?" I asked hesitantly.

"Of course not," Phyllis answered as she gritted her teeth. "I truly do believe we should forgive people for mistakes they make, but not when they continue to make the same mistakes without trying to get some kind of help."

I nodded in agreement. I felt the same way.

"I had to lie and say I forgave him, though," Phyllis explained. "I had just started dating Peter at the time and did not want any trouble."

"I understand," I smiled at her reassuringly. "It is not your fault that you had to lie."

She nodded and smiled at me through her tears.

I helped Phyllis carry the clothes upstairs, and then I hugged her and walked home. I was so disturbed by what I had just heard that I felt weak. What an awful man, I thought, and he is coming here to help with the baptisms. What right did he have to partake in a ceremony that was supposed to be pure and holy?

As I neared home, I was jostled out of my deep, moody thoughts by the sound of pigs squealing and people shouting. Afraid someone had been hurt, I ran over to the pig shed. As I approached, I was confused to hear laughter mixed with the sound of a pig groaning in pain. I was horrified when I turned the corner and saw Jacob with a sledgehammer. He was swinging it at the mouth of one of our boars. There was blood pouring from the pig's mouth, and the pig was in a corner cowering as Jacob continued hitting him with the sledgehammer.

"What are you laughing at?" I screamed angrily at Elam. "Ella, Ida, this is horrible." I climbed over the fence and jumped into the pig pen. I heard my dress rip as it caught on a nail, but I didn't care. "Dad, stop it. Stop it right now," I yelled at him, and I grabbed his arm as he started to swing the sledgehammer again.

Jacob, who was laughing, turned to me as if confused. "What's wrong?" he asked, kicking at the teeth he had knocked out of the pig's mouth.

"You are hurting this animal; that is what's wrong," I said with fists clenched. "I am so tired of watching how you and Elam abuse the animals. You are cowards and should be ashamed of yourselves!" I kicked a chunk of mud in his direction and stepped over to look at the pig. I could not help the tears that were forming in my eyes as I saw the blood running from the pig's mouth and the big eye teeth that lay on the ground next to him.

"He's just an animal, Emma," Elam laughed at me.

"Oh, yeah?" I replied, yanking the sledgehammer out of Jacob's hands. "Well, if that is the case, then you are just a human, and this should not hurt, huh?" I saw a worried look on Elam's face as I ran at him with the sledgehammer. I slammed the hammer into a wooden post just inches from his knee.

"That wouldn't have hurt, right?" I asked angrily as I threw the sledgehammer down and crawled out of the pig pen.

"Oh, don't be so soft," Jacob called after me. "It's just a pig, you know."

"Oh, yes, I know," I screamed back. "And you are just a man. I hope you go to hell. You are just a man, so it won't hurt." I screamed the words as loud as I could. I saw Lillian watching from the window, and when I stomped into the milk house, she didn't say anything but she looked pleased.

I did not care what anyone thought at that moment; I was right and I knew it. Of course, I did not really wish Jacob to go to hell. I was just trying to prove a point. I hated how Amish men treated animals, and when I glared at them, they would simply laugh and say, "It's just an animal." Pets are not allowed among most Amish, and whenever I was nice to the animals, I was laughed at.

"That is so wrong," Jacob had said one day as I knelt, petting our dog, Kate. She always walked with her tail between her legs and cowered whenever she saw Elam or Jacob.

"Why is it so wrong to be nice to an animal?" I had asked, remembering Brian and how horrible he had been to our animals.

"Because they are animals; they are here to serve man, not be our friends," he had explained as he kicked Kate in the ribs and told her to "get."

"You should be kind to all things," I had said as I got up.

"Oh, and where did you learn that?" Jacob asked with raised eyebrows.

I thought for a moment and suddenly realized I had never had such a role model, so where *had* I learned it? "It comes from inside me," I finally answered, "and from the words of Jesus."

"Oh, are you a prophet now?" Jacob had asked as he laughed.

"No," I answered defensively. "But it is a good motto to live by."

The evening after the pig incident, everyone acted as if nothing had happened. Even if something had been said, I was not about to apologize. I went through most of that evening without speaking, just to let them know that I was still seething inside. I wanted them to learn from this incident, but I knew they would not. Why should they? They truly did not care, and it was hard to teach people something if they did not care to learn.

The Baptism

"Conformity is the jailer of freedom and the enemy of growth."

— John F. Kennedy

The next morning, the children and I were walking toward the house with the milk buckets when I heard a car drive up the dirt lane. I stood and watched as four Amish people got out and walked toward Phyllis as she stood on her porch. I shuddered as they followed her into the house and closed the door behind them. *Poor Phyllis,* I thought to myself.

That evening we had the Bishop and his guests over for dinner. It was Amish custom to invite neighboring people that had visitors to your house for a meal, especially if they were visiting ministers. This was usually a fun event and a way for Amish families to catch up on gossip from other communities. As it turned out, Lillian had a brother and many cousins in the same community as Phyllis's parents, and she was eager for the visiting women to fill her in on the happenings in that community.

I tried to pretend I did not know anything about Phyllis's father, in order to protect Phyllis's secret and keep her from getting into trouble, but as I saw them coming down the lane that evening, I felt sick in the pit of my stomach. I saw Phyllis walking next to her mother, and the anger I felt toward that mother made my body shake. *How could this woman have stood by and done nothing to stop her husband?* I thought. Surely there was something—anything—she could have done to stop him and protect her children. Although there was no divorce or law enforcement involvement allowed among the Amish, I could not accept the fact that there was no way for a woman to protect her babies from an evil monster.

After dinner, Ella and I did the dishes while the smaller children played and the married couples talked about various things happening in different communities. After the dishes, Phyllis's mom picked up a game she had brought with her. The Amish love to play games like Pictionary, Dictionary, Monopoly and checkers in the evening, especially if there is company present.

"This is a game my *Englisch* neighbor gave me and I thought it would be fun to play," Phyllis's Mom said , opening it. I was surprised to see it was a game called Bible Trivia.

I saw Peter smile and nod to Phyllis's dad. "We will win this game," he laughed.

Phyllis's dad nodded. "Yeah, but we'll let them play anyway," he joked.

I rolled my eyes at him across the table, and he noticed and seemed perplexed as to why I might be angry with him.

"I think young Emma here thinks she might win." He grinned.

"Okay," Phyllis yawned, "but just a short game. We all have to get up early in the morning. Church is at the Mast's farm tomorrow."

As the game commenced, I could not believe the answers I was hearing to the questions.

"Elam, it's your turn," Phyllis's mom smiled at him. "Who built the ark?"

Elam thought for a moment. "Moses," he answered uncertainly.

I laughed into my hand, and Phyllis's mom looked at me with a frown. "Okay, then, Emma, who built the ark?"

"Noah and his sons," I answered with a smirk.

"Okay," Phyllis's mom looked at me with dislike. "Let's see if you can answer the next one. Who was the first priest to the Israelites'?" She smiled at me as if she were sure I would not know the answer.

"Aaron," I answered confidently.

"How do you know all this?" Phyllis's father looked at me with surprise.

I did not want to tell him I read the Bible, so I merely shrugged and told him that I had a good memory.

As it turned out, the Bishop and Phyllis's dad were fiercely competitive. One by one people left the game as they answered wrong, and finally the Bishop, Phyllis's dad and I were the only ones left. I liked competitions and really wanted to beat the ministers at what was supposedly their job: to know the Bible and to be able to teach others about it.

Phyllis's mom started pulling cards from the advanced category trying to finally end the game.

"Who wrote these words?" she asked. "If I am without love..."

Phyllis's dad frowned as he tried to recall where the words were from. "Uh, uh," he stammered. "I think it was in 1st Peter." He nodded his head. "Yeah, 1st Peter," he said again.

Phyllis's mom shook her head and looked at me. "Emma?"

It's from the letter to the Corinthians written by the apostle Paul," I answered with a smile of victory. Out of the corner of my eye, I saw Phyllis laughing into her handkerchief at the shocked look on her father's face.

"I can't believe you would know that," he shook his head.

"Oh, she really does have a good memory," Phyllis said, trying to keep a straight face. I saw Lillian grinning too as she watched the men soundly defeated by a mere girl.

So now it was between me and the Bishop. He looked at me with a worried look on his face. What if I knew more about the Bible than our bishop? *Wouldn't that be funny?* I thought.

"Okay, Peter," Mary turned to him. "What was the name of Jezebel's husband?"

The Bishop frowned. "I think we should skip that question," he fidgeted. "It is too hard. Neither of us knows the answer."

"I do," I raised my hand. I felt a little guilty since I really did have a great memory and could easily remember things without really trying.

Peter looked at me in shock. "Okay," he said challengingly. "Who is it?"

"King Ahab," I answered with a smile.

Phyllis and Lillian clapped. "Team Emma won!" they cheered, laughing and patting me on the back. Peter and Henry laughed, too, and tried to appear to be good sports. Among the Amish, if you show anger when you don't win a game, it is a sign of pride and is greatly discouraged. On the same note, the winner is supposed to be humble and say it was an accident that they won. I, however, was enjoying my triumph and must admit I felt at least a little proud of myself. I saw Jacob smiling at me from across the table, and I smiled back.

Mary seemed unhappy about my win and leaned over Ella to tell me not to be too proud.

Ella smiled from behind her hand, and I smiled back. *Creepy lady,* I thought. How dare she tell me anything?

The next morning, we got up early and hurriedly did the chores. After a quick breakfast of cinnamon rolls, the entire family was in the buggy and off to church. It was going to be a long day, and we had to be at church by eight. As we neared the church, I started to feel sick again, and despite the cool Minnesota April morning, I felt hot and stuffy.

I yanked at the string around my neck, loosening it as much as I dared. I did not know why I felt so uneasy, but I did, and I felt beads of sweat gathering on my forehead. I pulled a handkerchief out of my pocket. It was my present from Samantha; she had embroidered my initials in the corner. I smiled as I looked at it. The pretty yellow flowers were so beautiful. Samantha knew I loved yellow, and she had purposely picked the pattern out for me. I put the handkerchief to my cheek and blinked tears from my eyes. I had so many mixed feelings but did not know what to do about them.

When we reached the Mast's farm, Jacob instructed us to make sure the girls went in right after the women with no lollygagging. It was going to be a long service, and there was no reason to agitate the few ministers we had, almost all of whom were visiting from other communities.

When Ella and I joined the other girls, we were informed of the same thing again. Apparently, every father had offered the same instructions. One of the younger girls was elected to look through the window and tell us the minute all the women were seated so we could file in quickly. As we all took our seats, I found myself really missing Matty. I had other friends, but none like Matty. It would be far less stressful if she were here to cheer me up, I thought.

I was jolted out of my thoughts as the first hymn started. I was so nervous that I almost forgot to stand up and go upstairs with the other girls who were being baptized. As I climbed the stairs for my last instructions, a fleeting memory of an old dream passed through my mind. I had so wanted to be a medical missionary—an unlikely dream at the time, but now more impossible than ever.

After half an hour of instructions from the ministers, all of the baptism candidates went back downstairs and sat together, the boys first, followed by the girls and then the ministers. After another two-and-a-half hours of a sermon about John the Baptist and Jesus, all the baptism candidates were told to fall on their knees in front of the Bishop. One by one, the Bishop baptized the boys. When he was finished, he extended his hand and gave them a kiss of acceptance on the cheek.

I was the first in the line of girls, and when the Bishop got to me, Phyllis, as the Bishop's wife, came forward and removed my kapp. The Bishop asked me if I promised to obey the rules of the church and follow Christ's example by leading a low and humble life. I hesitated for a moment, and thought about how I was joining a church that silenced its sexual abuse victims. *What if I married such a man,* I thought; what would I do? So many thoughts raced through my mind in those two seconds. Then I decided, this is the only way to please God and go to heaven, so I whispered, "Yes."

"Then I baptize you in the name of the Father, the Son and the Holy Ghost," the Bishop poured water over my head three times. As the water rolled down my cheeks, it was mixed with tears. Most likely, everyone watching thought these were tears of joy, but they weren't. I felt a great heaviness and pain for everyone who had been hushed and humiliated in the name of religion. I did not understand these things, and most certainly there was nothing I could do about them. Any move I made or questions I raised would land me in the Bann and stamp me as non-marriageable for life.

The rest of the day I felt the same gnawing anxiety. It was like something was trying to tell me I had made a mistake. It was a very strange feeling, and one I could not quite figure out. I had joined the Amish Church, and I truly believed I had done the right thing. What other option was there? Everyone else was of the world, and that was pure evil. Still, the uneasiness and agitated feelings did not leave me for a few days.

I sent a letter to Samantha, telling her how excited I was, when in fact I really wanted to tell her about Phyllis's father. Of course, I could not for fear of it leaking out and getting Phyllis into trouble. Every time I saw him, though, I could not believe in my soul that he was truly elected by God, rather I thought it was just by chance. Would God really choose such a horrible, unrepentant man to lead his flock? No matter what anyone said, I knew the God I believed in would not do such a thing.

The letter I got from Samantha was all sunshine and good cheer. She said how happy she was in her new home, and how she looked forward to the future now that she finally belonged. I tried to read between the lines, looking for a subtle message that contradicted her happy words, but there was nothing. Sadly, I remembered a conversation I had had with Samantha when she first arrived in the community. I had relayed what Matty had told me about things not being as good as they seemed, but my words did not seem to bother her and she had just shrugged.

"It is way better here than with Mamma and Brian," she had told me, shaking her head. "There is nothing they can do to us here that could even compare to what we faced there."

"Yeah, this is better," I had acknowledged with a frown. "But it does not make it right."

"You are always worrying about what is right, Misty, and you have got to stop it. It is not your job to fix things; it is your job to follow the rules," Samantha had thrown her hands in the air. "You are just causing yourself a bunch of grief that you can't do anything about, anyway."

I shrugged. "I guess, but it makes me feel like an accomplice to evil."

Samantha had just shaken her head in exasperation. "The rules are the rules," she had stated. "Neither one of us can change them, so no sense trying."

Two weeks after the baptism was communion Sunday. Again, it was a very long day. Services started at eight. A little after twelve, the children went home and the members stayed to hear the Ordnung read and participate in communion and feet washing. It was announced that we would be selecting a new deacon that day, since we had visiting ministers to help with the load. I had finally lost the agitated feeling I had experienced two weeks prior and was eager to partake in my first communion. I got very sleepy, however, around three o'clock as the Bishop droned on reading the church rules.

"...The women's dress hem shall be four inches wide, and the dress shall be no shorter than six inches from the floor. No sleeves rolled up on Sunday. Men's shirt cuffs shall be two and a half inches wide. The horses' harnesses shall be black. The buggies shall be black with no trim or carpeting allowed. All house curtains shall be dark blue. No shingles allowed for roofing. No flowers allowed in the front of the house; only in the garden..."

It seemed the rules would never end, and a couple of times I jerked myself awake just as I started to fall off the bench. I looked around and smiled as I saw several people sleeping around the room. It just was not possible to sit for so long without losing interest. Finally, around four o'clock, the Bishop folded the paper that the *Ordnung* was written on and we had communion and the feet washing. Next, the tithes were collected and put away for any family that might have need of emergency funds. At the end of the service, we were all told to write a name on a piece of paper to put in the lot for a new deacon.

First the men voted, and then the women. I hesitated for a moment, not knowing how to vote. All married men were fair candidates. I knew people usually voted for someone in their family, but there was no way I was going to vote for Jacob or any of his brothers. Eventually I voted for Isaiah's dad. Although I had not liked the way his family treated me, I still saw some of the qualities in Isaiah's father that I had seen in Isaiah. The whole church waited in silence as the votes were counted by the ministers. The three men with the highest number of votes were asked to step forward. I swallowed hard when I saw Jacob step forward with two men from the Mast family.

Of course, I thought; they have the most family members here. Each man was then told to pick up one of the three song books that had been placed on the bench. One of the song books contained a small piece of paper. The wives of the men looked on with hands clasped as they each hoped their husband would not be chosen. The role of a minister's wife was not an envied one. It meant a lot more of the work load would fall on the wife as her husband made time in an already busy schedule to read scripture and attend to church matters, without any compensation in return.

I held my breath as I watched Jacob pick up one of the thick song books. All eyes followed him as he handed the book to the Bishop. The Bishop solemnly took it from Jacob's trembling hands, and after pausing for a second, he opened the book to check for the piece of paper. When he did not find it, he simply closed the book and shook his head. I sighed with relief, as, I am sure Lillian did. Next were the two Mast brothers. The minister took the song book from the youngest Mast brother. He looked at it briefly and then nodded his head to show that he had found the slip of paper. The entire church membership looked on with sympathy mixed with relief, as it became apparent that the young Abe Mast was the new deacon.

His face paled and everyone heard the sob that came from his wife of only two years. She quickly buried her head in the lap of one of the other married women. The prospect of spending her whole married life as the wife of one of the ministers was not an inviting thought.

After the deacon was chosen, church was finally dismissed. All of the church members were solemn as we prepared to go home. It was a sympathetic solemnness out of respect for the young family that had just been burdened with the responsibility for helping to lead the church.

That evening, everyone was silent as we ate cracker soup. We were supposed to be silent out of reverence for the new deacon, but I believe it stemmed partly from exhaustion.

That night as the girls and I got ready for bed, Ella whispered to me in the darkness.

"How is it being a church member?"

"Very tiring," I laughed as I snuggled into my pillow and drifted off to sleep.

BY MID-MAY, the garden was planted and we were ready for another long summer in the fields and the butcher shop. One morning late in May, Grandma Schrock decided it was time for me to see the homeopathic chiropractor to get help for my headaches. I did not want to go, but I did not want to hurt Grandma Schrock's feelings, either, so when the car arrived I followed Jacob and Lillian outside and hopped in the back seat next to Grandma.

The chiropractor was about fifteen miles away and located on a back road behind a large grove of trees. Grandma Schrock had informed me that his clients were primarily from the Amish communities. Many of the Amish came here to seek more advanced treatment than the Amish medicine person could give.

When we arrived, we walked around the side of what appeared to be a house. We were welcomed by a woman that was standing in the kitchen washing dishes. I was a little surprised that we were in someone's home rather than an office. The woman told us to sit on the couch and then called to someone down the hall. A few minutes later, a cheerful man in a white coat came into the living room. He smiled at us and waved us into a large bedroom that had been turned into an examination room. I walked in timidly and looked around, not really liking how it felt. It was so weird for his office to be in his home, I thought, and why is the guy wearing a white coat?

"Hi, Mrs. Schrock," the man smiled and nodded to Grandma. "How is your hip doing?"

"Oh, it is better," Grandma Schrock smiled in greeting as she rubbed her left hip. "But I am still having pain."

"Well, we will see what we can do for that," the man turned on one of his machines.

"By the way, this is my granddaughter," Grandma Schrock reached behind her and pulled me out from where I was hiding.

"Oh, nice to meet you," the man extended his large hand to me. "I am Dr. Rubinstein."

"Nice to meet you. My name is Emma," I said shyly as I shook two of his large fingers.

"And what can we do you for you, Miss Emma?" Dr. Rubinstein asked, smiling at me.

I looked at him for a moment. He seemed nice and cheerful, I thought...maybe a little too cheerful.

When I just stared at him, Jacob responded for me. "She has really bad headaches and she limps on one leg. We thought maybe you could find out what is wrong and help her."

"Oh, of course we can do that," Dr. Rubinstein smiled as he rubbed his hands together. "Who wants to go first?"

"I will," Grandma Schrock untied her crisp white cap and handed it to Lillian to hold.

Dr. Rubinstein helped Grandma onto a small table and let a few rollers roll over her back for a couple of minutes, then moved her onto a table where he twisted and pushed on her back. I winced hearing the sounds of popping bones. Now I was even less excited to take my turn with the cheerful doctor.

After he finished twisting Grandma's body, the doctor had her lie down flat on her back and told her to hold up her right arm while he placed some herbs in her left hand. Then he pulled on her right arm which went limp by her side. He did this several times, switching out the herb capsules each time. On the fourth attempt, when he pulled on her arm, it remained stiff and did not fall to her side. Lillian, seeing my perplexed look, nodded and said,

"It is just another technique like the fingernail clipper. It's a way for your body to tell you what it needs."

I rolled my eyes to show my distrust of this method and stood there with my arms folded in front of me and my lips pursed as Dr. Rubinstein motioned for me to come over to the table.

"Come on, Emma," he smiled at me. "Don't be shy. We just want to help you; that is all."

I looked into Grandma Schrock's smiling face and, not wanting to appear ungrateful for her concern over my headaches, I faked a smile and climbed up on the table.

"Okay," the doctor looked me over. "I just need a brief summary of any medical problems you have ever had."

"Uh, well," I stammered for a second, not wanting to go into detail about my traumatic childhood. "Um, right now I have really bad headaches and my left leg really hurts a lot."

"And when did all these things start hurting?" he asked as he began feeling around my neck and back.

I thought for a moment, wondering how to best answer the question without creating more questions.

"I was bitten in the head by a dog when I was little, and rammed in the back by a cow when I was fourteen."

"Ouch," the doctor shook his head. "That must have hurt."

I just nodded.

"Okay," Dr. Rubinstein said after a couple of minutes. "I need you to lie down so I can do a quick exam of you before we start treatment."

I lay down on the padded table, and I saw Lillian step forward and pull my black dress down so no part of my legs was showing. I was nervous and did not like this guy asking me questions. I clenched my fists as the doctor began palpating my stomach and asking me if there was any pain. After my stomach, he began pushing on my rib cage, and I flinched when he pushed on the ribs that Brian had hurt when he held me between his legs.

"A couple of ribs have been cracked, too, huh?" Dr. Rubinstein asked with raised eyebrows. "You really got banged up, kid."

I just nodded without commenting. After the doctor finished my adjustments, he said I would need further treatments, but he believed I would eventually be free of my limp and headaches. I had to admit, when he had adjusted my neck and hips, I instantly felt like pressure had been lifted from my head and shoulders, and when I got off the table and walked around the room, I felt less pain in my left hip. Dr. Rubenstein explained that my pelvis was lopsided and it made my left hip slip halfway out of socket, thus causing the limp.

"We usually see this sort of thing after a traumatic injury," the doctor frowned. "That must have been a very big cow."

I just nodded, not wanting to tell him about Brian constantly kicking me in the back and slamming me into walls.

"Okay, now test her," Grandma Schrock nodded at me . "See if the script saying will help her."

I frowned and refused to budge as the doctor patted the table for me to lie back down.

"I don't want to do that part," I protested.

"Oh, don't be silly," Jacob pulled me down toward the table.

I lay down on the table and held my arm in the air as the doctor instructed. Dr. Rubinstein came over to me with a list and started calling things out while he pulled on my arm.

"Feelings of anger," he pulled on my arm. My arm remained stiff, and he nodded to his wife, who held a notebook. "I feel sorry for myself," he droned on. "I do not love myself..."

After a few minutes, he asked me if anyone had placed a curse on my spirit. I tried to sit up. In the corner of the room, I saw Jacob shake his head at me, so I lay back down.

"I have been cursed in the last ten years," Dr. Rubinstein droned. My arm went limp. "I have been cursed in my lifetime." My arm went limp again. "Before I was born," he continued to pull on my arm. My arm stayed stiff.

"Oh, this is ridiculous," I sat up. "How could someone curse me before I was born?"

"Many spirits are bound by evil curses before they enter this realm," the doctor's wife said as she looked at me kindly.

I shrugged and lay back down. Who cares, I thought to myself. I will let them ask my arm all the questions they want if it will get me the hell out of here.

I listened, half amused, as the doctor asked me if a relative had cursed me. Eventually he came to the conclusion that it was a distant grandfather from Ireland that had been a satanic priest and, knowing I would be born in the future, he put a curse on me.

I frowned at the entire idea. "I am not cursed," I said defensively. "What would make you think that?"

"I feel it when I come near you," the doctor patted my shoulder. "Here." He reached for the piece of paper his wife was handing him. "Say this script every night before you go to bed, and it will weaken the curse and rid you of all the negative energy that you possess."

I kept frowning and looked at Lillian, Grandma Schrock and Jacob. I took the script and a book that the doctor's wife handed me, walked outside to the car, and got in while everyone else stayed chatting with the doctor. The driver looked up from his paper to turn off the radio and asked me if we were ready to go.

"I don't know," I answered vaguely as I looked at the book the doctor's wife had given me. The main point of the book was about ridding yourself of all negative energies. That was fine, I thought, but the more I flipped through it, the weirder it got. In the back I found a list of rituals and scripts that promised to help with the process of enlightenment. I couldn't believe that there were Amish that were into this kind of thing. The fingernail clipper, the pulling on the arm and the chanting of scripts all gave me a creepy feeling.

That night, Lillian asked me if I had recited my script. When I shook my head no, she frowned at me.

"You know, Grandma Schrock paid that man fifty dollars for you today, It is very ungrateful of you to not at least try it."

I pulled the script out of my pocket. "Does everyone here really do this?" I asked.

"No, not everyone, but quite a few."

"Well, I think it is phony," I shook my head and raised my eyebrows. "I don't believe any of this stuff. It's like the fingernail clipper," I pulled it from my pocket too. "I did a test with this."

"What test?" Jacob asked as he and Elam sat down at the table. "I thought you did not like the use of the fingernail clipper."

"I don't," I affirmed as I dangled it in front of me and over my outstretched palm. "But my point is that all of this is not to be trusted. Just watch: I can make this fingernail clipper go any direction I want. Go clockwise," I said, and the fingernail clipper began swinging around. Slowly it began to swing in a clockwise motion. I felt creeped out, as if I were performing some sort of magic trick, but I believed I needed to prove that the readings depended in part on the thoughts of the individual performing them and were therefore tainted.

"Now go counter-clockwise," I said after a few seconds. Slowly, the fingernail clipper started to change direction and was soon spinning in a counter-clockwise motion.

"Wow," Ella exclaimed from over by the stove. "You really have strong energy. Grandma Schrock was right."

"No, can't you see?" I insisted impatiently. "It does whatever I want it to, so if I am wrong, it is wrong with me. That means all these tests are merely the thoughts of the people applying them."

"You are supposed to have blank thoughts when you are doing this," Jacob said defensively.

"Well, that is impossible. I don't believe in any of this stuff, and I am most certainly not going to say this script," I stated as I tore it up.

Lillian shrugged. "You don't have to, but you are still being ungrateful."

"Hey, Dad," Elam grinned. "I bet Emma would be good with that book you and your friends had as kid. The one you used to do black magic."

"Black magic?" I frowned. "What kind of black magic?"

Jacob nodded thoughtfully. "My cousin in Pennsylvania is still really good with all that. Remember when Cousin Johnny came to visit, children?" he asked.

The children nodded. "Oh, yes," Moses seemed lost in a trance. "When Cousin Johnny was here, he made the cupboards open and close without touching them, and he hexed the buggy wheels so they wouldn't move and we all had to walk to church."

I shivered. "That does not sound like a good thing," I was still frowning. "But I bet it was just a trick of some sort, all magicians appear to be doing magic but it is always just a bunch of tricks.

"How do you know?" Elam asked. "I wish I could do stuff like that. I tried, but I can't."

"You tried?" I whispered in shock. "That's terrible. It's like witchcraft."

"I know," Elam grinned. "But it's neat to say a spell and have it really happen. Dad says all you have to do is go to one of those stores that sell satanic stuff and get the fifth book of Moses and read the whole thing backwards, and you will get these powers."

I put my hands over my ears. "That is witchcraft. I don't understand this nonsense. I don't want any part of it, and I can't believe this stuff is allowed," I shrieked. "Are you kidding me? I could be put in the Bann for wearing my dresses too short, and yet I can practice witchcraft and it is okay?"

Jacob shrugged. "There are whole families that seem to inherit the power or knowledge to hex and cast spells and there are plenty that can't. It's no big deal. I tried to do it as a young man and it did not hurt me."

I shook my head and began eating. I could not believe what I was hearing, and I did not want to hear any more about it.

As a result of my disbelief, Grandma Schrock never again invited me to learn from her vast knowledge of herbs. I had enjoyed that part of the training, but I was even more relieved to be left alone and allowed to forget about black magic and hexes and the crazy idea that my ancestor had been a satanic priest that had placed a curse on me. I did feel better from the chiropractor visit, though, and with time my limp completely faded and I was left virtually pain-free with a normal gait; for that I was extremely grateful.

Nevertheless, I was more than happy to push these things that were deeply rooted in Amish culture and history to the back of my mind. Who was I to judge? I thought. As long as I did not participate, I was fine.

An amish Wedding

"The most courageous act is still to think for yourself. Aloud."

— *Coco Chanel*

That summer was busy, and I found myself either in the slaughterhouse or the fields much of the time. It was fun, though, especially since the children were out of school and running everywhere trying to help. In the evenings we often made homemade ice cream with blocks of ice we took from the ice house. After supper, the whole family gathered to clean the eggs from our large flock of laying hens to get them ready for the store in the nearby town. Once a week, Jacob and Elam took the eggs to the store, where they were paid a flat rate. Mrs. Fletcher drove them and did her shopping while they dropped off the eggs. Mrs. Fletcher refused any kind of payment, saying she was only too happy to help out.

Despite the fact that I was happy and life was going smoothly, I always had an underlying nagging feeling I could not shake. Jacob was angry with me for rejecting to have talks with him and often went out of his way to be rude to me. I was not afraid of Jacob, in all I believe he was merely seeking someone to talk to and a hand to hold, but that was just something I was not willing to give. He had a wife, whom he had treated badly and now he was suffering the consequences of his actions, he was trapped in a loveless marriage that I doubted offered any form of physical comfort.

I spent quite a few days helping Phyllis that summer. She was swamped with her new baby. Her seizures came regularly twice a week now, and it was more than she could handle. Although her husband's sisters occasionally came to help or sent their daughters, it was apparent that, due to Phyllis's condition, she was starting to be looked at as lazy. Many did not believe her when she tried to explain how tired she was after

263

the seizures, and much gossip was started about her idleness. No Amish woman wanted to be labeled lazy, and I must admit I don't believe I ever met a *lazy* Amish woman.

I was sometimes there when Phyllis had her seizures, and knew she was not faking it. Since Lillian and Jacob had no small children, it was easy for me to slip out for a couple of hours here and there to help Phyllis, and she was very grateful.

I enjoyed my job writing for Die Blatt and began to include some of my poems in my column. At times the poems got too philosophical and questioned things. As a result, I was reprimanded by the Bishop and the new deacon and told not to write poetry that inspired people to stray with their thoughts and question things they had been taught. I would cool it for a while, and then start over again, penning my thoughts and doubts on paper only to be reprimanded again. Despite these transgressions, they did not remove me as the community's writer. My poems were also filled with my innermost longings to be a missionary and to help people around the world. The subtle hints in the poetry I put in in the Amish paper were my only outlet for my frustrations.

In mid-summer, Lillian received a letter from her mother with the news that her youngest sister was published in church to be married. Being published was how the Church let people know who was getting married and when. Usually the weddings were about two months after the publishing date and in the fall or early spring. Fall was the most desired time of year, since harvest was plentiful and feeding the large number of wedding guests would not be a problem.

An average Amish wedding ranged anywhere from two hundred to three hundred and fifty people, depending on how many relatives could make it from neighboring states. Weddings and funerals were occasions for the Amish to have family get-togethers. As more and more people moved farther afield in search of farmland, Amish families no longer lived in the same communities they had grown up in, so travel by van or bus to family events was becoming more commonplace.

Lillian smiled as she read the news. She was very happy to hear of her sister Ella's upcoming wedding. There had been much talk over the summer of who would be making the trip to Iowa if the wedding was scheduled for that fall. Jacob and Lillian had known this trip was coming, and they had been saving for it all year. They decided to take two of the children with them. Since Ella and Elam had made the trip three years ago, and since Ida was still too young, twelve-year-old Moses and I would go along. Ella and Elam would stay with Phyllis and Peter and come back to the farm to do the chores every morning and evening. I shuddered when I learned that Ella was going to stay at the Bishop's house, surely Lillian and Jacob knew what kind of man Peter was. They had known him much longer than I, and it was easy to see how he looked at the girls, but at the same time, it was easy to ignore if you so wished.

I was excited about going on the trip, but when I asked Moses if he was excited, he just shook his head.

"Moses," I stroked his light brown hair, "why don't you want to go? We are going to have so much fun on the bus to Iowa. Then we will swing down to Missouri to visit some other relatives." I continued washing the dishes as I spoke. "We are going to be gone for a while; how can you not be excited?"

Moses leaned into me as he was now in the habit of doing. Jacob often reprimanded him when he saw him doing this, but short little Moses continued to do it whenever he was feeling down, and I would just smile and put my arm around him.

"I don't want to go because I still wet the bed," Moses whispered after a couple minutes of silence.

I sighed and nodded in sympathy. Jacob and Lillian had taken Moses to Dr. Rubinstein several times to try to solve his bed-wetting issues, but nothing had helped.

"Don't worry, Moses," I dried my soapy hands on my apron. "I will be there and so will Lillian, so we will make sure no one notices, okay?" I gave him a quick hug. I was surprised to see tears in his eyes, and I bit my lip not knowing what to say that might help him.

"Dad says this trip will help me to grow up," Moses hung his head. "I think he hopes I will be so embarrassed that I will quit wetting the bed, but I don't think it will work; I am probably going to wet the bed for the rest of my life."

"No, no, Moses." I shook him playfully. "Listen," I got down on one knee so I could look into his tear-filled, brown eyes. "I have heard of boys in their late teens who were wetting the bed, and then one day they just got over it and that was it."

"Really?" Moses brushed the tears away with his chubby, tanned arm.

"Really." I nodded.

"Who was it?" he whispered as he watched my face to see if I was just saying it to make him feel better.

"Jacob Troyer," I whispered back.

"Really?" Moses raised his eyebrows in surprise.

"Yep. I heard his mom talking to Lillian about it when we were

265

cleaning for church one day."

"Okay." Moses was smiling now. "I guess it will go away then, huh?"

Just then we heard Elam calling Moses from downstairs and playfully I chased after him as he scampered off with a smile on his face. I finished the dishes and then went out to the butcher house to help Lillian and Ella with that day's chickens. I could not help but think of Moses and his sadness and embarrassment over the upcoming trip. I had noticed recently that Moses was a little different from the other boys, and Jacob and Elam had noticed it, too. I often made faces at them when they were rough with Moses, like the time they had tied him on a pony that was not yet broken and laughed as he screamed, "like a girl," they had said.

"He has to toughen up," Jacob had said one day when he came into the house. Moses was sitting next to me with his head on my shoulder, watching me sew a quilt for my hope chest.

"What?" I had put my arm around Moses as he wrapped his arms around my waist, seeking shelter from his angry father.

"Don't hug him like that," Jacob had said angrily as he pulled Moses away from me. "You have to stop hugging the children. It is a bad example; you know we do not hug children older than two years old. And you," he shook Moses roughly by the shoulders. "What are you doing in here? You know we have work to do outside."

"I just wanted to see the colors she was putting together in the quilt," Moses hung his head and wiggled his toes through the holes in his shoes.

"See, that's what I am talking about, Moses," Jacob shook him again. "You've got to cut this out. Boys don't care about sewing and quilt colors. You have got to stop this, you hear me?"

Moses nodded with a confused look on his face, and I saw him glance at the quilt spread across my sewing machine. He had such a good eye for combining colors, I thought, and although I had noticed his unusual behavior, I loved his company and his sweet nature.

Moses went downstairs with Jacob, and I went back to my sewing. About ten minutes later, I was startled to hear Moses scream in pain. I jumped up from my sewing machine and ran outside to the front of the machine shop, where Lillian, who had been in the garden, was already with Moses.

"What happened?" I cried as I looked at Moses. He was sobbing, and blood was dripping from his mouth.

"Oh," Elam was laughing, "he was sitting on the tire of that tractor we had jacked up. I let it down suddenly and he fell off and hit his mouth on the side board."

"That is not funny, Elam," I glared at him. "He is really hurt."

"Who cares?" Elam shrugged. "He needs to toughen up and quit acting like a girl. It is embarrassing."

"It still was not nice." Lillian echoed me as she wiped the blood out of Moses's mouth with her handkerchief and checked his teeth to see if they were chipped.

"Ah, come on," Jacob came over. "He's fine and does not need you women coddling him. Stop your crying," he barked at Moses. "Come on, we have work to do."

Moses stood up and swallowed his tears; I winced as I saw his split lip. As I walked back into the house I heard Elam taunting Moses.

"Only girls cry."

"You're just a meanie," Moses had said through his swollen lips.

Elam just laughed a mean laugh.

That night, I swabbed Moses's mouth and lips with peroxide. When he fell off the tractor, his teeth had clamped down creating deep gashes on the inside of his cheeks and lips. He tried not to cry, but everything was so swollen and red and I could tell he was in terrible pain. I was very angry with Elam and glared at him when he smirked as Moses started crying, despite his efforts not to.

"Elam," I snapped angrily. "You think this is funny?" I pointed to Moses's swollen mouth. "You want me to show you what it feels like? Because I will be more than happy to," I picked up the peroxide bottle and waved it in his direction.

"You two cut it out," Jacob said from where he was reading the Die Blatt. "And Moses, you stop your fussing before I give you something to fuss about."

I glared daringly at Elam, who was smirking and whittling a piece of wood into a car. His mean streak was getting worse and it worried me.

Lillian, who was holding the flashlight for me, finally turned toward Elam and told him she did not want to see anything like this again.

Jacob put down his paper and looked up, glaring at Lillian. "This is your fault," he snapped at her. "We knew he was like this and it comes from your family. If you keep coddling him, he is going to end up old and alone like your older brother. We have to cut this out now, and that starts by making a man out of him before it is too late."

"What is wrong with Mom's older brother?" Ida inquired from where she sat under the table, playing with her Amish doll.

"He is funny like Moses," Elam scoffed.

"What do you mean by funny?" Ida asked innocently.

"He is like a girl." Elam laughed.

"That is enough," Lillian said, turning off the flashlight. "And don't say anything more about your Uncle Isaac, Elam."

"Why not? It's true," Jacob turned the page of his paper.

Moses had a hard time eating for a couple of weeks, but he did not cry any more, and I sighed as I saw him trying to prove his toughness to his father and brother. It seemed that no matter how hard he tried, it could not impress them. Once, he came to me and asked me if there was something wrong with him. I did not know how to answer him. I knew Jacob would disapprove, but I could not let Moses feel so sad and out of place.

"No, Moses," I had said, stroking his hair. "You are a wonderful, sweet boy. Your brother could learn a lot from you."

"You really think so?" Moses had asked, putting his hand in mine.

"Yes I do," I turned my head so he could not see the tears in my eyes. "Kindness is one of the most precious gifts you can have. Don't ever lose that."

"Okay. Thanks, Emma," he smiled, and with the innocent trust of a child he ran out of the garden toward the barn.

I don't know why Moses felt so attached to me, but he always came to me with questions instead of Lillian. I knew that Lillian noticed and I felt she did not like it, but I did not know what to do about it.

THE WEDDING was scheduled for mid-September, and the summer seemed to fly by as Lillian and we girls worked on cleaning the chickens and other small animals that came through our butcher house. We completed the vegetable, meat and fruit canning we had to do, and then we made a few new clothes for the trip. I volunteered to do most of the sewing while Lillian tended to other necessities for the trip.

Samantha wrote me that she had gone on her first date, and asked me if I would go with a date to the wedding if asked. As it turned out the recommendation for us not to date till a year after baptism had all but been forgotten.

In response to Samantha's letter, I wrote back that I did not plan on going on a date. Samantha told Matty, who was also dating, and Matty wrote back with question marks all over her letter. I did not think they could understand my reluctance and fear, so I simply said that I was not ready.

On a Friday near the beginning of September, Mrs. Fletcher drove Jacob, Lillian, Moses and I to the Greyhound bus station, where we took an early morning bus headed to Missouri. The plan was to first go to Missouri to visit one of Lillian's sisters—she had married one of Jacob's cousins. We would stay for church that Sunday and then we would all take the bus to Des Moines, Iowa, where the rest of Lillian's family lived in a very large Amish community.

When we boarded the bus, Moses and I sat together behind Lillian and Jacob, and we glued our faces to the window, looking out at all the sights as the bus rumbled past city after city. I had only been to the local town a few times since I had come to the Amish community, so I was eagerly drinking up the different scenery. We made quite a few stops along the way and even talked to other Amish travelers on their way to one function or another. Several times as people passed, I saw them nudge each other and whisper, "Look at the Amish over there." I found it annoying, as it was a stark reminder that I was not like everyone else. As Moses and I roamed around wherever the bus stopped, for once I was grateful for my black bonnet. I pulled it down as far over my face as I could to hide my embarrassment.

We arrived in Missouri around one o'clock in the morning and were greeted at the bus station by Lillian's brother-in-law, who had come in a car with an English neighbor. Lillian's sister came out on the front porch as we tumbled out of the car half-an-hour later. We were all quiet as we entered the house, so as not to wake the nine children that were sleeping soundly. Lillian's sister, Anna, smiled at us graciously and showed Moses and me to the beds we would be sharing with their children.

That Sunday, we accompanied Lillian's family to church services and then spent the afternoon at another cousin's house. In the evening, I went with the cousin's daughter and her boyfriend to the singing. It was a fun-filled day and evening. The next morning came all too soon and we had to catch the bus northbound to Iowa.

That afternoon, an English neighbor who lived near Lillian's mother's farm drove us home from the bus station. Moses and I were very tired, and we both clapped happily as the large white farmhouse came into view. Lillian had been one of eleven children, but now the farmhouse was home only to her oldest brother, youngest sister and their widowed mother. After the wedding, one of Lillian's brothers and his young family were planning to move into the large farm house, and Lillian's mother and her unmarried son would move into a smaller one behind the house.

There was much hustle and bustle going on as we hopped out of the van. The wedding of the youngest child was almost always the largest, as well as the most lavish. Many women could be seen through the kitchen window with scrub brushes or paint cans in their hands. In the back of the house, girls were lined up at wash tubs, cleaning everything in the house that could possibly be washed. As we made our way to the front porch, we were greeted by Lillian's mother. She gestured to her two older daughters to come into the kitchen where plans were being made for the all-important wedding dinner, the seating arrangements, how the family would get from the wedding service back to the house and so on. Timidly, I followed the women into the kitchen. I did not know anyone, but for some reason everyone seemed to know me.

"Hi, Emma," a chubby lady waved to me from where she was peeling apples for the pies.

"Hi." I waved back, having no clue who she was.

The chubby lady laughed. "Oh, I am Matty," she smiled. "I am a cousin of Lillian's. I read your post in Die Blatt every month, and I really like your poetry."

"Oh, thank you," I said as I took the work apron Grandma Yoder fairly threw at me.

I looked around to see what task needed an extra pair of hands and jumped right in to help roll out pie crusts for the seventy-five pies we were making. The wedding was on Wednesday, so there was little time for dawdling, and according to Grandma Yoder, we were way behind schedule. One of the ladies that ran a bakery out of her house had a group of women with her that were making the bread, thus freeing up our oven for the very important cakes and pies.

A few minutes after we arrived, the bride-to-be came in and started helping as well. She was a pretty girl with light brown hair and bright blue eyes. At age twenty-two, she was already older than many girls when they married, but I had overheard Lillian and Anna saying that the Bishop had refused to marry her and her boyfriend of five years for some time now. Sarah's soon-to-be husband had been in the Bann several times for attending a local bar. It seems he rode his horse into the nearby town and tied it at a post while he spent a couple hours in the bar. For the last year, the twenty-seven-year-old had been on probation with the church, and when no bad behavior was detected, he had at last been granted permission to marry. According to Lillian, her sister, Sarah, had been secretly in love with him since she was fifteen, and he with her. *How romantic*, I had thought as the bus rumbled toward Iowa. *How very romantic indeed.*

That evening, when I went to help with the chores, I finally got the chance to meet Lillian's older brother whom I had heard so much about. Isaac Yoder was in his early forties, and a few streaks of gray were already present in his dark brown hair. Katie, Sarah and I were carrying milk buckets out to the barn to do the evening milking when I saw him standing inside the horse corral petting a large brown horse that was eating sugar cubes off his shoulder.

"Oh, there is Uncle Isaac," Katie waved in the direction of the corral.

Isaac waved back with a kind smile as he came out of the corral and over to us. I was surprised when he hugged his nieces, who seemed very happy to see him.

"Hi, Emma," he turned to me with a shy smile. I could tell he was searching my face to see my reaction to him. I smiled back.

"I like your poetry," Isaac said "I write poems, too. Maybe you would like to look at them sometime?"

"Sure," I nodded. "That would be very nice."

He grinned at me, and I could see he felt more at ease.

As we were milking, I saw Isaac doing chores by himself while Jacob and Anna's husband talked to each other as they did chores together. Once or twice, I saw Moses move to help Isaac give hay to the horses, only to be called back sharply by Jacob.

Isaac's life story was a rather sad one, from what I had gathered. At the young age of fourteen, he had kissed another boy at school, for which a group of boys had beaten him up pretty badly. From then on, he had been labeled as "funny," and did not attend many of the singings or youth gatherings. He remained unmarried and was, thus, available for labor to young fathers in need of help, but hardly anyone ever asked for him. Even his younger brothers were embarrassed by him, and his only friends seemed to be a handful of female relatives and his mother.

Now a man in his early forties, he spent much of his time either working the family farm or pursuing his hobby, which was training horses for the *Englisch*. He taught the horses fancy tricks that were quite impressive, and you could tell by the way the horses looked up and nickered in his direction whenever he passed the corral that he had a real connection with them. I felt really sorry for him, and even sorrier for little Moses as I recognized that he had many of the same mannerisms and behaviors. *Poor Moses truly had a lonely life full of rejection ahead of him, unless he was able to learn to suppress his behavior.*

271

THE WEDDING day dawned bright and sunny, much to everyone's relief. The wedding service was to take place at the house of a cousin that lived nearby. An Amish wedding service is pretty much like a church service and usually lasts from nine in the morning until noon. At the end of the service, the couple is asked to step forward with their witnesses, and they are asked if they agree to wed. If they answer yes, they are asked to make a few vows and then are pronounced man and wife.

Right after the couple was pronounced man and wife, the bride's mother, sisters, a few cousins and I immediately went back to the house to start putting the elaborate meal on the table. A few of us were in charge of the massive amounts of mashed potatoes and gravy. My arm was aching quite a bit after I scooped the last bit of fluffy mashed potatoes into one of the bowls on the long bench-like tables. In addition to the mashed potatoes, there was plenty of fried chicken, stuffing, deviled eggs, bread and butter, jelly, celery sticks and apple and cherry pies.

In the corner of the largest room is an area called the "Eck," (German for "corner.") This is a special place set up for the bride and groom where they can sit with their closest friends and still see most of their guests. The best and most beautiful foods are placed in the Eck for the enjoyment of the wedding party.

We had barely finished laying everything out when people started arriving. I helped the women replenish water glasses and food bowls as they were emptied. It was such a large wedding that we had to clear and reset the tables three times. As I went about the business of making sure the wedding dinner went smoothly and no one was in need of anything, I glanced at the blushing bride. She looked truly happy as she leaned on the shoulder of her husband of only a couple of hours. This was the only time it would be acceptable for her to show affection in public, and she seemed to be taking advantage of it. I smiled wondering if that would ever be me. In reality, being at a wedding almost made me want to get married and live happily ever after with the man of my dreams, but the finality of it scared me, and I knew I could not bring children into this culture and then have my hands tied if I was unable to protect them from monsters or defend them if something happened to them. I would not be able to do it, even if the thought of a large family made me smile dreamily.

After the wedding dinner was over, we cleaned up the dishes and cleared away the leftovers in preparation for the evening events. It is the custom on the evening of the wedding to invite all the young people from the district—and even from surrounding districts—for a long evening of singing. There was one variation to a normal singing: the married men took great pleasure in pairing the unattached young men up with the unmarried young ladies. I was a bit nervous about this since I was quite shy and never had much cause to talk to any members of the opposite sex unless they were in my immediate family.

As I went upstairs to change out of my soiled dress and apron, I could hear several girls that had stayed for the singing whispering about who they hoped to be paired with. I half listened to the girls' whispers while I pinned up my green dress and white cape and apron. I rolled my eyes as I heard a few of the boy-crazy girls squeal while they talked about young Adam Lambright, who was supposedly the cutest bachelor in the county. I was startled out of my eavesdropping when I heard a light knock on the door.

"Come in," I said as I hurriedly put the last pins into my cape and tied my stiff kapp strings in a neat bow under my chin.

"It's me," I heard Isaac whisper as he stuck his head through a crack in the door. "Do you mind if I come in?"

I smiled as I went to the door and pulled him in, laughing at the idea of a single man and a girl of my age being in a room alone together.

"It's just me. No one will care." Isaac walked behind me and tucked in the back of my cape as he if he were another woman. The back of the cape was always difficult to tuck in and get straight, and as I turned and looked in the mirror, I smiled at how even and neat it was.

"Oh, just years of practice," he grinned as he saw me admiring his work.

I laughed as he plopped down on the bed and started complaining about how much he hated weddings. I got my song book from the drawer and sat on the corner of the bed next to him. I felt so sorry for him. I had seen him out by the barn, standing alone some distance away from the group of men. He had been staring off into the sky as if he were miles away. Although Isaac was not officially shunned by the church, it seemed as if, unofficially, he was; and he was simply ignored by nearly everyone.

"Are you going to miss your baby sister?" I asked him.

"Yeah, a lot." He looked so sad. "It will just be me and Mom now... Emma," he propped himself up on one elbow, "you are from Washington State, right?"

I nodded. "How do you know that?"

"Oh, letters from Lillian," he grinned. "When you first moved in with them, she sent Mom a bunch of letters, and I secretly read all of them. I don't think she liked you much at first."

I smiled and shook my head.

"Yeah, Mom still does not like that you're living with them. I love my mom, but she is so meddlesome sometimes."

I just smiled and shrugged my shoulders. "It's okay."

"Yeah, I know the feeling," Isaac flopped back down on the bed.

We sat there in silence for a moment, enjoying each other's presence. The silence was broken by the sound of approaching buggies. I got up and looked out the window to see several open two-seat courting buggies turning into the lane. I started to feel nervous and looked over at Isaac; he was smiling at me.

"How do I look?" I smoothed out my white apron and pulled my kapp up on my head.

"Very sweet," Isaac smiled as he scanned me from head to foot.

I smiled back at him and found myself wishing he were *my* brother instead of Lillian's.

"You are probably going to get asked on a date tonight," Isaac said as he sat up. "I overheard a bunch of the guys talking about you. You are pretty popular."

I raised my eyebrows and shuddered.

Isaac frowned and cocked his head at my reaction. Our eyes met, and in that instant I knew he could tell that I had been severely hurt by a man, and I could see the sympathy in his eyes. As I passed him to go downstairs, he grabbed my hand.

"Don't let it ruin your future, Emma," his voice was soft. "You are too nice a girl to end up alone. Don't let that happen."

I smiled at him and squeezed his hand as I hurried to leave the room before he could see the tears welling up in my eyes. Those words from Isaac were the kindest and most sincere words of advice I had ever received, and the pure sweetness of his nature, combined with my own fears and dreams, made me burst into tears. As I got to the bottom of the stairs, I quickly dried my eyes with my handkerchief and went outside to join the other girls that were huddled together in groups, either waiting for their names to be called or to go sit with their boyfriends.

After about half an hour of standing outside, one of the young married men came to the door and waved the boys in. First the boys that had girlfriends walked in, and as they reached the door, their girlfriends joined them. They sat at the long table together as the married people looked on and commented about how the couple looked together or whose relatives they were and so on. Next, the boys that did not have girlfriends due to a breakup, being new to the young people's group or simply never having been able to get a girl to go on a date with them entered. One by one their names were called and then a girl's name was called, and as a pair they walked in and sat together. I waited nervously for my name to be called. About halfway through the list of single men I heard,

"Jonathan L Borntreger and Emma J Schrock." I looked around to make sure there were no other Emma J Schrocks in the group, and then quickly stepped forward to walk in with Jonathan. I looked up at him as we walked into the room, and he smiled down at me from his towering six-foot-plus stature. I smiled back. He seemed nice enough. As we sat down, I saw the paired couples whispering to each other. This was only allowed at weddings, and the young people seemed to be enjoying themselves immensely. This was my first time with youngie at a wedding singing since these pairings are not allowed until after baptism. Although I was nervous, I found myself starting to enjoy the fun atmosphere as girls on either side of me leaned past their boyfriends to crack jokes with each other. Jokes and funny articles circled around the table. I felt a little smothered when I felt Jonathan sitting as close to me as possible. Every time I started to move, though, I heard Isaac's words echoing in my ears and tried not to be bothered by his obvious advances.

That night, as the girls waited outside for their boyfriends and prospective dates, I waited for the inevitable request. When Jonathan's female cousin came over to me to ask if I would be willing to go on a date with Jonathan, I had been prepared to say yes..I fully intended to say yes, but at the last moment found myself shaking my head no. I felt bad when I saw her crestfallen face as she turned to go back to one of the boys Jonathan had sent to ask. I kicked myself afterwards, but I did not want to start a long distance relationship with someone I did not know. It was too frightening.

A HORSE NAMED TEARS

"No man has the right to dictate what other men should perceive, create or produce, but all should be encouraged to reveal themselves, their perceptions and emotions, and to build confidence in the creative spirit."

—*Ansel Adams*

The rest of our vacation time was spent cleaning up and getting ready for the construction of the small house that would be built on the side of the large house. I helped the other women as we packed some things which would then be moved into the smaller house. Sarah and her new husband were basically swapping farms with her brother. This larger farm was more suited to a family with children, rather than a young couple that was just starting out. As we worked, I could sense that Grandma Yoder was not accepting me as one of her new family members, and I felt a shift in Lillian's behavior. I just shrugged it off. What could they have against me?

We had plans to head home the next Friday, and much of our final week was spent visiting relatives and friends. The Thursday before we left, we planned to visit a cousin of Jacob's who lived a few miles away in a separate district. Everyone was going except Isaac. I was tying my bonnet to go with the rest of the group when Isaac came in from the horse corral and asked me if I could stay home and help him with a difficult horse. Surprised, I looked at Lillian and Grandma Yoder to see if it was okay. They shrugged and said it was fine if I wanted to stay. Happily, I nodded at Isaac and ran upstairs to change out of my good clothes and back into my

276

everyday dress.

When I came back downstairs, Isaac was waiting for me on the porch. As I came outside, I saw the sun glinting off the few gray strands in his hair. Despite being in his early forties, Isaac appeared more youthful than most of the married men his age. Because Isaac was single he did not have a beard, and his very smooth, white skin helped give the illusion of youth.

He smiled at me as I walked up to him.

"What horse do you need help with?" I asked as I skipped down the steps.

"Oh, silly Emma," Isaac pushed me playfully. "I don't need help with a horse. That was just an excuse to get you to stay here with me."

I smiled at him; I had figured as much. We spent most of the day talking about our dreams and what we wanted from life.

"Yeah," Isaac said when I had finished a brief description of my childhood. "What a mess, huh?"

We were both sitting haphazardly on the corral fence, watching the horses. I nodded and patted one of the horses that put his head in my lap.

"What is this one's name?" I asked, brushing its black mane out of its eyes.

"Oh, this is Tears," Isaac patted the tall, brown horse affectionately on its neck.

"Tears?" I looked at him and made a face "What a strange name for a horse."

"Well," Isaac explained, "I got him about five years ago. I was really sad the day I bought him. Originally, I was planning to resell him, but I felt such a connection to him...I felt he understood me when I cried, so I named him 'Tears.' I kept him and trained him to be my buggy horse, so he goes everywhere with me now."

We sat in a comfortable silence for a while, drinking in the Iowa fall sunshine.

"Emma, I have to leave the Amish," Isaac said abruptly as he hopped down from the fence.

"What?" I exclaimed in astonishment as I hopped down after him. "You can't leave the Amish."

"Why?" Isaac asked, turning to me as if he hoped I could convince him not to go.

"Because...because...you will go to hell." I stammered.

"They already believe I am going to hell," he shrugged. "And I can't live here any longer. What am I going to do when I get old? Who is going to care for me?"

I saw tears gathering in his eyes. I felt bad and nodded sympathetically. Although I really believed that anyone that left the Amish would go straight to hell, I was not so sure that would be the case for Isaac since his own people were almost forcing him out.

"No one will care if I leave," Isaac continued. "Not even my mother. She is embarrassed by me. Everyone is, and I don't know why I have to stay if they don't want me. I have been trying to get the nerve to leave for ten years, but every time I plan to leave, I dream I die and go to hell, and I just can't do it. But I have finally decided I have do it," Isaac clenched his fists. "I have to do it now, while I am still young enough."

"Where will you go, Isaac?" I asked, almost in a whisper.

"I always wanted to go out west and work on a ranch, maybe to Montana or Washington State," Isaac mused. "I would love to be a real live cowboy, you know, do something I want to do, have a little fun before I get too old."

I smiled at him and nodded. "Then you should do it, Isaac," I swallowed the lump in my throat. I feared I was giving him bad advice, but he was right. What would happen to him when he got older if he stayed here? He would die a lonely old man, regretting that he had never loved or been loved.

The day ended too quickly, and the approaching rattle of buggy wheels signaled the end of our open conversation.

THE NEXT day, we got up early to leave. Moses and I carried the suitcases to the waiting van while Lillian and Jacob said their last goodbyes. As I was closing the back of the van, I felt a hand squeeze my shoulder.

"Guess who?" I heard Isaac say playfully.

I turned around and smiled at Isaac.

"Well, this is goodbye, I guess," Isaac gave me a playful push. "I will probably never see you again, huh?"

I shook my head sadly. "Probably not."

Lillian and Jacob walked over to the van.

"Okay," Isaac pulled down his hat. "Here comes 'Mr. Nice Guy'. I better go. Take care of yourself, Emma."

Sadly I watched him turn and start walking away. "Isaac, wait," I called after as I pulled a new, pink-flowered handkerchief out of my dress pocket. I had been planning to give it to Sarah as a token of friendship but decided to give it to Isaac instead. This was an unusual gesture, but I wanted Isaac to have something to remember me by.

Isaac took the dainty handkerchief. "Pretty," he smiled at me. "Pretty like you, Emma. I will keep this always." He held it to his heart and walked away.

As we drove away, I felt really sad. It was not acceptable for men and women to write each other unless they were brother and sister, and even then, letters were usually written to the family; they were not personal letters. I knew I would probably never see or hear from Isaac again, but I really hoped he would leave the Amish and find happiness before he was "too old," as he had put it.

Although at that time I truly believed that anyone that left the Amish would most certainly go to hell, I was not so sure in Isaac's case. He was definitely the kindest, gentlest and most understanding man I had ever met, and I wished him happiness rather than the loneliness with which he was now surrounded. I felt I had made a true friend, and the warmth of that friendship made my eyes swell with tears. There *were* beautiful and nice people in the world, I thought with a sigh. I had just not been fortunate enough to meet many of them.

*W*E SAT in the bus station until it was time to board our bus. I was glad to be going home. The trip had been life-changing, but I was more than ready to get back to familiar surroundings.

"How about you, Moses?" I asked the quiet twelve-year-old as he sat next to me.

Moses shook his head. "No. I don't want to go home," he turned his back to me.

I frowned at his odd behavior. I was holding everyone's shawls and coats in my arms, but I managed to free a hand and pull Moses back toward me.

"Why don't you want to go home, Moses?" I asked, half frowning and half smiling at him.

Moses looked at his chubby hands for a moment and then looked around to see where Jacob was. When he saw Jacob standing far away looking at a map, he leaned in and whispered in my ear. "Elam is really mean to me, sometimes he really hurts me."

I sighed. I will never know why Elam was so heartless to his little brother. "Has he hurt you really bad, Moses?" I asked, watching his eyes for any hidden messages.

Moses shrugged. "Elam says I am half girl and I need to toughen up. I am really scared of him."

I was so angered by what I was hearing. What was wrong with Elam? I thought. In the last year he had turned into such a bully.

Moses just shrugged and put his tan hand in mine. "I am really scared of Elam," he whispered, and I saw tears forming in his eyes.

I looked at this little boy next to me. He was so sweet, a little shorter than average for his age and with a round stomach and chubby cheeks and hands. Every time I saw him, he made me smile because he was so sweet and innocent looking. Lillian had told me that he had almost died when he was born because he was so premature, and she believed he had slight brain damage due to his traumatic birth. Sometimes he did seem a little slow in thinking things out, but I believed it was due to his complex brain; he seemed to consider every possible detail before making a decision. As he sat there next to me in his dark blue shirt and suspenders that held up his black broadfall pants, he really did look scared.

"Listen, Moses," I said, wanting to comfort him. "If Elam does something to you, come and get me, and I will go after him and beat the c**p out of him."

Moses laughed at my choice of words. "I don't think you would be able to, Emma. He is way bigger than you."

"Yeah, well," I laughed with him. "I did not say I was going to fight fair. All I have to do is get one of those metal rods and sneak up behind him and crack him over the back with it."

Moses looked at me in surprise. "You would do that, Emma?"

"Of course I would," I nodded my head. "He has no right to do what he is doing. Matter of fact..." I looked Moses in the eye. "...you should do it yourself if he does something to you. Wait for your chance and hit him with something."

"Oh, no, he will hurt me even more," Moses shuddered.

"Bullies usually stop once you stand up to them, Moses," I said as I remembered the day Brian had nearly broken my neck.

"Okay, I will try it," Moses smiled up at me. "But if it doesn't work, you will still beat him up for me, right?"

"Anytime." I smiled.

"I feel better now, Emma. I am not scared anymore," he said happily as he hopped off the seat and ran to the bathroom.

I sighed and stared at the floor. Elam's behavior was getting worse, he was no longer just that *mean older brother* that some families have. He was now malicious and intentional and his treatment of animals was becoming so bad even Jacob sometimes chided him to "take it easy there." I did not know why but some of his actions made me shake inside and when I would frown at his behavior he would just laugh and continue. For the most part his parents chose to ignore it, something that was encouraged among the Amish. As long as he was not breaking the Ordnung he was considered a "good boy." Being a "good boy" in the Amish had nothing to do with kindness and decency, but everything to do with obeying the church rules with out questioning.

Moses tugged on my arm to jerk me out of my reverie. "Emma, come on, We are going to miss the bus."

I feigned a smile at him as I climbed aboard the bus. Everyone was quiet as we left the Iowa countryside behind and headed north to Minnesota. I looked out at the cars and *Englisch* houses as we passed by. I wondered how they spent their days. *How strange and different from us,* I thought. I could not even imagine how the *Englisch* lived with their bright lights, constant loud noises and worldly clothes.

I looked at the *Englisch* women and thought about how they all looked different. All of them had different hair, makeup and clothes. I wondered how they decided what to put on or how to fix their hair. I thought hard about this and wondered what it would be like to live among them. I had not thought about any of these things since I was a small child. All I had to do was dress according to church law every day of my life. The biggest decision I ever had to make was what color dress to wear on Sunday, and that usually meant whatever we had all decided to wear as a group. There was little individuality or sense of self-worth in the world in which I lived.

As I sat there, lost in my thoughts, I looked toward the front of the bus. I noticed a young, smart-looking woman, about my age, with a pile of books in her lap and a notebook in which she seemed to be writing notes. I frowned absentmindedly. How much I wished to be like that girl, smart and confident with the ability to live according to my own standards and speak my mind. She was worlds and worlds away from me, however, and even though we lived side by side, we lived in two very separate universes.

THAT NOVEMBER heralded the arrival of my twenty-first birthday. I was now considered a full-grown adult, and Jacob and Lillian were required to pay me three dollars a day for every day that I worked. This money was either put into an envelope on the desk or recorded in a tablet to be given to my husband after I married, or shortly before if we needed help with the purchase of a farm. Any quilting I did now was tracked, and I was paid for that and any other side sewing jobs I did as well. Many girls are in a hurry to make as much money as possible when they turn twenty-one in preparation for their upcoming weddings, but since I did not have an upcoming wedding, I did not care too much about the money.

For my twenty-first birthday, I was given a wall clock with a pendulum. I was happy as I stowed it away in my hope chest, but as I closed the lid on the chest, I could not help wonder if I would ever use any of these things to set up my own household.

Letters from Samantha and Matty told me how excited and happy they were with their new boyfriends. Matty had found an older boy in the community. Samantha wrote that he was overweight and a little slow, but he seemed very kind. I was happy for Matty. She was a kind, sweet girl and deserved someone that would be kind and sweet to her in return. Samantha had been on several dates with Daniel and was already dropping hints about becoming Mrs. Hostetler soon. Matty wrote that if I still had feelings for Isaiah, I had better get over them, because her cousin in Ohio wrote that Isaiah had been going steady with one of his second cousins for a while now and they were planning to visit and bring the girl's parents with them in the spring. That most likely meant wedding bells.

I was sitting on my bed when I read the news, and although Isaiah and I barely knew eachother, I could not help but think how different things would have been had his parents not sent him away. I had felt a connection with him, even though we never exchanged more than two words. I felt I could trust him and would have certainly dated him and most likely would have even married him, given the chance. I felt tears well up in my eyes, but I quickly brushed them away. I was not going to shed tears over something that could not be helped now, I thought.

THAT WINTER I spent a lot of time working on a quilt that I planned to sell for commission at the quilt shop. I was making my favorite sunshine and shadows pattern. I loved the mix of bright and dark colors, and since it was to be sold, I could use printed fabrics and any colors I wished. I had fun at Wal-Mart picking out the fabrics to be matched together. I put all of the creativity I could muster into that quilt and was repaid with oohs and ahhs from everyone that saw it.

My spirits, however, were dampened by the coldness I felt from Lillian ever since we had returned from Iowa. I did not know what was causing it until one early morning in January, when I was putting the cream in the ice house before going upstairs for breakfast. As I turned to go back in the house, I nearly ran into Jacob, who was standing in the shadows. He reached out and grabbed me, pulling me to him. I tried to yank away, but his grip was firm.

"Stop it, Emma." His words made me pause and look at him curiously. He had been going out of his way to be rude to me lately. I think he was trying to to prove to Lillian that there was nothing going on between us.

"What do you want?" I whispered, looking around to see if there was anyone around.

"You have got to patch things up with Lillian," Jacob said matter-of-factly.

"What?" I asked in confusion. "I have no idea what's wrong with her, and I definitely do not know how to fix it."

"Well, all I know..." Jacob paused as he kicked at a rock in front of him. "...all I know is that her mother convinced her that you are in love with me, and that is why you are turning down dates."

"How do you know that I turned down any dates?" I asked, feeling as though my privacy had been violated.

"Word gets out, Emma. You should have thought of that."

"Well, that is so far from the truth that it is laughable," I said as I turned to go into the house.

"Quit being a child, Emma," Jacob grabbed me by the shoulder again.

"Well, this is not helping matters any," I yanked away from him again and fixed the pins that had popped open on my dress collar when he grabbed me.

"Look here," Jacob towered over me. "It is not only your reputation that is being torn apart here... so is mine...and so is my family's."

"But it is not true," I repeated.

"You know that and I know that," Jacob scanned me with his eyes. I shivered a little as he did so. "But there has to be a reason if a young woman is turning down the very thing every Amish girl stays awake praying for every night."

I felt taken aback. Of course no one would understand the reasons for my hesitancy.

"I don't know what you want me to do," I said angrily. "First you are mad at me because of Isaiah, and now you want me to go on the first date offered me?"

"Oh, get over it, Emma," Jacob grabbed me again and pulled me toward him. "I don't ever want you to go on a date. All I want is for you to patch things up with Lillian somehow, so she can make her mother and her sisters shut up."

I yanked away again. "You have yourself to thank for how Lillian feels," I hissed at him. "And as for me, I can take care of myself. Just leave me alone and keep your hands off me." I turned on my heel and went into the house, slamming the door in his face.

I didn't know why I was so mad at him. I guess it was the sheer stupidity of the gossip. It seemed gossip was a favorite pastime for a lot of women, and they did not care who got caught in the crossfire of their treacherous tongues. Well, I thought, they can gossip all they want. What do I care?

"Wolves in Sheeps Clothing"

"Never rebel for the sake of rebelling, but always rebel for the sake of truth."

— *Criss Jami*

One day in March as Ella was helping me finish up my quilt, Lillian came upstairs with an *Englisch* woman that came by once a week to buy eggs and butter. It was unusual to have one of the *Englisch* in our house, and Ella and I stared at her for a moment.

Well, Mrs. Martin was telling me she was looking for a present to take to her granddaughter's wedding," Lillian explained as she walked over to us. "I told her about the quilt Emma was making, and she wanted to see it."

We unrolled the quilt from the frame, and I smiled as Mrs. Martin gasped when she saw the hues of green, pink, blue and purple surrounded by a border of deep maroon.

"Wow, it is so bright and colorful," Mrs. Martin exclaimed as she felt the hand quilting. "This is perfect. How much is it?" she turned to me.

"Uh..." I stammered. I had not thought of a price for it yet. "Uh, eight hundred," I said finally, remembering how much my quilt had gone for at the auction.

I saw Lillian wince when I said eight hundred, and I thought for a moment that I had overestimated the worth of my prized masterpiece.

"I'll take it," Mrs. Martin nodded and smiled at me. "It is truly one of the most beautiful things I have ever seen. How long before it is finished?"

"Two days, I think," I looked at Lillian, who nodded in agreement.

"Okay, I will pick it up next week when I come for eggs and butter," Mrs. Martin said as she turned to go downstairs. "And I'll bring cash," she added, smiling at me.

"Wow," Ella clapped her hands and threw her arms around my neck. "Eight hundred dollars. That is so much money for just a couple months' work."

I nodded, surprised myself. That was going to be nice chunk of money stowed away, I thought. For what, I did not know, but it was at least comforting to know it was there. When I went to help Phyllis the next week and told her how much I made from the quilt, she raised her eyebrows and smiled at me.

"You will make some young man a good wife," she smiled. I smiled back and tried to share her enthusiasm at the prospect of being a good wife.

THAT APRIL after communion service, all of the church members were asked to stay for an important announcement, something that must be discussed at length. I heard a moan from some of the young women beside me as we tried to stretch our backs after being seated for seven hours already. I fidgeted with the Halzduch (Amish for cape) that tucked into my neck string only a couple of inches under my chin. The stiff white organdy fabric always irritated my neck, especially when it was warm like this particular April day had turned out to be. I was only half listening as the Bishop stood up with a letter in his hand and began reading. Absent mindedly, I noticed that the letter was from out of the country and wondered why he was going to read it in church. I was suddenly jerked out of my sleepy, irritated mood when I heard the Bishop say solemnly,

"A couple of weeks ago, we got a letter from Larry, who has been living in Russia for the past year. He says he recently married a young woman from there and now requests permission to come back here to live among us as he did a few years ago."

The Bishop paused for a moment before continuing. "After much prayer and after we talked with the rest of the men, we believe his past transgression should not be held against him. Therefore, the ministers and I have written him to say it would be alright for him to live nearby if he wishes. He still dresses like us, and his wife will do the same; it is our duty to forgive him".

I sat stunned and looked around at the room of blank faces. No one seemed to object to this man moving back to the community. All of the

286

married adults knew what Larry had done, yet they seemed to think it was their duty to forgive him and let him live on the outskirts of the community just because he dressed like us.

Being a church member did have its advantages. It let us know what was happening in the community. As church let out, I saw several groups of women and men huddled together discussing Larry. I milled around, waiting for Lillian and Jacob. I felt too tired to walk home like most of the other young people were doing since none of them really knew or cared anything about Larry. I found myself eavesdropping behind the group of women Lillian was talking to.

"Remember what he did to Laura?" one woman said angrily.

"Yeah, but how is that different from one of our men with the same shortcomings?" another woman asked.

"Well." I heard Lillian's voice. "He went to prison in the eighties for holding those people from Asia on his farm and making them work while he molested their children. That is really weird. And we have to remember, he is a worldly outsider."

"So are Emma and Beth," I heard another woman say.

"Yeah," Grandma Shrock piped up. "But they were young girls who had been raised on a mountain somewhere. They were less worldly than our own children."

I raised my eyebrows surprised to hear what they thought of me and Samantha.

"Shhh," I heard Lillian whisper as she turned and spotted me standing behind her.

I looked at the women, who seemed embarrassed that I had caught them talking about me.

"We had better go," Lillian nodded to Grandma Schrock.

I smiled at Grandma Schrock. Despite her strange ways, I was happy that she had stood up for me; I could always tell she never believed the ridiculous gossip that constantly circled about me.

"Yeah, that's a good idea," Grandma Schrock glared at the woman who had made the comment about me and Samantha. "Come on, Emma, let's go home and get some supper," she tapped my shoes with her black cane.

I smiled and followed them to the buggy where Jacob was waiting with Grandpa Schrock.

About a month later I heard that Larry had arrived. He was leasing a small piece of property on the side of the Mast farm. He and his Russian wife would be living in a small mobile home he moved onto the property. They were not really living amongst us and following all the rules, but they were going to use a horse and buggy, dress like us and attend some of our social gatherings.

I was helping Phyllis when the couple came around in their new buggy to visit the Bishop's family. I was shocked to see a young, twenty-four-year-old Russian girl sitting next to the sixty-five-year-old Larry. I made a face when I saw them together, and Phyllis nodded in agreement. Zoya was a tall, pretty blonde girl; Larry was a little shorter than she was, he was chubby and balding with just a sparse amount of gray hair left on his head.

"How did he ever convince her to leave her home and family to come here with him?" I wondered aloud as I watched them walking toward the house.

Phyllis, who was watching them too, said that she had heard that Zoya was from a poor and remote village in Russia and had been only too happy to marry a man from the United States. However, Phyllis said she seemed shocked at how Larry expected her to live. Zoya had told Katie Mast that Larry seemed different in Russia, and that he had not dressed like this or told her she would have to.

"That's not nice," I frowned.

Phyllis shrugged. "It is good for her, although she does not know it, I guess."

"You really think so?" I asked, unconvinced, as I walked to the door and opened it for them.

I smiled at Zoya while trying not to look at Larry—I could not even stand thinking of him. Zoya smiled back at me timidly and stretched out her slim, beautiful hand to shake mine. She was only a couple of years older than I was, and I detected a look of confusion and helplessness in her eyes that I knew only too well.

"Are you Emma?" I heard Larry ask from behind me. I felt the hair on the back of my neck stand up, and I did not want to answer him, but I could not risk showing my feelings for fear people would realize I knew more than I should.

"Yes," I turned around and stared past his head.

"Good; you will be a good teacher for Zoya," he nodded at his wife. At his nod, she stepped forward and stood next to me as if we were playing follow the leader.

I frowned at him. "What do you mean?" I asked, not able to keep the iciness out of my voice.

I saw him study me for a moment as if he could see right through me into my very soul. I swallowed hard and tried to keep my composure. I did not want him to see how much he disturbed me. His gray hair, slightly chubby figure and those piercing eyes were so much like Brian's that it was eerie—especially the eyes...piercing...calculating eyes. I didn't like the way Zoya seemed to jump at his every whim. You b*stard, I thought to myself. How dare you talk to me like that? He had actually gone to prison for holding people against their will. *So much like Brian,* I thought.

"Well, I heard you were *Englisch* and joined the Amish, so I thought you would be able to help Zoya learn."

"Oh," I said in a sweet, innocent voice. "But you are not joining the Amish, and I was raised in the middle of nowhere, so technically I was a mountain girl, not *Englisch.*"

I saw him give me a look of exasperation and was pleased that he was getting my drift. I might have continued had Phyllis not stepped in, smiling like the gracious hostess she always was.

"I am sure Emma will have lots of tips for Zoya that will make her feel more at home around here," she waved everyone to sit down at the table, where she had placed some glasses filled with apple cider.

Larry squinted at me as he sat down, and I held his gaze defiantly. He was not a member of our church and never would be, due to his age and the fact that he was divorced. He could not do or say anything about me that would get me in trouble, so I was not going to let him think I was just another little lamb being led blindly to slaughter. I believe it was because he reminded me so much of Brian that I felt determined to let him know that I was fully aware of just what sort of man he was.

"So how do you like the United States, Zoya?" I asked as she sat next to me.

"It's not what I expected," she answered in a low, sad voice.

I was surprised at how well she spoke English.

"Oh?," Phyllis queried . "How so?"

"Well..." Zoya looked in Larry's direction "...I haven't seen anything of the United States, really. We came straight here, and then Larry made me wear these clothes that he bought from a catalog," she looked down at her blue dress and apron. The clothes he had bought, while not exactly in the same Ordnung with our dress code, were pretty close.

"I want to go back home," she whispered to me. "But I don't know how,

289

and Larry reads all the letters I send to my family."

"He can read Russian?" I asked in surprise.

Zoya nodded. "He knows five languages," she whispered. Just then Larry looked over at her, and she faked a smile for him.

"He can't keep her prisoner like that," I told to Phyllis and Peter after the couple left.

"It's not our business," Peter shrugged. "They are not part of our church. I explained to Larry he is allowed to live alongside us and attend social activities and church."

"Hmm," I sniffed as I tied my bonnet. "I think he is not being nice to Zoya, and she does not even want to dress Amish."

"Larry is her husband," Peter snapped at me, "it is her duty to obey him."

"We are condoning his criminal activity by welcoming him here while we know he is keeping that girl prisoner," I shot back at him.

"You will be respectful toward him and not judge him. You hear me, Emma?" Peter's voice was almost threatening.

I rolled my eyes and walked out the door. Although I did not know much about the outside world, I tried to learn as much as I could by reading scraps of newspapers that lay around. I knew all about the girls from poor countries of the world that were tricked into coming to the United States by creepy men promising them something other than what they found once they arrived. But I knew there was no reason for our community to care about this. There were so many men with the same so-called 'weaknesses in our church. One more would not make much difference.

AS THE weeks passed and summer approached, life became very busy again with all the work a farm brings during planting and birthing season. Zoya learned how to drive a horse and buggy, and since she was lonely much of the time in the mobile home she shared with Larry, she would often trot down to see me. She followed me and Ella around as we worked. I tried to be a good friend to her. Zoya was a sweet girl and she laughed with us as we worked and played practical jokes on each other, but I saw her face fall every time she hitched up her buggy to go home.

Once, when we were alone, I asked her why she did not just divorce Larry and go back home.

"I can't," she had whispered back. "I have no money for the plane ticket, and Larry took my passport and locked it in a safe deposit box somewhere. Besides, my father is dead and my mother and five siblings can barely feed themselves. It would break their hearts if they knew what happened to me here." She sobbed into her handkerchief. "It will be years before I get my green card, if I ever get it."

"Of course you will," I assured her, trying to remember what I had read in the paper about green cards.

Zoya shrugged and shook her head. "Larry drags his feet about filing papers and everything. It is going to take many years."

"Larry sounds like a j*rk," I whispered.

"You have no idea," Zoya whispered back. "I know you are Amish, but I really hate these clothes. I never even heard of Amish people before in my life,"she slapped her long, brown dress angrily.

"I am not offended," I smiled at her. "I was raised this way and cannot imagine much else, but I can understand how hard it would be to have something like this just pushed on you."

"I still trim my hair," Zoya took off her kapp and let her soft, light blonde hair down. It was cut in short layers around her shoulders and made her look so pretty.

"Larry hit me when he caught me doing it, but I felt I just had to. I felt so suffocated." Her lower lip began trembling. "Do you know he took my makeup out of my suitcase at the airport and threw it away?"

"Oh, I had not even thought about you wearing makeup," I furrowed my brow, realizing how dumb I probably sounded to her.

Zoya shrugged. "It was just the really cheap stuff, but I still miss my mascara and lip gloss," she looked at her face reflected in the shiny, stainless steel sink. "My eyebrows and eyelashes are so white." She frowned.

"Oh, Zoya. You are so beautiful." I smiled at her. "You don't need all that stuff to make you beautiful."

Zoya frowned and shook her head. "I used to be beautiful, but not anymore," she mused.

I smiled sympathetically as she stood there in her long dress and white kapp. She really was being held a prisoner, I thought to myself. Obviously she did not believe in our religion or think she had to dress this way in order to get to heaven. She was merely doing it to please her husband, and that must have been a miserable reality for her.

ON JUNE, the inevitable visit from Isaiah and his soon-to-be wife, Ruth, came to pass. The following church Sunday when I met Ruth before church services, I tried my best to be pleasant, even though it was hard. When I smiled and nodded to her in the washhouse, I could tell that she knew about me and Isaiah from the cold stare she gave me. Of course, I was biased, but I could not imagine what Isaiah saw in her. She was tall and heavyset with curly black hair. I decided she was probably nicer than she seemed, though. My very presence must have been a threat to her. During church services, I could not help but glance at Isaiah in the back row. I saw him staring at me, and our eyes met for a moment, but I looked away quickly, not wishing to start any new gossip.

That evening after the singing, I was waiting for Elam to come by with the buggy when Isaiah's younger sister came to me and nodded for me to follow her. I frowned for a moment and looked around to see if anyone had noticed. Ruth and a few of the other girls had their backs turned to us as they laughed about something they did not want us to hear. Perplexed, I followed Isaiah's sister out into the warm summer night. Stars twinkled across the sky, and a light breeze brought the scent of alfalfa through the air. When we got outside, she nodded to the side of the house where I saw someone standing in the shadows, and then she jumped into the buggy with her boyfriend. Slowly I walked into the shadows and smiled hesitantly when I saw Isaiah's face reflected in the moonlight.

"Isaiah," I whispered. "We can't be seen like this."

"Just a moment," he whispered back as he grabbed my hand. "I just wanted to see you before I left. I wanted you to know I wish things had been different."

I bit my lip as I looked around the corner of the house and saw Elam trotting over with the buggy.

"I know, Isaiah," I whispered back. "I have to go, though." I pulled away, not wanting to reawaken the feelings that I had once had.

Isaiah grabbed my hand again and yanked me around. "I will never forget you, Emma," he whispered. "I have to marry Ruth, though. My mother would ruin you if I tried to see you."

"Goodbye, Isaiah," My voice was trembling. "I won't forget you, either, but we can't meet like this again." I pulled away and ran to the waiting buggy.

A VISIT FROM THE FBI

"Indifference is more truly the opposite of love than hate is, for we can both love and hate the same person at the same time, but we cannot both love and be indifferent to the same person at the same time."

— Peter Kreeft, Prayer for Beginners

A few weeks later as Ella and I were pulling weeds in the garden, I looked up to see a cloud of dust coming down the dirt lane. Two black SUVs stopped in front of the Bishop's house. Curiously, Ella, Moses and I watched as a woman and a man wearing suits got out of the SUVs and walked up to the porch, where Phyllis had come out to greet them. We watched as she pointed down the lane towards our place, where Peter was helping Jacob and Elam work on a neighbor farmer's tractor. The man and woman got back in their SUVs and drove to where the men were working.

"Who do you think they are?" Moses asked curiously.

"I don't know," I answered as we hugged the garden fence in order to better hear what was being said.

"Hello. I am Agent Morrison, and this is Agent Kendrick," the woman said as she walked up to Peter and flashed her badge.

"I think they are FBI," I walked to the garden gate.

"I am looking for the Bishop of your church."

"I am the Bishop," Peter took off his straw hat and wiped his sweating brow.

"Okay." The woman turned to him in a confident, no-nonsense manner. "I am here in regard to a Larry Flint who recently moved into this area. I am told he has affiliations with your church."

"Well," Peter said slowly, "he does dress like us, but he is not a member of our church."

"I see," she wrote something down in a notepad. "And are you and your people aware that he is a sex offender?"

"Yeah," Jacob shrugged at them. "We know that, but we believe a man can change through forgiveness, and we don't want Larry's transgressions to permanently label him."

"Regardless of what your beliefs are," Agent Morrison said matter-of-factly, "we are taking Larry in for failure to register as a sex offender, and we want you to be aware that you have a potential predator living amongst your group. We know that you do not have internet or television, so we wanted to be sure you were aware of the situation."

"Yeah, okay," Peter nodded toward them as they turned, got in the vehicles and barreled down the lane out of sight.

"What is a sex offender?" Ella asked as we walked back toward the garden.

"Um," I stammered, not knowing how to answer her. "Um...you should ask Mom."

"Why can't you tell me?" Ella frowned at me.

"Well, it is something someone does to make the government mad at them, I guess." I shrugged as if I did not really know.

"Oh," Ella was still frowning. "I wonder what Larry did?"

I shrugged again. I wished that I could tell her but I could not risk being called to the barn for having an indecent talk with an unmarried girl.

We heard that Larry was going to be in jail for a month. I figured no one would bother to visit Zoya, and that she would be all alone in her mobile home, so I hitched up the buggy a couple of times and went to see her. The first time I pulled the buggy up to the front of their place, I found her sitting on the steps, just staring around and hugging her knees.

"Oh," she exclaimed as I hopped down from the buggy, "I am so glad you came over. I was not sure what to do, so I have just been staying here."

I went over and hugged her. "How are you?" I asked, sitting down next to her.

Zoya just shook her head. "I am so confused," she wiped a tear from her cheek. "I had no idea about Larry's past. When they came in and arrested him, the woman took me aside and questioned me to see if I was okay. I think she thought I was being held hostage or something."

"Well, you kind of are," I looked into her clear blue eyes.

Zoya shook her head. "I can't do anything to upset my green card status,"she stared across the hay field. "Even if they did get me back to Russia somehow, he knows where my family lives. He would come after me."

"Where does he get his money?" I asked curiously.

"He sold a ranch he had a long time ago, and he has been working as an English professor off and on," Zoya shook her head in dismay. "I don't know how much he has, but he told me it is quite a bit and that we don't need to ever worry about money. That's how I know he has enough to come after me if I leave here."

We both just sat there for a while, and then I helped Zoya put a small wall hanging into a quilt frame and showed her the basics of quilting. I figured she could at least have something to do and would not be quite so lonely. Larry had left her with no money, so she was unable to go anywhere or do anything except stay at the mobile home and wait for his unwelcomed return.

One day in mid-July after Larry's release, I was getting the mail when I noticed a man in a pickup truck stapling signs to trees and mailboxes. I was even more surprised to see Larry's picture on them.

"Hey, you," he called to me as I was turning to walk down the lane. I turned back to him and raised my brows in inquiry.

"You people know about this guy, huh?" he shouted at me.

I smiled at him innocently, not knowing what to say.

"I know this guy is dressing like you guys and everything, but do you know he is a sex offender?"

I bit my lip, still not sure what I was supposed to answer. Whatever I said would be spread amongst the *Englisch* and would eventually get back to the church, so I just stood there, looking at the man. He walked over to me and smiled.

"You scared of me or what, girl?"

"Oh, no," I smiled up at him. "But you probably should ask my dad these questions because they don't really tell us much about what is going on."

"Oh, yeah, my bad." He smiled at me again. "Come on, I'll give you a lift," he waved me over to his truck.

I hesitated for a moment, but then walked over and hopped in. He seemed like a nice guy. He looked to be in his mid-thirties, and his roughened, callused hands were certainly an indication that he was someone that worked on the land like we did.

"I'm new to the area," he said as his noisy truck bounced down the lane. "I just moved here with my family from Montana so I could help my wife's family on their farm. It's a couple miles that way." He pointed to the south.

I just smiled at him, and he grinned back at me. "You will have to pardon me Miss, but I am not accustomed to talking to Amish ladies, so excuse me if I am rude."

I smiled again and shook my head to show that I did not think him rude. He seemed very nice and sincere. He wore faded blue jeans and a gray T-shirt with a cowboy hat sitting on the back of his head. I thought he looked more like a Montana cowboy than a Minnesota farmer and was probably only here out of respect for his wife and in-laws.

The noisy truck came to a halt as we drove up to the front of the house.

"Thanks for the ride," I said as I gathered my dress skirt in my hands to jump to the ground.

"Any time," he smiled at me and touched his hat.

I went into the house with the mail. After a couple of minutes, I heard shouting outside. Ella, Lillian and I walked over to the open bedroom window so we could hear what was going on.

"You knew this guy was a sex offender, and you let him just waltz in here and be part of your group?" I heard the *Englisch* man yell at Jacob.

"Well, we do not believe in labeling people as you *Englisch* do," Jacob calmly stroked his beard. "We believe in forgiving and forgetting. It is our way."

"Well," the other guy shouted back, "that might be your way, but it sure as h*ll is not mine. My wife and I have three pretty little girls, and if this creep so much as looks at one of them, I am going to put a bullet straight between his eyes."

Jacob shook his head solemnly. "We would never seek revenge like that. Revenge is the Lord's, not ours."

The man started to walk to his truck, but suddenly he turned on his heel and walked back to where Jacob was standing.

"Oh, is that so?" he shouted. "And if that guy came in here tonight and raped that sweet girl I just gave a ride to, you would be just fine and dandy with that?"

"Well, we would not be happy, of course," Jacob answered in his irritatingly calm voice. "But we would not seek revenge."

"Revenge? You have got to be kidding me man," the guy was clenching his fists. "What about honor? What about justice?"

"That is not our way," Jacob shook his head slowly.

"Well," the man shouted angrily, "you know what? Screw you, and screw your ways. I have never understood you people, you know that? I have an older brother who died defending this country so you people could look down on him and on us while you farm here, enjoying the very things my brother died for."

"We did not kill your brother," Jacob said with a little laugh.

The man was getting more and more irritated. "Oh, you think that's funny, do you?" he shot back. "Well, if people like my brother didn't die for you, you would not be enjoying the freedoms that you have here."

Jacob just shrugged. "That's your opinion."

"No, that's a fact," the man shot back. "I don't understand why you people look down on us, call us the *Englisch* and keep to yourselves. When you need a ride or a telephone or something, you have no problem running to us, but it is a sin to have these things yourselves. That's just weird."

"That is our way," Jacob said again with a shrug.

"Yeah, exactly," the man replied, walking back to his truck. "Maybe someone needs to let you guys see the real world of taxes and government and how things really work for a while. Maybe then you would appreciate your country a little more."

"We are not citizens of this country," Jacob called after him.

I smiled as I saw the man lift his head heavenward, as if begging God to help him understand what seemed to him to be utterly ridiculous.

"Well," the man started his truck, "just tell this sex offender friend of yours if he comes near my property, I cannot vouch for his safety. My daughter's mean way too much to me to care about whether I hurt his feelings or not." He then turned his truck around and disappeared in a cloud of dust.

"Why is he saying those things about Larry?" Ella asked Lillian.

"Because he thinks Larry is a bad man," Lillian closed the window.

"Is he?" Ella asked.

"It is not for us to judge him," Lillian replied, walking back into the kitchen.

I rolled my eyes and Ella saw me. "Do you think he is a bad man, Emma?" Ella asked me.

I looked into her wide, innocent eyes, and then I looked at Lillian, who was giving me a warning look. I could be put in Bann for divulging member-only information to a non-church member.

"Oh, at least he doesn't roll his sleeves up on Sundays," I finally said sarcastically.

"What?" Ella asked with a perplexed look on her face. "That doesn't make any sense."

"Exactly my point."

I saw Lillian grin and she seemed to agree with me.

THE SUMMER passed with all the usual summer work. We were up as early as 3:30 in the morning sometimes and would not fall asleep until nearly eleven at night. The egg business was proving to be more than we could handle during hay season and butchering time.

At least once a week, Zoya would come by to spend the day helping us. At first, Jacob and Lillian did not like her coming by so often, since they thought her to be *Englisch* and a possible influence on the children and me. But once they saw how quiet and withdrawn she was, they did not mind. She did not talk very much, so she fit in quite well, and our company helped fill the utter loneliness she felt in this new country. We did not see that much of Larry—mostly only on church Sundays and occasionally when he came along with Zoya. I wondered what he did all day. When I was at their place, I noticed a lot of books and figured they must both spend a lot of time reading.

SOON IT was fall again in rural Minnesota. Letters from Samantha hinted that she felt her boyfriend might pop the question any time. I was happy for her. She had finally found some sense of security and was looking forward to a future as an Amish wife and mother. As she had told me before, "You can learn to live through things. Just don't over think them, follow the rules and everything will be okay." This seemed to be working for her, but I was starting to feel restless. With each passing birthday, I felt as if I had lost something; it seemed like I was running out of time to do something...but what? I asked myself this question over and

298

over again.

Life was much the same every day. Work changed with the seasons, but life changed very little. I could not pinpoint what was bothering me, so I dove into my work and tried to find a sense of fulfillment that just was not there. Please help me, Lord, I would whisper into the dark, starlit nights. I don't know why you gave me this drive to do something without telling me what it is I am supposed to do. I thought of Isaac when I felt restless. I was sad that he had not found the courage to leave the Amish yet. Although I was not allowed to write to him, the letters from Lillian's mother and sister would most certainly have mentioned such an important topic. I could imagine how happy he would be on a ranch out west and sincerely hoped he would go before he became an old man.

For my twenty-second birthday, I got a full set of pretty, flowered dishes. I smiled as I put them in my hope chest, but I also sighed. At twenty-two years old, I was fast on my way to becoming one of the oldest girls at the singing table without a boyfriend. I saw many glances directed my way in church, and although I pretended not to care, I felt like crying.

That evening at the dinner table Ella commented on my pretty new dishes. I saw Lillian make a face out of the corner of my eye.

"I don't know why she's collecting things," she said in an irritated voice. "She is never going to marry anyone."

"Why not?" Moses looked over and smiled at me. "Emma would be the best mother in the whole world."

"Oh, you think so?" Lillian sniffed. "Well, your Emma here says no when she is asked if she wants to go on a date. Obviously she has her eye on someone else."

"You don't want to go on any dates Emma?" Ella asked with wide, surprised eyes.

I sat there uncomfortably for a moment. No one would understand even if I attempted to explain myself, and I could not believe Lillian would spill my private business like that.

"Lillian, that is not yours to tell," I yelled in a hurt voice as I stood up from the table.

"Well, it's the truth," she shot back at me. "You are simply waiting for me to die so you can take my place."

"That is the most ignorant and stupid thing I have ever heard," I snapped back at her.

Everyone at the dinner table was watching us in shock. After a moment, Jacob shouted at both of us to sit down and be quiet. Lillian sat down and looked as though she were embarrassed for what she had just said in front of the children. Children were just as good at spreading gossip as anyone else, and one way or another, I was sure what had just happened was going to get out to the entire church.

"Sit down, Emma," Jacob ordered me.

"No," I shook my head.

"Emma! I don't want to tell you again," Jacob shouted, standing up. "Sit down!"

"No," I yelled again as I turned and ran for the door. I was sad and full of anger at the same time. I ran out the back door and kept running as fast as I could through the snow-speckled hay field.

"Emma, come back here!" I heard Jacob calling after me. "Emma! Emma!"

I just kept running, as if I could outrun all my troubles and somehow leave them behind. I crossed the hay field and ran into the darkened woods. I started shivering from the cold and sat down with my back to a large tree trunk. What I had just done did not hit me until I sat there for a minute. What kind of behavior had I displayed? But more importantly, what was I trying to prove? I sat there shivering for about half an hour, lost in my thoughts. The complete solitude felt refreshing but I was getting very cold and I could feel a few snowflakes landing on my face and hands. I felt slightly feverish as I sat there with my teeth chattering; I was too proud to go back and pretend everything was okay.

Eventually I saw a lantern coming across the hay field and into the woods toward me.

"Emma! Emma!" I heard Moses calling.

I sighed, feeling embarrassed by my actions. "Over here, Moses," I called out wearily.

Moses came running toward the sound of my voice. "Oh, Emma, I was so worried about you," he gasped as he handed me my coat. "I know you get sick so easily if you are cold."

"Thanks, Moses," I said as I quickly put my coat on. "I am freezing."

"Dad was going to come after you, but Mom would not let him," Moses had a confused look on his face. "I don't understand what is going on."

I saw another lantern bobbing toward us in the dark. The yellow flicker of the lantern light danced on Elam's face.

"Come on, you two," his voice was angry. "We've got to get back to the house."

As we walked back Elam whispered to me, "That was really theatrical, Emma."

I glared at him. He would never understand anything I was feeling and he was one of the last people I wanted to talk to at that moment.

The BISHOP'S MAID

"You may choose to look the other way but you can never say again that you did not know."

— *William Wilberforce*

The next day I went to help Phyllis, as I did every week. In the afternoon, I saw Jacob and Lillian walk over. I stood in the middle of the room as they walked in with Peter. It appeared that Jacob had told Peter what had happened the previous night before he heard it from the gossip that was sure to start floating around. Peter sent the children upstairs and motioned for us to sit down.

"So," Peter began, "this is getting out of hand. It appears that Lillian cannot handle having Emma in her house, and it is unfair for Emma to be caught in the middle of your marital spats."

About time, I thought to myself.

"Phyllis and I have given this some thought," Peter continued, "and we are willing to take Emma in. She is a good friend to Phyllis, and with the new baby and Phyllis's seizures, we really need the help. We think it would be best if she moves in with us for a year or so and then, perhaps, she can move back. Who knows? By then she may have a boyfriend, and it will put an end to all this jealousy."

Jacob was not happy with the idea of my moving out for an entire year but he finally agreed knowing it would help squash the rumors, and it would help Peter and Phyllis who were just barely making it with their seven children, one of whom was only two months old.

"The children are going to miss her," Jacob commented sadly, although I could not help but think it sounded more like he was going to miss me.

Lillian seemed pleased at the thought of my leaving for a while and offered to have the children help me move my things over the next day.

The next morning Jacob told the children that Phyllis needed my help and that I would be staying at the Bishop's house for a while.

"How long?" Moses and Ida asked together.

"We don't know," Jacob shrugged. "It may be a few months or it may be a year. We will see how it goes."

"But she can't," Ella grabbed my arm. "She just can't. I will miss her too much."

Jacob smiled at Ella. "Well, what if she were getting married? You would miss her just as much."

"But then I could be her maid sometimes," Ella frowned at him.

"It has been decided already," Jacob stood up from the breakfast table. "You children will help Emma move her things this morning."

"I don't want to," Moses whimpered as he came over and put his arms around my waist. Ida started crying, as did Ella who was still holding my arm. I smiled at them, trying not to be sad for their sakes.

"It is only for a little while," I hugged them. "And besides, I am just down the lane a little ways."

"Oh, can we go see Emma sometimes?" Ida begged Jacob.

"Of course you can," he smiled at her. I saw Lillian make a face as if she disagreed, and I just sighed. I told myself I would take the next date offered. My life was starting to get too complicated and an unmarried girl would always suffer the brunt of any rumors.

After doing the breakfast dishes, Moses got his red wagon and helped move my sewing machine to the Bishop's house. Next we moved my hope chest and my Sunday clothes, and that was about it. I took the small Bible from under the corner of the bed where I kept it. Although I would be returning in a year, taking my few earthly belongings with me made me feel more like I was in charge of my life, even if this was just an illusion.

As I went to the closet to get my chore scarf, Lillian walked up to me with an envelope in her hands.

"Here is the money you have made so far," she said, handing it to me.

I looked down at the envelope that held the eight hundred dollars from the quilt I had sold and the fifty dollars a month that I had been receiving from Jacob and Lillian since I turned twenty-one. There was also some extra money I had picked up from quilting and odd sewing jobs. There were many figures and dates scribbled on the front of the envelope, and at the bottom of a column of numbers I saw the sum of fifteen hundred dollars written out.

"That's okay," I handed it back to her. "You might as well keep it till I come back."

Lillian shook her head. "Phyllis will keep track of it till you return here. Give it to her right away and don't lose it."

I don't believe Lillian thought for a moment that I might not give it to Phyllis. An unmarried girl had no need for money and there was nowhere to spend it even if she had it. I did not even think of keeping it when I nodded to Lillian and put the envelope in my pocket. It seemed strange that Lillian gave it to me in the first place, since the norm was for Peter to simply pay Jacob the three dollars a day for my work. But I figured Lillian must not have wanted the responsibility for the money since she had already been accused of treating me unfairly.

When I got to Phyllis's house with my arms full of dresses, I went to my new room to hang them up. I was just about to go into the main room to give Phyllis the money when I stopped. I stood there at the door thinking for a moment. Chances were Phyllis did not know how much money was in the envelope. Sometimes parents used their child's money if they needed it and then returned it when they had the available funds. I don't know why I did it, but suddenly I found myself removing a thousand dollars from the envelope. I put it in one of my stationery envelopes and, kneeling down next to my hope chest, I took out several things until I reached the clock, which was still in its box. Carefully, I taped the money to the back of the wall clock, put it back in its box, and then piled everything else on top. I was careful to pile all of the loose dishes across the top in order to discourage anyone that might wish to search my things. Of course, I would have to return the money when I moved back to Jacob's house, but for now I felt safer having the thousand dollars hidden in my hope chest. I did not have any conscious thought of ever using the money, but I could not shake a feeling that my life was going to change in the near future. It was like a premonition but without a definite image.

Phyllis did not even glance into the envelope when I handed it to her. She simply put it in the desk drawer and then helped me make my up bed with warm quilts. My room had a lean-to shape that slanted off the side of the house. The family that had lived there before Phyllis and Peter had used the room as an outlet to sell baked goods. Since it was used as a store, they had failed to insulate it and it got terribly cold. Phyllis had been using it as a storage room, but she asked me if I would mind staying there, since it was on the first floor. She thought it would make it easier for me to help with the baby at night.

I agreed eagerly. It was like having my own tiny house. The room was about fourteen feet long and ten feet wide. There was a tiny stove in the middle of the room and it had a few counters and cupboards as well. Phyllis helped me hang sheets on the windows. They would have to do until we had time to make dark curtains. I pushed my bed into a corner and then, just for fun, put a couple of my dishes in the cupboards. The room had a door leading outside that had been added for the bakery. I sat on the edge of my bed and let my imagination run away with me. I fantasized that I was in my own little house, completely disconnected from the main house. Of course, this daydream was short-lived, as it was Saturday and there was much work to do.

The sounds of children skipping through the house and arguing with each other pulled me back to the real world in which I was merely a maid. I did not really mind being a maid. It made me feel strangely liberated. I was no longer living under a roof with people that could claim they were my parents, at least for now. I was so tired of having someone else decide everything for me. At least as a maid I had chosen to help someone else.

I smiled at the children as I walked into the main room.

"Aunty Emma's going to be staying with us," I heard the children saying happily as they jumped around the house.

"Children, children," Phyllis was shouting in a tired voice. "We have to get to get our work done."

I jumped right into the work and could tell Phyllis really needed my help since the baby cried almost nonstop. Grandma Schrock visited the baby and thought that it seemed to be having a lot of stomach aches, but nothing seemed to relieve them, and the baby only slept a few hours during the day and at night.

There proved to be much more domestic work at Phyllis's house than what I was used to on a daily basis. Due to the number of small children in the house, there was always a never-ending line of dishes in the dish washing bowl. There were school lunches to prepare, bread to bake, breakfast, lunch and supper to cook. Then there were the chores and the house to clean, not to mention the vast amounts of laundry and sewing that needed to be done. I was up for the tasks, though. There was nothing I liked more than tackling a mountain of work and then stepping back to enjoy my accomplishments.

As the days passed, I settled into my new routine. Sometimes Zoya stopped by, but not very often. I think that since I was living at the Bishop's house she felt uncomfortable being there. Ida, Ella and Moses popped by quite often at first, but eventually their visits slowed because Lillian told them they were annoying Phyllis.

I spent the holidays back at home with Lillian and Jacob like a normal maid would do. Being back for Thanksgiving and Christmas was nice, and I could see that Jacob and the children were very happy to have me in the house again. Lillian, however, did not even talk to me. I felt kind of sad, since we had had a good relationship for quite some time, but somehow she had gotten it in her head that I was after Jacob, and although she probably did not love Jacob, the very idea that I might give him any sort of happiness in life seemed to drive her mad. Of course, I could not blame since he treated her rather badly; but I also could not stand by and let her take her frustrations out on me.

The holidays came and went, and January set in with a vengeance. The incredibly cold northeasterly winds seemed to rip through every bit of clothing I wore, no matter how many layers I put on. Phyllis's seizures seemed to be getting worse, and many nights Peter would knock on my bedroom door with a screaming baby in his arms. I started to sleep in my dress because Peter stared at me and pretended he did not mean to touch my breasts as he passed me the baby. I didn't know how to react to him, so I pretended not to notice. I just took the baby and walked away from him. I certainly understood what Matty had been talking about now.

Eventually, Peter quit knocking on my door and just walked in and shook me awake when it was my turn to care for the baby. If he had not been so creepy, I would not have minded, but whenever he touched me, my skin started to crawl. He would always tell me he did not want to wake the children by knocking, and then he would stay there, standing over the bed and holding the baby and the lantern while I crawled out of bed. The first couple of times he did it, I saw his eyes light up because he could see through my night dress. That was when I wised up and began to keep my dress on when I suspected the baby would be really fussy. Locking doors was not allowed among my Amish group, but this was one time I really wished for a lock on my door. Phyllis did not notice Peter's strange behavior, and like most Amish girls I did not tell anyone, but I had no idea what to do about it.

Normally, I was very good at quieting babies, but this one was proving to be extremely difficult. Even I, so well known for being able to quiet the most difficult babies, had to exert a lot more effort to quiet this one. Many nights I fell asleep in the rocking chair with the baby in my arms. I often thought Peter could have done a lot more to help out than he did, but who was I to say anything to him?

During the day, I was busy doing most of the household work, and although Phyllis tried to help, she seemed to be getting worse instead of better. I was very worried as her seizures were coming more regularly—

306

usually in the early mornings and twice a week or, on occasion, as many as three times per week. After a seizure, she would sleep for a few hours and then tend to the baby or do some other light household work. When I suggested that she go see a specialist that could help with her seizures, she shook her head sadly.

"We don't have the money, and I have already been to a few. They just want to put me on expensive medication that we cannot afford."

"But you can't go on like this, Phyllis," I said while I washed the dishes and she sat next to me in the rocking chair. "I won't be here forever. What are you going to do?"

"Well," Phyllis replied in her tired voice, "Katie will be out of school next year and she will provide much more help around the house. We will manage."

I bit my lip worriedly. Although Peter was the bishop of the church, they were by no means well-off, and they certainly did not have any extra money. Out of regard to Phyllis, I told both of them not to bother paying me my three dollars a day while I stayed with them. I knew they barely had it, and what did I need it for anyway? Their food supply was also very low. It was only the beginning of January, and the canned meat and vegetables were already growing sparse on the basement shelves. Phyllis told me to serve more bread with every meal since it was cheap to make and would stretch the potatoes, meat and canned vegetables further.

Peter and Phyllis seemed to be in a bad place where money was concerned. Their property taxes were coming due, and they would probably soon have doctor bills for the sick baby. I thought about offering them the thousand dollars hidden in my hope chest but I could not make myself do it. Once, I had even knelt by the chest to get the money, but I just could not bring it out of its hiding place. I kicked myself for being so selfish but in the end I decided to not give it to them.

Finally, an answer to our prayers seemed to come along when a couple asked to rent a workshop on Peter's property. They had a not-for-profit horse rescue company that they had been running for a few months at their current location, but their landlord had raised their rent when he found out. They were a couple in their early forties, and they were both "live off the land" kinds of people. The wife, whom I had met a few times, always wore a scarf on her head and had a long braid hanging down her back; she usually wore either skirts or flowered dresses. She was a tall, friendly woman and she told me she was half Choctaw Indian and half Swedish. Her husband was always dressed like a backwoods, outdoors man and was very friendly as well.

The Amish had adopted several horses from her over the last couple of months. One day when she delivered some of the horses she noticed the abandoned workshop and thought they could fix it up to live in. Peter agreed to let the couple stay there for three hundred dollars a month and gave them permission to build any out buildings they might need. The shop was down past the barn, so Phyllis and Peter agreed that it was far enough away from the main house so that they wouldn't interfere with our routine. I was excited to have the horse rescue so close. This was going to be interesting.

That week, Phyllis let me go over with Peter and some of the children to clean the shop and help Karen and Carl move their stuff in. Peter was letting them use the barn for the horses they had at the moment, but the next week he was planning to gather some of the local men together and build them a small stable.

I was surprised when there was so little stuff to unload from the horse trailer. I mentioned as much to Karen as I carried a box in behind her.

"Oh, I know," Karen answered, smiling at me. "I have only been out of prison for a year, so I have not had much time to collect a lot of things."

"Prison?"

"Oh, I thought Peter told you all," she set her box on the rough wood floor.

I smiled, embarrassed at how nosey I must seem. "It's none of my business," I shrugged.

"Oh, no, you need to know," Karen had a serious look on her face. "When my probation officer comes to check on me, I don't want him to think I'm hiding out here."

"Probation officer?" I asked with even more shock.

"Yeah, I was let out of prison, but I still have two years of probation."

"How long were you in prison?" I asked, unable to contain my curiosity.

"Three years," Karen stared out the window. "It was supposed to be ten, but I was lucky." She turned and looked at my inquisitive face. "Okay," she laughed. "You want to know what for. Well, I was a doctor and I took some government documents I was not supposed to." She sighed. "And that was that."

"You were a doctor?" I asked in surprise.

"Yeah, but not anymore," Karen sighed.

"Oh, that is so exciting," I clapped my hands together in delight. "I always wanted to be a doctor."

Karen just smiled at me and looked me over from head to foot. "I did not think Amish could go to college," she looked confused.

I looked down at my shoes as my cheeks grew warm with embarrassment. "Oh, we can't, I always wanted to, though."

"That's okay, honey," Karen patted me on the back. "We all have unattainable dreams."

Quietly, I helped Karen unpack her dishes. As I was pulling paper from between her plates, a pamphlet with little African children on the front caught my attention. I picked it up and opened it. "Come join us at YWAM in Jacksonville, Florida," it said across the front. Eagerly, my eyes flew across the page as I read that YWAM stood for 'Youth with a Mission'. It was a missionary training school that took people overseas for three months and gave them the opportunity to live the life of a missionary, helping people all over the world. I did not know there was such a school, and I squealed in happiness as I read it. Karen looked over to see what I was reading and smiled.

"Oh, a friend of mine has a daughter that went there and she is now a full-time missionary with the organization," she peered over my shoulder.

"Oh," I sighed. "I have always wanted to be a missionary."

"I thought you wanted to be a doctor," Karen laughed.

"Yes, a doctor too..." I smiled, "...a missionary doctor."

"You are for sure the strangest Amish girl I have ever met," Karen laughed again as she took some plates out of my hands.

"Yeah." I frowned. "Not the first time I have heard that."

"That's okay." Karen smiled at me. "Different is what makes people interesting."

"Do you mind if I keep this?" I asked, waving the pamphlet in the air.

"No, you can keep it if you want. I have no use for it."

"Well, I don't either,"I folded it and put it in my pocket. "I just like to look at it, I guess."

The next day, when I when I saw the truck and horse trailer pulling up with the last of their things, I ran down to the shop to see if they needed any more help. As I got to the front of the shop, I was greeted by a huge, reddish-brown dog that ran up to me and nearly knocked me over. I laughed as he barked happily and licked my face as if I were his long-lost owner. Karen laughed at the dog's reaction, too, and she came over and pulled him off me.

"Come, Simba," she patted him on his giant head.

I knelt down and put my arms around Simba's neck. He was so big and fluffy and friendly. Karen told me he was half wolf and half Saint Bernard and that he was a rescue dog. She had three other full-blooded wolves, too. Karen and Carl were keeping them in a fenced pen they built in front of the shop.

"Better be careful," I said as I stood up and dusted the dog hair off my dress. "There are many farmers around here that will shoot wolves if they see them running around."

"I know," Karen nodded as she put Simba in the pen with the other wolves. "That's why I have to keep them in here."

I petted the other wolves and was surprised at how friendly they were. I was hugging one of the black wolves when suddenly Simba ran over to the fence and started growling menacingly. I saw Peter walking up to the shop and Simba staring at him with ruffled fur and bared teeth. *That was really strange*; I thought as I went over and petted his head. Simba wagged his tail at me and licked my hand, but when he turned around, he bared his teeth at Peter again.

"Better keep those wolves in check," Peter's voice was irritated. He seemed particularly annoyed at how Simba was staring directly at him.

"Oh, I know," Karen snapped her fingers at Simba. "I don't know what is wrong with him. I have never seen him act like this."

Finally Simba lay down, but ever after that he always gave a low growl whenever Peter came near the shop.

As I walked back to the house about half an hour later, I heard Simba whining after me. Karen told me later that if I'd had my own house, she would have given Simba to me, since he seemed to have adopted me anyway. She said this was quite common in wolves—that they connected with certain people and that it was always best to give a wolf to whomever they adopted. She said that that person would be forever blessed with the wolf's undying loyalty.

Of course, I could not take Simba, but I wished I could have. The way he growled at Peter made me wonder if he sensed something about him that we humans could not see.

KAREN AND Carl settled into the shop. They had a generator In the back of the shop, and had hired someone to install the Internet so Karen could use the computer for her business. At first Peter was not happy with the Internet installation, but when Karen said it would be disconnected if and when they moved, he agreed to allow it.

I would often go over to Karen's for half an hour or so in the afternoon. After I finished doing the lunch dishes and while Phyllis sat in the rocking chair with the baby and Peter took a nap with the younger children. I would play with Simba, who barked excitedly when he saw me coming in the distance. Karen and Carl would either be in the stables with their horses or in the shop, where Carl would often be reading and Karen would be doing online classes to complete a veterinary license. Once while I was there, her probation officer showed up and asked her a few questions. He also asked me who I was.

"Oh, this is my new friend, Emma Shrock," Karen said as she waved for me to come to the door.

I smiled at him and shook my head when he asked me if I was living at the residence. I thought he seemed surprised to see me there, and I wondered for a second if Karen was telling us the whole truth about why she had been in prison, but she was nice so I really didn't care.

I felt more alive when I looked out the kitchen window and saw Simba lying in his pen, looking toward the house where I was. I also liked to see the activity that seemed to be constantly going on over at their place. However, inside the bishop's house, life was taking a drastic turn for the worse, and suddenly I found myself facing one of the greatest decisions of my life, one that would totally change my life forever.

Poisoned

"If not us, then who?

If not now, then when?"

— *John E Lewis*

As January slipped into February, things with Peter took a swift turn for the worse. Alarmingly, Phyllis's seizures began to happen more frequently. One week she had seizures three days in a row. Her seizures somehow seemed odd to me. She would have one major seizure and then several smaller ones for a few hours after the initial one. I felt there was something unusual about this, but I had no real medical training and did not know what it could be.

At the breakfast table the morning after a seizure, Peter abruptly asked the children if they thought I would make a good mom if something happened to their own mother. I was sitting in Phyllis's place, trying to calm the baby and feed little Edna at the same time. I looked up, startled, when Peter said that, and then I looked at the children who were smiling and nodding at me.

"Emma is more fun," four-year-old Eli said with a giggle.

"Children!" I admonished as I glared at Peter. "Your mother is in the bedroom sleeping. She is not dying."

I frowned at Peter, who was thinking about the children's answers with keen interest. I could not believe what he had said, and suddenly I became suspicious of Peter and of the frequency of Phyllis's seizures. I had not thought of it before, but some of Phyllis's seizures seemed to happen after Peter had been alone with her. I felt a little dizzy as I noticed Peter looking at me arrogantly, as if he had some scheme he was planning. *Well, I* thought to myself, *if this creep thinks I will become his next wife, he has another thought coming.* There was no way would I ever marry him, but he was the Bishop of our church, and if he asked and I refused who would care for his seven little ones? I would be considered proud and ungrateful. The one thing he didn't know was that I no longer cared. That short conversation left me terribly shaken. I will never be able to fully explain just how much. I felt shaken to the core.

The next morning I got up early to make breakfast. It was very cold that morning and Peter had awakened me extra early but he told me not to wake the children. He said that he would do the morning chores himself so the children could sleep. After I got the potatoes and biscuits started, I stood at the wood stove stirring the tomato gravy. Phyllis was still sick and sleeping, and I was lost in thought about her declining health. Grandma Schrock had been over with some herbs the week before, but they seemed to be making her worse instead of better. When I suggested she stop using them, Peter refused and insisted she try them for at least two weeks.

I was beginning to believe that Peter was giving Phyllis something other than the herbs Grandma Schrock had given him, but I did not want to tell Phyllis, as I wasn't sure how she would react.

After a while, I heard Peter come in through the back door with the milk buckets and go down to the basement to strain it. I was startled out of my reverie a few minutes later when I heard Peter call my name. Wondering what had happened I took the gravy off the stove and went down into the dark basement.

"What?" I asked in a sleepy, annoyed tone as I came to the bottom of the stairs. I looked around in confusion when I saw that the basement was completely dark.

"The lantern went out and I can't find the matches," Peter said as he seemed to be fumbling about. "I think the milk spilled, too."

"Here," I handed him some matches from my pocket. It was very common for Amish women to carry matches in their pockets for starting the fires or lighting lamps.

Peter took the matches and lit the lamp. As the lamp lit up the dark basement, I gasped in horror as I saw that the entire front of Peter's pants was open. He was not wearing any underwear and he was in full erection. I swallowed hard, and Peter looked at me piercingly as I stumbled backwards and ran up the stairs.

I grabbed the railing on the front of the wood stove for a moment and tried to calm my trembling limbs. After a couple of minutes, I heard Peter start to come upstairs, and I looked around the quiet, sleeping house frantically. *The children*, I thought, and I ran upstairs and noisily called for the children to get up. I was so noisy that Phyllis came out of the bedroom and asked if everything was okay.

Peter was angry that I had awoken the children and told me I should ask him next time instead of just doing whatever I wanted. Phyllis told him not to yell at me as she tasted my tomato gravy and nodded with approval. I just stood there, feeling weak and awkward and ill at ease. I acted as if nothing had happened. What else could I do? If I said anything, I would break Phyllis's heart and I would be no better off for it, since it would somehow turn out to be my fault in the long run. At the same time, my inaction went against everything I believed in, but, for the moment, I had no idea how else to proceed.

From then on, Peter seemed to constantly try to flash himself at me. When he took his coat off, if the children were not around, his pants would be unbuttoned with everything hanging out. A few times, he snuck up on me and sat on the wood box behind where I was standing at the stove, cooking. I would turn around to get more wood, and he would just be sitting there with his pants unbuttoned and legs spread wide open. I would immediately call for one of the small children, who would come pattering happily around the corner as Peter hurriedly turned sideways and buttoned his pants. Another time I was taking a bath and he entered and just stood there staring at me. I had been standing washing myself, according to Amish rule there was no lock on the door but everyone new not to enter the pantry at bath time. I felt nascious and really hoped that Phyllis would catch him. He stood there for several moments grinning. I stood frozen in place, covering myself the best I could. I felt trapped, alone and scared. No one would ever believe me if I came forward and even if they did I knew with certainty that it would be my fault for seducing him, that knowledge left me terrified.

It was getting really bad, and every night I lay awake, afraid he would come into my room. I no longer liked my room downstairs and wished I was upstairs with the children. Only now did I realize why Peter had been so adamant about my sleeping downstairs.

ΘN EARLY March, I came down with thrush. My mouth was covered with a white coating, and the pain was so bad I could not eat anything that could not be consumed through a straw. Karen told me my immune system must have been extremely low, since not many people my age got thrush. She asked me what I had been eating, and when I told her mostly white bread and potatoes, she shook her head and gestured toward the dark sky.

"Not many vitamins in that, you work way too hard to be eating only starch."

Karen urged me to go to the doctor, but Peter told her that was an unnecessary expense, so she gave me some walnut bark to rinse my mouth with twice a day instead. She said it would take about two weeks for the thrush to clear up. When I talked to her later, Karen shook her head and told me I was lucky it had not reached my heart and killed me.

As time went by, there was no improvement in Phyllis's seizures. As I had suspected, Phyllis rarely seemed to have seizures randomly during the day. Rather, they always happened about a half an hour after Peter came out of the room. Usually Peter gave her the herbal medicine from Grandma Schrock before he went to do the chores, and by the time he got back, she would be having a seizure. This scene played out at least two times a week, and I was finding it strange that she always had her seizures the same time in the morning.

That week Karen had even mentioned that she thought Peter was giving something to Phyllis. She had squinted at me and searched my face for an answer. I could tell she was slowly becoming suspicious of him even though I had not told her anything. She had offhandedly remarked that Phyllis's seizures were strange and with her knowledge of medicine she thought that Peter was doing something to cause them. This had shocked me to the core but I did not say anything. I had no proof, and I knew that Karen would not get involved because she was on probation. But I did feel she was telling me what I already knew deep down.

The previous week Peter had told Phyllis that he thought she was possessed and that was what was causing her seizures. While she had seized I had watched in dumb founded silence as Peter held the bible in front of her and commanded that the devil come out of her. I feared that his screaming was somehow making her seizures worse because it lasted much longer than normal and during and afterward she moaned in pain for a long time. Peter had even remarked that some people died during exorcisms. I had stood transfixed to the spot. Fleetingly I had seen myself as Peters next wife. How long before I to would meet the same fate? Besides, Amish did not believe in exorcisms. I had heard of them from the early days of the Catholic church but knew they were not part Amish customs. The whole thing was very bizarre.

IT WAS the last week of March when my life changed forever. It all started one evening when I went downstairs to the basement to see what was keeping Katie so long. She was supposed to be skimming the cream from prior days milk and bringing a pitcher of it upstairs for the supper table. I was still weak from the thrush and was not yet able to eat much of anything. Slowly I walked down the stairs and suddenly stopped mid-way when I saw Peter standing in front of her messing with the pins on the front of her dress. Katie saw me right away, and Peter, seeing that she was looking up the stairwell, looked to. His face grew a few shades redder. I felt I would faint as I watched him continue to be pretending to fix the pins in Katie's dress. I don't know why he did not stop. It seemed like maybe continuing would make him look less guilty. After a few seconds I continued down the stairs and walked towards them. I am ashamed to say that I was sort of frozen. I did not want to believe what I knew to be true. As I walked closer Peter hurriedly turned away and mumbled something as he exited the door of the basement.

I just stared at Katie who was fidgeting nervously and seemed to be pretending nothing had happened. I wanted to reach out to her, but I didn't and she went upstairs without so much as a word. Her nervous smile was masking her real feelings. I had seen her like this before, and it reminded me of Samantha's reaction to stress. I did not make any effort to go after her, I will always regret that. I know I should have went after her and offered my help, but what could I say? I could not even help myself.

That night at the dinner table, Phyllis asked me what was wrong when she saw that I was not eating anything. I just told her that I was not feeling well again. She seemed to suspect that something was wrong, however, as Peter seemed irritable and terribly short with the children. I wondered if Phyllis really knew nothing about Peter's deviant behavior, or if she were just ignoring it. Phyllis was my friend, and I was trying to work up the courage to tell her what I had seen Peter doing with Katie and what he was doing with me.

The only problem was what could she do about it? She could not divorce him or move in with an in-law or anything of that sort. The only thing she could do was tell the church what he had done. The ministers would place him in the Bann for six weeks, after which he would be welcomed back as a full member of the church, and the sins he had committed would never be spoken of again. There was one really big problem with the Bann, though: It did not offer any counsel for the victim. Peter would still be at home; the only difference would be that he would have to sit at a different table from the rest of the family. He would still have total access to his victims. They would most likely not speak out against him because they wanted to save themselves from embarrassment, and they didn't want to be considered unforgiving of a man that had repented.

All of this was whirling through my mind as I sat there at the dinner table. I knew that Phyllis would probably get mad at me and want to believe I was lying instead of believing that her husband was a monster much like her father had been. My hands shook as I tried to swallow some milk. I had a real dilemma, but I knew I had to do something. I was just not sure what or how or when.

The next morning, my heart was pounding as I stood outside the closed door of the bedroom where Peter was giving Phyllis her medicine. The very fact that he closed the door was suspicious, since Amish do not believe in having secrets, and bedroom doors are rarely fully shut and never locked. I noticed that there were days when he did not shut the door, but he always did on the days that Phyllis ended up having seizures. I was almost one hundred percent sure that he was giving her something to make her seize, but I could not figure what it might be.

After all that had happened the night before, I was not even going to consider giving Peter the benefit of the doubt; and I was not going to let Phyllis die and allow Peter to go off and find a younger, healthier wife which would most certainly not be me.

After a couple of minutes, I mustered enough courage to turn the doorknob and push the heavy wooden door open. There was a small flicker of lamp light that just barely lit the room. Peter had a glass in his hand. He turned and looked at me in surprise. Phyllis was moaning and turning her head from side to side. My gaze landed on the glass that was in Peters hand. I squinted at him. He turned and looked at me, instantly he read my expression and immediately I could see a guilty look on his face. He did not stop giving Phyllis the liquid in the glass though. I could felt quivering in the pit of my stomach. I felt slightly dizzy and I could tell that he knew, that I knew what was happening. I could not move for a moment as I continued to stare.

Even though I had been subjected to terrible abuse my entire life and seen awful acts of violence that moment left me shaken and makes me tremble every time I think of it. It was in that moment that I knew for sure. He really was poisoning her and know he knew that I knew. My shocked face said everything. Briefly I remembered the way Jacob and Elam had callously talked abut the Amish man that had tied his wife up in the house and set it on fire. Everyone knew he was a murderer and even talked about it behind closed doors, yet no one did anything about it.

I began to shake uncontrollable and quickly closed the door. The question Peter had asked the children about me becoming their mother was just to clear. He was planning on me being his next wife. The only poison that would cause such terrible seizure was rat poison. It was said to be a painful death and matched Phyllis's symptoms perfectly.

A few seconds later Peter came stomping out of the bedroom. "What is wrong with you, barging in our bedroom like that?" He yelled at me.

I was terrified. Peter was looking at me without blinking, almost as if he were laughing at me. I backed up a little and shrugged.

He looked at me with that same cool, unblinking stare. It would have been better if he had gone into a screaming rage. I felt very scared but thankfully he turned and went out to do the chores and I shakily went back to the kitchen to finish making breakfast.

I knew that Phyllis really did have an underlying seizure problem. But when I had first came to the community they had seemed more random and less intense. It was only the past couple of months that she had taken a strange turn and Peters actions seemed suspicious. I think he had started to give her something to just aggravate them at first, but know, I could just tell from his face. Something was very off and I knew deep down that it was very bad and dark and I was very worried.

I was torn from my thoughts by the sound of milk boiling in the pan. My hands were trembling as I stirred the milk. I wondered if Simba the dog knew more about Peter than any of us ever would.

As if on cue, about thirty-forty-five minutes after Peter had been with her, Phyllis began seizing violently. I heard the familiar sounds and ran into the bedroom that was adjacent to the kitchen. These seizures lasted about a minute and then she would just collapse in exhaustion. Sometimes she had another one a few minutes later, and this was one of those mornings. About five minutes after the first seizure, she went into another. I wrung my hands with worry at the second one. Now that I feared she was being poisoned, I was really afraid she might die. Just as her second seizure ended and I was putting her back under the blankets, I heard Peter and the children coming inside.

I did not want to face Peter so asked Phyllis if she wanted to get up. She shook herself sleepily and complained that she was in pain. I finished tucking her in, and felt my hands begin to tremble when I sensed Peter watching me from the doorway. I stood up straight and looked at him demurely. He grinned at me maliciously as if he was a cat and I was a corned mouse. I wanted to slap that look off of his face, but pretended everything was okay.

After breakfast, I was thankful to see Phyllis come out of her room and pick up the screaming baby. She sat in the rocking chair most of the day, complaining that she was still feeling extremely weak and was having left shoulder pains. I bit my lip—not wanting to comment on her condition— and continued to iron the church clothes. Peter sat in the other rocking chair, reading for Sunday's sermon, and I noticed he seemed particularly interested in our conversations that day.

Later that afternoon, I went to see Simba. I put my arms around his huge neck and let tears run down my cheeks. He whimpered and wagged his tail as if he understood. After a couple of minutes, he pulled away from me and began barking and growling violently. I turned and saw Peter standing a few feet from the fence, watching me.

"Emma," he half shouted in an irritated voice. "The baby is crying, and

Phyllis is looking for you."

Karen came out of the door and shouted at Simba to be quiet, but he wouldn't listen. I winced when Simba tried to lunge at Peter. There was white foam dripping from his bared teeth, and I had no doubt that if he could have gotten out of that pen, he would have ripped Peter's jugular out. It made me sad to see this, because I had seen Simba act the same way toward Elam and a few other men from the community. It was as if he had a hidden radar that could detect men like Peter.

I looked Peter straight in the eyes and then started to walk toward the gate to open it. Peter looked a little frightened until Karen yelled at me to wait to open the gate until Peter was gone. I sighed. I would not have let Simba out of course, but it did not hurt to let Peter think I might.

"Whew. You have got to be careful when you come out of the dog's' pen, Emma," Karen grimaced and shook her head. "If one of my dogs kills someone, I might go back to jail."

"Oh, sorry," I felt slightly remorseful. "I wasn't thinking."

"Oh, that's okay." She put her arm around my shoulders. "I don't understand why, but Simba looked like he wanted him for dinner, huh?"

"Yeah, I wonder why?" I asked, as if I did not know.

I walked slowly back to the house. I wanted to go home to Jacob and Lillian. I sighed. Even if I told everyone what was going on, chances are the men of the community would find something that would discredit me. It seemed the ultimate wish for any man was to have a strong and healthy wife that could bear many children and still get all of her work done. If a man was not this fortunate, he was pitied and viewed as less successful than the rest of the men.

Again I thought of the story about the man that had set his house on fire with his wife tied up inside, and everyone had just looked the other way. I was so angry about these rules of the church as I walked toward the house on that dark and cloudy spring day. I could see Phyllis lighting a lamp through the living room window. *She looked so thin*, I thought. What kind of strange church was I in that preached such strict adherence to church rules, right down to the very last apron seam, but looked the other way when someone was raped or nearly killed. It did not make any sense to me.

Suddenly it hit me, what about the baby? If Peter really was poisoning Phyllis then the baby must have been getting some through the breast milk. It made total sense and I was certain that was what was happening. Why else would Peter ask the children if I would make a good mother for them if their own mother died? I shuddered, it had been such a creepy question.

Poor little *baby,* I thought; *stupid Peter probably had not even thought of it getting some of the poison too.*

I had no idea who I might be able to confide in. I thought about telling Grandma Schrock, who had proven to be someone I could count on, despite her strange ways. But no, her first reaction would be to go to the church elders and then to make sure I was silenced about the whole ordeal. Even if Peter admitted to what he was doing, he would only get the six weeks' Bann, and who was to say he would not try it again? Phyllis would have to forgive him and remain with him or be put in the Bann herself for her unwillingness to forgive. It was a horrible situation I found myself in, and I was scared. I wanted to write to Samantha and confide in her about what was going on, but I did not, because I knew she would also be silenced and it could cause her a great deal of trouble. I stood on the porch, biting my lip. My only option seemed to be to pretend I knew nothing, but that was not who I was. I felt sick to my stomach as I walked in the house.

Silenced no Longer

"There comes a time when one must take a position that is neither safe, nor politic, nor popular, but he must take it because conscience tells him it is right."

— *Martin Luther King Jr., A Testament of Hope:*

The Essential Writings and Speeches

That evening, I had a hard time pretending everything was okay. I could not even bring myself to be happy around the children. Phyllis commented on how extremely pale I was and felt my forehead to see if I had a fever. I finished the dishes and told everyone I was going to bed. The children were a little upset that I did not play with them like I usually did, but I just couldn't. I felt strange, and I could not stop my hands from shaking. I just lay in my bed with the quilt pulled over my head and quietly cried myself to sleep.

I awoke suddenly, unable to breath. I opened my eyes and felt I could not move or breathe. I was frozen in terror as I gazed up at Peter and felt his hand under my night dress. I opened my mouth to say something but nothing came out. *What was he going to do to me?*

The house was quiet; I assumed I had slept through my alarm and that Peter was the only one up. After fondling my breasts for a couple of minutes, he pulled me up to sitting position. My mind was racing. Was he already expecting me to fulfill the duties of his next wife? I remained stiff and felt as if I would pass out. As his hand went back up my night dress I tried to pull away. I was almost afraid to move, I just wanted him to go away and I was afraid if I struggled to much I might make him angrier. I

321

felt I was in a dream. Sometimes when something really, really bad was happening I used to try and make my mind go blank. If I did not acknowledge it, the fact that it was happening, maybe it would make it untrue. The room spun around me. But the feeling of Peter's hot breath on my neck and the steal like strength of his arms were all to real. My blank mind finally began to panic. What if I became pregnant? What if the baby was taken away from me? Who would protect my baby? I felt my pulse began to race. I had to get away from him. I don't know why I did not scream, but I didn't.

All of a sudden I heard a little boys voice outside.

"Is Dad in there?" I heard Henry shout from the back of the house.

"No," I heard Katie shout from the direction of the barn.

Hurriedly Peter stood up and put on his hat. He looked into my terrified face, his face was so strange and I was so scared.

"I will start coming to your room during the night to check and make sure you are Okay, you know not sick or anything." He looked intently into my face and I could read what he really meant in his eyes. He was going to start coming to my room now in the middle of the night. *No! No!* I felt to vomit but kept my face blank and did not make a sound. I felt totally paralyzed.

He turned from me, seemingly satisfied by my reaction. He figured I would not say anything. Numbly I watched as he looked out the window to see where the children were and then quietly slipped out the side door. I just sat there in my bed, hugging my knees. The thought that he would be coming back that night or some other night paralyzed me with fear. As I sat there, I realized I was not about to lose myself for the sake of religion. I had been through so much already; I could not risk the possibility of becoming pregnant.

A possible pregnancy was something that haunted me. I figured I could take care of myself, but not if I were pregnant and vulnerable. And what if they forced me to give the baby to a married couple? Who would protect my baby then? In most cases of rape, that's what happened. The girl was either taken to a female relative where an abortion was performed, or the baby was given to a married couple that would raise it as their own.

But what could I do. Shakily I got out of bed. *I would go to Karen's. Dare I tell her my situation? What could she do?* With shaking fingers, I tried to put in the pins in the front of my teal dress. My thumb started to bleed as I poked it with the pins, and I stood there holding it for a moment. All of a sudden I turned and saw Peter standing inside the doorway, he had reentered and closed the door behind him and I had not heard a thing. My heart began to race as he stood there looking at me. He was menacing and I was so terribly frightened of him. I think he was trying to show me how easy it was to come into my room. I could not even ask for a lock to keep him out. That would only draw suspicion upon myself. I would most likely be accused of hiding things I was not supposed to have and then he or any other church member would have the right to go through my things.

I swallowed hard as I hesitantly looked over at him. He did not say anything or move from his spot in front of the door. He just stood there looking at me in a threatening and intimidating manner, judging what my next move would be and silently warning me not to make any mistakes. I was very afraid I could possibly end up dead, I had no doubt that he was capable of it if I crossed him badly enough. Besides all he had to fear was being shunned for six weeks, if at all. It seemed that suspected murder cases were never punished at all.

I turned away from him for a second. I wanted to leave, to run away as fast as I could and never come back. But I could not do that, I was Amish and I had to remain so or I would go to hell. Slowly I began to pin my apron. *Just pretend you are getting dressed and nothing else has happened.* I could not let him know I was going to Karen's. I did not know what he would do if he knew. After I finished pinning my dress I slowly turned back to the door. I jumped, he was gone. I put a shaking hand to my forehead, His behavior was beyond unsettling and I was scared to the core. I waited a couple of minutes and then slid on my coat and stood there for a while longer, looking at the door. I was trying to gather enough courage to open it. *What if Peter is waiting for me on the other side? Should I go through the kitchen? What if he is waiting there?*

I waited another moment and then slowly opened the door and stuck my head out. I did not see anyone. With shaking hands, I pushed the door farther open and walked down the two little steps. As I was closing the door, I suddenly felt a hand go over my mouth and someone grab me by the back of my coat. It was Peter. He had been waiting for me to come out, as if he knew I was going to use that door. He drug me around the side of the house and shoved me into a corner.

"Where do you think you are going?" he hissed at me.

"It's none of your business," I hissed back.

Suddenly some of the fear I had was replaced with anger, and I lunged to try to get past him. He grabbed me and tried to throw me back into the corner, but I resisted violently. He began pinching my breasts and trying to put his hands under my dress. I was much smaller than he was, and he seemed to be as strong as an ox. All of a sudden he grabbed both of my breast and pinched and twisted with incredible force. I gasped as the pain shot through me. The attack was violent and extremely painful and for a moment I was temporarily set off balance. Peter grabbed me with both arms and began pulling me back towards my room. For a second I wondered where Phyllis was and why he was not worried that she would come around the side of the house and see what he was doing. What had he done to her and what was he planning to do to me?

Again I did not scream, I only struggled. My only thought was to get away from this madman. Finally I wriggled out of his arms and took off running toward Karen's. I could hear Simba barking as if he knew something was wrong. If Peter attempted to come after me he would be seen, so he decided not to follow me.

I reached Karen's house panting and out of breath. I banged on the door. Simba was barking frantically in the direction of the barn where I assumed Peter had gone. Karen came to the door with a biscuit in her hand.

"Emma, what is wrong?" she pulled my trembling body into the house.

"I am so scared of Peter," I gasped for breath.

"What happened?" Carl jumped up from the table, where he was eating breakfast.

Karen pulled me upright and grabbed me by the shoulders. "What has happened, Emma?" she cried.

I stared at her for a moment. I almost didn't tell her because what had just taken place had not quite sunk into my brain yet. He was the bishop of my church, the one true church, and yet it was a church where it was all to easy to commit serious crimes and get away with them. It was so crazy even I did not want to believe it. If I did not talk about it, maybe it would seem as if it had never really happened.

"Emma, Emma, tell me what happened. Why is your dress ripped? What is wrong with you?"

I looked down at the front of my dress, which could be seen through my open coat. The thin, worn-out material had ripped in the struggle with Peter, and my white under dress could be seen beneath it. I don't know what happened, but in that moment I felt dizzy and started to fall forward. There were so many things racing around in my head, fleetingly I thought about asking Karen to take me to the police station but I could not, it was forbidden. If I committed such a horrible crime I might never be trusted by the church ever again, I would forever be known as the girl that went to the police—committing one of the worst offenses an Amish person of my order could carry out. Since Amish do not believe themselves citizens of any country, most have little respect the laws of the land and abide by as few as possible.

324

Karen caught me as I started to fall and sat me in a chair. I could hear her and Carl mumbling and felt a cool washcloth bathing my face.

"Peter came in my room this morning and was feeling me up under my dress, he was going to undress me but then the children were calling for him. And then when I was leaving my room he attacked me. He told me he will be back tonight. I know he is going to rape me tonight. I cant go back there and I cant go back to Jacob's. Even if they believe me he will only be shunned for a few weeks and then I will have to forgive him. What if he tries it again? I am so mad at myself I should of screamed when he was in my room..." I was sobbing and Karen and Carl, were kneeling on the floor in front of me.

After a moment Karen and Carl stood up, I watched in a daze as they put their coats on. "It is common for sexual assault victims to not scream when they are being assaulted. Karen's voice was soft and it sounded like she was biting back anger. "Stay here we are going to confront this piece of s****

"No, I shook my head at Karen. "Karen he is a dangerous man you shouldn't get mixed up in this. I don't know what would happen to you if you crossed him.

"Carl smirked. "We can take care of ourselves Emma, don't worry."

The door closed behind them. All of a sudden I felt very alone and scared. I wished that Samantha was there, but even then I knew she would frown at me for going to an outsider. Truth be told the outside world felt safer in that moment than the supposed gentle people that I belonged to.

After about fifteen minutes I saw Karen and Carl leave Peter's barn and walk back towards the shop. Numbly I watched as they entered. Both of their face looked startled and they just stood for a moment looking at me.

Slowly Karen came over and sat down next to me. Her lips were pursed. I had never seen such distress in her face before. Her lips became sort of whitish from her pressing them together so hard.

"I never thought I would get mixed up in something like this, out here in Amish country." She shook her head slowly. "That is why we asked to live out here while I finish my probation. I cant get mixed up any sort of violence or these kinds of situations, it could jeopardize my probation.

"I know." I nodded. "I shouldn't of got you mixed up in this. I have to go tell Jacob and hope that I can move back in with them. I have no other choice, I have nowhere else to go. But what if he says he is sorry and I am forced to still live there?" I looked around the room. I was in a nightmare and there seemed no way to escape.

"Emma you can't do that." Karen looked me in the eyes. "You have to go the police. He readily confessed to us that he attacked you." Her eyes widened as she talked. "He told us that he has sex with the animals too. He has done it his whole life and he said he confessed many times to the church and was forgiven. I think he is immune to church discipline now. And..." Her voice faltered. "He told us that it would be so easy to smother you in your sleep one night. No one would ever know, even if they did he would only get a few weeks shunning and all would be forgotten. Her face was white and she looked like she had just seen a ghost.

I felt as though I would vomit. She had confirmed what I already knew to be true. I knew that Peter sometimes had sex with the calves. He had alluded to as much one day when one was sucking on his finger. I had tried to ignore it. I knew he was not the only one and I did feel bad for the animals but what could I do about it?

Carl came over and his face was just as disturbed. "He knows we can't do anything Emma. He knows that we can't get mixed up in any crime because of Karen's parole. We told him as much when we moved here. But he is a bad man, he really needs to be stopped. I have no doubt in my mind that he is going to try and kill you, you have to got the police Emma."

I looked up at him. "I can't Carl, it is against the church rules. I will be shunned."

"Well do you want to end up dead?"

I looked at my trembling hands. All of a sudden a certain surge overpowered me. I would do it. I would go to the police. I had witnessed so much pain, so much suffering. Someone had to stop it. I tried to block out the consequences I would face. I would think of that later.

"Okay, I will go to the police. I will tell them about Peter. I said as if in a dream. I had a dazed feeling I could not seem to shake. "Karen, can you drive me?" I asked as I got up and started to open the door.

"Hold on," Karen grabbed my arm. "I want to make sure you have thought this through and that this is your decision. You know you could be put in the Bann if you go to the police."

I turned and jerked my arm away. "Don't touch me!" I screamed at her. I felt bad when I saw her back up in shock, but I felt sick to my stomach every time she or Carl tried to touch me. I knew my reaction had nothing to do with them, but right now I could not stand having anyone come near me or touch me.

"I'm sorry," I said quietly, feeling guilty for yelling at her. "I just don't want anyone touching me, okay?" They nodded as if they understood. "You are not even Amish," I frowned at Karen. "Why should you care if I am put in the Bann?"

"I just know you have to live here in this community," Karen shook her head. "And I know it is not easy for a girl to be put in the Bann."

"But you think I should go to the police right?" I looked at her. *Was I doing the right thing? I would be in so much trouble.*

Karen nodded her head vigorously and started to pull on her coat. "I just want to make sure you aren't going to clam up when they start questioning you...that's all. If I weren't on probation and I had a gun, I would go up there and put some buckshot in his a*s. That's the best solution to this problem," she pulled a baseball cap down on her head.

I frowned. "Why are you wearing that?"

"I am taking you to the police, but I am not going in with you," Karen looked at her reflection in the window. "I can't be associated with any violence; I can't have anything to mess up my parole."

We got in Karen's rattling old pickup and headed for town, which was about seven miles north of the farm. We rode in silence the whole way. I saw Karen look over at me a couple of times, but I did not want to talk so I just hugged the passenger-side door and looked out at the beautiful spring countryside. It was cloudy that morning, but it was still so beautiful. My eyes were brimming with tears, and a couple spilled over and rolled down my cheeks. Anyone driving down this road would probably smile as they looked around at the scattered Amish and *Englisch* farms.

They would probably feel they had stepped back into a simpler and quieter era, as the *Englisch* were so fond of saying. Never would they suspect what had happened this very morning in this idyllic community, and I was sure that if the police drove out here, they would not believe it either, just like they had not believed what I told them about Mamma and Brian. I did not know why people think the Amish are such innocent and kindly people; I guess it is because they are a religious community steeped in secrecy. They only allow the *Englisch* to see what they want them to see, thus appearing to be quaint and innocent people from a different place in time.

I shook my head at the thought... simpler time...why did people always say that? The 1500s and 1600s were a time when people died from plagues and were tortured for their beliefs. There were very few human rights; the crusaders were slaughtering thousands in the name of God. Sure, there was no technology, but that did not mean there were any fewer psychopaths, murderers and rapists than there were now. It is likely that people were even more likely to get away with these crimes then than they are now. And who better to know how to get away with these crimes than these people that had remained practically unchanged for the past three hundred and fifty years?

I was jolted from my thoughts when Karen turned off the motor and pushed her seat back. I pushed open the truck door and started to slide down off the seat when Karen reached over to grab my arm. I jumped and squealed loudly. Embarrassed, I looked around to see if anyone had noticed. No one had, and I breathed a sigh of relief.

"Sorry," Karen apologized.

I stared at her blankly.

Karen pulled the baseball cap farther down over her face and then looked at me. "I just wanted you to know that just because you are going to the police does not mean they are going to arrest him."

I shrugged. "I have to try," I said as I got out and closed the door.

I trembled as I walked into the police station. It was very small and appeared to have only two or three rooms in it. The town had less than two thousand residents, so I figured there must be a low crime rate as well. I walked through the front door and went over to a heavy wooden counter where a middle-aged policewoman sat at a computer. She looked up as I stood there watching her. I saw a surprised look on her face as she took in my appearance.

I imagined I was very different from most of the people that normally walked up to her desk. I was a young Amish woman, just a little over five feet tall, wearing an ankle-length, plain, teal-colored dress and apron. I had on knee-length black socks and black shoes, and my coat was of homemade denim with a high collar and hooks and eyes to hold the front closed. On my head I wore a stiff, white Amish kapp that covered nearly all my reddish-brown hair and it was tied in a small bow under my chin. I was shaking as I stood there, looking at the woman. I tried to get up enough courage to say something, but my mouth was so dry I could not form any words.

"Can I help you with something, honey?" the woman asked me as she took off her reading glasses.

I stared into her bright blue eyes, which crinkled up on the sides when she smiled. *She seems like a nice lady*, I thought, and I felt a little better.

"Um," I swallowed hard as I tried to block out the mental image of possibly being put in the Bann. "Um," I said again. I placed my trembling hands on the counter top.

"Yes, dear. What is it?" the woman asked.

"Um..." I said again. "Um... I would like to talk to the police, please," I pressed my hands down on the counter to stop them from shaking.

"Okay, In regards to what?"

328

"Um..." I hesitated. "I need to talk to someone because the bishop of my church attacked me and is threatening to kill me, and I think he is also poisoning his wife and molesting his daughters."

The woman raised her eyebrows in shock. After looking at me for another moment, she got up and came around the counter.

"Are you okay, honey?" she asked as she reached out to put an arm around my shoulders.

I backed up, not wanting her to touch me. I saw her nod as if she had seen this reaction before.

"Okay," she waved at a chair. "Just have a seat here for a minute."

She brought some paper and told me to write down what had happened, and after about half an hour, she waved me into a room and said that someone would be there in a few minutes. I sat there, looking blankly at the wall, until an officer walked in. He was a tall man—I guessed he was in his mid-forties, and he was scanning my report as he walked through the door. He sat for a couple minutes, drinking his coffee and reading what I had written.

"Well," he looked over at me. "I am Officer Jensen, and you are?"

"Emma Schrock," I said flatly.

"Okay." He nodded, looking back at the report. "So, you are saying that the Bishop of your church assaulted you and he is threatening to kill you?"

I frowned, not liking the tone of his voice. It seemed like he thought this was some ridiculous story that I had made up.

"Yes," I nodded. "That is what happened."

He nodded and looked at me for a long moment. "Do you have any evidence to support any of these allegations?"

I stared at him and shook my head. To this day I kick myself for not telling him about my badly bruised breasts. They were extremely painful and would be for a couple of weeks. But no Amish girl in her right mind would ever dream of doing such a thing and it honestly never even crossed my mind to mention such a thing to a man. At that time I was not taken seriously enough and no female officer offered to look me over or take me to the hospital. I myself had no knowledge of such proceedings. I was just looking for help and hoping they would at least scare Peter so he would not hurt me or anyone else ever again.

"Well," he looked skeptic, "we can't just go out and arrest someone for unsupported claims made about them."

"What do you mean?" I asked, standing up. "This man is going to hurt me, and I am absolutely positive he has been poisoning his wife, and you are saying there is nothing you can do?"

"Hold on, Emma," Officer Jensen said. "Just sit back down. I didn't say there is nothing we can do. I just said we cannot arrest someone without evidence to support the accusations."

"Well, what kind of evidence do you need?" I asked trying to think of any evidence I could possibly get.

"For instance, if you had been raped, we could do a rape kit, and that would give us physical evidence."

"So you are saying I should have let myself get raped?" I asked indignantly.

"No, no, I'm not saying anything like that. I am just saying that right now it is just your word against his. I am not going to go haul the bishop of the Amish church in without any evidence to prove he has committed a crime."

"Can I just tell you briefly what is really going on?" I asked through clenched teeth. I was trying hard not to get angry at his skeptical behavior. After all I had been through and all I risked to come here, I was not in the mood for his skeptical attitude. I spent the next ten minutes explaining what had happened and how the Amish church dealt with such things.

"I don't know," Officer Jensen was still skeptical when I had finished. "I find all of this a little hard to believe. We have a good relationship with our Amish neighbors and have never had any trouble with them."

I shook my head in frustration. "Of course you haven't had any trouble with them," I stood up again. "Do you think they are going to tell you if someone is raped, murdered or poisoned? You know that we are a society set apart from the rest of world; what would make you think they would ever let you know what is really going on out there?"

Officer Jensen seemed taken aback by my outburst and sat thinking for a moment.

"Do you think anyone else from your community would come forward and support these claims you are making?"

I thought for a moment and then shook my head. No one was going to risk it.

"Well, I really don't know what we can do except go out and question his family to see if everything is okay, but even I hate to do that to an Amish bishop."

"Why?" I asked. I was very angry now. "If he were not Amish you would not hesitate to bring him in, right?"

"Well, it's just that anyone could make the case that you are an Amish girl that is angry about something and has decided to falsely accuse the bishop of her church of a crime for revenge."

I was furious now, and I spun around, slammed both my palms down on the table and leaned toward him.

"Why is it so hard for you people to believe the Amish are just as capable of a crime as any other human being? The only difference is that they don't have to pay for their crimes. And, ironically, these very people you hold in such high regard think you are all going to hell because you are of the world."

"Well, I am sure that is probably true," Officer Jensen nodded his head. "They are regular people, but they are raised with a strict doctrine they have to follow."

"Or what?" I snapped. "Can you tell me the Amish policy on rape and murder?"

"Well, I never thought of them like that," he nodded again, as if he might finally be getting my point.

"Exactly," I straightened up. "I am so tired of you *Englisch* putting cameras in our faces and taking our picture like we are cute little puppies or something. We are people with all the same faults the rest of the human race has to offer." I looked him straight in the eyes. "Do you really think they would even bother to tell you if I died tonight? No," I shook my head. "You would never know. I would simply be buried in an Amish cemetery and it would be thought that I died from some unknown cause."

"I find that a little hard to believe," Officer Jensen looked at me in shock.

"Oh, really?" I asked with raised eyebrows. "How many Amish autopsies have you had done? How many Amish do you have walking in and out of your office every day? Don't you find it strange that the rest of the world traffics through here on a daily basis, but the Amish never darken your door?"

"I have to admit you are the first Amish I've ever interviewed," He leaned back in his chair.

"So you must agree that the Amish are closed off from the rest of the world?" I asked.

"Well, yes, I already knew that. I just didn't think of them as being harmful." Officer Jensen looked thoughtful as we both stood up to leave

331

the room.

He held the door open for me, and I pulled my coat tighter around my small frame. I stopped and looked up at him before going through the door.

"Just remember that we are humans like everyone else," I whispered, and then turned and walked back out to the car.

Karen was sleeping in the front seat and jumped a little when I knocked on the window for her to unlock the door. I got in, and she asked me how it had gone. I just shrugged and said I did not know. We drove the rest of the way home in silence.

Karen pulled up next to the horse shed, and we both got out. Simba was wagging his tail and whining for me to come over to him.

"So what are you going to do, Emma?" Karen asked me.

I just shook my head and looked around the wide-open field. "I guess I will have to go back to Jacob and Lillian's," I mumbled as I hugged Simba.

Karen nodded in agreement.

About ten minutes later, we were both surprised to see a police car turning into the lane and driving toward us.

Karen's face went pale, and she motioned for me to see what they wanted.

"Excuse me, Miss," one of the officers called to me as I walked up to the car. "Do you know which house belongs to Bishop Peter?"

"Uh, yeah, it's right over there," I pointed toward the white house that looked so peaceful and innocent from where I was standing. I watched as the police car drove down the lane and stopped in front of the house. I could see Peter as he came to the door. They stood there talking for a couple of minutes, and I frowned as I saw Peter welcome them in his house as if he had nothing to hide. I could just imagine the charming scene that greeted the officers when they went inside the house. There were probably little Amish children peeking at them shyly. Phyllis was probably offering them tea. Peter was most likely solemn as usual and maybe even holding the baby. *Certainly they would not be presenting the picture of crime these officers were used to,* I thought to myself.

I went to the dog pen and sat next to Simba, who put his giant head in my lap and wagged his tail as if trying to cheer me up. After half an hour or so, the policemen came out and drove away. I sighed when I saw them waving to Peter, who stood on the porch with his hat in his hands. I watched as Jacob and Lillian walked over to see what was going on. I felt sick to my stomach. What I had done was slowly starting to sink in, and

332

now Jacob and Lillian were going to find out. It wouldn't matter whether they believed Peter was guilty of the crimes or not. What would matter was that I had involved the authorities in a matter that should have gone in front of the church.

I sat there for what seemed like a very long time but was, in fact, little more than thirty minutes. I watched as Jacob walked to his farm and came back with Ella. My stomach tightened. That had to mean they were planning on coming over to talk to me. I felt I would be sick. I hugged Simba close and wished I could stay like that forever.

LEAVING THE AMISH

"Each time a person stands for an ideal, or acts to improve the lot of others, or strikes out against injustice, they send a tiny ripple of hope, and crossing each other from a million different centers of energy and daring, those ripples build a current which can sweep down the mightiest walls of oppression and resistance."

— *Robert F. Kennedy*

I stepped out of the pen and went into the house. I did not want to talk to them. I had to... eventually, I knew. Or did I? Suddenly, something seemed to come over me, a thought I had not even considered this whole time. *Did I really have to stay Amish? Of course I do*, I told myself. I will go to hell if I don't. If I become worldly, I will be proud, and God will be angry with me, and I will have no purpose in life.

I was holding on to the back of a chair and looking out the window. I could see Karen and Carl talking to Peter, Jacob, Lillian and Phyllis. I could see Phyllis's thin, white face. She was devastated. Lillian was standing there with a worried look on her face, and Jacob and Peter looked as if they were trying to explain something to Karen, who was standing in front of all of them with her hands on her hips. Through the open window, I could hear what they were saying.

"This is a church matter, Karen," I heard Peter say. The sound of his voice made me want to scream, but I resisted the urge.

"A church matter, huh?" Karen snapped at him. "You just assaulted sweet little Emma, and you come over here and dare to even mention the word church in front of me?"

"I have confessed to Jacob and Lillian what I have done," Peter said

334

solemnly. "I have asked God for forgiveness, and now Emma must forgive me too and drop these charges she has filed against me."

"Oh, it's just that simple, is it?" Karen scoffed at him. "I should have told that to the judge so she would not have put me in prison for three years."

"But we are not *Englisch*," Jacob informed her. "We have our own church rules that Emma must follow, or she will be shunned until she repents of this evilness she is bringing into our church."

"Karen, stop talking to these men," Carl spat angrily. "You son of a bi*ch," he turned his fury on Peter. "You threaten to kill that little girl, and then you come here telling us she has to forgive you? If my wife wasn't on probation, I would kick your a*s from here to the North Pole and back." Carl looked very angry, and it occurred to me that this was the first time a man had ever stood up for me. It was a good feeling to know there was someone who cared enough to tell these men to get lost on my behalf.

"We want to see Emma now," Jacob pushed past Karen and Carl.

"Emma! Emma, come out here right now!" Jacob shouted. He saw me through the window, and I shook my head at him. I was scared and confused at the thoughts that had just entered my head. *Did I really have to stay Amish? Were these people really God's only chosen people?* I remembered Ella's comment from a couple of years ago. Jesus was not Amish; did he go to Heaven? Jesus was just like everyone else in his time, although perhaps he was more humble; he was not living in a different time period than they were. If he had dressed as differently as we did, everyone would have laughed at him and he probably would have been labeled as crazy. So much of our religion was based on how we dressed and on not letting modern technology into our lives, and now as I saw the angry bishop of my church, I knew why. We were truly our own society, government and country, all living within another country called the United States.

My head was spinning with all these thoughts as I watched through the window and clung to the back of the chair. I could hear Simba barking and lunging at the fence. Jacob backed up a couple of steps when Simba's pearly white teeth snapped at him. Suddenly, my fear was replaced by rage. The world, as I knew it, was crumbling down around my feet, and the strong faith I had always clung to, was going with it. I still believed fervently in God, but I did not believe it was the same God these people believed in. I had not made up my mind yet, though. I was only thinking and trying to determine what I really believed.

Karen came to the door and asked if I wanted to talk to them. I nodded without uttering a sound. I moved over to the far side of the room as they entered the house. I stood with my arms folded in front of me; I was going to show no weakness, I told myself. I was not going to be intimidated. My hands started to shake a little when Peter entered, but I balled them into fists to still them. I wanted to cry when I saw Phyllis, but I had to stop myself. I loved Phyllis as a sister, but I could not help her by saying I was sorry and pretending everything was okay. Her husband wanted her dead and he wanted me to be his next wife, or at least had. Now he was furious and I seriously feared for my life.

"Okay," Karen addressed the room. "I am not going to have any violence in my house. Emma, you stay over there, and the rest of you stay here by the door. If anyone starts to get rowdy, this meeting is over."

Karen got a chair for Phyllis to sit on, and the room was quiet for a few minutes. Jacob was staring at me angrily, as if he were my real father and I was a wayward daughter that had brought shame to his family. I stared back at him, unashamed of what I had done. Peter was acting strangely and flashed his malicious grin at me. I was shocked by this and was not quite sure what he was trying to prove, but I did know he did not look one bit sorry for what he had done.

"Okay," Karen said again when no one started talking. "Someone has to say something, or we're going to be here all day." Karen and Carl were standing off to my side, and out of the corner of my eye I could see Carl glaring at Peter.

Jacob cleared his throat but still no one made a move to speak. Finally, he looked at me and started speaking in our Amish dialect.

"Oh, no, you don't," Karen shook her head at him. "This is my house and you will speak English here." She turned to me and asked me what he had said. I swallowed and stared at her for a second. I was so scared and confused. Jacob had just told me Karen was not a church member, and I was committing a grave sin by involving her like this. I just shook my head at Karen and looked at the floor. I did not know what to do.

"All right," Peter said after another moment of silence. "If you do not drop these charges against me, we will have no other choice than to place you in the Bann until you do. As it is, you are already facing six weeks of Bann, and this will only make your punishment longer."

I became angry. Using my anger was the only way I would be able to stand up to these people. It took a lot to make me angry, but once it happened, I would not back down. I felt the terror that I had been feeling all day leave me; it was replaced with indignant rage. My hands were still trembling, but not with fear, and I clenched them so hard that my knuckles were as white as snow. I glared at Peter.

"How dare you!" I took two steps toward him with my fists clenched at my sides. "How dare you talk to me about the severity of punishment I will receive if I do not drop these charges against you? You threatened to rape me and kill me...and now you dare to come in here and act like you have the authority to punish me?"

"He does have the authority," Jacob snapped at me. "He is the bishop, and these are our ways."

"No, he does not," I snapped back. "He is an evil man that must be stopped."

"It is not your place to judge a man once he has confessed to God," Jacob shot back at me. "He will be placed in the Bann for six weeks as well. But you," he shook his head at me. "You have committed a grave sin and are not repentant, you will be in the Bann until we see you have repented for what you have done."

"I have committed no crime," I stomped my foot. "You cannot punish me. I am the one who was assaulted, and not one of you has bothered to say you are sorry for what happened to me. You only want me to drop the charges. It is not fair."

"Emma," Phyllis stood up. "You will be silent and come with us. This is enough." I thought she looked weak, and I was sure she had had another seizure that morning. Most likely while Peter had been in my room or attacking me by the steps.

"No, Phyllis," I shook my head. "I will not go back and pretend everything's okay."

"This is ridiculous," Phyllis was angry. "I thought you were my friend, and then you turn my husband over to the police. Emma, how could you do such a thing?" Phyllis looked very concerned and sad for what I had done, I thought. I hated to see her that way, but it could not be helped.

"Phyllis," I said in a softer tone. "You have to know the truth."

"About what?" Phyllis asked me.

"No," Peter shouted. "This is enough. We are leaving, and I am going to meet with the elders and the deacon, Emma will be placed in the Bann until she repents."

I had to tell Phyllis that I feared she was being poisoned, so I walked over and stood in front of the door. "Phyllis," I grabbed her hand. "The real reason Peter attacked me is because I have been ignoring his advances for weeks now."

"I don't believe that," Phyllis shook her head and pulled away.

"That's not all." I grabbed her hand again and looked into her eyes. "I believe Peter is poisoning you at least two times a week, and he is molesting Katie."

"What?" Phyllis gasped as she stared back into my eyes. We had had so many heart-to-heart conversations since I had moved here that I knew she realized I was telling the truth.

She shook her head frantically. "No," she said, backing away from me. "It can't be true. Peter would not do that."

I nodded at her. "One day at the table, he asked the children if they thought I would make a good mother if you died. He was going to replace you with me, Phyllis. Go ahead," I pleaded. "Ask the children if he said it if you don't believe me."

"Let's go," Peter tried to reach past me to open the door.

"No, wait," Phyllis said in her weak voice. She grabbed Peter's arm and gazed up at him with her clear blue eyes. "Peter, tell me. Did you say that?"

Peter hesitated for a minute. If Phyllis were to ask the children, he knew they would certainly confirm what I had said, so he confessed.

"Uh, yes. I guess I did say that," Peter nodded his head slowly. "But," he glared at me and then looked back at Phyllis, "I just said that because you were so sick and I knew how much you liked Emma, so I thought she would be a good choice."

Phyllis's eyes filled with tears, and she shook her head in sorrow. "Peter, how could you do this to me?" she put her face in her hands.

"Phyllis, you do believe me, right?" I reached out for her.

Phyllis looked at me in anger. "Yes, I believe you," she snapped. "But it does not excuse what you are doing to us, Emma. You should have come to me, not the police."

"Phyllis," I was in shock, "I just told you that your husband is poisoning you and molesting your daughter, and this is how you respond?"

"It does not concern the outside world," Phyllis said angrily.

I got angry, too. "Phyllis," I snapped. "This man is just like your father. He is molesting your daughter. Tell me, did the church ever help you or your siblings?"

"That is none of your business," Phyllis snapped back.

"Oh, no," I shook my head. "It is my business. If you know your daughter is being hurt by this man, and you just stand by and let it happen...I am sorry, Phyllis, but I don't have any sympathy for a mother that would do that."

"He will repent," Phyllis said as if she were reciting a script.

"How many times did your father repent, Phyllis?" I asked her.

She shook her head. "It is a church matter."

I could not believe what I was hearing. It was so bizarre to me that this woman would stand by a man who was poisoning her and molesting her daughter. It was crazy.

"Phyllis, listen to what you are saying," I grabbed her by both shoulders. "This man is hurting you and your children. You have to leave him. You can't let your children suffer as you did."

"It must be God's will," Phyllis shook her head and pulled away from me. "Peter was chosen by God to be my husband and the leader of our church. We have no divorce. I can't leave him, Emma. You know that."

"Your husband was not chosen by God," I said angrily as I turned toward Peter and Jacob, who were standing behind me. "It was just chance that caused him to pick up the book with the paper in it. There is no way God would want any of this to happen. I can't believe that." I shook my head and squinted thoughtfully.

"Emma," Jacob said as he grabbed my hand. "You will be silent and come with us now. The longer you drag this out, the worse it will be for you. You may never regain the trust of the church, and then you will never marry and have a family of your own."

Family! I stared at him and pulled away. The thought of bringing children into this church made me sick to my stomach. I stepped away from the door and backed a few steps toward Karen and Carl.

"Come, Emma," Jacob ordered. "If you confess right now and drop the charges, it will be better for you."

"No," I shook my head. "No, I will not confess, and I will not drop the charges."

"You will be silent and do as you are told," Peter shouted at me.

"No," I said again. "I cannot bring children into a society that prevents me from protecting them; a society that only seems interested in protecting the predators."

"Emma, what are you doing?" Lillian asked me as I reached up and untied my head covering. I did not fully comprehend what I was doing; it was as if I were in a dream. I pulled off the stiff white covering and looked down at it for a second, watching as a few of my tears fell on it.

"Emma," Peter said in a warning voice. "Don't do this. You will be

339

excommunicated and shunned for life."

I thought of Samantha. She would probably be getting married soon. If I did this, we could no longer write as often. I could not attend her wedding. If I showed up at her house, the church members would turn their backs to me. It was a very hard decision I was making in that split second, but I knew I had to do what I thought was right.

"No," I let the covering fall to the floor. "You will not have the pleasure of excommunicating me, because I am excommunicating myself."

Everyone in the room stood in stunned silence. I was kind of stunned, too. I had just left the Amish. What had I done? But as shocked as I was, I felt in my heart that I was doing the right thing. This was the only way to stand up for what I believed in. It was the only way I could live with myself. I could not go through life belonging to a church that hurt people and then silenced them. It just was not in me; I could not do it.

"Emma, don't do this," Phyllis pleaded with me. "I know you are angry and sad because of what happened, but you will go to hell for what you are doing."

I shook my head at her. I had made up my mind.

"If you leave the church you will go to hell, Emma." Peter informed me solemnly.

My resolve was growing stronger by the second, and I just looked back at him. "Not before you do." I watched as his face became a little worried, for a split second my comment made him think of his own soul, perhaps even beyond the Amish tradition which he clung to as his salvation

"Emma," Jacob looked at me angrily. "Going to hell is no laughing matter. And it is clear that is where you are going if you leave the Amish."

"Well, I don't think it will be much worse than living here, full of regrets and fear."

"You have nowhere to go, Emma," Lillian said from where she was standing behind Phyllis.

I bit my lip; I had not thought that far ahead yet. I stared back at Lillian. This woman had caused me so much grief, but I could not help feeling a twinge of sorrow for her and all that she had been through. But Lillian was just like Phyllis. No matter what her husband did, it was her job to stand by him. There was no escape for them. They believed too wholeheartedly in what they had been taught.

"She can stay out back in our trailer until she figures it out," Karen piped up.

"Yeah," I fiddled with my apron. "I will stay in the trailer." Such foreign-sounding words for an Amish girl. I was going to stay by myself in a travel trailer. What a scandal.

Peter looked angrily at Karen. "I want you to get off my property."

"Nope," Karen shook her head. "Not going to happen. We have a two-year lease agreement, and if you force me off the land, I will haul your a*s into court and tell the judge everything that went down here today. Do you really want that?"

They stared at me for a long moment, and then Jacob went to the door. "You are now in the Meidung (this is a punishment worse than the Bann and it involves shunning a person lifelong, unless they repent and confess in front of the church) "I don't want you at the farm until you have confessed and repented and agreed to your punishment. The official shunning will be set on Sunday, but I consider it in place now."

"I wasn't planning on coming by," I answered from where I was standing with my kapp at my feet. My hands were sweating, but my resolve was not broken.

"God have mercy on your soul," Lillian shook her head and followed Jacob out. Phyllis trailed after them. Peter was ready to leave as well, when he suddenly turned and stepped over to where I was standing. My first reaction was to back away, but I did not. I didn't want him to see how much he scared me.

He just stood there menacingly, his eyes reminded me of Brian's. There was something very wrong and very threatening in the way he looked at me.

I felt sick. The very thought that he was the bishop who had punished and admonished me and then had assaulted me and now was standing in front of me in such a threatening manner was almost too much to bear, my body began shaking violently.

I heard Karen move up behind me as she ordered Peter to get away from me. He looked at me for another long threatening moment, and then turned and left with the others. I was terrified, I felt in my soul that if I stayed in the area Peter would make good on his threat to smother me in my sleep. If I had remained Amish I have absolutely no doubt that at some point, somewhere I would have succumbed to an awful accidental death. It was to clear and to apparent in his eyes.

I watched them as they walked a few hundred feet away and then huddled together to talk. Suddenly I felt so alone. I was no longer a member of their society. What was I going to do, and where was I going to go? For the first time in my life, I had no book of rules to follow. All of this finally proved to be too much, and I ran outside and vomited in the tall grass.

I sat there for a few minutes and looked out over the rich farmland—everything that I loved and knew so well. I knew I would miss these familiar surroundings and my daily activities. I knew nothing beyond being an Amish girl. I knew how to cook, take care of children and I loved quilting and sewing. But all of that was not going to matter anymore. I was no longer Amish. That very thought was shocking, and I felt as if I were in a dream. It did not seem real. Did I really have what it took to leave everything I knew behind and start out on my own? I knew I did not possess this strength on my own, but my firm belief in God would get me through; I truly believed he was guiding me to do this.

I thought of Brian and Mamma and wondered if they would ever find out I had left. I did not plan to tell them, but I knew Samantha sometimes wrote them and would probably tell them, eventually. I could just imagine Brian's gloating face as he nodded to himself and told Mamma that he had always known that I had the Jezebel spirit.

I shook myself out of my reverie. I had left the Amish; that was all there was to it. Now I was going to pursue the dreams I had been repressing all my life. I was going to find a way to be a medical missionary. I knew it would be a long, hard journey, but I believed it was my true destiny, and I believed that my intense faith in God would guide me through the rough, trying days ahead.

Eventually, I went back into the house, where Carl and Karen were waiting for me.

I sat down in a chair and just looked at the floor.

"Emma," Carl addressed me after a moment. "We have to figure out where you are going to live.

Karen shook her head. "It is not safe for you here, Emma. Where can you go?"

I shrugged my shoulders. "I don't know," I said in the same numb voice. I thought hard for a moment. Where *was* I going to go?

"Well," Carl thought for a moment, "there is that halfway house you stayed in for a month, Karen. I'm sure we could talk to the lady in charge; they would probably take Emma in and help her get situated."

Karen nodded at first, but then shook her head. "Look at her, Carl," she pointed to me. "She does not look a day older than fourteen. Those women would eat her for lunch."

Carl nodded. "Well, she can't stay here. It isn't safe."

"Is that what you want to do, Emma?" she asked me.

I nodded. "I'll contact the YWAM School while I am at the halfway house and find out what I need to do to get into their missionary training school."

"Okay," Karen got up slowly. "I will take you there, but you are going to need different clothes."

I looked down at my Amish dress and apron. I wanted to take them off, but I was afraid. I had worn these clothes for so long and had always been taught that to wear anything different was following the ways of the harlot. I had not left the Amish over a desire to dress like the rest of the world, but rather because I wanted to stand up for all the people who had been hurt and silenced.

"I don't want to wear any pants," I hesitated, what would I wear?. "I will still wear dresses, just not Amish ones."

"You are going to have a hard time out there like that," Carl shook his head. "Karen only gets away with it because she doesn't care, but you're a young girl. It's going to be different for you."

I put a hand to my head, and Karen told Carl to shut up as she rummaged through a box. "Here," she held up a purple dress with blue flowers on it. "This dress was one of the first I tried to make, and it is too tight and too short for me. You might be able to wear it."

I took the dress and asked Karen if I could borrow one of her scarves. Not having my head covered made me feel naked and as if I were doing something very bad. She handed me a white one, and I went behind their room divider, took off my coat and unpinned my teal Amish dress and apron. My hands trembled as I looked in the large mirror that leaned against the wall. I looked at the tear in the front of my dress and at my ashen-colored face. I kept asking myself what I was doing—my body seemed to be acting without my direction. I looked down at the dress and apron that lay on the floor.

I felt that everything these clothes represented had been a lie. It was heartbreaking that now, at twenty-two years old, I was just beginning to realize that my entire life had been based on a lie. I had been told that the Amish way was the only way to heaven, but now as I thought about it, I realized that almost everything they claimed was in the Bible was not there. I had always known this, but I had never let my mind fully process it before.

I slipped into the flowered dress and stared in the mirror as I fastened the pink pearl buttons. The dress did not have a collar, and the neck line fell below my collar bone making me feel a little uncomfortable. The dress was huge on my small frame, but at least it was not Amish, I thought. Having the flowers on the dress was a strange feeling, too, but I was sure there was nothing in the Bible that said women had to wear solid-colored clothing. I knotted the white scarf and then balled up my Amish dress and apron and put them in the bucket Karen used as a trash can.

"Well, don't you look different, Emma." Carl smiled.

"That's not my name," My eyes opened wide at the remembrance of my own name, and not just my first name, but also my last name that I had not been able to use since I was four years old. "My name is not Emma. It's Misty...Misty Griffin."

"Misty Griffin?" Carl said with a perplexed frown.

I nodded and spent the next fifteen minutes telling them my life story.

"Wow. We had no idea." Carl shook his head. "That is a crazy story, and you are quite a remarkable young woman."

I sighed. It was a crazy story, and what I was doing now seemed even crazier. But suddenly I had an idea. What about calling Aunty Laura to see if I could stay with her for a few months? Carl and Karen thought it was a fantastic idea; the only problem was that I had no idea how to reach her. Carl turned on the generator so Karen could look online for the phone number of Laura's furniture store near Seattle. I sat next to her, fascinated by how fast things popped up on the computer screen.

"You are going to need to learn about computers," Karen said as she saw my fascination. "Everyone is online these days."

I looked at her and then back at the screen. The idea was foreign to me, but I knew she was right. I was just not ready to process everything yet.

"All right, here we go," Karen clicked on the name of the furniture store. "Is this the right one?"

I nodded and felt a little panicky as Karen dialed the number. I didn't want to have to explain what had just happened to Aunty Laura, and I was worried because she was Brian's sister. I felt as if I couldn't trust anyone. I took a deep breath to calm my nerves as I heard Karen say, "Hello. Um, yes, I would like to speak with Laura...It is in regards to her step-niece."

There was a pause, and I put my ear to the other side of the phone. What if she said no? What if Brian had convinced her I was a bad person? I would have no choice but to go to the halfway house—I didn't want to go, but I would have no other option. Breathlessly, I waited.

"Hello?" I heard a familiar voice on the other end of the line.

"Hi. Yes, I am calling on behalf of your step-niece, Misty Griffin,"

Karen said in a professional voice. It was easy to tell she had not always been a horse rescuer in a flowered dress and scarf.

"Okay?" I heard Aunty Laura say hesitantly. "Has something happened to her?"

"Well, sort of," Karen glanced over at me. "Hold on one second, please." She put her hand over the phone and turned to me. "What should I tell her?"

I swallowed and reached for the phone. "Aunty Laura," I said in a nervous voice.

"Yes, honey, what is it?"

"Hi, it's Misty, and I was wondering if I could come and stay with you for a few months?"

There was a pause. "Of course you can stay with me," Aunty Laura tried to sound cheerful, but I could tell that she knew something was wrong. Relieved, I nodded at Karen and gave her the thumbs-up.

"Where are you right now?" Aunty Laura asked.

"I am in an Amish community in Minnesota," I explained. "But I am leaving the Amish, and I don't know where else to go."

"Does Brian know you called me?" Aunty Laura asked.

I swallowed hard; Mamma and Brian were my only problem now. I would no longer be sheltered in a community. What if they came after me for calling the police? Aunty Laura had no idea about the torture Samantha and I had endured at the hands of her brother. I felt like I was going back into the past and fervently hoped I was not making a mistake.

"No, he doesn't know, Aunty Laura," I was shaking. "And I hope you won't tell him till I get there and explain what happened."

"Well, okay," Aunty Laura relented. "Are you okay, honey? Did someone hurt you?"

I didn't feel like explaining anything and put a hand to my forehead. I had told the story to the police already and did not wish to retell again. Karen took the phone from me and whispered, "You are going to have to tell her what happened."

I just nodded numbly. I listened while Karen talked to Aunty Laura.

"Hi, Laura. It is Karen again. Yes, Misty is staying with me right now. This morning she was hurt and assaulted by the bishop of her church. The man that did it is threatening to kill her in her sleep. No, she is okay, but she is in shock. Yes, she has definitely left the Amish. She is wearing one of my flowered dresses right now. Okay, we will call you back when we have details for her arrival. Thank you so much. Bye."

"Your Aunty Laura wants to know if you need money for a plane ticket," Karen said as she set down the phone. "But I just realized you can't even get on a plane because you don't have any form of ID."

"ID?" I queried with a frown.

"Yeah. You know, picture identification card."

"Oh," I just looked at her blankly. "I didn't know you had to have that."

"Yeah. In the real world you have to have it. Do you even know your social security number?"

I shook my head. Mamma had given me my social security card when I turned eighteen, but when I joined the community, they made me put it in the wood burning stove.

"What the heck?" Karen shook her head. "You are like an illegal alien, and we have no way to get your social security number because we have no way to prove who you are."

I shrugged. I had known that Mamma and Brian had driver's licenses, but I had never known it was mandatory for everyone to have picture IDs and social security numbers.

"You are not going to be able to get a job without it." Karen sighed. "And you won't last long without a job."

I bit my lip and stared at her. What she was saying was all so strange to me; I was a girl that had spent her entire life detached from society. I did not comprehend the seriousness of what she was saying and reassured myself that everything would be fine. God would get me through this. He always did...all I had to do was follow His lead.

"Don't worry, Karen," I said. "Once I get to Seattle I will ask around and figure out how to do everything. It will be fine."

"You are so brave." Karen smiled at me. "I am not sure I could do what you are doing. It's going to be a whole different world out there for you."

I nodded. That it was, but I was glad for what I had done. I believed God had finally answered my prayers, and now I knew that the desire to be a medical missionary had not been just a fleeting dream, but rather an unforeseen destiny.

"Okay," I stood up and stretched my back. "I need to go back to Peter's house to get my hope chest. I have a thousand dollars in it."

"A thousand dollars?" Karen raised her eyebrows in surprise.

"Yes, a thousand dollars." I nodded. "It will pay for my bus ticket and a few necessities to get me to Seattle."

"Well, that is awesome," Karen nodded. "That definitely helps. I thought you had no money."

"I wasn't supposed to," I explained. "But it was mine, and I hid it away. And now I am glad I did."

"You are one smart cookie," Karen said as she put on her coat.

Carl and Karen drove their pickup truck over to Peter's house, and I watched as they seemed to argue with him for a few minutes. Then they went inside and came out with my hope chest. A tear spilled down my cheek as I remembered the birthday I had received it, and how much it had meant then. Now it was just a big cedar box that would most likely be left behind as I embraced my new life, unlike the Amish women who keep their hope chests as lifelong treasures. Before marriage, it stores the dishes and quilts that will grace her future home, and after marriage, it holds the Sunday quilts that are placed on beds when church is being held at her house or when guests spend the night.

This was the life I knew, that I had embraced and that I was now leaving. Unless you have been Amish, you will never know the emotions that well up when leaving. Although I had not been born Amish, nearly my entire life had been spent dressing like them, acting like them and eventually becoming one of them. It truly was the only life I knew. Life with Brian and Mamma had been like a prison; I had been sealed off from the real world. I had no outside knowledge to guide me during these trying times, and I felt scared and vulnerable. At the same time, I was full of resolve to do the right thing. It was the only way I could live with myself.

Truth be told, it would have been much easier to go back and confess that I had done wrong by calling the police. I would have been punished, but I would not have been on my own. My life would have continued as it always had. There would have been no frightening decisions to make. In fact, as an Amish person, there are rarely any major decisions that you have to make. Everything is laid out for you. But now I felt pummeled with decisions I had to make. It was so hard, I thought, but like Karen said, "Welcome to the real world."

SHUNNED BY THE CHURCH

"When a man is denied the right to live the life he believes in, he has no choice but to become an outlaw."

— *Nelson Mandela*

After much discussion, Carl and Karen decided they would drive me to Seattle. It would be a long drive, but if they took turns driving they said we could make it in a little over a day. Karen said there was a horse rescue they wanted to see in Montana, and this was the perfect opportunity to go. The only problem was that she had to call her probation officer and get permission to travel. She said it usually took about a month before she could be cleared to leave the state. I did not want to stay there for a month, but decided I might as well accept their kind offer to take me to Seattle instead of getting on a bus all by myself.

The next month went by in a haze. Karen said she was not allowed to have anyone living in the house with them, so I stayed in the small, eighteen-foot trailer in back of the shop. At night I stayed awake, terrified that Peter would make good on his promise to come in the night and smother me in my sleep. I sat on the tiny bed, holding a broom to defend myself. Sometimes I dozed off, only to be jerked awake when the horses made noises in the barn behind me or by Simba's deep growl. I left my kerosene lamp on low and would read much of the time. The door of the trailer was thin, and I was afraid that Peter could just rip it off if he really wanted to get in.

At night, when I went to the trailer, I would put a two-by-four that ran nearly the length of the trailer in front of the door. Then I tied it to a long piece of twine which was, in turn, tied to the door handle. I fastened several aluminum cans on the piece of twine and I hoped they would make noise if anyone tried to get in. I thought of asking Karen if Simba could stay with me at night, but I knew that if he managed to get out of the trailer and was found on one of the local ranches, he would be shot, and that would be an unbearable loss.

During that month, I counted at least three times when, during the night, Simba started barking and growling like he did whenever Peter came near. Once, I fell asleep and dropped the broom. Frantically, I reached for it. My hands shook, and I dropped it again. I jumped down and grabbed it again, and then sat on the bed, waiting for someone to try to open the door. To my relief, no one did, but I was badly frightened and very tired from being unable to sleep. It was one of the longest months of my life.

During the day, I took naps and helped Karen and Carl with the horses. I went to town with them a few times, and Karen took me to a thrift store to get some different clothes. I chose a few long skirts, blouses and T-shirts, as well as a couple pairs of flats. As I tried them on in the dressing room, I thought of how *worldly* I looked. I tried on a pair of jeans but could not stand the feeling of having something so close-fitting around my legs.

I really liked the denim skirts; paired with a T-shirt or blouses, they made me feel more like the rest of the world. I still wore the scarf on my head though. I was going through so many changes and I was not ready to let go of everything just yet. As it was, with every new choice I made, I could constantly hear a small voice in the back of my head saying, "*You are going to hell*".

᛭HE DAYS seemed to drag on. I was anxious to get to Seattle and a couple of times I thought about telling Karen and Carl that I would just buy a bus ticket, but that seemed ungrateful, so I did not. When I was not helping with the horses or visiting the nearby town, I read some of the novels Karen had lying about. Karen studied for her veterinary class, and she left the radio on. I was intrigued by the radio. I had never realized how much fun it would be to have a radio on while you worked or sat reading. We mostly played gospel songs, and I found myself singing along to this new kind of Christian music.

I sent a letter to the YWAM in Jacksonville, Florida, asking them what I needed in order to attend their next missionary training school. They wrote back that all I needed was a high school diploma or GED and fifteen hundred dollars. Karen nodded in approval and told me it would be easy to save up fifteen hundred dollars over the summer, so I should be able to attend the next class that started in January.

"Okay," I said happily, starting to feel excitement now that a plan was starting to form. "But they also say I need a GED. What is that?"

"Oh, it's a high school equivalency test," Karen was studding the picture of the African orphans at the top of the page. "You went to the eighth grade, so you should do fine on it, although you may need to take a few classes at the college first. I am sure you can get the GED by January."

I frowned. "But I didn't grow up here, Karen," I looked at the floor in shame. "I don't have an eighth grade education."

"Oh?" Karen bit her lip. "What grade did you go to?"

I shook my head. "I went through the second or third grade, I guess. I really don't know. I learned how to write. I can add, subtract and multiply single digits."

"You didn't learn anything else, like how to write a paper, or science or history?" Karen looked completely mortified.

I shook my head. "No, but I did write for the Amish paper, and I read a lot of history books."

Karen looked pensive. "Well, I don't know," she tried to mask her shock, "but I am sure your aunt will help you once you get there. You just may not be able to get your GED by January."

"Why not?" I frowned.

"Well, you have to learn almost eight years of school first. Maybe, if you really put your head in the books you could do it in a year, but not in six months. And besides, you don't even know how to study for a test, do you?"

I shook my head. "No, but it can't be that hard."

"Yes, it is that hard," Karen said. "You were never in school, so you never learned the discipline or the skills it takes to study. You have no academic skills. I am just being honest with you, Misty. It's going to be very difficult."

I was frowning, but not discouraged. "Don't worry, Karen. I will make it by January, just you wait and see." I started to smile again.

Karen smiled back and shook her head. "Is there anything you think you can't do?"

"Well, where there is a will, there is a way," I said as I stood up. "I believe everything is possible as long as you follow what is right and your intentions are good."

Karen nodded. "I guess you are right, Misty. I am so going to miss having you around. You are a real inspiration."

I shrugged. I did not feel like I was an inspiration, but I did feel fortunate to have everything falling into place.

I SENT a letter to Samantha two days after everything had happened. I wanted her to hear this news from me, as I knew word that I was leaving the Amish would soon start flying from community to community through family letters. I was sure it was one of the most interesting things that had happened in our community in a long time.

I sent the letter with a sigh. I did not know if I would ever see or hear from Samantha again once I was excommunicated. It was the only thing that really made me wish I had not left. I would miss many things, but nothing as much as my little sister. It was what I had to do, though, and I hoped by doing so I would set a good example for her. I felt like I was being blackmailed—either come back to the church or lose my sister forever. It was definitely hard, but I couldn't say that what I had done was wrong, and I could no longer be associated with people that bound a person the way the Amish did.

Some people will disagree with me; some might say that I was free to leave at any time. No one was holding a gun to my head and making me stay. I beg to differ on this, though. Leaving someplace when you have no money or knowledge of the outside world does not mean you're free. The likelihood of anyone leaving the Amish is very doubtful. The fact is, that it takes a lot of courage and faith in oneself to successfully transition out into a world so different from your own. This is what makes it so easy for people to fall prey to predators. Now that I think about it, the probability that an Amish person would ever go to the police was even less likely than the possibility that the person would run away.

The Sunday evening after I left, the ministers all gathered outside Karen's house to tell me I had been placed in the Bann. I had been feeling so much stress that I did not think I could stand anymore, so I told Karen and Carl that if anyone came by to see me to tell them I did not want to talk to them.

I watched as the women got out of the buggies to stand next to their husbands. How could they? I wondered. How could they stand there beside these men? I just could not understand it. I was in the house with Karen when they all trotted up to the hitching post. I had been expecting them and had told Karen and Carl that I would not give them the pleasure of putting me in the Bann. I had left the church of my own accord and I was not about to let these people lecture me and tell me I was going to hell.

My words had been rather harsh and I felt angry, but at the same time

I knew they were not doing this out of meanness. They were not doing it to torment me, they truly believed in what they were doing. I knew in my heart that most of these people would never have done the things that Peter had and most likely they felt disgusted by his actions. Yet, the reality remained, they were Amish and they had to carry out the rules of the church. I was breaking those rules now, and that made me the one to be outcast. Even though the rules of the Amish church had been written by mere men, they could not see that. The *Ordnung* was law, the only thing that could possibly save your soul from hell.

Karen and Carl walked out to where the buggies were. I was sitting under an open window so I could hear the conversation without being seen.

"Why are you here?" Carl asked them abruptly.

"We are here to see Emma," The Deacon said solemnly.

"She does not want to talk to you," Karen snapped at them.

"That is between us and Emma," The Deacon replied.

"No, it is not," Karen retorted. I couldn't see her, but I could imagine her with her hands on her hips and lips pursed, daring the group to try anything.

"We did not come here to talk to you," I heard one of the ministers say, his voice rose slightly. "Emma, come out here," he shouted in the Amish dialect.

I sat, shaking and clenching my fists. I did not answer. I wanted to scream at them to leave me alone and go away.

"Leave her alone. She does not want to talk to you," Carl shouted . . "Haven't you done enough to her? Just leave her alone already."

I was choking back tears as I waited to hear the words that would cut me off from Samantha forever unless I repented from my 'supposed' evil and agreed to come back to the Amish.

"Well," the Deacon cleared his throat, I detected a twinge of sadness and for a second almost felt guilty. "We were going to give her one last chance to repent before we placed her in the Bann, but she leaves us no choice. Tell Emma she is, as of now, placed under the Meidung of the Amish church until such a time as she returns to the fold and repents of the evil practices she has adopted."

I felt the air leave my lungs, and I gasped for breath. I had known it was going to happen. I knew that as a result of my choice, I was now excommunicated from the Amish. I was cut off from my sister and Matty and all the children that I loved so dearly. The severity of that action had not yet set in, but over time it would, and the sting of it would surely cause more than a few tears to run down my cheeks. When that happened, I would remind myself of why I had made this choice, and I would be comforted knowing that I had done the right thing.

SEVERAL TIMES during that month while we waited for Karen's permission to travel, people from the community would stop by to warn me of my wayward ways, but I was in no mood to talk to any of them and just stayed in the house. Once Zoya came by and we talked for a while. She told me she wished she could go with me, but her troubles far exceeded just leaving the Amish. I wished I knew how to help her, but I barely knew how to help myself at the time.

Letters from Samantha were the hardest to open. I was now shunned from my sister, it was so hard to accept especially when she wrote that if I did not confess now, I would not be able to attend her wedding, and that would all be on me. Of course, it made me sad, and in truth I *was* the one leaving, but I found it so frustrating that no one cared why. Even though Peter had confessed his crimes to the church, the fact that he had confessed to the ministers and the Deacon made the other members nod at him in approval, while I, the victim, was scowled at for going to the police and leaving a church that would act in such a manner.

I wrote Samantha, telling her as much, and with the next letter she sent me, there was also a letter from the Deacon with whom she lived. In it, he outlined why my going to the police and leaving the church was worse than Peter attacking me and threatening to kill me. He said that because Peter had confessed, he was open to being forgiven by God, but I was holding anger toward him and therefore I must repent, or I would surely go to hell. Peter would be forgiven and reinstated in the church, but I had involved the outside law, which meant that I wanted revenge for what had happened to me, and such behavior was unacceptable in the eyes of God and the Amish Church.

After that I did not write to Samantha again before I left for Seattle. There was no use arguing with people if they were not going to budge on their beliefs. They would never be able to understand that I had done what was necessary to stop Peter, not to seek revenge. I did not understand how fathers in the community could stand in the barn with Peter before church services and not think that maybe one of their daughters was next, or that maybe he had already molested one of their daughters. What about Phyllis's father? He was a known serial rapist and was now hurting his grandchildren, but he was also a deacon in the church.

It seemed that these men were calloused to the severity of these deeds, calloused by years of hearing confessions such as Peter's and silencing the victims so they never talked of the matter again. It was the perfect way to sweep these devastating happenings under the rug where everyone would forget about them. But the pain that lingered in the hearts of the victims who would never be able to talk about what happened to them was a lifelong prison sentence—especially if, like Phyllis, your attacker was someone in your own immediate family and whom you had to see frequently. If the victims were children, they would have to live with their predators until they married. It was a terrible tragedy and I was glad I was leaving it all behind me. At that time in my life I was angry with the Amish church. Now that anger has subsided and been replaced with such sadness. I feel so sad for those who must blindly follow the Ordnung every day without thought to their own conscious.

ℱINALLY, THE end of the waiting period came to an end. I was very nervous about leaving, but at the same time, I was really happy to go. I was so tired from the lack of sleep. I had barely slept at all in the past thirty days, and when I did, I had nightmares so terrible that I woke up screaming and sweating. Karen and Carl said they were both worried about me and were afraid I was suffering Post Traumatic Stress Disorder. Carl had been in the army when he was younger, and he said I showed all the classic signs. I jumped and screamed at the slightest noise, and if someone reached out to touch me, I backed away from them like they had a knife in their hands. I hated this, but I did it without thinking, always apologizing afterwards. It made me uncomfortable to think I was not in complete control of my actions, since I had always prided myself on my self-control and being able to stay calm and logical in a crisis. However, after Peter attacked me, I was a little broken inside, and I was at a loss as to how to fix it. I hoped that once I got to Seattle and a safe environment, some of my fears would go away.

It was one of the last days of April when we set out on the road trip to Seattle. Karen and Carl were excited to get started. They said they loved to travel and were expecting this to be an exciting trip. It was spring and the hillsides were blooming with wildflowers. It was a great time of year to travel. I was glad I had set aside the thousand dollars—I had spent less than a hundred dollars so far. I gave two hundred to Karen to pay for the gas; she said she was very grateful but she did not want to accept it. I told her I wanted to pay my way and said it would make me feel better, so she nodded and accepted the money. It felt good to be able to pay for something. It may seem strange to the average person, but paying my own way gave me an incredibly good feeling...like I finally had some control over my life and my finances as a single girl. It made me feel independent and as if I mattered just a little bit.

As we packed my things into the back of the small truck, Karen commented that I did not have many belongings and asked if I was sure I did not want to bring any of my Amish clothes for the memories. I frowned and shook my head. The only item of Amish clothing that I brought with me was a light blue apron that Samantha had made for me. I took my hope chest, my sewing machine and the new clothes I bought at the thrift store. I don't know why I took the hope chest and sewing machine, but I thought they might be useful. Just shows how Amish my thinking still was, and how much I was going to have to learn about the new world.

It was a long drive, and Karen and Carl took turns napping, but I did not sleep the entire time. Although I was exhausted, I was excited and unable to sleep. I stared out the window as the familiar countryside was replaced with more countryside that looked similar to what I had left behind years prior, but that seemed to be from a different lifetime. It felt as if I were moving in reverse. I kept telling myself I was not going back to the mountain to live with Brian and Mamma, but the closer we got to eastern Washington, the more anxious I felt. I tried to sing along with the radio—my new found friend—but it did not stop the tears that started rolling down my cheeks as we entered Washington State. I had thought I would never be back here, and I had tried my hardest to block out the memories of Fanny and Grandma. Although it had been hard, I had been somewhat successful. Sometimes a certain smell or sound would bring terrible flashbacks of their tear-stained faces, and I would run to a corner where no one could see me and try to choke back the tears. I would tell myself there was nothing I could do and that I would never see them again. But now I was on my way to Brian's sister's house and I felt as if I was headed back in my old life.

As we started the ascent up the Cascade Mountain pass that would take us into western Washington, I felt sweat beads forming on my forehead, even though I was not hot. My hands were sweating profusely, and I was gasping for breath. Karen looked into the back seat and, seeing me gasping, told Carl to pull over to the side of the road. She got out of the car and then pulled her seat forward and reached in and pulled me out.

"Carl, get me that bottle of water," she ordered. "I think she's having a panic attack."

Karen poured some water on a handful of napkins and dabbed my face with it. I started to calm down, and my breathing got easier. I shook myself and looked at Carl and Karen in embarrassment.

"I'm sorry," I said as I crawled into the back seat.

"No." Karen shook her head as we hit the road again. "Carl and I have been waiting for something like this to happen. You have been so strong since everything happened. You have to fall apart sometime. It's a release mechanism for the brain."

I shrugged and stared out the window again. I was still ashamed of myself but I did feel surprisingly better.

*W*E PULLED up to Aunty Laura's house in the early afternoon. I remembered the house from many years earlier. It seemed smaller than I remembered, but it was still the house that I used to imagine I lived in. It was a medium-sized, three bedroom house. Aunty Laura always kept it spotless, and I remembered that her house always smelled like fresh flowers. There was also a large magnolia tree that graced the front lawn and the driveway. Memories from so many years ago started floating through my mind. Sadly I recalled the image of my small, seven-year-old self that had been badly beaten and was rarely seen out in public.

I shivered as I remembered Brian driving up into the driveway and turning to tell me and Samantha to dry our tears and smile. We knew what we would get it when we got home if he caught us doing anything other than smiling while we were at Aunty Laura's. It was our second time coming to Washington for the summer, and we stopped at Aunty Laura's to get the keys to Grandpa's shop. Samantha and I had been caught talking to each other without raising our hands a few hours earlier, and Brian, in a fit of rage, had cut down a blackberry switch and switched us both so badly we had had to change our clothes because there were blood spots that could be seen coming through our dresses. About forty-five minutes later we were at Aunty Laura's; little Samantha could not stop whimpering and, afraid she would get another switching, I pretended to be angry with her.

"Samantha! You shut up this instant," I yelled at her as I shook her chubby shoulders.

Surprisingly, she got quiet, and I quickly dried her face and gave her a hug.

Aunty Laura came out, all smiles, and hugged Brian while she pretended Mamma was not even there. Samantha and I smiled at her from the back seat. It was not hard to pretend to smile at Aunty Laura because she was always so nice to us.

"Hi, honeys," she said as she opened the truck door and pulled us out, one by one, to give us a hug.

I winced as she hugged me. The searing pain from the blackberry switch was terrible.

"What happened to your leg?" Aunty Laura asked as she bent over to hug me.

I looked down and saw that the long skirt of my dress had ridden up a little when she hugged me; the wide track mark from the thick blackberry branch was bright red and purple across the calf of my thin leg. A few dried droplets of blood could be seen as well, but as bad as this welt looked, there were several others on my upper legs that looked much worse.

"Oh," I stammered, not knowing what to say. What if she pulled my dress up farther to take a look?

Mamma came over and put her arm around Samantha and me.

"You know little girls," she said with a sigh. "They were playing hide and go seek in the blackberry bushes this morning, and she was running when a giant branch snapped her on the back of the leg."

"Ouch," Aunty Laura made a funny face at me; I could not help laughing. "Did you put anything on it, Sue?" she asked Mamma. "It looks like it might get infected."

Mamma scowled at her indignantly. "Of course I did, Laura," she had snapped.

Aunty Laura shrugged and waved us into the house to eat some of her freshly-made strawberry pie. I looked around the clean, peaceful house and wished I lived there and that Aunty Laura was my mother. Good thing I had not known then all the horrible things I would have to go through in the next fifteen years. It may well have broken my seven-year-old spirit.

Now, as I got out of the backseat of the small truck, Aunty Laura was again coming down the walk to greet us. She looked much the same as she had fifteen years ago. There were a few more wrinkles here and there, but she was still the radiant, smart, kind lady she had always been. She came up to me with outstretched arms and gave me a giant hug. I gritted my teeth as she hugged me. I could still not stand to be touched, but I didn't want to worry her, so I just closed my eyes as I hugged her back. I felt so numb inside. I was trying to be happy, but I couldn't even fake it. I was so exhausted I felt like I was going to fall over. I saw Uncle Bill coming out of the house and felt him grab me and give me a giant bear hug. I gritted my teeth again until he was finished.

"So?" Uncle Bill looked at me. "How long are you going to be staying with us?"

"Until January, if that's okay," I tried to smile.

"Okay? Of course it is okay," Uncle Bill said as he put his arm around my shoulders and playfully dragged me over to where the others were huddled and whispering together.

Karen looked up at me and commented on how tired I looked. Aunty Laura nodded and said I should lie down. I was suddenly feeling completely exhausted and agreed when Aunty Laura said she would take me to my room. I waved goodbye to Karen and Carl and told them I would call them once they got back to their house. I knew that after I lay down, they were going to explain everything to Uncle Bill and Aunty Laura. I was glad. I did not feel like telling them myself.

I closed the door to the bedroom I would be staying in and locked it. I checked to see if it was locked at least three times. I locked the windows and closed the curtains. Still not satisfied, I moved a few boxes that were near the closet to block the door. I knew it was dumb, but it made me feel better. I lay down on the twin-sized bed and thought how *Englisch* everything was before I drifted off into a deep sleep. I did not wake up for the next eighteen hours.

A MODERN WORLD

"Even if you are on the right track, you'll get run over if you just sit there."

— *Will Rogers*

I awoke suddenly and sat up in bed. I could see sunlight streaming in through the cracks in the frilly, light yellow curtains. For a split second, I was confused about where I was. I frowned and looked at the twin bed with the flowered bedspread. I wondered why it was flowered and why I was in a flowered blue dress instead of my Amish clothes. I could hear the doorknob rattling and a woman's voice calling for me to come and unlock the door. Suddenly, everything came back to me in a rush, and I jumped out of bed and moved the boxes so I could open the door.

Aunty Laura was standing there with a screwdriver in her hand. "Wow, thank God," she sort of gasped. "I was worried about you. It's eleven o'clock."

"Eleven o'clock?" I felt embarrassed and uncomfortable being in a strange house. "I'm sorry, Aunty Laura," I shook out the skirt of the long dress I was wearing. I tied the thin, white scarf up and under my hair so it was not around my face. I noticed that Aunty Laura was staring at me. I realized that although I knew Aunty Laura, we did not really know each other well, and I believe she was realizing the same thing.

"I just can't believe you are here in my house," Aunty Laura put her hand on my shoulder. "You always stood out to me as a bright, sweet girl, but I never had the chance to really get to know you."

I smiled at her with as much kindness as I could muster. This was harder than I thought it would be. She reminded me of such sad times in my life. It was not her fault, nor mine; it was just how it was. Tears formed in my eyes and I could not blink them away fast enough for her not to see them. Aunty Laura nodded when she saw the tears and put her arms around me.

"I am so sorry, honey," she soothed. "I am so terribly sorry." She rubbed her hand up and down my back. "Karen and Carl told us everything before they left last night."

"Did they tell you about Brian and Mamma?" I asked, pulling away from her.

Aunty Laura nodded. "Yes, they did tell me what my brother did to you. I just don't understand why I didn't see it. I knew they were weird, but they told us that you girls went on trips with friends and went through a homeschooling program and stuff." Aunty Laura kept shaking her head. "You have to believe me, honey. I honestly didn't realize that you girls were prisoners up there."

"It's okay, Aunty Laura," I reached for her hand. "No one knew. Mamma and Brian used their religion to cover up the heinous crimes they were committing."

Aunty Laura nodded. "They have my mother up there, though," she looked at me with a frown.

I nodded and put a hand to my head. My headache was coming back.

"Okay, enough of this. We'll talk later," Aunty Laura patted me on the back. "You go ahead and take a shower and then we will talk about what needs to be done."

I nodded and went to get some clean clothes. I walked into the bathroom and closed the door. *This is amazing,* I thought. It was so different from sponge bathing in a tub. I fiddled with the knob for a few minutes, trying to remember how to get the water to come out of the shower head. I jumped back, startled, when I pulled a knob on the top of the water faucet and suddenly scalding hot water came cascading out with a roar.

I stood in the shower for probably ten minutes letting the hot water pour over me. It was so relaxing and refreshing, and I remember thinking how long it would have taken to heat all that water on top of the wood burning stove. How proud I was for using so much hot water and lathering up with the good-smelling soap. I actually laughed. I was starting to feel better and even a little excited about my new life.

When I got out of the shower, I combed my long, brownish-red hair. It reached halfway to my knees. I saw the hairdryer lying on the counter next to the sink and decided to try it. I was a little scared to plug it in, though, since I had heard how easily people could get electrocuted. After carefully plugging it in, I pointed it at my head and turned it on, but it was so noisy it scared me, and I decided not to use it after all. Instead, I just rolled my hair up and tied my scarf back on. Then I walked out into the kitchen where Aunty Laura was making sandwiches.

As we ate, Aunty Laura told me that she had a job for me at their furniture store. She said she needed someone to dust furniture, vacuum and take messages for her. I was excited at the prospect of already having a job and told Aunty Laura I would do a good job for her.

"I know," Aunty Laura smiled. "I've seen you working around the farm, remember?"

Aunty Laura asked me about my plans, and I told her about wanting to go to YWAM in January. She told me it would be easy to save the fifteen hundred dollars over the summer, since I would be making ten dollars an hour at her store.

"Ten dollars an hour?" I exclaimed. "That is a lot of money. An Amish girl who is working as a maid only gets three dollars a day!"

Aunty Laura laughed outright. "Well, you certainly won't get by with three dollars a day out here. You will learn soon enough that money just slips away without you knowing where it went."

I raised my eyebrows. *Ten dollars an hour still seemed like an awful lot of money*, I thought.

The rest of the week, I went to work with Aunty Laura and Uncle Bill at their large furniture and interior design store. Aunty Laura and Uncle Bill were often gone, advising people on how to remodel their homes or overseeing furniture deliveries. Their grandson worked for them too, and he was in charge when they were not there.

I found my job to be extremely easy. I had to vacuum the store every day. At first I was a little scared of the noisy vacuum cleaner. I hated being around something so loud and I constantly looked behind me to see if anyone was standing there. I dusted and polished all the furniture and sometimes I answered the phone. My twenty-seven-year-old step-cousin, Blake, talked to customers when they came in and made sales. It was said that Uncle Bill was grooming him to take over the business when he and Aunty Laura retired.

I usually got all my work done very early and then walked around, looking for something to do. As a result of my boredom, I started taking it upon myself to tend the flowers we had out front. Once when Aunty Laura and Uncle Bill came back to the store and laughed to see me kneeling in the flower beds pulling out some weeds. I did not see what was so funny, but Aunty Laura took a few pictures of me and said she wished all of her employees were as concerned about the place as I was.

On Sunday, I went to church with Uncle Bill. Aunty Laura said she was too sleepy and was glad I was there so Uncle Bill would not pester her to go with him. The store was closed on Sundays and Mondays, so we did not have to go to work on those days. In the afternoon, I went along to visit Aunty Laura's youngest son and his wife. I sat most of the time watching the television. I knew they were talking about me, but I didn't care.

I loved watching the history channel. It was so fascinating to watch history books brought to life like that. The first few times I tried to watch television, it hurt my eyes and put me to sleep, but I was getting used to it. I found I enjoyed sitting with Uncle Bill and Aunty Laura in the evenings and watching TV. While we ate dinner, we often watched shows called *CSI* or *Law and Order*. I thought it was amazing how the bad guys were always caught and put in prison. *So much different from real life,* I thought, but I still cheered as the crooks were led away in handcuffs.

On Monday, I cleaned the house. Aunty Laura seemed amused at how I always did the dishes without her asking. Sometimes, she would come into the bathroom and see me cleaning it for no real reason. I asked what she wanted me to cook for dinner, and then cooked it. I knew my behavior seemed strange to her, but like my version of the saying goes..."You can take a girl out of the Amish, but you can't take the Amish out of the girl." So it was with me. Even though I had left the Amish behind, it was still all I knew, and it was not going to be easy to leave my habits behind.

I realized I would probably never be completely like everyone else and I told myself that that was okay. The culture we grow up in is always with us, no matter how far away we move or how much we try to change. In part, there would always be a little piece of the Amish girl left in me, the girl that loved to quilt and sew and play with children, the girl that loved to drive the horses in the fields and loved the smell of fresh-cut grass. I would always be that girl, no matter where I went.

Even though I had no regrets about leaving the Amish, I found the noisy city to be a little unsettling. The feeling would fade with time, but during my first few weeks in the city, I was acutely aware of every sound, and it made me feel strange. Also, the constant use of electric lights hurt my eyes. Aunty Laura kept coming behind me and turning on the lights. She laughed once when she found me in the kitchen peeling potatoes as the sun was setting with barely a smidgen of light left on the horizon.

"You know I don't mind if you turn on the lights," she said with a smile.

"Oh," I said innocently, "I know, but I am used to not lighting the lamps until the sun sets. It saves on kerosene and really isn't necessary."

Aunty Laura stared at me, as if I had just told her I was an alien from Mars.

"Uh... okay, Misty," she shook her head. "Just don't go and buy any kerosene lamps and bring them here. This is not 1820, you know."

I looked at her, perplexed. "I have one in my hope chest."

"Oh, my God," Aunty Laura laughed and grabbed her head in playful exasperation. "I don't even know if my grandmother had a hope chest, and now I have a twenty-two-year-old girl standing in my kitchen, talking about hers."

Uncle Bill had come up behind her and he was laughing, so I laughed too—whenever Uncle Bill laughed it was hard not to laugh with him, even if you did not know what he was laughing about.

"Just think, Laura," he came over to me and put his hands on my shoulders. "We have our very own Pilgrim girl, teleported to us from the 1620s."

We all laughed then. It was funny, but little did they realize that was exactly how I felt. Even though I tried, I did not understand what people were talking about half the time, and I was not very good at sitting and relaxing. I felt I had to be constantly busy. I sighed within myself. Eventually, I would figure all this out. But in the meantime, I tried to be a cheerful person. I was starting to feel safer and did not flinch as much anymore when someone touched me, but I still screamed when someone came up behind me unexpectedly. I hoped that would fade as well.

*T*HE *BISHOP* *E*SCAPES

"Courage isn't having the strength to go on - it is going on when you don't have strength."

— *Napoleon*

During the week, I began asking around about how to get my GED. I knew I needed to get started on it if I was going to have it by January. Aunty Laura and Uncle Bill shook their heads in disgust when they learned what a paltry education I had. Uncle Bill said I made up for my lack of education by being just plain smart and quick to figure things out. He said my lack of knowledge was not noticeable until someone started talking about going online or something similar, and I just stared at them nodding my head without actually knowing what they were talking about. Aunty Laura said the best way to find out how to get a GED was to go to the local community college and ask someone there. She said she didn't know how I was going to make up for eight years of missed school, but I told her, "Where there is a will, there is a way," and she nodded at me and commented that she wished her five grandchildren had my determination for getting things done.

Aunty Laura dropped me off at the community college one morning later that week. I remember the powerful feelings I had as I walked up to what appeared to be the main entrance to one of several large buildings. I saw people my age going in and out of the giant sliding glass doors carrying books in their arms. I was so excited knowing that I might be one of those students one day soon. I looked at the sign out front that said "Community College," I went over and put both of my palms on it and just stood there for a moment. I don't know why I did this, but it was as if I were trying to convince myself I was really on a college campus. I could not believe it; it was like a dream. I am sure that the people passing by were staring at me...wondering why the girl in the long dress and white scarf was standing there touching the sign like that. They had no idea how much it meant to me to be there, and that was okay. Even if I told someone why I was touching the sign, I would never be able to convey the deep emotions that were running through me in that brief moment.

After I brushed away a few tears, I walked into the building and asked to talk to someone about getting my GED. The lady asked me for an ID so she could make an appointment for me. I frowned and told her I did not have any picture IDs. I noticed she was staring at me curiously and, not knowing what else to do, I told her that I had just left the Amish and wondered if there was any way I could possibly talk to someone about how to get my GED. She told me to wait, and then a few minutes later she called me to a back room. I followed her timidly. When we reached the room, I was met by a friendly, middle-aged lady. She motioned for me to sit down, and I did so nervously. I was afraid she, like everyone else, was going to tell me it would take a long time to get my GED and I did not want to accept that.

"So," the woman looked at me as she sat down in her chair in front of a computer, "I hear you just left the Amish and are now in pursuit of your GED?"

I nodded.

"Good. Good," she nodded. "So what level of education do you have so far?" she asked as she typed something into the computer.

"I guess second or third grade," I said as my cheeks flushed with embarrassment.

"Ouch," the woman frowned. "And what subjects did you study?"

"Math," I said as I thought hard. "I guess math, and some phonics to learn to read."

"Nothing else?"

I shook my head. "There were some other books, but my mom just kept them in case the state asked to look at them." I did not realize at that moment how strange this must have sounded to the lady in front of me. She stared at me for a couple seconds and then typed something else into her computer.

"Okay," she said a couple minutes later. She turned fully toward me and took off her reading glasses. "I am going to be honest with you," she looked very serious. "Normally, people who come in looking to get their GED have at least completed the eighth grade, and they have some grasp of how to study for a test. But..." She paused. "You're telling me you only learned a little math and how to read?"

I nodded. "I also learned to write," I interjected, as if it would help my case. "I learned by tracing letters and then eventually writing them."

"All by yourself?" the woman asked.

I nodded. "My mother gave me a book, and I figured it out."

"Well, that is impressive," the woman stared at me trying to hide her shock.

She handed me a poem and asked me to read it for her. I read it without a problem, and she seemed impressed and told me that my reading was at a very high level. She recommended that I take night classes to get my GED and told me it that, realistically, it might take at least a year or two before I would be ready to take the exam. I was not happy to hear this and asked her if there was anything I could do at home that would speed things up. She told me there were a few books in the library on how to get a GED and I could try that, but, she said that without classroom instruction, she was doubtful that I would be successful. I thanked her for her time and left. I was a little discouraged, but I was determined to get the books from the library and get my GED as soon as possible. I figured that after all I had been through getting a GED could not possibly be all that hard.

That afternoon, Aunty Laura agreed to take me to the local library; it was only a few blocks from where we lived. Aunty Laura told the librarian I would be using her library card for a while, and the librarian said that was fine. I checked out three books on how to get a GED, hoping they had everything that I needed in them.

When we got home, Uncle Bill was standing outside the garage, dusting off an old, pink bicycle he had found.

"I thought you would need your own wheels to get around in case you want to go somewhere by yourself." He smiled at me as he patted the seat.

I jumped on the bike and although I was wobbly at first, I eventually gained my balance and happily drove around the driveway. It was going to be great fun to have my own transportation to go to the library or the dollar store or wherever I wanted. I thanked Uncle Bill and sped off on my bike headed for the Walgreens that was a few blocks down the street.

On the way home from the library, Aunty Laura told me that she had made an appointment to meet with someone at the congressman's office to see about getting my social security number and a picture ID. She also said that the next day she and her daughter-in-law, Denise, were going to take me out for a girls' day. When I asked her what that was, she said they were going to take me shopping for a few new clothes. She asked if I would be willing to try on some makeup and to get my ears re-pierced. I agreed. I had noticed that all the women I saw were wearing makeup, and I was keenly aware how plain I seemed in comparison. I looked at makeup in the drugstore, but I had no idea what to use, where, and I was afraid to try anything out.

When I got to Walgreens, I purchased a bag of razors, some deodorant, a nice smelling fragrance and a pair of scissors. I noticed that Uncle Bill and Aunty Laura took showers every morning and almost every night. I was shocked at the number of showers they took, but I copied it as if it were normal for me, too. I also noticed that they used this stuff called deodorant, and that they never seemed to smell at all. The only contact I had ever had with deodorant was when some Amish girls used it as perfume to wear before a young people's gathering because that was the only time it was permissible to wear scent. Even then, I remembered, too, that when Matty and I used hers before the singing, we had not put it under our arms, but on our wrists and neck as if it had been perfume. While I was Amish, I had not thought much about body odor, although at times, particularly during the summer, things had been very rank; it was a normal and an accepted part of everyday life. But here in the modern world, I noticed that everyone seemed to smell good all the time, and a lot of women wore perfume every day.

THE NEXT morning I was still in the bathroom when I heard Denise come in. I nervously finished up, wondering what she would say about my new look. I had shaved my legs and underarms and used my new deodorant, and I felt quite sophisticated as I combed some strands of hair over my forehead and trimmed some bangs. To be honest, my bangs were definitely not the best, but for me it was something drastic and I thought it looked quite nice. I let the rest of my hair fall around my shoulders and down my back. Then I sprayed on my new fragrance. I smiled at myself in the mirror. I looked so incredibly different. My face fell a little, though, as I looked at the white scarf that lay on the counter next to the sink. My head felt so naked. It was not that I believed I needed to wear the scarf anymore; it was just that I was more comfortable with it on. It was like a security blanket, and I felt a little anxious without it.

After a moment of just standing there, I finally grabbed the scarf, put it in the trashcan next to the sink, opened the door and walked out. My hands were shaking a little at the thought of going out without a head covering, but at the same time it was liberating to know that I would not be stared at anymore. Aunty Laura and Denise turned and looked at me as I entered the kitchen. Aunty Laura's mouth fell open, and I saw a happy smile spread across her face as she gave me a hug and told me she was proud of me.

"I was wondering when this was going to happen," she said as she sniffed me playfully. "You smell really good, too. I thought I was going to have to have a talk with you about deodorant."

"Your hair is so beautiful," Denise came over and took handfuls of it in her hands.

"Yeah," Aunty Laura laughed. "She only washed it every week or so. It should be pretty healthy."

My cheeks flushed with embarrassment as I saw the shocked expression on Denise's face. Denise was a nurse at one of the local hospitals, and she was very modernly dressed. Whenever we visited her house and something about my past came up, she always seemed so shocked, as if she had no idea what the Amish were, or that there were horrible people out there, like my step-dad and mother. She was very nice, however, and said she was excited to help bring me into the twenty-first century.

Our first stop was at a clothes shop. I don't remember the name of it, but I do remember thinking that I had never been to a store that sold new clothes before. The skirts I was wearing were from a thrift store, and I had only paid a few dollars for each of them. Because of this, the price tags on the new clothes were an incredible shock to me. I had no idea that clothes could be so expensive.

Aunty Laura and Denise went around picking things out that they thought would look nice on me. I cringed when I saw them picking up sleeveless shirts they called tank tops. When they weren't looking, I hid most of them under some clothes on a table nearby. I was equally hesitant when they picked up shorts and jeans. I shook my head violently, but Denise laughed at me and said I should just try them. I picked out a few light, summery dresses, and we all went to the fitting room. Denise handed me a pair of jeans and nodded at me to put them on. I took off my skirt, slid into the jeans and looked into the mirror. I did not like the feeling of being in something that hugged my figure so well. It felt as if I were naked.

"Wow," Denise exclaimed as she looked at my reflection in the mirror. "I wish I looked that good in a pair of jeans."

"You and me both," Aunty Laura smiled and pretended to pout.

I saw them both looking at me, and suddenly I panicked. I had thought I might try wearing jeans, but the very fact they were saying I looked good in them made me feel afraid.

"Very sexy," Denise said as she came up behind me for a better look.

I started trying to get out of the jeans, but they were tight and seemed to stick to my legs. I started shaking, and I tried to blink back the tears that were forming in my eyes. If they were looking at me like this, I was afraid men would look at me the same way, and that was so scary. I knew it was irrational, but I could not seem to help it. Thankfully, Aunty Laura and Denise seemed to figure out what was wrong and helped me out of the pants. I could tell Aunty Laura had told Denise what had happened to me before I came to stay with her.

Denise hugged me and told me she was sorry and that I didn't have to wear anything I was not comfortable in. I felt better after that and became my cheerful self again as I tried on the summer dresses and a few pretty T-shirts to wear with my denim skirts. Denise and Aunty Laura said they were excited to get my makeup done and my ears pierced, so that's where we headed next.

We went to Aunty Laura's hairdresser, who ran her business from her home. Aunty Laura said she had been going to this same lady for years. She was retired now, but she still had a few loyal customers that made appointments to go to her home, where one of the back rooms had been converted into a small salon. The woman met us at the door and waved us in. She was a very kind woman that appeared to be her mid-sixties. She told me that Aunty Laura told her I had just left the Amish and was in need of all the basics. I smiled at her, although I had no clue what the "basics" were.

I sat in a black salon chair and watched as the women chattered about what they should do to me. They brought over a bunch of makeup samples and held them to my face. Then they talked about my hair and piercing my ears.

"Okay, honey," the hairdresser came over to me. "What exactly do you want to look like when we are done?"

I furrowed my eyebrows and looked at her blankly. "Uh, like me," I answered innocently.

They all laughed as if I had said something really funny.

"Girls. Girls," Aunty Laura said, playfully slapping them on the back. "You know what she means."

"Okay," the hairdresser came over and looked at my eyebrows. "You have very nice, thick eyebrows. I think this is a good place to start."

"What are you going to do with my eyebrows?" I asked.

"Wax them," Aunty Laura nodded encouragingly.

I frowned, not understanding.

"You don't really think these are our real eyebrow shapes, do you?" Denise asked.

I just smiled. I had no idea what they were talking about. I was in for a shock when the hairdresser put wax on my eyebrows, followed by some cloth, and yanked it off. I almost wouldn't let her do the other one and everyone laughed as they thought how funny I was going to look walking around with one arched eyebrow and one thick eyebrow.

It took about two hours before we were finished. The hairdresser trimmed my hair up to my waist, fixed my bangs, pierced my ears and helped me put on some light makeup. When everything was done, I got up and stood in front of the mirror. I could not believe it was me looking back. I was so used to seeing an Amish girl in the mirror. The girl that looked back at me now seemed to be a different person. I was wearing a gray polka-dot blouse and a black skirt. The bangs framed my face nicely and reflected a dark auburn color in the sunlight. My long hair was wavy at the ends. I leaned in closer to look at the makeup. I was very pleased with it. It looked very natural—there was just a little foundation, some pink blush, mascara and clear lip gloss. My ears were still stinging from the piercings, but I liked the tiny sparkling earnings the hairdresser had put in.

"Well?" Aunty Laura asked. "What do you think?"

I nodded happily. It was just what I wanted. "Do you like it?" I asked her.

Aunty Laura smiled and nodded back. "Your hair is beautiful, and the makeup makes you look very sweet. You might look fifteen now instead of fourteen."

I frowned playfully. It was true: I did look much younger than most women my age, but I didn't know how to remedy that.

Uncle Bill gave me a big hug when he saw me that evening and said he was going to have to get the shotgun out because now the boys would come sniffing around. I blushed, and he said I looked very cute. I was happy with my new look and felt less self-conscious at work. I knew that I would eventually have to start wearing pants, but I was just not ready for that, yet.

I STARTED studying for my GED in the mornings before work and in the evenings when I got home from work. I chose the thickest book I could find, figuring it must have the most information. When I opened it for the first time, I was in shock at all the different topics I would have to study.

"What is a-l-g-e-b-r-a?" I asked Uncle Bill.

Uncle Bill shrugged and shook his head. "It's been so long since I went to school, but I do know algebra is math."

"Math?" I was in shock as I glanced at what looked more like drawings and letters. "How can you add up letters? It says here solve for X. That doesn't make any sense."

Uncle Bill laughed. "That's what I said when I was a kid, but no one would listen to me."

I frowned as I read down the list of subjects—social studies, science, writing, reading, and something called an essay. I did not know what any of that stuff was. Social studies would be easy, I thought. It was just reading and learning. *Couldn't be that hard*, I told myself. I decided to make myself a schedule to follow. It was the only way to get this done. I got up at six in the morning and studied for an hour and a half, and then I made breakfast for Aunty Laura and Uncle Bill. I was at work Tuesday through Saturday from 9 to 5, and after work, Aunty Laura and Uncle Bill liked to go out for dinner or to one of their children's houses. After they went to bed, usually around eleven, I turned on my bedside lamp, studied until the early morning hours, and then slept for a couple of hours before getting up again at six.

I had horrible nightmares and did not really want to sleep, anyway. I dreamed that Brian found me and shot me, or that Mamma was beating me up, or that I was back with the Amish and someone was being hurt and I could not help them, or worst of all, that Peter managed to kill me by smothering me with a pillow. I would wake up in a cold sweat, and sometimes Aunty Laura would be leaning over me and shaking my shoulders. It was bad, and during the day I was exhausted, but I forgot all of my tiredness because I was so excited about getting my GED, attending the missionary school and eventually, starting college. Although people kept telling me it would be hard to get my GED, I never doubted myself even for a second. I knew I could it.

I called Karen and Carl about once a week to see how they were doing. Karen told me that the Amish community did not have much to do with them anymore but had not tried to force them off the property due to the lease agreement. Karen said she thought Simba missed me; he walked around pen looking out as if trying to see where I was and why I was not coming to sit with him. I missed him, too, and sometimes wished I could wrap my arms around my fluffy friend. Maybe then I could sleep without the horrible nightmares.

Two weeks after I left the farm, I got a call from Karen. She told me there had been a new development in the case against Peter. She said that the previous day, the police had come out again to question Peter, and they had been there for a while. Karen said she didn't know why the police had come, but they seemed pretty serious this time. She said that just that morning she had seen Peter and his entire family leave in a van driven by one of the neighbors. A couple hours later, she saw Elam and Jacob walking the horses and cows down to their farm. Later that afternoon, the police came back and stopped at Peter's house again, only to find no one there. After looking around they drove over to Jacob's house. When they left, Karen said, Carl walked over to the barn where he had seen Jacob's children. Carl pretended to be looking for something and stopped to say "Hi" to the children. He casually asked the children where Peter's family was going, and Moses told him they were going to visit relatives in Canada.

I swallowed hard when I heard the news. It was obvious the police had decided to take another look into the case and were most likely going to arrest Peter, but, catching wind of this, he had fled to Canada where he had some distant cousins. When I was living with them, I had seen letters from these relatives, but unfortunately I never bothered to study the address.

The next morning, I called the detective's number and left him a message to call me back at the store. When he called, he told me that he had thought a lot about our conversation at the police station, and he had finally decided to take the case to one of his supervisors. After quite some time, the supervisor sent some more policemen out to question Peter again. They felt he was hiding something and that his wife looked a little rattled. He said they planned to take him in for questioning but when they got to the farm, they were shocked to find he was gone. When they talked to Jacob, he had told them that Peter and his family had gone to visit family in Canada. Jacob said he did not know the exact address. He asked me if I knew the address by any chance, but unfortunately I had to say no. All I knew was that they were in Ontario somewhere.

I closed my eyes and tried not to cry as the detective told me what I already knew. Most likely Peter and his family were not coming back, at least for a long while. There was no way to track someone who had no social security number, passport, picture ID or credit cards. The Amish were allowed to travel back and forth through Canada using the family Bible where the records of family births were kept. Many were ushered through without anyone even looking at their credentials. They were considered harmless and not worth the time it took to ask them to identify themselves. Besides, there was no picture of Peter available and he had no fingerprints on file. There would be no way to identify him.

The detective asked me if there might be something far worse in Peter's past that would cause him to pull up stakes and run like he had. I told the detective that I thought poisoning his wife and threatening to kill me were bad enough. The detective, however, believed there must have been something else, and if the police were to connect the dots all the way

372

back to when Peter was a young man, they were confident they would find a series of crimes in his wake. Of course, this was mere speculation, but it could be possible since among my Amish order all crimes were forgiven and are never spoken of again. The fact that Peter had fled the country spoke volumes, but unfortunately, there was not much that could be done without a picture of him. I asked if a sketch artist might help, but the detective told me they would probably have to bring in thousands of Amish men, and I would have to look at each one. Even then, we would most likely never find him.

I sighed and hung up the phone after thanking the detective for at least believing me. It made me angry that they had come so close to arresting Peter, and then he got away. I wondered where he found the money for all the bus tickets; but then I figured he must have met with church officials and been given money from the church treasury, which was kept at the deacon's house. That would have been the fastest way to get that much money so fast.

I went into the bathroom and shed a few angry tears. First Brian and Mamma were off the hook, and now Peter had escaped. Why did the bad guys always seem to get away with doing such bad things? I wondered. I had spent my whole life trying to do the right thing, but it seemed that every which way I turned I met some sort of roadblock, while people like Brian and Peter seemed to get away with their evil deeds and continue to thrive. It seemed so unfair, and I sobbed into my hands. It was unfair that I had to live with the trauma and flashbacks while Peter settled into a new life in Canada with all the sympathy and support of the church. Peter would go on molesting Katie and probably some of his other children; he might even go after someone else's children, yet he was welcomed with open arms merely because he had confessed his sins and been forgiven.

I could not help feeling that I had failed again, and it made me very sad. No one could say that I hadn't tried, but the fact that I had been outsmarted by Peter really irritated me. I really missed the children and felt like I had left them to the wolves, but I was doing the best I could, even though it seemed less than adequate.

A VOICE FROM THE PAST

"You never fail until you stop trying."

—*Albert Einstein*

The whole ordeal was extremely upsetting, but I could not let myself get depressed over it. I was far too busy. Aunty Laura managed to set up an appointment at the congressman's office about a month after I came to Seattle. We needed some way to get my social security number so she could put me on payroll. And the fact that I was an undocumented alien seemed to really bother her.

The morning of our scheduled appointment, I gathered whatever evidence I could find to prove who I was and put it in a bag. There were a few letters from Samantha, the Amish apron I had kept and my German Bible and songbook. My hands shook as I flipped through my song book and remembered the young people's gatherings. It seemed worlds away from where I was now. I shuddered and quickly placed the book back in the bag.

As we left, Aunty Laura handed me a few pictures that she had found in her photo album. I looked down in shock to see a picture myself when I was seven. I had my arm around a five-year-old Samantha; she appeared to have been crying.

"Why do you have a picture of us?" I asked Aunty Laura.

"Oh, you girls were always so cute and sweet," Aunty Laura smiled and looked at the picture over my shoulder. "You were both in the alley behind Dad's shop with your mom when I took that."

I gazed at the picture and looked deep into my own eyes. It was so strange to think that the seven-year-old girl looking back at me was *me*. Mamma had pictures too, but they were always put away, and we never looked at them after we became Amish. As I looked at the picture now, I saw something that only I would be able to detect. I could see that Samantha was crying and leaning into me, and my arms were around her. To anyone passing by, it looked as if I were hugging Samantha, but although I could not remember the specific day the picture was taken, I could tell that I was protecting her from someone standing off to the side.

"I wonder why Samantha was crying." I mused as if I didn't know.

"Oh, I was driving around the corner taking pictures of Dad's shop when I snapped that one. Your mom said Samantha had fallen in the alley and that was why she was crying."

I rolled my eyes as I looked at myself in the picture. It looked as if I had seen Aunty Laura coming around the corner with the camera. Mamma most likely shouted at me to smile at the camera; but my eyes were diverted to the right, and the eyes told a very different story than the fake smile plastered across my face.

There were a few other pictures that Aunty Laura said Brian had sent her. They were some of the pictures we had taken for the state when they wanted to come up and see Aunt Fanny's living conditions. There was one of me hugging a cow, and one of me and Samantha holding a cow's halter. I sighed. These pictures brought back such bad memories, but I was glad Aunty Laura had them. It was very obvious it was me in the pictures—my facial features were very distinct—so I hoped they would serve as some form of ID.

On the way to the congressman's office, Aunty Laura and I discussed ways to get Grandma away from Brian and Mamma. I told her and Uncle Bill the many horrors that took place on the mountain, and Aunty Laura cried and told me she had not known. She was now terrified to let her mother stay with Brian any longer. The only problem was that Grandma had signed papers putting Brian in charge of all her affairs, and seeing how the police had not done much the first time I contacted them, it did not seem likely they would try again.

Aunty Laura said she had been up there at the beginning of March and noticed that half of Fanny's face was bruised, and when she asked her what had happened, Fanny had told her that Mamma hit her in the face with a plastic bucket. I gripped the arm rest until my knuckles became white and closed my eyes, hoping the gnawing feeling in my chest would go away. I could see Fanny's sweet face in my mind, and the thought of the abuse she was suffering was so hard on me.

"I really thought it had to be an accident," Aunty Laura said as we got out of the car. "I know Sue is an evil b*tch, but I could not imagine she would purposely hurt her own sister so badly."

"Hmm..." I sniffed. "That's pretty mild compared to some of the other things she does."

Aunty Laura looked horrified as she held the door open for me. "Those two are insane," she shook her head in dismay. "I don't know how they found each other."

I shook my head to, and as I sat in the waiting room, I thought of what I could do. Aunty Laura said Mamma and Brian were still planning on getting foster children, and their application was being processed. Somehow the police report I had filed had not stopped them. Mamma had to have fixed the fake address she had given the state. I figured she had most likely updated her records and told the state she moved after Samantha and I left since there was nothing to hide now. Brian's children were all well over eighteen, and the only checks they received now were Brian's social security, Grandma's one thousand dollar check from the postal service, Fanny's SSI check and Mamma's disability check.

I was outraged when I heard they might be getting foster children and knew I had to do something that would stop them permanently. Aunty Laura said the house and farm looked really gorgeous, and that Brian had hired a few men to do work for him a couple days a week. She said she could really see how they could fool the adoption agency into letting them have foster children, or even to adopt children. There was such a shortage of families in that part of the state that were willing to be foster parents.

After a short wait, we were ushered into an office where a man was talking on the phone. He was an assistant to the congressman, and he smiled and waved at us to sit down.

"He looks the same as he did when he was a kid getting into trouble with my Mikey," Aunty Laura mused fondly. "You would not have convinced me then that that little troublemaker would ever end up here."

I smiled, grateful that Aunty Laura knew someone that might possibly be able to help me.

"So this is the girl you told me about?" the assistant asked as he hung up the phone.

"Yes, this is she," Aunty Laura smiled as she bumped me with her elbow so I would stop looking so petrified. I had asked Aunty Laura if she thought they might mistake me for a terrorist and arrest me for not having any documentation. Aunty Laura thought that was an hilarious question, but I was still nervous that the person in charge would not believe me.

When Aunty Laura nudged me, I picked up the bag containing all the things I had brought along with me.

"Here are some pictures that show I was Amish," I handed them to him as I began rambling. "And here is my Amish song book, an apron, a Bible and some letters from my sister."

I looked at him anxiously and was surprised to see a half smile on his face as he looked curiously at the pile of things in front of him. There was a minute of silence that Aunty Laura broke by telling him that I was afraid he might think I was a terrorist. He seemed to find that as funny as Aunty Laura had.

"Don't worry," the assistant laughed. "You are the most innocent-looking girl I have ever seen. If you were a terrorist, we would really be in trouble."

We talked for a while, and he asked me a few important questions such as my birth date, mother's maiden name and so on. Aunty Laura told him she really needed my social security number so she could put me on the payroll. He told us that he needed to file a lot of paperwork and it might take a few months to get everything ready, but, he said, it should all be ready before January. Until then, he told us we could run everything under Aunty Laura's ID, and that she could vouch for me.

"Are you one hundred percent sure you want to vouch for this girl?" he asked Aunty Laura with a smile.

Aunt Laura grinned at me and nodded. "She is so well behaved it is unreal." She laughed. "Can you believe that last week I found her mopping the kitchen floor at six-thirty in the morning? I was stumbling into the kitchen, and she had already coffee made and she thought she would mop the floor because it was getting late and there might not be enough time before we left for work."

They both laughed. I smiled, too, although I didn't get what was so funny. The assistant said his daughter, who was my age, could not even put her plate in the sink, let alone mop the floor at six-thirty in the morning. Aunty Laura and he seemed to be having a laughing fit of sorts, and I could not help but laugh with them.

As I sat there and thought of the times the Amish leaders had given me a stern talking-to and all of the beatings I got from Mamma and Brian for just talking or laughing. I had been told there was an evil world out there, but I could not help noticing all the people here seemed genuinely kind and concerned for my well-being. No one frowned at me, or told me I had unknowingly broken some minor rule. I was sure there were people here that were not nice, but all of the people I had met so far seemed kind and pleasant—so very different from what I was used to.

The assistant gave us some paperwork to take to the social security office, and with Aunty Laura's ID, we were able to get my social security number. The assistant said he would send us the rest of the paperwork through the mail and to just be patient, as these sorts of things usually took a couple of months. Aunty Laura helped me open a checking account which was joint with hers—that way I would at least be able to use a debit card without needing any form of ID.

I was very happy as I deposited all of the money I had left over. Things were taking shape for me, and I was starting to feel really alive and happy, despite the sorrow that still lurked in the shadows and assaulted me when I least expected it. Terrible flashbacks popped into my mind several times a day. Certain smells or sounds would trigger them, and when they did, I had to clench my fists and close my eyes to block the images. They only lasted for a few seconds, and then I could take a deep breath and move on. After these episodes, I always put on my perpetually cheerful smile and worked hard at being happy until the next time they occurred.

AROUND MID-JUNE, Aunty Laura and Uncle Bill went to see Mamma and Brian. They planned on trying to bring Grandma back with them for a couple of weeks so they could have her checked over. I had told Samantha where I was and asked her to not tell Brian and Mamma. She wrote them once or twice a year (why, I did not know), but she promised not to tell them anything.

They were due back on Sunday, and I stayed home studying and getting Grandma's bedroom ready. We had decided that I would stay at home with Grandma for a week, and then Aunty Laura would try to get her into a nursing home. They hoped that she would say she wanted to stay there, and then, perhaps, Brian would not be able to take her back. I was not too sure about the plan. I knew how much Brian and Mamma depended on Grandma's check and just how mad Brian would be if Grandma managed to escape them. Aunty Laura had said it was going to be okay, because she was Brian's older sister and that he would not risk doing anything stupid in front of her. I merely raised my eyebrows, but I hoped she was right. We had all agreed it was critical that Brian and Mamma not know I was there, or else they would never agree to let Grandma come to Aunty Laura's house for a two-week visit.

Still, I was very surprised when Uncle Bill and Aunty Laura drove into the driveway with Grandma in the backseat.

"They said we could have her for one week," Uncle Bill said as he got out of the van. "They have to come over here next Monday for a meeting with someone and insisted on picking her up."

I froze in place and looked anxiously at Aunty Laura.

"Don't worry," Aunty Laura opened the back door. "You can stay with Denise from Saturday through next Wednesday; just to be sure everything is okay."

"What about work?" I asked.

Uncle Bill shook his head. "We can't run the risk that they might stop by the store and see you there. You are doing so well, and we don't want them messing you up again."

I walked around the side of the van and blinked back tears as I saw Grandma's small frame. She was in a light blue dress and black apron. Her white kapp was haphazardly placed on her head, and her long white hair was falling down over her shoulders.

"I took the pins out of her hair," Aunty Laura stoked grandma's soft white hair. "I saw that there were some small sores on her head. I think Sue has been leaving those pins in for days without checking them."

I nodded. "Most likely."

"That b*tch!" Aunty Laura grumbled under her breath. Uncle Bill carried Grandma into the house and we all followed.

Aunty Laura and I put a nice flannel nightgown on Grandma and helped her into the hospital bed that Uncle Bill had rented. The side rails were very handy, I thought. At least we would not have to worry about her falling out of bed like she had done many times at home. Grandma was rambling, and she did not seem to recognize any of us. Aunty Laura said that for the first time, she was glad that Grandma had dementia. At least she could not remember all the terrible things that had been done to her or the things she had seen. I nodded. It was small comfort.

That night I could not sleep at all, and after everyone else was asleep I took my study books and a small coffee table into the room where Grandma was sleeping. I turned on the bedside lamp and studied most of the night. It was an eerie feeling to have Grandma with me. I was overjoyed to have her here; sitting next to her made me feel at home. That in itself was very strange, since no one would ever want to live in the home where I grew up. Still, I sometimes felt uncontrollably lonely and as if I didn't really belong anywhere. Grandma was a living part of the family that I had once belonged to—no matter how horrifying and tragic that family might have been.

I was awakened the next morning when Uncle Bill shook me and asked if I was okay. I jumped up, startled and unsure of my surroundings. I had been dreaming that I was home with Mamma and Brian. Samantha and I were being beaten and Grandma was yelling at them to stop. For a split second, I thought Uncle Bill was Brian and I screamed and tried to get away from him. Aunty Laura came running in to see what was wrong as Uncle Bill grabbed me and hugged me, telling me it was okay. I was very shaken and leaned into his giant bear hug, enjoying the comfort I found there.

"I don't know if this was such a good Idea," Uncle Bill pursed his lips and shook his head at Aunty Laura. "This girl was sleeping in here next to Mom and was terrified of me when I woke her up."

"Are you okay, honey?" Aunty Laura asked as she came up and stroked my arm.

I nodded. "I'm fine," I was a little embarrassed at my reaction. "I will go make breakfast."

Aunty Laura and Uncle Bill stayed in Grandma's room and talked for a bit, and while we were eating breakfast Uncle Bill asked me if I would be willing to see a counselor about my PTSD. I frowned and shook my head.

"Why not?" Aunty Laura asked.

"There is no way any counselor is going to understand what I have been through," I stared out the window.

"You have to talk to someone, Misty," Uncle Bill's look was stern. "You can't just get over what you have been through. It was just too traumatic."

I finally agreed to see a counselor, but just so they would stop pestering me about it. I hated the thought of needing someone else to help me with the flashbacks and nightmares. I could get over it myself, I thought. To need someone else was a weakness, and I could show no weakness at this point in my life. Even though I had many people around me that truly wanted to help me, I did not fully trust anyone yet other than myself. I felt as if I were waiting for these good times to come to an end only to be replaced with something terrible. Nothing ever worked in my favor for long it seemed, and I couldn't believe this would last. I knew these were all mental issues, but I didn't know how a counselor could help someone like me—someone with such an insane, crazy past. What could a counselor possibly tell me that would make everything better?

After Uncle Bill and Aunty Laura left for work, I got Grandma up and gave her a sponge bath. Then I dressed her in some of the new clothes we had bought for her. She was irritable and kept trying to slap me. I did not mind, though, and I wondered if somewhere in the back of her mind she subconsciously thought I was Mamma. It made me sad to think she could not understand that she was safe now. After I dressed her, I tried to get her to eat a little. I remembered that she always liked mashed potatoes, so I made her some, even though they were a strange breakfast offering. She refused to eat anything though, and all I could get down her was a little bit of a chocolate vitamin shake. As I maneuvered her out of bed and into her wheelchair, I estimated her frail frame could not have weighed more than ninety pounds.

We both sat in front of the TV for an hour or so, watching the news. Grandma fell asleep again, and I was nodding off where I sat next to her in Uncle Bill's recliner. Suddenly, the jangling of the telephone jolted me out of my sleepy state. I answered it thinking it was Aunty Laura checking on us.

"Hello," I said, trying not to sound as sleepy as I was.

There was a pause. "Hello?" I said again, thinking maybe it was a wrong number.

"What are you doing there?" I heard an all-too-familiar voice say on the other end of the line. I had not heard that voice in years. I suddenly felt dizzy, and my visual field went black for a second.

"Misty is there, at their house," I heard Brian say to someone in the background.

"Son of a b**ch!" I heard Mamma say. "How do you know it's her?"

"That voice is unmistakable," Brian sounded like he was gritting his teeth.

I stood there, frozen in place and listening to their conversation.

"I don't think so," I heard Mamma say. "Why would she be there? That does not make any sense!"

"Misty?" I heard Mamma shout into the phone. I did not answer for a moment. We had not thought about them calling, and now that they had, I did not know what to do. I decided that they might as well know it was me. It would be too hard for Aunty Laura to try to convince them it wasn't me.

"What?" I said, trying to keep my voice from shaking.

"What the h**l are you doing there?" Mamma exploded.

It made me angry that she was yelling at me like I was a bad little girl. I was a full-grown woman now. I was no longer a scared child with nowhere to turn. If something happened to me now, there would be hell to pay and that gave me comfort.

"I left the Amish and I'm staying here for a few months until I leave for a missionary school in Florida," I answered her. It sounded just important enough to make them raise their eyebrows, I thought.

"You left the Amish?" Brian yelled into the phone. "You stupid b**ch." I heard the phone click on the other side.

I was a little panicked after they hung up. I knew they would be on their way over the mountain pass to get Grandma as soon as they hung up. I knew it would take about four hours even if they went over the speed limit, so at least I had enough time to get ahold of Aunty Laura. Hurriedly, I checked on Grandma and then called the store. Blake answered and said Uncle Bill and Aunty Laura had left and told him they would be back in a few hours.

I figured they were probably looking at nursing homes, and since they did not have cell phones I had no way to contact them. I explained what had happened to Blake, and he told me to call 911 if Brian showed up at the house and tried to get in. He said he would call all of the places that my aunt and uncle might possibly be and see if they were there. I was scared, although I knew that if Brian and Mamma tried something I could call the police and maybe have them arrested. The only problem was that Brian had power of attorney over Grandma and could possibly say we kidnapped her.

I carried the phone around with me as I closed all of the windows and locked them. I pulled all of the curtains closed and made sure the back door was locked, and I even went into the garage and shook the door to make sure it was secure. Then I sat in the house, waiting anxiously for a call from Aunty Laura or Uncle Bill. I kept the lights, TV and radio off so I could hear and see everything that was going on outside the house. Then I sat on the couch, peeking out at the driveway through a crack in the drapes. I was very sad. *Why did all these things have to happen, one right after the other?* I thought. It made me wonder if I had done the right thing by coming to stay with Aunty Laura. In a very strange way it seemed as if I had stepped back in time instead of leaving my past behind me

Some three hours later, the phone rang. I answered hesitantly, not sure who would be on the other end. (To this day I have trouble answering the phone if I do not recognize the number on caller ID). Thankfully, it was Aunty Laura on the other end of the phone. She said she was at the furniture store and should be home in less than twenty minutes. She said if Brian showed up to keep the doors locked and call the police.

By now it was getting dangerously close to the time I had estimated for their arrival. It normally took five hours to get to Seattle from the mountaintop, but that was with bathroom stops and at a time when we weren't in much of a hurry. I knew that there were few police cars patrolling the pass going from eastern to western Washington, and I was afraid that Brian would speed the whole way. A sudden thought occurred to me, what if they had been in Wenatchee when they called? That means it would only take them two and a half hours to get here. I sat on the couch nervously fidgeting with the phone I held in my lap and poised to dial 911 at any moment.

I wasn't sure anyone could understand just how dangerous Mamma and Brian were. I had spent an entire childhood with them and vividly remembered how they taunted me with the hints of murder. Even now, as a young woman, I have no doubt that they were completely capable of committing murder.

I breathed a sigh of relief when Aunty Laura pulled into the drive.

"Everyone okay?" she asked as she hurried through the door.

"Yeah," I was shaking. "I'm sure glad to see you, though."

Aunty Laura looked around the dark house with all the curtains closed and lights turned off. "What is going on in here?" she asked.

"I was scared they might try to get in," I said sheepishly.

"My God," Aunty Laura opened the drapes covering the window that faced the driveway. "They're not ninjas or CIA assassins."

I could tell she was trying to lighten the tension, but it was hard for me to lighten up.

Aunty Laura said we could not act as if we were scared of them. She said she was not afraid of her little snot-nosed brother, and that if he tried anything she would kick his a*s. I was not so sure she could do that, but I agreed that we could not act like we were afraid.

Aunty Laura suggested we make stew for dinner to keep busy until they got there. I wheeled Grandma into the kitchen, and she woke up and began to ramble about things we could not comprehend. I smiled when I saw Aunty Laura hugging her mother tightly. This is how Brian should be with his mother, I thought. I asked Aunty Laura what she thought was wrong with Brian, and Aunty Laura just shook her head.

"I don't know," she stopped peeling the potato and gazed out the window. "All I know is that he was never a nice kid. He was a brat from the very beginning. I was two and a half years older than he was. I remember trying to play with him when we were little, and he would pinch me really hard and laugh. Sometimes he pinched so hard I was left sobbing and had bruises for a week."

I nodded. Sounds like Brian.

"When he grew up," Aunty Laura continued, "I could never connect with him, even though God knows I tried. He was just very odd. After he moved to Arizona, I did not see him for years, and frankly, I never thought I would see him again until he showed up with you guys and your mom."

"You never liked my mom, huh?" I asked as I peeled a potato.

"Not even a little." Aunty Laura shook her head. "She is an angry, evil woman, and I could see that right off the bat. She always tried to act like she was in charge of everything, but she did not have the common sense God gave a jack**s."

I could not help but smile a little at that, and Aunty Laura smiled back at me.

"You know it's true," she said. "I didn't like how harsh she was with you girls, but I didn't feel I could interfere because Brian said it was part of your strange, new religion."

I nodded and shrugged. "It's okay," I smiled at her.

"No, it's not," Aunty Laura shook her head sorrowfully. "Honestly, I actually thought about calling child protective services a couple of times, but Brian is my brother and I just could not make myself do it."

I smiled at her reassuringly. "You could not have known, Aunty Laura."

Suddenly I heard the sound of car pulling into the driveway, and froze. Aunty Laura put down the knife that she had been using to cut up the potatoes and went to the door. I saw Mamma and Brian jump out of the van almost before it came to a complete stop. It was so strange to see them after all this time, and I was astonished that I was interested to see whether they looked well or not. Actually, they looked pretty much the same—Mamma had gained some weight and Brian had lost some, but other than that they looked pretty much the same and, as they often were, they were mad as hell.

Aunty Laura called for me to take Grandma into the bedroom and close the door. I hurriedly did so, but I did not stay there with her. I was worried about Aunty Laura's safety because I knew how violent Brian could get and I was not sure he would take time to think about the consequences of his actions in the heat of the moment.

I stood next to Aunty Laura as they approached the house. Most of my fear evaporated as I saw those two miserable people walking toward me. I felt a twinge of pity for them as I could not imagine how they could possibly live with themselves, knowing all the horrible things they had done.

"Hi, Brian," Aunty Laura said in a civil tone. "Did not expect you here so soon. Misty and I were just making some stew if you want to stay for dinner."

"Don't be cute with me, Laura," Brian snapped as he came to the door. "You know exactly why I'm here."

I saw Brian and Mamma staring at me in shock. I figured I probably looked quite healthy compared to how I had looked when I was all beaten down and still living on the farm. I was wearing a denim skirt that had a few pearls scattered around it, a light pink T-shirt and flip flops, and my toenails were painted a bright pink. My long hair was blowing lightly in the breeze, and my small crystal stud earrings sparkled in the sunlight. I was keenly aware that they were both staring at my clothes, but they seemed most shocked at the makeup I was wearing. Makeup was the ultimate sin. I just let them stare but I felt the anger starting to stir in me as I saw their judgmental looks.

Mamma finally stopped staring as she came up to the door and pushed past both me and Aunty Laura without saying a word.

"Hey!" Aunty Laura yelled. "You can't just walk into my house like that, Sue. Get your a*s back out here."

Mamma just walked back to the bedrooms, and when she found Grandma she started wheeling her out of the door. Brian pushed past us too as Aunty Laura tried to stop them.

"Stop it!" Aunty Laura yelled. "You can't just take her out of the house like that. She's my mother too, Brian, and just so you know...Misty told me everything!"

"Yeah?" Brian shouted back. "Misty is a little whore that needs to be punished and sent back to her community." He grabbed the wheelchair from Mamma and tried to push it past Aunty Laura as she stood blocking the hallway.

"Get out of my way, Laura," he said in a threatening voice.

"No!" Aunty Laura shouted, putting her hands on her hips.

I was standing behind them, not knowing what I should do. I was afraid if I did anything, things would get very ugly. Brian, in a fit of rage, swung at Aunty Laura. She backed up into the kitchen table, dodging the blow, and I could tell she was completely shocked by what he had just done.

"Call 911," she yelled at me.

Hurriedly I dialed 911 as Aunty Laura grabbed the knife she had left on the table.

"You son of a b**ch," she screamed at Brian as he wheeled Grandma out of the door and over to the van.

Mamma stood in front of the door, blocking Aunty Laura so she couldn't go after him. I told the dispatcher to hurry and hung up the phone, then went over to stand next to Aunty Laura. I glared at my mother. She was at least four inches taller than I was, but I didn't care. I was over being scared and now was just plain mad.

"You are nothing but an overgrown bully," I screamed at her as I tried to push her out of the way. Angrily, she slapped me across the face and told me to never talk to her like that. I don't know why, but I was so enraged I spit on the ground in front of her. "That is what I think of you," I said as Aunty Laura pulled me back. "You will never have any respect from me. Respect is earned, and you sure haven't earned even a micro second of it."

"I gave birth to you," Mamma screamed back at me.

"Well, I wish you wouldn't have," I screamed back.

I could not believe my own actions, but I could not stand the thought of Grandma going back home with them. I felt it was my fault, as if I had...once again... failed somehow. *If only I had not answered the phone,if only...why was I always such a failure...*I kept thinking.

Brian picked Grandma up and then dropped her back into the wheelchair. I saw a trickle of blood on one of her frail, white legs. Brian turned and saw his sister watching in shock, and he seemed to get even madder than he already was. Finally, he managed to throw Grandma into the backseat, and Mamma stepped away from the door when Brian told her to get in the car. He looked at me in disgust, and I glared back at him.

"You," he came over to me and jabbed me in the chest with his finger. "You are a curse to this world. You should never have been born."

I raised my eyebrows defiantly at him. "Why not...because I am trying to stop evil people like you from hurting innocent people?"

"You are a Jezebel spirit," Brian spat. "And what you are wearing proves it." He looked me up and down and hissed, "You always were a great little whore."

I bit my lip in anger but only glared back at him in response. What a vile human being he was, and no matter what he said to me or how he put me down, he knew it was not true...and so did I.

Suddenly I realized that Fanny was not with them. I figured she was most likely locked in the house so she could not get out. *Poor girl,* I thought, all alone on that lonely mountain top. It was so hard for me to bear, and tears started to stream down my cheeks as I watched Mamma climb into the back seat with Grandma. My heart sank even more when I saw Mamma put Amish clothes over the clothes Aunty Laura had put on her. Brian backed out of the driveway and sped off. I knew if the police stopped them now, they would be reluctant to do anything merely because they looked Amish. The whole ordeal had lasted less than five minutes but I was disappointed that the police were not yet there.

Revisiting a childhood Nightmare

"Change will not come if we wait for some other person, or if we wait for some other time. We are the ones we've been waiting for. We are the change that we seek."

— *Barack Obama*

The police showed up a couple minutes after Brian and Mamma left, and I stood there impatiently while they questioned us. I thought they did not appear too concerned about what had happened after they found out that Grandma had given Brian power of attorney and that he was her primary caregiver. After a few minutes of questioning they agreed to go after Brian and Mamma to question them, just to make sure everything was okay.

"They are not going to do anything once they see them dressed in plain clothes," I said as I watched the police drive away. "It's as if people get star-struck when they see Amish or people who appear to be Amish."

"Well, let's just hope something gets resolved," Aunty Laura's face was extremely sad. "This has to stop. It has gotten way out of hand."

A couple of hours later, the same policemen returned. Aunty Laura and I had been waiting anxiously to see what had happened. The policemen told us that they caught up to Mamma and Brian on the mountain pass and, that after they questioned them, they had seen no reason to detain them. They said Brian had documentation with him showing that he was Grandma's caregiver and that he also had power of attorney over of all her affairs. Mamma told the police that Aunty Laura did not like that Grandma had chosen to join their religion, and that was why she was creating these problems.

388

When I asked if they checked for the cut on Grandma's leg, they merely said that Grandma looked fine and happy and there was no cause to look under her clothing and that doing so would have been a violation of their religious rights.

I just stood there, squinting at the officers. One of them seemed annoyed at my behavior and asked me if I had any further concerns. I bit my lip and continued squinting at him. I realized it was not really his fault, but at the same time I felt that if Mamma and Brian had been in ordinary clothes, things would have been handled differently.

"So, anything else?" the officers asked as they turned to go back to their car.

"Just one thing," I stepped toward them while trying to keep the anger out of my voice. "If they had been dressed in regular clothes, would you have treated them differently?"

"Well," the officer's looked at each other, "I wouldn't say we would have treated them differently, but they really looked like peaceful people; it was just your word against theirs. There wasn't much we could really do."

"Uh huh," I huffed. "I just want you to know that those 'peaceful people' are good actors and that they tortured me and my sister for years. Those people you just talked to should be put in prison for the rest of their lives, and you just let them go because you thought they looked harmless. What gives you the right to make that judgment?"

The officer looked at me curiously. "I would be happy to take you down to the station where you can file a police report. I have to be honest with you, though. They do have the upper hand in this. They say that you don't approve of their religion, and they also have the necessary documentation."

"What about them just barging into my house and slapping Misty?" Aunty Laura asked in exasperation.

"I'm sorry, ma'am," the officer said as he opened his car door. "Like I said, it's your word against theirs, and they say that is not how it happened. Again, I would be more than happy to take you to the station and let you file a formal complaint, and we can see what we can do then."

I turned on my heel and stomped into the house. I knew it was not really the officer's fault, but I could not believe this was happening again. It did not seem possible that these awful people could go through life able to get away with these horrible crimes. I did not understand how it was possible for such mean and evil people to appear so kind and loving when confronted by authority figures. Where did they get that particular talent?

It was so confusing and awful.

From that day on, I was terrified to answer the phone, and Uncle Bill told Blake to answer the phone at the store whenever possible so I would not have to.

Uncle Bill and Aunty Laura decided it would be a good idea to go up the mountain and confront Brian on his own turf. Aunty Laura thought maybe she could reason with him. I didn't believe it would work but decided to go along with the idea, and I told them I wanted to go with them. At first Uncle Bill refused to even consider the idea. He said it was not a good idea for me to go back to the house where so many bad things had happened to me, but I told him I needed to return now as a grown woman; that maybe by doing so some of the intense fear and dread I remembered from that place would dissipate. I was not sure myself if this was a good idea, but finally Uncle Bill agreed. We decided to leave in two weeks, thus giving the dust enough time to settle after the last confrontation.

IT WAS sometime in July when we drove over to eastern Washington and up the mountain where I had spent so many awful years. As we passed farm after farm and orchard after orchard, I was flooded with one terrible memory after another. I had to close my eyes and blink a few times to get the sounds of screams out of my head. Sadly, I remembered Fanny screaming as Mamma stood there, laughing as she beat her with the fly swatter. I blinked a few times as I saw the tears streaming down her chubby little face, while I stood helplessly by.

As we drove down the long lane toward the house, my heart started beating rapidly in my chest. Seeing the familiar sight was like reliving a nightmare. There were definitely fewer animals than when I had lived there, but there were still a few cows and goats in a small pen in front of a cute, white barn. The house looked gorgeous as it stood beneath the large, cottonwood tree. I bit my lip and shook my head. Anyone stopping by the farm would likely gasp and comment on how utterly beautiful and peaceful the place looked, without ever realizing that it was truly a house of horrors.

I got out of the van to open the gate that led up to the driveway. As my hands touched the metal, I felt a shiver run up my spine. It was the exact same gate that had been there when I was still at home. For a split second it felt as if I had never left the mountain and I was opening the gate for Mamma or Brian to drive through. In that second, I realized that Uncle Bill had been right. I should never have come back, but it was too late now.

390

With trembling hands I closed the gate and then turned and walked slowly toward the house. I saw Mamma and Brian standing on the porch, staring at me. I was wearing a gray checkered cotton summer dress with black flats; so different from the clothes I had worn when I live there as a girl.

I stood under the cottonwood tree until Brian opened the door and everyone started inside. No one said a word. I hesitated at the threshold of the door. I saw Grandma's room off in the corner, and my eyes settled on the place in front of the stove where Brian had tried to break my neck. I saw the same wooden table that Brian had thrown Samantha over when she jumped on his back to save me, and I blinked to try to get these images out of my head. I felt dizzy and struggled to keep my balance as I stepped into the house, closing the heavy wood door behind me.

As I closed the door, I looked around for Fanny but did not see her anywhere. Mamma saw me looking for her and impatiently yelled up the stairs for her to come down. I smiled when I heard a pattering of feet as Fanny came down the stairs. When she came around the corner and saw me, she ran up to me and put her chubby arms around my waist. She looked much the same as she had when I left, with the exception of a few more gray hairs. I put my arms around her and hugged her close. It felt so strange to be hugging Fanny. It seemed I had lived an entire lifetime since I had seen her last.

I frowned as Mamma came over, pulled her away from me and told her to go sit down. I noticed that as soon as Mamma touched her, she seemed to lose touch with reality. When she did not sit down, Mamma slapped her on the back of the head and then looked at me as if to say, "And what are you going to do about it?" I just glared at her. One of the worst memories for me on this day was that I had tried to stop them from hurting others, and had failed. Now they seemed to think they could get away with anything. I figured that is why they had let me in the house, to prove to me that there was nothing I could do to stop them.

I sat down next to Fanny and waited for Aunty Laura and Uncle Bill to come out of Grandma's room. Mamma and Brian were sitting across from me on a wooden bench and were blatantly staring at me.

"So you're going to missionary school, huh?" Mamma asked.

I just nodded, not wanting to speak to her.

"We wrote Samantha and she told us you were excommunicated from the Amish," Brian scowled at me.

"I left of my own accord," I looked at him defiantly. "I am a grown woman and have the right to make my own decisions. When I finish missionary school I am going to college, and then I am planning to start my own medical outreach for sick people all over the world."

I saw their eyes widen in surprise, and it made me feel good to be telling them my plans.

"You are misguided," Brian informed me as he leaned forward in his seat. "What you have become is a disgrace to your mother and me. You need to go back to your community and beg for forgiveness for your terrible sins."

"And what about their sins?" I queried.

"That is not for you to question," Brian said angrily.

"Don't talk to me like I am a child, Brian," I shot at him. "Neither one of you has the moral right to tell me about right and wrong." I was very angry, but I quieted myself when I saw Aunty Laura and Uncle Bill standing in the doorway, listening.

"I am the only father you ever knew," Brian shot back at me, "and you are completely disregarding everything I taught you."

"None of what you taught me is even in the Bible," I shook my head at him. "And besides, you were never a father to me. How dare you sit there and pretend I don't know what happened in this house? You and my mother are a disgrace to humanity."

I saw that Mamma and Brian were becoming furious, but I did not care.

Uncle Bill seemed worried and told everyone to calm down. Aunty Laura tried to talk to Brian about how they were treating Grandma. She asked them about some of the things I had told them and said she was not trying to blame anyone, but thought it would be best for Grandma if she were put in a home where she could be cared for without causing anyone any stress. Brian and Mamma said I was a liar, but Uncle Bill told them that no matter what they said about me, they knew that what I said was the truth. Mamma and Brian kept trying to engage me in the conversation, but I refused to speak. I was not about to play this game with them.

All during the conversation, I saw Mamma and Brian watching me when they thought I was not looking. I could see they were surprised that I had enough courage to do the things I was doing. They had not been able to kill my spirit; I could see that this made them very angry, but they also acted a little awestruck.

Our stay did not last much over an hour. Aunty Laura and Brian got right up in each others faces and were screaming so loudly I couldn't tell what they were saying. Uncle Bill separated them, but then he and Mamma started yelling at each other. Brian shouted that we were all going to hell for our evil ways, and to get out of his house. As we were leaving, Fanny looked at me, and I could tell she was lucid in that moment. She seemed to be pleading with me to help her. I felt as if someone had reached into my chest and was tearing my heart in half. I was filled with disgust for the terrible people that had raised me. I turned to Brian, who was holding the door, and asked.

"Do you believe in God, Brian?"

"What?" he spat at me. "Of course I do. The question is, do you?"

"Oh, yes, I do with all my heart," I answered, nodding and smiling. "It's just good to know that you believe in God, too," I continued. "Because you won't be surprised when he sends you and Mamma to hell for all the sorrow and pain you have caused for so many innocent people."

I saw Mamma's mouth drop open, and Uncle Bill and Aunty Laura turned around in surprise. I kept my gaze locked on Brian's face, and his eyes shifted as if he were uncomfortable. At last I turned, walked to the van and got into the back seat. Aunty Laura and Uncle Bill followed. I saw a smirk on Uncle Bill's face as he slid into the driver's seat.

"That was a good exit, Misty," he said as looked at me in the rear view mirror. "I am proud of you for standing up to them."

I did not answer; I just looked at Fanny, who was watching me through the living room window. It was so hard for me to leave her. I was quiet the whole way home. I felt nauseous and had to keep rubbing my eyes to get terrible images out of my head. I didn't know what I could do to help Fanny and Grandma, and it was so frustrating.

When we got home, I went to my room, closed the door and burst into tears. I overheard Uncle Bill tell Aunty Laura that that they should never have allowed me to go with them. I knew he was probably right as I knelt in a corner and put both hands over my aching heart. I heard the door open, and Aunty Laura came up behind me. I told her to please go away. When she reached out to touch me, I pulled away and told her not to, but she hugged me anyway even as I tried to push her away.

"Misty, stop," she said as she hugged me. "It's going to be okay. Don't let this set you back."

"No," I cried. "It's not fair that those horrible people get away with these things. I have to stop them somehow."

"You have already tried more than once," Aunty Laura soothed as she stroked the back of my head. "Look at what happened to the Bishop. He is walking around scot-free in Canada. You have to stop wasting your time on these people. They don't deserve it."

"No," I screamed, pulling away from her. "Then they win. I have to do something."

"No," Aunty Laura grabbed me by the shoulders. "They win if you spend all your energy obsessing about them. Look at you. You got away. You are beautiful, kind, smart, funny, and one of the most optimistic and inspiring people I have ever met. You can't let them get to you like this."

I looked at Aunty Laura in surprise. "You really think those things about me?"

"You bet I do." Aunty Laura nodded at me. "You have to realize that you have great potential and you can't just let these people ruin it for you."

I agreed with Aunty Laura. I knew that I could not keep mourning over what I couldn't fix, but at the same time I could not, in good conscience, do nothing. I ended up making a lot of phone calls to child protective services telling them about Mamma and Brian. I informed them that they were in the process of trying to get some foster children and sent them a twelve-page document detailing many of the horrible things they had done to Samantha and I. Everyone I talked to told me there was nothing that I could do to stop the paperwork from going through, but eventually I got through to someone that said she would review the paperwork and see what she could do.

I also called adult protective services again on Fanny's behalf, but got nowhere since Mamma had full custody of her and she was no longer a ward of the state. I could not help but feel the government had been relieved to be rid of one of its mentally ill wards and was thus reluctant to investigate. I was a little disheartened by the whole thing. It seemed I was getting nowhere, and I felt no one really cared.

Finally, this time, my attempts to stop Mamma and Brian were not totally in vain. About a month and a half after I first called child protective services, I got a letter from them saying that their application to become foster parents had been denied and that the government would not grant them the right to appeal. I was so happy at the news that I barely noticed all the horrible things they called me. It was one small victory; but finally, something had worked. For once my persistent nature had paid off. Thank God, I whispered heavenward as I tore the vile letter into a hundred little pieces. I did not reply. Like Aunty Laura said, they were not worth it.

A CALL FROM THE COMMUNITY

"Victory isn't defined by wins or losses. It is defined by effort. If you can truthfully say, 'I did the best I could. I gave everything I had,' then you're a winner."

— *Wolfgang Schadler*

I opened my eyes and sat up in bed. Frowning, I looked at my white night dress. I blinked a couple of times and looked into Phyllis's face. She was sitting in a chair next to the bed, holding a damp washcloth in her hands. As I sat there she reached out and pressed it against my face. The washcloth felt cool on my skin, and I put a hand to my forehead to see if I had a fever. It was boiling hot, and beads of sweat were trickling down my face despite the cool morning air. I looked down at my night dress and saw that it was soaked with sweat. Confused, I looked back at Phyllis, who was wringing out the washcloth in a stainless steel bowl on the floor.

"Phyllis, what are you doing here?" I whispered weakly.

"What do you mean?" Phyllis asked me with a furrowed brow.

"What are you doing in Seattle?"

"Seattle? What are you talking about?" Phyllis asked as she put the washcloth on my forehead again.

"No, this can't be true," I tried to crawl out of the bed. "I left the Amish. I went to Seattle; I am getting ready to take my GED test. I am going to Florida to a missionary school. How can it be that I'm in bed in the middle of an Amish farmhouse? This does not make any sense." I stopped for breath and looked into Phyllis's confused face.

"I left the Amish, right?" I asked her.

Phyllis looked at a loss for words. "Emma, I don't know what you are talking about," she gently stroked my face with the washcloth. "Remember, last night you didn't feel well, and went to bed right after supper?"

"What?" I asked, I was confused as to why she was talking about the night before Peter had attacked me and I had gone to the police. "That was months ago," I told her.

"No." Phyllis shook her head. "That was three days ago. You have been running a high fever ever since, and we were very worried."

I stared at Phyllis, and the lurching feeling in my stomach made me want to throw up. I had dreamed everything!

"So I never went to the police?" I whispered. "I never told you what Peter was doing? I wasn't brave and I never accomplished any of those things that I thought I had?"

The feeling of sorrow was so great it cannot be explained. It had all been a dream, all of the things I had done that had taken so much courage and strength. I was not sure I could do it now, no matter how much I longed to. I would simply be Amish forever, no matter how much I disagreed with them. Just thinking back on my dream and all of the confusing and difficult things I had encountered after I left the Amish made me shiver. I could not breathe; I stood up despite Phyllis's attempts to pull me back down.

I had traveled down a long, dark road in order to expose the truth about these people and the Amish as a whole, and now I was finding out I had not done any of it. How was it possible? I saw Peter standing in front of the barn, and it made my blood boil. I could not believe I was still here in the same house with him. I was weak, but I struggled to open the door.

"Emma, where are you going?" Phyllis called after me.

"I'm leaving," I yelled back at her. "I won't stay Amish. I have to go to missionary school; I have to become a doctor. I can't stay here."

"That is ridiculous," Phyllis grabbed at my arm. "You can't leave the Amish; you will go to hell."

"No," I shouted as tears streamed down my cheeks. I was thinking of my dream and the happy days I had experienced while in Seattle. I thought of the fun I'd had planning my future, how excited I had been to learn so many new things and the satisfaction I felt at finally being in charge of my own life. It had been amazing, but it was only a dream.

In the distance I saw Karen's place and I could see Simba waiting at the fence for me. I was not happy. It only made me more certain that I was still Amish. I pinched my arms to make sure this was not a dream, and winced in pain. Still not convinced, I slapped myself as hard as I could across the face, and then had to blink back tears from the sting.

"Emma. Emma, where are you going?" I heard Peter say from behind me. I screamed as he reached out and grabbed my shoulder.

"Get away from me, you horrible monster!" I screamed at him as I began running.

I stopped abruptly when I got to the road. For some reason, there was now a high wire fence around the farm. I turned and looked behind me. Several Amish had gathered and were staring at me and shaking their heads in disapproval. I grabbed the fence with both hands and shook it as I screamed "No!, No!" over and over again. *What had made me think that I could be that courageous?* I thought to myself. I just stood there, shaking the fence and thinking of all the things I thought I had done and those I had not had the chance to do yet. It was utterly devastating.

Suddenly, I awoke in a cold sweat. I was on my hands and knees beside the bed in my bedroom in Seattle. From the way I was holding onto the bed, I figured I must have been shaking it. The house was quiet, so I must not have been screaming out loud.

I got up slowly. My legs were trembling, and my flowered nightgown was soaked with sweat. I was so confused. Had I fainted or fallen asleep again and now I was dreaming that I was back in Seattle, or was *this* the reality? I pinched myself with my fingernails and winced at the pain, but then the same thing had happened in the other dream. I went through the dark hall into the bathroom and splashed cold water over my face. I felt the cold, but in the other dream I had been able to feel the coldness of the washcloth, too.

I decided to go outside. The cool, late summer breeze greeted me, and I closed my eyes as it swept across my face. I walked over to the giant magnolia tree and rubbed my palms along the bark. I felt its roughness and decided this had to be real. I sat under the tree for a long while and thought how terrible it would have been if I had not decided to leave the Amish. What if I was still there? I sat there, shaking at the thought. I felt so stressed and tired. As much as I loved my life here, it was hard to talk to anyone about my past, so I avoided it as much as possible. Any time I opened up to someone, he or she just looked at me in stunned silence, as if unable to comprehend what I was saying. I felt so alone at times. I could not expect people to understand, yet at times I wished there was someone that had been through something similar so I did not feel so peculiar.

I couldn't help but think that if Mamma had never met Brian, maybe my life would have been more normal. Although I tried not to wallow in self-pity, that night I felt really wounded because my mother and Brian had stolen my childhood from me. I did not even have memories of becoming an Amish teenager. My teenage years blurred into one another and they had no real significance. They had all been spent on top of a mountain in the middle of nowhere. I began sobbing uncontrollably. I felt like I had been robbed, and there was no way to recover what had been stolen. It was gone forever.

After that night, I had the exact same nightmare three to seven times a week, and each time it took at least a minute to calm down and realize that it had only been a dream. I believe going back to the mountain and seeing the place where I had been so badly abused was almost too much for me. I did not realize it then but the overload of trauma had resulted in my brain causing these horrible dreams to recur over and over again. By stepping back into the past I had somehow caused my brain to question if I had really left or not.

As the dream evolved, the list of things that I told myself I had not really done grew to include all the endeavors that were relevant to my accomplishments. This made the dream that much worse. Even today I have this frightening nightmare at least twice a week, and I find myself sitting up in bed in a panic. What if I had never left the Amish? Well, I do know that if that were the case, I would not be writing this book.

SUMMER CAME to a close, and with the beginning of September there was a significant change in the Seattle weather. It began to rain a lot making it hard for me to get around on my bike, but still I had fun peddling around in the rain wearing my pink raincoat. Aunty Laura laughingly scolded me, but she knew how much I enjoyed my freedom and did not protest too much. I was continuing to study for my GED. I had already managed to get through the study guide twice and was starting on my third round. The paperwork for my ID was taking a long time and my passport would not arrive until October; I was starting to get anxious because January was fast approaching and I could not take the test until I had some sort of picture ID.

I was positive I could pass the GED test, but it seemed I was the only one. Aunty Laura and Denise were trying to coax me to stay in Seattle for another year and take the test next fall. They said they were afraid that if I took it and failed, I might lose my motivation and not take it again. I just shook my head at them and told them I appreciated their concern, but that I was anxious to stay on track.

One day at the beginning of September I got a call from Samantha. I had been sending letters back and forth to her all summer, trying to explain my reasons for leaving. With each letter I sent Samantha, I included the phone number of the house and the store, hoping she would call me. The Deacon wrote me and told me to quit sending phone numbers; he did not want Samantha to call me. He explained that Samantha's boyfriend's father had expressed concern that his future daughter-in-law was in contact with a member that had been placed in the Meidung. This made me sad, of course, but I had suspected this would happen.

Because of this, I was very surprised one day in early September when Blake came to the basement where I was dusting to tell me Samantha was on the phone. Excitedly, I ran up the stairs and stood with my hands clasped, waiting for Aunty Laura to give me the phone. Aunty Laura seemed to be trying to have a conversation with Samantha, but apparently she was not having much success. After a few minutes, she shrugged and handed me the phone.

"She's not very cheerful, is she?" Aunty Laura said with a frown.

"Someone is probably listening," I whispered back as I put the phone to my ear.

"Samantha?" I said hesitantly, not sure if this was going to be a pleasant conversation or a scolding.

"Emma! How are you?" Samantha said in Pennsylvania Dutch.

"I'm okay," I answered, without realizing I had switched languages. After a few seconds, a little melancholy swept over me at the sound of the familiar language and Samantha's voice. There were a few things I missed about being an Amish girl—it was definitely less stressful. For an Amish girl, decisions that needed to be made were few and far between. It was ever so much easier not to think and to let your mind just go blank. But I could not dwell on those thoughts now, as Samantha's stern voice traveled to me through the phone.

"Emma, what the h**l are you doing?"

"What do you mean?" I asked.

"You know what I mean," Samantha scolded. "Brian and Mamma wrote me and told me what is going on. I thought you would have returned to the church by now. You have got to cut this out and come back before it's too late."

"Why are you even writing to them?" I shot back.

"Everyone deserves forgiveness," Samantha said in a superior tone.

"Everyone except me, I guess." I bit my lip in anger.

"You are in the Meidung," Samantha reminded me. "We cannot forgive you until you return and repent."

"I did not do anything wrong, and I am never returning!"

"You left the church," Samantha stated flatly. "You broke an oath to God."

"I would have been placed in the Bann regardless of whether I left or not, and you know it," I said.

"You involved the police, and that is unacceptable," Samantha continued in the same robotic tone.

"Yeah, right," I shot back sarcastically. "I would love for you to show me where in the Bible it says you may not go to the police and turn someone in if he is a danger to other people."

"It's not our way," Samantha said solemnly.

I shook my head in exasperation. "Can you even hear how ridiculous that sounds, Samantha?"

There was a long pause. I pressed my hand to my forehead and told myself to stop arguing. There is no way to get through to people if they don't want you to.

"Okay, Samantha," I sighed. "What is the real reason you are calling me?"

"I wanted to tell you that I have convinced the Church to let you come and visit for a few days," Samantha's voice was anxious.

I raised my eyebrows. "That's against church rules."

"Yeah, but I found a loophole," Samantha continued nervously. "You would still be in the Meidung, but you could stay for a few days on the pretext that you are considering coming back and repenting."

"I am not coming back to the Amish Samantha," I protested weakly as I moved my hand to my heart. It was hard to keep telling her this, but I had to stand my ground.

"Yeah, yeah, whatever," Samantha switched to English.

"I am sorry, Samantha," My tone was apologetic. "I never meant for this to come back to you and cause you any trouble."

"Well, it has." Samantha paused. "Can you come back for a few days though?"

I felt tears starting in the corners of my eyes. "Samantha, there is nothing that you can do to bring me back to the Amish," I said in a broken voice.

"I get that," Samantha pleaded. "But we can pretend, Emma. No one will know. It may be the last time we will ever be able to see each other. I miss you so much."

I thought for a moment. Maybe I could use a loophole to go back and talk face-to-face with Samantha. Maybe I could convince her to come back with me. I nodded to myself. This could be a good idea or, on the other hand, it could be a very bad idea. I imagined the ministers gathering around me with looks of disapproval on their faces. It would not be easy, but I had to take advantage of the chance to see Samantha again.

"Okay," I relented. "I will come back for a visit if you are sure I will be allowed in."

"Yes, I am sure," Samantha said enthusiastically.

"Okay," I hesitated. Was it a good idea to back? "I will look into the details of the trip, but I want to wait until I get my ID and pass my GED test, so it will probably be the first part of November."

"Can't you leave tomorrow?" Samantha asked.

I smiled. "No, Samantha. I don't want to travel that far without any ID."

"Why?"

"It's not a good idea," I tried to explain.

"But we travel all over without IDs," Samantha said in a genuinely confused voice.

"Yes, I know. But I am not Amish anymore, so it is not a good idea."

"Well, okay, So you promise you will come see me?"

"I promise," I said, trying not to let my voice break.

"Okay, bye then."

"Bye."

DENISE HELPED me get the bus tickets for my trip to Wisconsin. I was scheduled to go in mid-November and would be gone about a week. I would return home just in time for the Thanksgiving holiday. Uncle Bill, as always, was thinking about my mental well-being and adamantly stated that he thought the trip was a bad idea and that it would not be good for me. I knew he was probably right given the recent encounter with Mamma and Brian and the number of nightmares I was having; but I also knew I could not live with myself if I did not at least try to get Samantha out. I had thought I would never be able to see her again, since Amish church members do not socialize much with ex-members that have been placed in the Meidung, out of fear for their *wordly* influence and because it is forbidden.

I finally convinced Uncle Bill that this was the right thing to do, and he agreed that I needed to do all I could to help my sister. I did not tell him that it was an emotional set up to get me to come back to the Church. There was no reason to share that with them, I thought. It would be too hard for either of them to understand just how great the tug was going to be.

*I*T WAS a happy day in mid-October when I finally received my passport in the mail. I was so excited to have a form of identification and to finally be able to take my GED test. I had practiced all the examples in the book three times and I was sure I could pass. I was able to set up an appointment for the third week in October, and for two days before the test, Aunty Laura and Uncle Bill refused to let me go to work. I laughed and told them they were more anxious about this test than I was.

I decided my weakest point was math and spent those two days practicing the same problems over and over again. I literally studied for about eighteen hours a day. Aunty Laura commented that she never needed to prod me to study and praised me for my self-motivation. I raised my eyebrows in surprise as I always did when she made such comments. I was just very determined. When I set my mind to something, it was hard to pull me away from it. That was just how I had always been.

The morning of the GED test, I arrived at the college an hour early, and despite all my professed confidence that I could pass the test, my hands began sweating. I stood outside the test room door with about ten other people that looked to be around my age. There were three girls that were annoyingly loud. I listened as they talked about the classes they had taken in order to get ready for the test. My stomach tightened as I overheard them say that they had all dropped out of high school during the last year or in the last few months. I felt myself starting to panic and went to bathroom to calm down.

I took a few deep breaths and stared in the mirror. The girl looking back at me was the same girl that had lain in the back of a pickup truck at five years old, writhing in pain from cracked ribs, the same girl that had once been a nobody living on top of a mountain, the same girl that had been threatened by the bishop of her church and the same girl that had had trembled as she walked into that small police station in rural Minnesota. I blinked as I found courage in what I had already endured in life. Compared to many things in my past, this test would be a piece of cake, I thought as I ran cool water over my sweating palms.

Finally we were ushered into a room; we were told to leave our things outside. I sat at the table; in front of me there was a pencil, some paper and a strange-looking, long piece of blue paper with letters all over it. I looked at the piece of paper curiously, and out of the corner of my eye I saw others start writing on it. I frowned. I had seen a piece of paper like this in the book I had been practicing with but had not bothered to read what it was for. Carefully, I read the top of the test. What did it mean to 'bubble in' my social security number? I thought. I started to panic; I was really afraid that I would fail the test, and I was struggling to hold back tears. I did not even know how to start the test, and the only thing I could think to do was raise my hand. I sat there for about a minute with my hand raised before someone came into the room and told everyone to put their pencils down.

"What's wrong?" the woman asked me impatiently.

"Uh..." I said in embarrassment as I saw everyone staring at me. "What does it mean to bubble in your answer? Where am I supposed to write my answers?"

The woman, that appeared to be in her late twenties, stared at me for a moment. "What?" she asked me as if I were mentally handicapped.

"Where am I supposed to write my answers?"

"Okay, this is weird," she snatched the pencil from my hand and looked at me suspiciously. "Look, you just pick A, B, C or whatever, and then fill it in like this. Got it?"

I nodded in relief, and she rolled her eyes at me, saying she couldn't believe that I could not remember how to use a *scantron*. I heard giggling from a couple of the girls in the corner and could not help but blink away a few tears as I began bubbling in my answers. It's okay if they laugh, I told myself. They have no way of knowing why I don't know what a *scantron* is.

I concentrated as hard as I could on choosing the best answers, and I found myself wishing I had taken Aunty Laura's advice and slept more than an hour the night before. I got very sleepy halfway through the test. I thought the test seemed easy, but I was afraid I was just choosing all the wrong answers. When I got to the math section, I found the algebra questions to be a little more difficult and I hoped I would get at least a few of them right. At the very end of test, I reached the essay portion. I was still confused on this subject. I did not really understand what a thesis was and had not known how to study for this part of the test.

I read the question I was supposed to write about. The question was something about what I thought should be done to help prevent DUIs. The test said to write at least three paragraphs on the subject. I sat stumped for a moment. I didn't know too much about DUIs, but thankfully I did know what it stood for. Finally, I started formulating a plan to cope with the problem and tried to write it as if I were writing a legal document. I did not know if that was what I was supposed to do, but I hoped it would at least be passable.

I HAD to wait three business days before I got the results back from my test. I got a little annoyed when everyone kept telling me not to worry if I did not pass because I could always take it again. I knew they were only trying to help, but I still didn't know why they were so convinced that I wouldn't pass. When I said as much to Denise, she laughed and said it was because it was crazy to expect a girl that had never been to school to study on her own for four and a half months and then pass a high school equivalency test. I frowned, afraid maybe I had not passed after all, but hoping against hope that I had.

GOING BACK FOR MY SISTER

"If you don't stand for something you will fall for anything."

— Gordon A. Eadie

That September was when Hurricane Katrina hit Louisiana, and our local Red Cross was giving classes on disaster relief. That was also when I was waiting for my test results, so I signed up for the classes thinking I might go New Orleans and volunteer for a week if I passed my test. I enjoyed the three-day training program, but afterward, I did not go to New Orleans because Uncle Bill begged me to take it easy since I was going to Wisconsin soon to see Samantha. I agreed with him, but it still made me feel very happy to look at the Red Cross training certificates I had earned. For me, they were a major accomplishment, so I tucked them into my photo album with all the other keepsakes I was beginning to collect.

At the beginning of the next week, I hurried to the college to get the results of my test. I waited anxiously until noon which is when the woman at the desk said they would be ready. I found myself waiting with the same three girls that had been so obnoxious the day of the test. I tried not to notice as they eyed me curiously. They were the ones that had giggled when I asked about the scantron, and although I was slightly embarrassed, I shrugged it off.

Finally it was noon, and I waited in line as the woman printed off our results for us. I felt my stomach tighten as I saw the girls in front of me scream as they saw the results. Only one had passed. The other two girls ripped up their papers and angrily threw them in the trash.

"I spent months in those stupid classes," one girl said as she kicked a chair in frustration.

I smiled nervously as the lady handed me my results. Hurriedly, I scanned the page as I held my breath. Beads of sweat were forming on my forehead, and I could feel my heart pounding. In order to pass the test, I needed a cumulative score of fifty percent correct. The test was worth one thousand points. Please, God, let my score be five hundred points, I whispered as my eyes darted to the bottom of the page. My eyes widened in surprise when I saw the number 730 at the bottom of the column. I looked more closely to make sure I was looking at the right number, and it definitely said 730. I even confirmed it with the woman at the desk. She assured me that it was 730 and was above the passing grade. She congratulated me with a big smile and a nod.

I was so happy I could not help but jump a few inches in the air and squeal with pleasure. The three girls, that did not seem to know how to smile, looked over at me with their glowering faces.

"Did you pass?" one of them asked me.

I smiled happily and nodded.

"Let me see," she snatched the paper out of my hand and looked at the scores.

I saw a surprised look cross her face when she saw my score.

"How is it possible that you passed and I didn't?" she asked as she handed the paper back to me.

I knew it was supposed to be an insult, but I was in no mood for dampened spirits.

"Well," I answered, "I just left the Amish about five months ago. I had a second or third grade education, but I have been studying for the past four months and I was lucky enough to pass." I paused, enjoying the shocked look on their faces. "And I probably passed because I studied for hours every day...before and after work."

I smiled at them one more time, and fairly skipped away. I hoped they, too, would be able to pass someday, but all I knew at that moment was that I had worked very hard for this and it had paid off.

As I walked to the furniture store, I read the individual grades for each subject. I was shocked to see that in the area of language arts and writing, I had received 99%. I had not even known how to write an essay, but it must have looked like I did. In reading comprehension, I received somewhere in the high eighties; in the science and social studies categories, I received high sixties. Only math was a really low score, coming in at forty-nine percent. I was really pleased with my writing score of ninety-nine percent. For me, that was a huge pat on the back. I now had a piece of paper in my hand that told me I was as smart as the majority of the rest of the world. It made me feel really good.

I believed that I was able to learn fast because I was a fast reader, and I sincerely believed that I had become a good reader due, in part, to the vast numbers of books I had read. Many of these books had come from the collection the school teacher had dropped off at the end of the driveway or that Mamma had sometimes brought home from the library. The wide selection of good, old classics such as *Uncle Tom's Cabin, Tom Sawyer* and *Anne of Green Gables* forced me to learn difficult words, different styles of writing and a lot about our American history.

When I got back to the furniture store, Aunty Laura and Uncle Bill were out on a call. Blake was opening some new shipments that had just arrived so I stopped near one of the couches to talk to his girlfriend. When he saw me, he looked at me anxiously.

"Did you pass?" he asked.

I smiled at him and jumped up and down, waving the paper in my hand. "I passed. I passed," I squealed excitedly.

"I can't believe it," Blake said as he hugged me and grabbed the paper out of my hand. "What the heck?" he exclaimed as he looked at the scores..."99% in writing!"

I smiled happily.

"You got close to seventy percent in science. How do you even know any science?"

I shrugged. "I read about it in the book."

"Well," Blake smiled at me, "I think you got better grades than I did all the way through high school."

Uncle Bill and Aunty Laura were in shock when we told them I passed. Uncle Bill smiled as he read my test results.

"We have ourselves one smart cookie here," he said proudly.

It felt really good to know that everyone was so proud of me, and I basked in it for several days.

Ɔ WAS scheduled to leave on a Greyhound Bus to visit Samantha in mid-November. I had decided to take the bus instead of a plane because I thought it would be nice to travel across the country.

I was turning twenty-three that month, but I was so busy thinking about visiting Samantha that I had not given much thought to my birthday. I'd had so many birthdays that had never been so much as mentioned that I did not think too much about them anymore, so I was totally surprised when Aunty Laura held a surprise birthday party for me.

It was a chilly Tuesday in November and Uncle Bill asked me to stay at the store with him after work to go over an order that had to be ready the next morning. We were finally finished around six-thirty and were both very hungry. Uncle Bill said Aunty Laura was meeting us at our favorite Mexican restaurant, and we would have dinner there. I was glad, as Mexican food was one of my favorites.

I was tired and mentally exhausted that evening. There was a light, drizzle falling, and my face felt flushed and I was slightly feverish. I always seemed to feel this way when the weather was cold and damp. When Aunty Laura had taken me for a checkup I had asked a doctor why. After he took some of my background information he told me it was probably due to the fact that I had been hypothermic so many times, and more than likely, the ice baths Mamma made me take were one of the main causes.

I pushed my bangs out of my face and pulled my jacket hood up, hoping I would not get one of my full-blown fevers since I was scheduled to get on the bus for Wisconsin on Thursday. I had already packed most of what I would need on the trip; there wasn't much since I was going Amish clothes while I was there. As I got into the van, Uncle Bill asked me if I was okay. I nodded at him and smiled, but I fell asleep as soon as he started the engine. A little while later, I awakened as Blake playfully dripped water out of a straw onto my face.

"Wake up, birthday girl," he said as he stepped out of the van.

Sheepishly I crawled out of the van behind him, laughing at myself for falling asleep. I looked around, confused as to why Blake and his girlfriend were there.

"Are you guys having dinner with us?" I asked as I followed them in the restaurant.

Blake just grinned at me as he put his arm around my shoulders and half-dragged me to the back of the room. My mouth dropped open in surprise as I saw a large poster on the back wall that read HAPPY BIRTHDAY MISTY and CONGRATS ON PASSING YOUR GED. There was a long table with over twenty people seated around it. Denise smiled and waved me over to sit next to her. Aunty Laura was smiling happily at my shocked face and gave me a hug as I passed her to sit down. I looked around, smiling at everyone at the table. Most of them were people I had met through Aunty Laura, Uncle Bill, Denise and her husband, and Blake. It made me feel good to know that so many people seemed to genuinely like me. I forgot the stress of the upcoming trip and joined in the merry laughter.

"Here, try this," one of Blake's friends handed me a drink he had ordered for me.

I took the drink hesitantly not knowing what it was, and smiled at him. He was always staring at me and trying to get my attention, but I was in no position to pay attention to him, even though I thought he was a funny, nice guy.

"What is it?" I asked him as I smelled the drink, which was full of chopped strawberries.

"Oh, it's just strawberry lemonade," he smirked at me.

I smiled and furrowed my brow questioningly at Blake as he grinned at me from across the table. I tasted the drink. It was really good and I was very thirsty, so I drank most of it straight down. After about thirty seconds, I felt my extremities start to tingle with a warm sensation. I saw that everyone was smiling at me mischievously, and although their faces were slightly blurry, I could tell I had been the brunt of a joke.

"Honey, those boys over there just slipped you some alcohol," Denise said as she playfully shook her head at Blake and his friends.

"Aw, come on, Denise," Blake laughed. "That was a strawberry daiquiri. There's hardly any alcohol in it."

I blinked, trying to get the fuzzy feeling to go away. I smiled with embarrassment as everyone laughed and said how easy it was to get me tipsy.

"I think that was her first alcohol, ever," Aunty Laura said as she put a basket of chips in front of me and told me to eat a few.

I sat quietly for a few minutes and ate some chips while my dizziness faded. It was true: I did not drink and was wondering how Denise and everyone else could drink so many margaritas without passing out.

It was definitely the best birthday I had ever had. There was a giant chocolate cake that said "Happy Birthday Misty," and after we had cake, everyone piled presents in front of me. I had so much fun opening the presents. Everyone knew I was leaving for missionary school in a couple of months and it seemed they had based their gift selections on what I might need in the middle of an African jungle. I squealed happily as I opened gift after gift. Everyone laughed when I opened the present from Denise's husband—it was a first aid kit.

"That is a fantastic present...something every girl wants," Uncle Bill said sarcastically, shaking his head.

"Well," Denise came to her husband's defense, "he thought that if she got scratched by a lion or something, it would come in handy."

Everyone laughed as I nodded in agreement and hugged the first aid kit to show how much I liked the present. Denise got me a fold-up, battery-operated lamp that could be attached to a book. From Uncle Bill, there was a Bert's Bees lotion and lip balm set, and from Aunty Laura I got a pair of low, black heels that she said would be nice for church. When Blake came over and handed me his present, he turned to the rest of the table.

"I just want to make a short speech," he tapped a glass with a fork. He turned toward me and put a hand on my shoulder. "I just want you to know that you have been a real inspiration for me and all the rest of us over the summer. We have watched you grow into a beautiful, young woman as you struggled to learn new ways and customs. Never once did I see you sitting in a corner, pitying yourself or making up excuses for why you could not do something. You just dove in, feet first, and did whatever it was that needed doing, all the time maintaining your sweet and innocent nature."

"Hear, hear," I heard Uncle Bill and the others say as they toasted each other.

I felt tears of joy fill my eyes. I was not sure I was as nice as Blake was letting on, but it felt really good to be recognized for my small accomplishments. I brushed away a tear, and then I opened Blake's present and pulled out a small, sparkling wire motto that read "Believe."

"I saw it and thought of you," Blake said as he sat back down.

I smiled at him and stared at the motto for a minute. It was true: I had believed in God and still did, and I was very thankful that He had finally delivered me from evil. I had struggled so much and now suddenly, over the past year, I was finally seeing that it had all been worth it. I strongly believe that if you have faith in God and enough belief in yourself and your abilities, that you can accomplish most anything.

Aunty Laura was going around the room taking pictures, and I hooked the motto onto the cross necklace I was wearing. To whoever might see that picture in the future, I wanted them to believe in believing. Believe—I love that word so much.

THURSDAY MORNING finally came around, and Uncle Bill drove me to the bus station. He was not comfortable about this trip back to the Amish and was adamant that Samantha should have come to see me instead. I just smiled at him and tried to soothe his concerns by pretending I was not at all concerned myself. I was not really worried about my physical safety, but I was very anxious about my mental state. I knew they were going to try every psychological trick they could think of to entice me back into the Church, and that made me slightly nervous. Just to be safe, I told Aunty Laura that I would call her every evening, and if she did not hear from me by midnight each day to send the police to the address I had given her.

Aunty Laura nodded and told me not to worry. She said if she did not hear from me, she would call the police, the Marines and the Coast Guard. I laughed, knowing she was trying to make light of the situation, but I also felt reassured, knowing that she would do whatever it took to find me if something happened.

As I sat waiting for the bus, the minutes ticked by and my anxiety grew. *There was still time to call everything off*, I thought. No one would blame me. *What kind of person knowingly walked back into something that had caused them so much pain?*

Just the thought of seeing and being surrounded by Amish again made me shiver. I sighed as I battled in my head. *What kind of person, that professed to want to help others, left her sister behind without doing whatever she could to get her out?* In the end, I got on the bus and decided to enjoy my cross-country trip. It would take thirty-six hours to reach Wisconsin, so I had a lot of time to collect my thoughts. I had a pillow and a blanket with me, so I snuggled into the blanket and watched the countryside as it began rolling by.

Denise had purchased the cheapest tickets she could find, and as a result I had many layovers in major cities. I was having fun, though, as we stopped every few hours for short breaks. In Montana, I walked around a gift shop, enjoying my freedom to do or buy whatever I wanted. When we reached the Dakotas, the freezing November winds cut through me like a knife. It was so much colder than Seattle. I had almost forgotten how cold those winters could be. I had a six-hour layover in Minneapolis and almost got lost when I wandered away from the bus station, trying to see as much as I could of the giant city. I got back to the station barely half-an-hour before my bus was scheduled to depart. As I sat in the waiting area, I heard a familiar language behind me. I felt my hands begin to sweat before my brain even registered what I was hearing.

"Where is the bathroom?" I heard a little boy say in Pennsylvania Dutch.

Slowly, I turned and saw a small group of Amish sitting in the corner of the bus station. Their backs were turned so they were not facing the giant television screen. I stared for a moment, feeling shocked to suddenly see Amish people as an *outsider*. That had been me less than a year ago, and now I was on the other side of the fence looking in at them for the first time. One of the women saw me staring at her, and I could see the same annoyed look on her face that I used to have when people stared at me.

I looked away and took a deep breath. It had only been a few months, but it seemed like I had left an entire lifetime ago. From the clothes they were wearing, I could tell they were from the same Ordnung of Amish that I was. Maybe they were even from a neighboring district. I tried not to look at them for the rest of the wait, although their chatter floated over to me. Finally, I had to walk past them to get to the restroom. As I walked toward them, I was imagining their shocked faces if they knew I was an excommunicated church member. As I neared the restroom, I watched as two of the smaller children chased each other around the rows of seats. I was right next to them when the smallest one slipped on some spilled juice and started to fall. Instinctively I reached out to catch her; I was afraid she would hit her head on one of the seats.

"Gib acht [be careful]!" I said without thinking.

I saw the children and their parents all turn and stare at me curiously. I was an *Englisch* lady speaking Amish. How odd.

"You speak Amish?" one of the women asked me in surprise.

I straightened up as I saw the little girl I had caught cringe back into the group. If I had been Amish, she most likely would not have cringed, even if she did not know me. But I was an *Englisch* girl, and for a second I had almost forgotten as much myself.

I felt my cheeks get warm now that I was on the spot. I didn't know why I felt embarrassed; I was not ashamed of my decision to leave. I turned toward the group and said with my most polite smile, "I am Emma Schrock. I left the West Hills community seven months ago."

"You are Emma Schrock!" the oldest man said in shock. "You are the girl who used to write for Die Blatt!"

I locked eyes with him and nodded. I knew what was coming next and wanted him to know that I did not care, even though I did.

"I used to read your posts," one of the younger women said to me.

"Sarah, shh..." a man I presumed to be her husband shushed her.

I stood for a moment as they all slightly turned their backs toward me and began mumbling together.

"It was the bishop of her church," I heard one of them whisper.

I swallowed hard as I continued to walk toward the bathroom. I went to the sink and stared into the mirror. My long hair was wrapped up in a bun, my bangs hung down to my eyebrows and I was wearing light makeup. I was in an ankle-length blue skirt, flowered blouse and thick

412

green coat. Even though I was still dressing modestly, to them I must look extremely worldly and was most assuredly going to hell. I did not know it would affect me so much, but it did.

My hands were shaking as I got on the bus for the last few hours of the journey. On one hand, I was angry that these people would judge me so harshly even though I had been trying to stop a madman, and on the other hand I felt rejected when they turned away from me. It was like they were part of my family, and they were turning their backs to me, telling me I was not worthy of their attention.

I was thankful that they got on a different bus. I lay my head against the window and tried to blink back tears. I didn't know why I was crying; I just felt so broken inside. I took a small mirror out of my purse and looked at myself. For some reason, I began listing in my mind all of the things that Samantha and the others would be whispering about when they thought I was not listening. 'Did you see she has bangs...she was wearing earrings when she got here...I heard she was wearing lipstick...Oh, my goodness, she is so far gone....' And with all of this, no one would care about the real reason I had left.

I rested my head on my hand and tried to drown out all the scenarios that were playing through my head. I could see the bishops all gathered in the barn, their black hats pulled down intimidatingly and their solemn faces staring at me as if I had committed a horrible crime. In my mind, I knew I had done nothing wrong, and I could not figure out why my thoughts were racing so. Suddenly I felt sweat begin pouring down my face. I started shaking and I felt nauseous...as if I were going to throw up. I swallowed hard trying to quell the urge to vomit. I clenched my fists as I felt my heart palpating. I was soaked in sweat, and then suddenly everything went black...

I JERKED awake not knowing how long I had been out. My face was slumped against the bottom of the window, and I could feel a long groove on the side of my face where the edge of the window had dug into it. I sat up slowly and looked around the bus. Most of the people seemed to be sleeping. I blinked as I looked around and tried to figure out where I was. I did not know. I looked at my hands, and then at my skirt and shoes. I did not even know who I was. My mind was totally blank, as if there were zero information in it. I sat there for about five minutes, fighting the urge to fall asleep. Think, I told myself. Who am I?

Nothing registered. I kept looking out the window of the bus, hoping something would come to mind. I felt scared. What was I going to do if I could not remember who I was? How would I know when I was supposed to get off the bus? Why was I even on the bus in the first place?

Finally, after about ten minutes of worrying, my eyes landed on the purse that I was wearing across my body. I opened it and took out my wallet. I looked at my ID and debit card. It did nothing to jog my memory, but now I knew I must be Misty Griffin. I dug further into my purse and found some pictures and the envelope with my GED and test scores. When my eyes landed on a picture of me and Samantha and the envelope with my GED in it, everything suddenly came rushing back. I felt shocked as everything fell into place. It was as if I had returned to myself after being absent for a few minutes. It was such a strange feeling. The whole episode gave me a real headache, and I almost wondered if I would have been better off not remembering anything.

I decided to get some sleep before reaching the Lacrosse station, where one of Samantha's neighbors would be picking me up. Before I fell asleep, I saw a few snow flurries outside in the dark. The sounds of an early winter storm resounded in my ears as I drifted off into a much-needed sleep.

I dreamed that I was standing outside in a blizzard and was knocking hard on a door trying to get someone to let me in. Through the window, I could see Peter and Jacob and Phyllis's dad, along with a lot of other Amish people. They were all eating and laughing. Samantha came to the door, and when I asked her if I could come in, she said, "No."

"But I am freezing," I cried. "I might die."

"You should have thought of that before you left," she told me as she closed the door in my face.

I remember thinking how unfair it was that these men, who hurt people were sitting there in that warm house, eating while I, the one that had been injured, stood out in the cold and was most likely going to die in the blizzard. "I won't die," I kept telling myself. "This is not how my life is supposed to end. I was made for greater things than dying in a blizzard." I huddled next to the house for warmth as I kept repeating, "I am not going to die like this."

I woke up suddenly, just as we were pulling into the Lacrosse bus station. I gathered my things and thought about my dream. I was no analyst, but I knew enough to realize that my dream was playing off my subconscious. I felt a new resolve as I stepped off the bus and felt the rush of the icy Wisconsin wind washing over me. I was done cowering and feeling rejected. I had nothing to be ashamed of. I had only been trying to stop a bad man.

I was no scared little girl, running for the comforts of home. I was on a quest to get my sister. Although the chance that she would come back with me was slim at best, I had already planned everything out. If she would come with me, I had more than enough money in my bank account to pay for her bus ticket. I would put off going to Florida for a year, and we would rent an apartment together. I planned to tutor her for her GED test and help her get an ID while I continued to work at the store. I thought it was a good plan, and although I wanted to leave for Florida in January, I was willing to put it off until Samantha was on her feet. I thought it was a good plan and I hoped it would work.

As I stepped off the bus, I saw a woman standing nearby with a sign that read "Emma Schrock." I rolled my eyes and smiled a little when I saw that they were using my Amish name. I walked over to the woman, who appeared to be freezing.

"Are you Emma Schrock?" she asked.

I nodded hesitantly, knowing there were probably a lot of Emma Schrocks in these parts. "I am going to see my sister Beth."

"Yep, you're the one I've been looking for." The woman nodded. "Your bus is over half-an-hour late, and it's freezing out here."

"Oh, I'm sorry about that," I apologized.

"Oh, it's okay." The woman smiled at me. "I have had the heater blasting and the radio cranked up, so it wasn't so bad." She looked at me curiously. "I don't know why, but I was expecting an Amish girl. Beth did not tell me you weren't Amish."

"I left a few months ago," I said offhandedly, not really feeling like chatting.

"Oh ... so you don't mind if I leave the radio on?"

I shook my head and smiled at her.

"So how is it being on the outside?" the lady asked as we drove out of town toward what was one of the largest Amish communities in the Midwest.

I smiled politely. "I like it."

"So..." She looked over at me. "Are you shunned?"

I smiled and nodded as I shrugged, trying to show that it did not bother me.

"Oh, I'm sorry, honey," the woman reached over and patted my shoulder. "That's one thing I could never understand about the Amish. How they can turn their backs on family just because they want a different life, is strange to me."

I just smiled at her again without responding.

"You seem like a sweet girl." The woman continued to chatter. "I have two daughters, and I can't imagine not being there for them, and they're not even nice half the time," she sighed.

"How old are your girls?" I asked, trying to deflect the subject from myself.

"One is nineteen, and the other is twenty-four."

"Oh, that's nice," I yawned. I saw the lady looking at me sympathetically. She was a nice, motherly woman I thought, and I was happy she lived close to Samantha.

We arrived at the farm a little after two in the morning. As we approached, I saw the lamp light on the kitchen table grow stronger as if someone had turned up the flame. I got out of the car and tried to pay the kindly neighbor, but she refused and told me I could use her phone anytime if I needed to. I thanked her and told her I really appreciated her help.

I turned toward the house and stood frozen in place. Everything was so quiet; I could not help but shudder. On one hand, the familiar look of an Amish farm reminded me of good food and playful children, but on the other hand, it reminded me of all the people I knew that were trapped behind a wall of rules and sworn to silence. It was a strange feeling for me to be returning now as an *outsider*, and I clenched my hands to stop their trembling.

THE STING OF BEING SHUNNED

"Some things you must always be unable to bear. Some things you must never stop refusing to bear. Injustice and outrage and dishonor and shame. No matter how young you are or how old you have got. Not for kudos and not for cash: your picture in the paper nor money in the back either. Just refuse to bear them."

— *William Faulkner, Intruder in the Dust*

I walked toward the house, my heart pounding. I had not been on an Amish farm in seven months. After the neighbor drove away, I was in complete darkness, save for the lamp light that was radiating from the house. There were no electric lights on the porch and only an occasional car could be heard in the distance. Somehow it felt as if I had come home. I guess that so much of my life had been spent on the outskirts of society that I felt slightly nostalgic for these familiar surroundings, even though I did not want to.

I saw Samantha in the lamp light, and my heart skipped a beat. She was in an ankle-length, dark blue dress, a green apron and had on a stiff white kapp. I was so happy to see her. It had been more than two years since I had seen my baby sister; she had recently turned twenty-one. Instinctively, I reached out to hug her but she quickly stepped back and held up her hand in a motion for me to stop. I sighed. I was shunned, and she was not allowed to hug me. *It is as if I'm contagious,* I thought.

"Samantha, I am so happy to see you," I whispered excitedly.

Samantha smiled slightly and looked at the ground. "I am happy to see you too, Emma." She paused. "Just promise me while you are here you will observe the Meidung rules closely and not cause me any trouble. My future father-in-law will call off the wedding if he believes I am leaning toward your way of thought."

I nodded. "He sounds really strict."

Samantha nodded. "He *is* Emma, but at least Daniel is not like his father and he is nice to me. Besides I might not get another chance at marriage since you went and messed everything up."

"Samantha, that is a terrible thing to say," I chided. "You can't marry just because you might not get another chance."

"Oh, yes, I can," Samantha whispered back. "Even though I really do care about David It's still my only chance. I don't plan on becoming an old maid."

"You could come with me." I looked at her hesitantly, trying to test the waters.

Samantha swung around. "Don't you let anyone hear you say that," she snapped at me.

I shrugged. "Just letting you know there are other options."

Samantha stiffened her lips and opened the door slowly. Quietly, we crept up the stairs. It reminded me of when we were children, trying to outsmart Mamma and Brian. How much I had missed my sister.

Samantha motioned for me to go down to the end of the hall where her room was. I shivered. The house was freezing as the wood stove was only allowed to smolder during the night in order to conserve wood. I opened the door to Samantha's room and walked inside. Samantha set the lamp on her dresser and closed the door behind us.

"Okay, we can talk now, unless you are too tired."

"No, I am okay," My teeth were chattering. "But I sure am freezing!"

"You are always freezing." Samantha laughed as I put my blanket around my shoulders and sat on the cot that had been placed next to her bed.

For a minute she seemed to forget I was shunned, and we just acted like sisters again. I looked at the cot, realizing it was for me. Despite the fact that Samantha had a full-sized bed and that it was normal for Amish sisters to sleep together, especially in winter, I would have to sleep separately because I was in the Bann.

I sat on my cot, rubbing my freezing feet as Samantha looked curiously through my things. She took out my makeup bag and opened and smelled the contents curiously.

"You're wearing makeup, huh?" she asked, staring at my face.

"Just a little bit."

She peered at my eyes. "Wow, that black stuff really makes your eyes look green."

I thought she was going to try some of it on for a moment, but she quickly stuffed everything back in the bag and zipped it up. I was afraid to say much for fear of making her angry and spooking her before I had a chance to tell her everything that had happened over the past seven months.

"You should see these," I handed her the pictures I had of us as teenagers.

Without thinking, Samantha reached out and took them from me. Our eyes met at the precise moment when we both realized she had just taken something from my hand. It was forbidden to take anything from the hand of a shunned person, to sit and eat at the same table with them, to have any kind of business transaction with them or to socialize with them unless an emergency arose. A shunned person was allowed to attend church services, but they had to sit in a chair set apart from the rest of the community, usually off to the side of the minister's bench.

I was in the Meidung, which was the strictest form of shunning, because I had left the Church. The only reason I was allowed in the house at all was because they were trying to lure me home. I also knew that if I ever returned, I would be under close supervision for the rest of my life and would probably not be accepted back as a church member for two to five years, and there would be almost no possibility that I would ever marry. No Amish mother or father would ever allow their sons to marry one that had strayed as much as I had. Luckily for me, I had no intentions of returning to the Amish, despite the happiness I felt being in familiar surroundings and talking to my only sister.

When Samantha realized she had taken the pictures from my hand, she dropped them as if they were so many hot potatoes. I watched as they scattered across the floor. *This is ridiculous*, I thought to myself as I gathered them back up. But I had promised to respect the rules and realized I would not gain anything by disregarding the rules of the church that I knew all too well. I set the stack of pictures down on the floor where Samantha could pick them up. She reached out for them. I could see that she really wanted to look at them, even if they were a reminder of our horrible past. Despite the awfulness of our mountain home, it was still a part of us that we would carry with us forever.

Samantha's eyes filled with tears as she looked at the pictures. I could tell she was remembering the day they were taken. I tried to bite back tears, but to no avail. Again I reached out for Samantha to give her a hug, but she shook her head as she wiped away her own tears.

"Emma, don't tell anyone I took those pictures out of your hand, or I will get in trouble," she said as she continued rummaging through my stuff. She took out a pair of small, sparkling hoop earrings that I had stowed in a side pocket and held them up to her ears as she stared into my little mirror.

"Don't be ridiculous; of course I won't tell anyone, Samantha," I said as I smiled at how funny she looked with hoop earrings and her Amish clothes. Samantha laughed, too, and looked at the rhinestone studs I was wearing.

"You really aren't coming back to the Amish, are you?"

I shook my head and let down my long hair. "No, Samantha." I looked her straight in the eyes so she could see how serious I was. "Did you think I was?"

"Not really." Samantha looked down at the sparkling earrings in her hand. "I know how you are when you make up your mind."

I nodded. "I want to be honest with you, Samantha. I came here to take you back with me."

"I know." Samantha was still looking at the earrings as the lamp light played across them. "You know," she mused, "I always secretly wanted to wear those really long diamond earrings."

"Really?" I smiled in surprise. "I never knew that."

"Yeah, I know. I never told anyone, but once when I was in Wal-Mart, I tried to put a pair on." She rubbed her earlobe where the piercing had grown over. Our dad had pierced our ears when we were babies, and I remembered seeing pictures of us wearing little heart earrings.

"You know, Daniel does not like that I have these old piercings," Samantha continued to rub her ear. I thought she looked sad. "I try to keep them covered well underneath my kapp, but I see him looking at them sometimes."

I bit my lip, not wanting to say anything rude about someone I had never met. Samantha saw my expression and looked away.

"He's not bad, Emma." She sighed. "I could do way worse. He is nicer than most men around here."

"Do you even really know him, Samantha?" I asked.

"Do we ever really know anyone?" she asked me back. "What about Peter? I can't believe Peter did those things you said he did. I always knew he was creepy but I never thought he was like that."

We spent the next two hours talking about everything that had happened over the past two years.

"That b**tard," Samantha said in English as I haltingly told her about Peter threatening to kill me and the fact that he ran to Canada to avoid the police.

"Exactly, Samantha," I agreed. "How can you pretend to stay in a church that allows this sort of thing to happen? How can you believe this is the only way you can get to heaven?"

"Well, I don't think what he did was right, but you have got to let the Church handle these things. That's what the rules are for—so we know what to do when something happens."

"So you think I was wrong to go to the police?"

Samantha nodded. "You risked everything, Emma, and you could have been killed. What were you thinking?"

"No, Samantha," I shook my head violently. "You are just settling for the easy road. You know these things are wrong, yet you don't want to do anything about them."

"I can't do anything about them," Samantha snapped at me. "There is nothing I can do unless I want to be shunned with you."

"You can come back with me," I ventured, as I began telling her about my plan for both of us. "I promise you, Samantha," I looked at her earnestly, "I will never leave you alone until you are ready. I promise." I held up my GED proudly. "Look. I got this in just a few months, and I will help you get yours."

"I am not as smart as you are," Samantha said forlornly. "I would never make it out there."

"Samantha," I chided her. "I will be there. I know you can do it."

"No." Samantha shook her head. "I have a life here. My life is planned out all the way to the grave. If I marry Daniel, I will have security, status, in-laws... I will have everything."

"Samantha, that's not everything." I clenched my fists in exasperation. She was so brainwashed she could not begin to comprehend the depth of the things I had accomplished in the past few months. To her they meant nothing, because her world did not include such things.

"Samantha, listen to me." I reached my hands out to her to symbolically draw her into what I was saying. "Getting married is not everything. It is something nice, for sure, if it is the right person, but do not give your own personal self away for it. You are an individual,

Samantha; you have the human right to stand up for what you believe in and to pursue things in life that interest you."

Samantha was only half-listening to me, as if she were fighting my *worldly* influence. I understood completely. That had been me two years ago, I would have done the same thing.

"That sounds prideful," Samantha said, trying not to look me in the face. "My place is here...for my future husband...to give him children."

"That's not all you are worth, Samantha," Tears streamed down my cheeks.

"You don't know that." Samantha looked at me. Tears filled her eyes, and her lips were quivering. "You have always had ambitions and had dreams, Emma. You knew what you wanted from life when you were six-years-old. I just want to be safe."

"Safe?" I said sarcastically. I knew this was one of my last chances to get her to see my side. "Samantha, tell me exactly how safe you will be if you have a daughter and she is raped and the Church orders you be quiet about it and to forgive her rapist. Will you feel safe, then?"

"I would kill the son of a b**ch," Samantha said angrily.

I just looked at her.

"We have two guys like that here in our community," Samantha admitted slowly. "I know Phyllis's dad is one of them. I have been in church when they confessed to a sin of the flesh and of course, I knew what it was."

"How can you live with that, Samantha?" I asked. "Those poor children either have to live with that person or at the very least they have to see them at social functions and in church. Those poor children. No one ever tries to help the children; they just order them to stay quiet."

Samantha stood up and changed out of her day dress and into her night dress. "It happened to you and me, and we are okay. They will manage, too."

"So you think it is okay that Peter threatened to kill me, poison his wife and was molesting his daughter... that Phyllis's dad molested all of his girls...?"

Samantha held up her hand. "Stop it, Misty!"

I looked at her, surprised that she had used my real name.

"Just stop it. This is the way of our church. It is not my fault, and to leave would certainly mean going to hell."

"Is that what you think of the Mary Schrock case?"

"Yes. What she did was wrong, just like you."

Mary Schrock (name has been changed) was a case I had recently read about on the internet. I had heard about it when I was still Amish, but it had been hushed up throughout the communities. Mary Schrock was a girl from a district close to Samantha's, and she had lived only a few miles away. She had been raped most of her life by her brothers. When she tried to tell her mother, her mother merely said that little Mary was not praying enough. Finally, Mary decided to go to the police, after hearing her four-year-old sister say that their brothers were bad to her. Somehow she got authorities to listen to her, and she agreed to wear a wire and confront one of her brothers. She got him on tape, admitting that he had raped her at least fifty times. At the end of the trial, her stepfather, her brothers and even her mother, were sentenced to jail or probation. Some of her brothers were currently serving their sentences in a Wisconsin prison. Contrary to popular belief, there are Amish that end up in prison, but only if someone is brave enough to step forward.

Samantha looked at me blankly—as if she did not want to think about it—and then crawled into bed. "Mom said we could sleep in," she said as she looked at the alarm clock that already read 4:30.

As I drifted off to sleep I could hear soft footsteps and noises from downstairs. Such familiar sounds, I thought. I was tired, but I was also a little disheartened. Samantha was not going back with me. She was too scared of the outside world and she honestly believed she would not be good at anything other than being a mother and housekeeper. That was fine, too, I thought. She was a cute girl. I was sure she would have a lot of chances to do just that in the outside world, but there was no getting through to her. She believed this was her one and only shot at avoiding a life as an old maid. At least she thought Daniel was nice though. I knew his family was extremely strict, but maybe Daniel would be nice to my sister. That would be a great comfort.

$\mathfrak{I}$ WOKE to the sound of children squealing and racing through the halls. I sat up on the cot and blinked my eyes; it took me a minute to remember where I was. I looked at the white walls and the blue curtains over the window and the royal blue quilt that was on the bed. So familiar, I thought as I stood up. I always loved the Amish way of having clean, crisp white or light blue walls contrasted with dark blue curtains, wood floors and deep, rich quilts. I sighed. These were things I loved and missed, but I could not let myself dwell on them.

I looked at the clock. It was only a little past 6:30, meaning I had been asleep barely two hours. I was still sleepy but I figured there was no use trying to sleep with the children running about in the hall. I began taking off my worldly clothes. Samantha had left a royal blue dress, green apron and white kapp hanging on the door with a note.

Tomorrow is church Sunday and the bakery is open today, so I have a lot to do. Please wash off your makeup and don't forget to take out your earrings. Put all of your belongings on the high shelf in my closet so the girls don't get into them.

Beth

I sighed after I read the note. It was as if she had not been present during our conversation the night before, I thought. Slowly, I took off my skirt and flowered blouse. I stopped when I got to my bra and lace slip. I was not about to walk around without a bra for anyone. I hoped no one would notice. My hands shook a little as I slipped the dress over my head and out of pure habit I gathered the collar at the front and deftly began pinning down the front of the dress. I took the towel off of Samantha's mirror and gasped when I saw myself in the Amish dress. It was like I was living out the nightmares that had been haunting me so. I was Amish again!

I wished that I had not agreed to dress Amish while I was there. I felt like I had let my guard down and allowed them to reach out and reel me back in using my sister as bait. It could not be helped now, though, I thought as I tucked in the front dress bodice and pinned the blue apron at the side. I put the light green work apron over the front of the dress. Methodically, I brushed back my long hair, rolled it into a flat bun and secured it in place. As I was taking out my earrings, little Sarah popped her blonde head through door to tell me it was time for breakfast. Her eyes lit on the sparkling earring that was still in my ear, and I saw her eyes widen in surprise.

"What is that?" she asked, pointing at my ear.

"Oh, nothing," I smiled at her as I quickly removed it.

She stood there staring at me for a moment, and then scampered down the stairs. Quickly I wiped my face with one of my disposable towelettes and then stowed everything high in Samantha's closet. I looked in the mirror one last time and fiddled with my bangs, which were falling insistently down over my face.

At the top of the stairs, I stopped for a moment. Familiar morning sounds floated up to me. The muffled sounds of Pennsylvania Dutch chatter danced about my ears, and the cozy winter morning with its wood stove smell not only reminded me of my life in the Amish church but also of my life on the mountain. These things represented the first twenty-two years of my life, no one would ever understand why they were important, even if I tried to explain it to them in depth. Even though those years had been full of terrible things, being back amongst familiar surroundings also brought with it reminders of the things I had loved in life. I always loved the smell of the wood stove in the early morning hours, the coziness of soft lamplight and the smell of breakfast before it was even light outside. All of those things made me feel at home.

No matter how bad home was, it was still home, and home is something that will always be a part of you, something that helps define your life. Whether or not you chose to repeat what you learned at home in your life—whether you did better or worse—home would always be there with you. It was so hard to resist the tug that pulled at my heartstrings that morning.

Slowly I walked down the steps, not at all anxious to meet Annie or the Deacon. I knew the older children would remember me from when they lived in our community, and I hoped that they would not ask any questions. I guess that they had already been given a stern warning not to talk to me, but I was not sure if they were aware that I was under the Meidung. Usually, non-church members did not know too much about these happenings, except that if someone was in the Bann, they had done something bad.

As I walked into the kitchen, my gaze fell on the long table. Blue- and black-speckled metal plates and plastic cups were lined along its length in anticipation of the great-smelling breakfast. I stopped mid-stride when I saw a small coffee table set off to the side of the room. It was set up for breakfast as well. It was the table for the shunned. I looked up to see Annie and the Deacon looking at me solemnly. There was no smile as there would have been for any other house guest, only a look of sternness that spoke volumes about their disapproval of my new life.

"Where is Samantha?" I asked, purposely in English.

Annie looked at me curiously. "She is in the store," she answered in Amish as she motioned toward the side of the house where the small baked goods store was located.

"Thank you," I said, again in English.

As I walked to the side door, I heard Ella say, "Emma looks different, and she is speaking English again."

"Shh..." I heard Annie shush her as she handed her a pot of oatmeal.

Samantha was in the store, putting stickers on the bread and pies which were ready for the day's sale.

"Looks nice," I commented as I entered.

"Yeah." Samantha nodded. "I really like it. I wish you lived with us. You could help me in the bakery here. You always made the most beautiful pies."

I winced slightly at the comment. "Is it Annie's business or yours?" I asked.

Samantha dusted off the wooden table in the middle of the room. "Since I am twenty-one now, I have split the shop with Mom, fifty-fifty. I make the bread and noodles and she makes the cookies, pies and jellies."

"That's a great idea," I nodded as I gazed around the old fashioned store.

"Yeah," Samantha agreed. "We are lucky we live so close to the road, so we usually sell out on the weekends. After we are married, Daniel and I will live here for a year or so until our place is ready on his dad's farm. After we move, I will just bring my stuff down here, or bake it here with Mom."

I nodded. It sounded like Samantha had everything planned out. I knew now that she was not coming with me, so I was glad she at least had some good Amish woman business sense going for her. It would keep her husband in good status and give her an outlet outside of her own home.

"How much have you saved since August?" I asked.

"About three hundred dollars," she nodded happily. "It will go a long way toward buying material for our new house."

I smiled, remembering the quilt I had sold for eight hundred dollars not long after I turned twenty-one. Samantha saw my smile and remembered my quilt too.

"Oh, I know it's not as much as you would have by now," she frowned. "But Daniel said he is proud of me for earning so much."

"Samantha, that is a great deal in such a short time," I said, trying to make her feel better. "Besides, how many unmarried girls do you know that have deals like this with their mom and have their own businesses going before marriage? I think you are doing something amazing here."

Samantha smiled at my approval, and I winced again. I did not want her to stay here, but I was smart enough to know when I was on the losing end of an argument. If she was going to stay here, I might as well make her feel good about herself, I thought. It was never my intention to leave her depressed.

"Breakfast." Ella fairly yelled at us from the door.

Everyone gathered at the table for the morning meal, which was a little

426

late on this Saturday morning. I sat at my table, and all the children stared at me with wide, innocent eyes. I smiled at them, trying to show that I was not at all bothered by it.

"Why is Emma sitting over there?" Little Rebecca whispered to Samantha.

"Oh, she wanted to sit there because she is tired," Samantha whispered back.

Rebecca seemed confused and kept looking over at me throughout breakfast.

I was hungry and dug into my plate of food, savoring the familiar taste of potatoes with tomato gravy, molasses oatmeal and country fried eggs. I saw Samantha, Annie and the Deacon look over at me, hoping to see that I was uncomfortable sitting away from the group, but they were disappointed. I smiled at them and complimented Annie on the good breakfast. It was strange behavior for an Amish girl, but then I was not Amish, was I?

After breakfast, I knelt with my face on my chair as the Deacon recited the Saturday morning prayer. Some families said prayers before the meal, some after the meal. I closed my eyes tightly as I listened to the Deacon recite the German prayer. It was a nice prayer, and I liked the words. The only problem was that no one ever listened to the words of the prayer or cared enough to translate the High German into Pennsylvania Dutch. I had done just that one Sunday when I was bored using my German and English Bible. I had been curious about what Jacob had been saying each morning and decided to translate it. It took me a while to finish it, and when I read my rough translation out loud, I was surprised to see that no one was particularly interested in what the words meant. The only thing they were interested in was making sure they said it each morning and evening, because that was the rule.

I sighed as I knelt there in my Amish clothes, listening to the Amish prayer. I was thinking how hard it was going to be to leave again. It was so much easier to wear this simple dress and go about the day's work. Once I left, I would probably not see my sister very often and I would definitely not be able to attend her wedding. That was a painful thought, but something that could not be helped.

INJUSTICE

"In keeping silent about evil, in burying it so deep within us that no sign of it appears on the surface, we are implanting it, and it will rise up a thousand fold in the future. When we neither punish nor reproach evildoers, we are not simply protecting their trivial old age, we are thereby ripping the foundations of justice from beneath new generations.

— *Aleksandr Solzhenitsyn, The Gulag Archipelago 1918-1956*

After breakfast, I helped the girls do the dishes and straighten up the house. Since none of them were baptized members yet, I could work freely with them without fear of touching them or handing them something.

Annie and Samantha stayed busy with customers in the bakery and doing other Saturday chores. The bakery closed at noon on Saturdays to ensure that the womenfolk had enough time to get everything ready for the upcoming Sabbath. At noon, I sat again at my little table again. Rebecca tried to sit with me because she thought I was sad, but a firm swat to her bottom from the Deacon sent her whimpering over to the main table. I could see that the adults were a little irritated that I was showing no signs of remorse and had expressed no desire to come back to the fold. Annie and the Deacon all but refused to talk to me. When they did speak, their words were short and they glowered the whole time. I knew they saw me as a threat, and I was a little sorry for that. But I am positive that in their own way they meant well.

Annie and the Deacon were actually really nice people. They only acted the way they did out of concern for my soul. Just like I had, they truly believed that leaving the Amish was a grave sin, one that you could never recover from. They believed that if I were to die without coming back to the Amish I would go straight to hell, no exceptions.

I cant help but think that if I had been adopted into a home like theirs

428

I would most likely still be Amish to this day. Only pure terror had finally convinced me that were to many holes in the Amish doctrine for it to make sense. If I had not been so emotionally tired from living so long at Jacobs and then threatened by the bishop, I don't think I would have ever left. I would have been too scared that I would go to hell. However during my stay I had not yet quite grasped all of this insight and instead let some of their actions irritate me a little.

In reality, If Samantha was going to stay Amish she was very lucky to have these two people in her life. I knew that not all of the Amish families were like Jacob or the bishop, or Phyllis's dad. The real problem that I had with the Amish church was their refusal to punish the *bad apples* and remove the victims from abusive situations. Instead *The good people* of the church looked the other way, convinced they were doing their duty by holding the world at bay and punishing from within. And why was the given punishment was so light, only six weeks for such brutality.

AFTER LUNCH I took out my disposable camera and secretly took pictures of myself in my Amish clothes. I took a picture of Samantha's room and of the house. I really wanted to take pictures of Samantha, too, but I could not bring myself to betray her trust like that, so I tucked the camera back into my suitcase, happy that I had been able to capture a few small moments of my trip so I could remember it later.

In the evening I worked with Annie cleaning all the lamps, while Samantha took over the weekly braiding of the girls' hair. Annie told her that she needed the practice, so ever since Samantha had gotten engaged, she had been doing all the braiding.

Cleaning with Annie proved to be a very uncomfortable task. I instinctively tried to hand her things from time to time without thinking, and I was amazed at how good she was at remembering that she must not take anything from my hand. She would motion for me to put it down on the table and then she came over and picked it up, all the while giving me a long, hard look. Her behavior made me rather sad; I felt she was purposely asking me for things to test me. This went on for some time until she gestured for me to get the scissors out of the drawer. I tried to hand them to her—this time on purpose—and, as usual, she motioned to the table with her eyes. I put the scissors down on table, but not before I rolled my eyes at her. She looked angry at my reaction, but I didn't care.

"I know what you are doing, Annie," I told her in English.

"What do you mean?" she asked, pretending not to know.

"I know you are using the Bann to try to shame me back to the Church, and I just want you to know it is not going to work."

"It is your soul that is at stake," Annie shook her head sadly. "We are just trying to help you."

"No, you are not," I said firmly as I moved to stand in front of her. My green eyes were snapping with frustration. How many women in this church were willing to cover up the evil deeds of some of their male members? Unfortunately, it seemed to be one hundred percent. "You are just trying to coax me back in because you are afraid I am bad example to other young people and because I am a threat to Samantha."

"You have strayed so far." Annie shook her head. "I am not sure there is any hope for you."

"I thought we are not supposed to judge," I raised my eyebrows at her.

"We do not judge God's children," Annie said with conviction. "But we do judge the world, for the evil that it brings."

"So I am evil?"

"If you are a part of that world." Annie nodded.

"And what about the creeps you are protecting in this church?" I asked, my temper rising.

"They are humans with struggles, and we pray for them."

"That is so contradictory it is ridiculous," I told Annie as I turned away from her.

"Listen to me," Annie came around to stand in front of me. She was a big woman and fairly towered over me. "You are in our community, and you will behave while you are here. I don't want you filling Beth's head with nonsense."

"You forget," I stepped toward her so she could see I was not intimidated. "Samantha is my sister. She is my flesh and blood, and blood runs deeper than any ridiculous church rules."

"We will see about that," Annie said as she wiped a lamp chimney and continued to stand in front of me.

"No, we will not see about anything," I shot back at her. "You invited me here. I never planned on coming until you guys called me. I want you to know that I am not under your authority and I will not be harassed by you or anyone else in this church. I am no longer Amish, and I will say anything I want to my sister." I paused for breath. "If you want me out of your house, let me know now and I will leave, but don't think for one minute that I'm conforming to any hypocritical Amish rules out of conviction, because I am not."

Annie was staring at me, and out of the corner of my eye, I saw Samantha and Ella standing by the stairwell, looking on with big, round eyes. I knew full well that Annie would not ask me to leave because their hopes were to coax me back to the church.

"Just be sure you respect our rules as you agreed," Annie mumbled into the lamp.

I could see she was absolutely shocked that I had put her on the spot like I had. It was not the Amish way. It was better to gossip behind someone's back than to confront them directly.

After a couple of minutes I began to feel a little guilty. I knew I had been disrespectful and rude to a woman who was really kind to my sister. It was Annie's house after all, how could I blame her for sticking to her beliefs and obeying the church rules? She truly believed me to be a soul lost in the dark, her intentions were nothing but good, that I knew to be fact. It was confusing and sad and I felt my head begin to pulse with a headache.

Quickly I finished cleaning my half of the lamps and went to help Samantha start dinner. Samantha had told me earlier that her boyfriend and his family were coming for dinner. Normally, this would have taken place on the following evening, but they had decided to have it that night in stead.

Even though I was trying to appear to be brave and acting like things didn't bother me, they still did. I hated sitting at the table on the side of the room. I was not ashamed, but I still felt like such an outsider amongst people that were family. I had not known they were planning a dinner with a bunch of people and felt peeved at Samantha for putting me in this situation, but I also knew she would do just about anything to impress her new family, and by having me eat off to the side of the room, she could show them how much she disapproved of my actions.

While Samantha and the rest of the family did the choring, I went upstairs and took a nap on Samantha's bed. I was exhausted from the long trip and even though I had a headache I fell asleep as soon as my head touched the pillow. I awoke to the sound of a rattling buggy as it turned onto the lane. Slowly, I sat up, straightened my dress and apron and put my kapp back on. I sat there for a moment, not wanting to go downstairs to meet Samantha's future in-laws.

They seemed to be one of the strictest families in the community. Among the Amish there are church rules, and then there are family rules. Some families obey the rules just enough to stay out of trouble, and then there are families that are run like the military. They go above and beyond the church rules, creating the strictest of environments.

I had been fortunate in that I had not had to live with one of those families during my time among the Amish, but I had known of a man and his six sons that were this type of family. Every time I saw them together, it made me shudder. They never smiled or played with their children. Very often, they could be seen hitting one of their sons or daughters and no one ever said a thing because they were believed to be one of the holiest of families, due to their overly-strict dress code and their extremely well-behaved young people.

I remember thinking how sad their wives had looked. How unfortunate for them to have married into that family as it was rumored that they were also wife beaters. Once, when I accompanied Elam and Jacob to a nearby auction, I ran into one of the younger brothers that had just married. He had such a cold face. I had just witnessed him whipping a sick horse that had refused to stand up. It had made me so angry I had purposely gone down the steps and into the holding area to see the horse. He was coming up the narrow stairwell as I went down and he flashed me that cold look he always wore.

"Is the horse going to be okay?" I asked him through narrowed eyes.

"What do you care?" he asked, trying to push past me.

"I care because he is sick and doesn't feel well," I answered as I glared at him. He seemed uncomfortable, but he wasn't embarrassed like he should have been, he was angry. As he pushed past me, he told me my dad should not allow me to come to auctions, and that I should be home where I belonged. It made me furious, but I was afraid to say too much because I knew he would tell his father, and he would, in turn, go to the Church and probably get me in trouble. I went to the pen where the horse was and patted his head. The poor horse looked so sad and so sick, I thought. What a j*rk. There had been no reason to beat this horse.

I got up from the bed, went across the hall and peered out the window. I was anxious to see Samantha's future husband and was hoping against hope that he would not be a harsh man. I watched as a woman bundled in a shawl and wearing a wool bonnet stepped out of the buggy, followed by a few teenage girls. The men stayed in the buggy and drove over to the barn; I was disappointed that I did not get a peek at them. I went to the bedroom door and stood there for a time, not wanting to go downstairs. In that moment, I wished myself back in Seattle with my friends. Finally, I took a deep breath and went downstairs.

As I walked into the kitchen, the comfortable chatter came to a complete and sudden halt. I saw Samantha's future mother-in-law and her daughters stare at me with probing eyes. I stood there, trying to keep my small frame from trembling. I straightened my spine and stood as tall as I could, looked back at them and smiled. They seemed put off by my smile.

432

I rolled my eyes as the mother turned her back to me without even saying hello. Samantha saw my reaction and gave me a slight shake of her head as she sliced the bread her mother-in-law handed her. Of course, I was not allowed to help for fear of corrupting a church member, so I sat with Rebecca and looked at a picture book with her. I saw Samantha's mother-in-law looking at me with disapproval, but there was nothing she could do. Rebecca was not a church member, so I was allowed to sit with her and even hug her if I wanted to, but I suspected that in her family, that would not have been allowed.

After a few minutes, I heard muffled male voices in front of the house. I watched anxiously to see Samantha's betrothed. Even though I was now in a separate world from Samantha, I still had all my sisterly instincts and was already coming to the conclusion that this family was not good enough for my sister.

I watched as the men walked into the kitchen and sat at the long table. The Deacon was followed by the father of the groom. The father looked at me with icy disdain. His gray eyes were cold, and in just one glance he made it clear that he did not approve of my being there. Out of irritation, I smiled my sweetest smile at him and enjoyed his look of shock and his utter disapproval of my attitude. He expected to see a girl cowering in shame, but I would not give him the satisfaction of that, ever. Following them was a small man that, at first, I thought was a little boy. I was shocked when he turned and looked at me, and I saw that he was a young man. I smiled at him hesitantly. He just stared back at me, but seemed to have a kind face.

As he sat down with the men, I decided he must be at least an inch shorter than I was. That would make him barely five feet tall, and he looked as if he couldn't weigh more than a hundred pounds. Not that there was anything wrong with that since Samantha seemed to really care about him.

I looked at Samantha's tall, big-boned frame and then back at her husband-to-be. Well, if she was marrying into this sort of family, maybe it was better that she was bigger than her future husband, I thought. I felt really sad for my sister, though. Somewhere between Washington State and Wisconsin, her spirit had been completely broken, and she seemed anxious to please with no regard to her own happiness. I watched as Daniel called her over. She stood in front of him with a look of total submission, nodding her head as they cast sideways glances in my direction. I could not hear what they were saying so I pretended I did not see them. As Daniel spoke to her, I saw her future father-in-law say something as he waved his finger and looked straight at me.

I stood up, a little upset now that they kept pretending I was not there, yet were staring right at me. *I was not a caged lion on display at a zoo, I* thought. I was a human being in a room with other human beings. *Really, who did these people think they were to ask me here and then send me off into the corner?*

I walked over to the table and, smiling sweetly, went over to the groom's father. "Did you want to ask me something?" I asked in English.

"What?" He stared at me in shock.

"Oh, I saw you looking at me. I thought you were talking to me," I shrugged.

I saw Samantha's horrified face. *Come on, Samantha,* I thought to myself; *show a little backbone.* But I did not push the matter. I didn't want to make Samantha any more uncomfortable than I knew she already was. I smiled smugly to myself, though, as I saw Daniel's father steal glances at me when he thought I was not looking. *That's right,* I thought to myself. *Even though you think Samantha has no backbone, just remember her older sister has enough for two.*

I sat at the small table and picked at my food. The roasted ham and pineapple with creamy mashed potatoes and gravy was one of my favorites, but I had a lot on my mind so I barely touched my food. I sighed, as they seemed to purposely be taking hours to eat. They were talking about plans for the upcoming wedding, and that made me sad. I had a small book that I had taken from Samantha's room and I sat at my table pretending to be very interested in turning page after page, even though I barely read any of it. I was not about to let them think they were getting to me...not even a little bit...but they were. I wished I was sitting at the table making wedding plans with my sister. It was the one thing that made me very sad, even though I pretended it didn't bother me.

I saw the mother and father glancing at me in exasperation when they noticed that I was reading a book. It was like they knew I was outsmarting them, and it made them feel powerless. I smiled into the book a couple of times and once I almost burst out laughing. That would have been terrible, but the whole thing seemed so ridiculous and childish that I had to bite my lip to stay in control.

I sat there for about an hour before I stood up from the table and yawned. "I am going to the neighbor's to call Seattle," I said in English as I reached for the Amish coat Samantha had brought out for me.

"But we are not done eating yet," Daniel's dad glared at me. He looked like he wanted to order me to sit back down, but then thought better of it when he realized I would not have done it and it would have clearly made a fool of him.

"That's okay," I smiled back at him. "You guys finish, and I will be back

434

in half-an-hour."

"Who are you calling?" Daniel's mother asked me pointedly.

"Oh, I'm calling some of my friends in Seattle," I answered.

"Seattle." I heard the mother repeat the word as she squinted at me. That was far away in the western United States. What a *worldly* place, she must have thought.

I stepped out into the frigid Wisconsin air. I closed my eyes and drank in the silence. There were no prodding eyes out here—how relaxing. I walked to the neighbor's house and called Aunty Laura. I told her I was fine and having fun with Samantha. Uncle Bill must have asked me at least five times if I was sure I was okay. Aunty Laura finally told him to stop it, and told me to have a nice time. I smiled. It was nice to hear their cheerful voices, and after that evening's dinner, I was happy that I was leaving soon to go back to my new life.

THE NEXT morning, everyone arose early. It was church Sunday and the house in which church was being held was half-an-hour's walk away. I wanted to help with the chores, but it seemed the family didn't want me to help, so I stayed in Samantha's room until I heard the plates clattering as the little girls set the table. I sat again at my little table and thought to myself that this was getting pretty old.

We ate breakfast hurriedly, and then after doing the dishes went upstairs to change into our church clothes. As Samantha and I ran upstairs, I remembered the first few days we had spent together in the community—I could see that Samantha was remembering them, too.

"Don't you miss it just a little?" she asked me as we pinned our stiff, white organdy capes.

I sighed. "Sometimes," I admitted.

"Are you sure you won't come back?" she pleaded. "You could live here and find a husband like me. We could even be neighbors."

I bit my lip and looked at Samantha. "I can't, Samantha," I said softly. "I don't believe in the church rules anymore, and I will not back down on my principles for the sake of a secure life. I just won't do it. But that does not mean I love you any less. I will always love you."

I saw tears form in Samantha's eyes. "But you are my older sister. You are supposed to be there for me, to help me." She burst into tears, and I began crying too.

435

"I am here for you, Samantha," I choked out as I started to reach for her.

"No, you aren't," Samantha said angrily as she pushed me away. "You left me!"

"I did not leave *you*. I left the Amish!"

"That *is* leaving me," she said as she stomped out the door and down the stairs.

I closed my eyes and fervently wished I had never come to Wisconsin. It was so hard to hear my little sister accusing me of abandoning her. I did not know what to do about it. I felt very sad and even wondered if I was being a bad sister. In reality Samantha and I reminded each other of our horrible childhoods. I knew she thought of it when she looked at me. I could see it in her eyes and I am sure she could see it in mine.

No one would ever be able to truly understand the horror we had experienced there on that mountain. Even I myself cannot fully describe it, I lived it and that respect it was my normality. Only the eyes of an outsider looking in could truly explain the total sorrow of those two frightened girls that had lived on that mountain. Despite the fact that we both loved each other, we had never truly been sisters in the full sense. We had spent almost our entire lives not being allowed to talk to each other unless we snuck away out of earshot of Mamma and Brian. I brushed away a tear. How could that have really been my life, I felt a slight panic beginning to well up in my chest. The thought of Mamma and Brian and the fact that I was once again in an Amish farmhouse. It was almost to much for me.

We walked to church in silence. As we approached the wash house, I saw a group of girls entering and I felt a little nauseous. I didn't want to sit in this church and listen to them admonishing to the members to put away with their worldliness, obey the Ordnung and the Church and so on because all the while, I would know from Samantha's own confession that there were at least two or three child molesters in their midst, and one of them was Phyllis's dad. I did not want to see him, and I was mad at myself for giving in to their coaxing to get me to come to church in the first place. It was even worse that Phyllis's dad would be sitting on the ministers' bench, looking at me with stern disapproval. Ever since Samantha's family had moved to this church, it had two deacons. Samantha's dad did most of the work since he was younger, but Phyllis's dad was still an acting member of the clergy.

I was surprised when Samantha told me to file in with the rest of the girls instead of sitting apart from the church members like I was supposed to.

"Why?" I asked her in surprise.

"Don't be stupid," she replied in English. "You know what kind of game they are playing here. By making you feel part of the Church, they are hoping you will come back."

I sighed. "Don't you wonder why they want me back so badly, Samantha?"

"Yeah, because you are notorious, and they want to show the young people that even you came back, so there is no reason for anyone else to leave."

"I nodded my head.

I took my place on the wooden bench and remembered a time, four years ago, when I struggled with the German hymns and tried to fit in. Now I was just the opposite. *How strange life was,* I thought. It was not as if I didn't have any fond memories of being Amish...because I did, and these memories made me blink back tears. I loved it when the babies used to be passed up to me during church services, I was energized by the seasonal work, I enjoyed frolicking with the children and my animal friends. Those were all such treasured memories, and I thought of them now as I sat there and bowed my head so no one could see the tears trickling down my face.

I tried to fight these emotions, because I knew breaking down was what they were trying to accomplish, but I couldn't help it. I thought of Isaiah, who was now married. What if I had married him? I thought. Although he was very nice, I knew I would never have been able to accept the practices of the Church, and being married would have made it nearly impossible to leave. "Thank you, Lord", I whispered heavenward. What had been a disappointment at the time turned out to be a blessing in disguise.

I was looking at the floor, lost in my thoughts, when I felt someone staring at me so hard it felt as if a hole were being burned into my forehead. I looked up to see Phyllis's dad looking at me. I stared back. It made me sick to see him sitting on the ministers' bench, and I did not understand how this could be allowed. Two of his children were in the same church district; I wondered how it made them feel to see him sitting on the ministers' bench every Sunday. Did they have terrible flashbacks? I was sure they must, and now, as parents themselves, they must be terrified of this man.

After church, Samantha told me they would set a little table aside for me to eat lunch if I wanted to stay, but I told her I would walk home and wait for them there. When I got back to the house, I went straight to the barn and I sat on the fence feeding handfuls of sweet grain and old cookies to the horses. I really missed the horses, one of the horses was especially friendly and kept nuzzling me. I smiled and put my arms around his neck.

Such a comfort, I thought as I breathed in the distinct aroma of horse. They were so nonjudgmental and totally accepting of me just as I was.

I stayed in the barn for a while and then went into the house and walked around. I was bored and found myself wanting to watch the evening news. *How sinful*, I told myself with a laugh. The sound of the children's laughter signaled the return of the family, so I sat down on the wood box until they came into the house.

"Do you want to come to the singing." Samantha asked as she took off her bonnet. "You cant go with me and Daniel but you can go with dad and mom and sit in the back.

I looked over at her and shook my head. I wanted to leave. Even though I loved my sister dearly I just could not stand to be there any longer, dressed in Amish clothes and remembering every horrible thing that happened to me and how this church covered up such crimes and would continue to cover them up in the future.

After Samantha and Daniel had left for the singing I ran upstairs and fairly ripped the Amish clothes off my body. I let my hair down and sighed with relief as I pulled a bright green knit sweater over my head and buttoned up my favorite denim skirt. I put on my cross necklace and my crystal stud earrings, and finally I put on a pair of nylons and my black flats with the little pink bows on top. I looked in the mirror for a moment and breathed a silent prayer of thanks that I was no longer Amish. I swallowed hard. It might have seemed like a funny thing to do, especially at night but I could no longer stand pretending I was still Amish.

I looked out the window at the dark Wisconsin sky. Despite all the things I had told Samantha, all the abuse I had witnessed and suffered, she was still steadfast and unwavering in her belief that she had to remain Amish. I could not believe she was willing to stay here, but I knew, given our nightmarish childhood, this seemed like heaven to her. I fully blamed my own mother and Brian for what had happened to Samantha. *Talk about awful people,* I thought.

There was one difference that Samantha was failing to piece together. When we were living with Mamma and Brian, we knew that they were crazy. We had been terrified of them and scared of what they might do to us if we tried to escape. It was one thing to know your family was crazy, but the Amish were something else. To an Amish child, the world began and ended with the Amish. There was no higher authority. The Amish was your life, your government, your country, your world.

For abused Amish children of the stricter orders, they were not only forced to live with the fact that their family members or church members were harming them, but also that the church members would not help them. Rather they would tell them to keep quiet and that the predators had been forgiven and that they must forgive them as well, or they would surely go to hell. These children must cry when no one is looking and they know that their entire world says it is okay for these awful people to go free, while the children are eaten away inside by what had happened to them. It was all so awful...I closed my eyes at the thought. It was a crime against humanity. It had to be stopped, but how?

I decided not to go back downstairs. I knew Annie and the deacon would want to corner me and talk to me about my sinful ways. I just could not bare it. The slight amnesia I had suffered on the bus was a sign that I was putting myself under to much stress. I just did not have any strength or fight left in me.

I stayed up late reading, and I heard Samantha and Daniel come in around eleven. Their muffled voices carried up from downstairs for about two hours. Finally, I heard Samantha coming up the stairs. I took my lamp and went out into the hallway. She just looked at me.

"I can't stay in the same room with you tonight," she looked at the floor. "I promised Daniel I wouldn't, so I will stay in Ella's room."

I nodded. Only now was the severity of the Meidung beginning to sink in. I studied Samantha's face as she stared at the floor.

I went back to the room and crawled in bed and pulled the heavy blankets over me. As I snuggled into Samantha's bed, I let the tears flow, some out of sadness and some out of pure anger. I was glad I was returning to Seattle the following morning. I could not take much more of this, of that I was sure.

The next morning, I quietly went downstairs for breakfast but could not eat. The sadness that enveloped me was tremendous and all I wanted to do was run out of that house and never stop running. I had lost my sister, my church, and the only world I really knew how to function in. One side of me wanted to let myself be lured back into familiarity but the other side of me fought on principle. I was so sad and kept blinking back tears. I know Annie and Ezra saw them. But I could not help it.

After the dishes I tried to shrug off my sadness as I walked outside and then down the country road. A few English neighbors drove by and waved at me, and I waved back. It was a nice feeling, I thought. As I walked I could see for miles across the vast, rolling Wisconsin landscape. I saw Amish farmhouses everywhere I looked. My heart ached. I felt I was not doing enough to stop the injustice, but I was only one young woman and did not know what I could do to help these people who were so intent on blocking me out rather than looking for ways to improve their culture. I am failing again, I told myself as I walked with tears streaming down my cheeks.

Finally, nine o'clock came around. I was upstairs gathering my belongings when the neighbor drove up. I was so happy when she arrived that I grabbed my things and fairly flew down the stairs. No one was in the house. I went around to the side to the wash house and found Annie and Samantha doing the laundry. They turned and looked at me blankly. Annie turned her back to me. Samantha hesitated briefly, and I saw a tear sparkle in her green eyes. This was good-bye, maybe forever, or at least a very long time.

I saw Ezra standing by the barn as I climbed into the truck. When he saw that I had caught him watching, he turned away as well. I clenched my teeth, trying not to flat out burst into tears. Even if I did come back, the next time I would not put on Amish clothes and stay in the same house or go to church with Samantha. I would be a worldly outsider, held at a distance for the rest of my life. "Oh, God," I whispered as I tried to choke back the tears. Why is everything always so hard?

As we drove to the bus station, the kind woman did not say anything. She had seen a tear rolling down my cheek and had turned up the news on the radio, to signal me that we did not need to talk. I rested my head against the window and watched the farmland roll by. I was mentally exhausted. When we got to the bus station, the lady turned and smiled at me as I was opening the truck door.

"I can tell you are very brave, honey," she looked at me sympathetically. "Keep your chin up and you will achieve a lot out there. I know you will."

I smiled at her. "Thanks," I said as I slid off the seat. "That means a lot to me."

I closed the door and watched her drive away. It was nice of her to say that, and it cheered me as I thought about my up coming trip to Florida. I was excited at the thought. She was right: I hoped to accomplish many things. My life was not over; it was just beginning!

Feeling a little lighter, I walked into the diner that was next to the bus station. I still had an hour and a half and thought I might as well get some breakfast. I was starving, since I had only been able to swallow a few bites of food in the last 24 hours. I sat there and happily ordered whatever I wanted from the menu. I felt great satisfaction as I paid for the food with my own money...money that I had earned myself. It made me feel good, indeed. As I boarded the bus for the long ride home, I turned and waved in the direction of Samantha's home. "I love you, Samantha," I whispered.

The cold morning breeze swallowed my words as I spoke them, and I fantasized that that same wind would whisper them in Samantha's ear. I settled back into my seat and gave a great sigh of relief. I was going back to Seattle and to my new life. I was so happy and felt so sleepy. I fell asleep thinking about going overseas with the missionary group. It would truly be a dream-come-true. I could not drown myself in thoughts of what I might have done differently, although I was sure I hadn't handled things as well as I could have. I had made many mistakes in life I knew. Some times I had been irritated with Samantha and had not been the best sister I could have been. I knew that and sometimes I obsessed about it. I always thought if I had just done some minor things differently maybe we both would have had a better life. But I could not change the past and I had to focus on the present. My present now consisted of getting ready to embark on a whole new adventure, and for that, I was ready!

CHRISTMAS IN SEATTLE

"You may be the only person left who believes in you, but it's enough. It takes just one star to pierce a universe of darkness. Never give up."

— Richelle E. Goodrich, Smile Anyway:

Quotes, Verse, & Grumblings for Every Day of the Year

On the way home I made a quick detour, which Denise had programmed into my travel plans at the request of Karen and Carl. They picked me up at the bus station and then drove me back to their place to spend the evening. I didn't want to see any of my former Amish community so I stayed low in the truck as we drove to their place. I figured no one would recognize me anyway, but I did not want to take any chances. As I got out of the car, I heard the sound of Simba whining with excitement like he used to when I walked over in the afternoons. I went into the house so no one would see me, and Karen brought the dogs inside. Simba jumped up on me like he was trying to hug me and nearly knocked me over backwards. He was so happy to see me, and I him. I buried my face in his long, winter coat. It was like hugging a bear.

That afternoon, Simba stayed attached to me while Karen, Carl and I talked about everything that had transpired over the past few months. They listened in shock as I told them about my trip to Wisconsin.

"Wow." Carl shook his head. "I don't know how they continue to get away with this stuff. An Amish deacon molested all his daughters, that is beyond belief."

"They're Amish," I shrugged my shoulders.

Proudly, I showed them my GED and test scores, and they both told me I really had something to be proud of. I nodded happily. There was still a part of me that thought I was being prideful, but I told myself it was not pride; it was merely satisfaction for something I had worked very hard to accomplish.

As the evening grew later, I tried not to look out the window that faced Peter and Phyllis's old place, but there was a time or two I couldn't resist. Afterward, I found myself staring into space for a few moments. I was remembering the morning that had changed my life forever—the morning I had gone to the police station. It seemed so long ago and yet it seemed as if it had happened only yesterday. Around 7:00 that evening, I saw an open buggy coming down the lane, and my heart skipped when I saw Jacob driving. It brought back so many memories, some good, and some bad.

Karen saw me watching the buggy as it trotted over to Jacob's farm. She put an arm around my shoulders, and we just stood there watching together. Life had so many twists and turns... It was a mystery.

I slept on a pile of blankets on the floor next to the wood burning stove. I lay awake for a while, listening to the howl of the November, Minnesota wind and the crackle of the stove. Simba lay snuggled against me, wagging his tail every time I moved. It was hard for me to go to sleep. I had not realized how hard it would be to return here, and I was constantly reminded of the nights I spent terrified in the small trailer. Finally, I fell asleep snuggled against Simba. No one could harm me with this giant dog next to me, of that I was sure.

Early the next morning, Karen drove me back to the bus station. I hugged her goodbye and promised to keep her updated on my travels. I waved as the bus pulled out of the station. I was so happy to be on my way to Seattle once again. I watched as Karen got smaller and smaller in the distance, and I wondered who she really was and what she had done that put her in jail. I knew she had not told me everything, but that didn't matter. When I was in trouble, she had helped me, and for that I would be forever grateful.

When I arrived at the Seattle bus depot the next morning, Uncle Bill and Denise were waiting for me. They both ran up and hugged me, and I hugged them back. I was so relieved to be home.

"Your uncle has been fretting for hours," Denise said as she punched him playfully on the arm.

I smiled at them, and Denise commented on how tired I looked. I was happy they didn't ask me too many questions about the trip. They wouldn't have understood anyway, I thought. That morning, I breathed a sigh of relief as I stood in the shower, letting the steaming hot water run over me. Surprisingly, this had been one of the main things I missed on my trip, and it was my favorite of all the modern technologies I had embraced. The hot water was relaxing, and I smiled as I aimed the hair dryer that I had finally adjusted to, toward my long hair. As I stretched out in bed afterward, my eyes were heavy. For a while I thought about what it might have been like if Samantha had come back with me. I imagined her reactions to things like the shower and hair dryer as I remembered what my own reactions had been. Finally, I drifted off into a deep sleep. I had slept very little over the last two weeks, and what a long two weeks it had been.

I went back to work at the store the very next morning. No time for dwelling on what I could not change, I told myself. I was happy to see Blake and his girlfriend again. Their cheerful faces made me feel happy. Aunty Laura was going over a list of things she thought I might need for my trip, and I kept shaking my head in amusement. I didn't need anything she had on the list. I liked to travel light and was told room at the mission would be cramped. Uncle Bill just laughed and told me to let her have her fun, and I did. Aunty Laura was such a good-hearted woman, and I owed her a great deal. I hoped she knew just how much she had done for me.

The holiday season was upon us, and it would be my first one outside the Amish. I happily went shopping with Aunty Laura and Denise as they got things ready for Thanksgiving dinner. It was so much fun! Holiday music was playing from the stereo in the living room as we made plans for the family feast. Aunty Laura's granddaughter was coming into town with her two small boys, and her daughter was driving up from Utah, and of course all of the local family members would be there as well. Aunty Laura put me in charge of the baking, saying this was the first time they could have fresh Amish baked goods for Thanksgiving.

When Thanksgiving came, I had fun watching funny movies in the living room with the women while the men watched football in one of the bedrooms. As I sat on the couch, squished between Denise and Aunty Laura's daughter, Eva, I felt happy and I was finally somewhere I belonged. I even took a sip of the wine that was being passed around between outbursts of laughter caused by the comedy we were watching. I blinked with dizziness, and everyone laughed at me.

That evening as I helped Aunty Laura put the food on the table, everyone ooh'ed and aah'ed over the rolls and pies I had made. I smiled to myself, thinking it was a talent befitting an Amish girl. I winced for just a moment as thoughts of Samantha crept in. I blinked back a tear and then dug into the delicious dinner with everyone else. I could not help but think of Mamma, Brian, Fanny and Grandma as well. Today was a day for family, but mine was scattered to the four winds. I wondered where my dad and brother might be.

After a few seconds of being lost in my thoughts, I shook my head. It was so sad and so unnecessary. I blinked to block out the thoughts. I couldn't let my former life ruin the present one, I told myself as I choked back a tear.

*N*OVEMBER TURNED into December, and with every passing day I got more and more excited about my trip. I started counting down the days on a calendar, and soon I had only a little over two weeks left to go. It was such an exciting time for me.

I found it funny when, a week before Christmas, Blake and Uncle Bill both enlisted my help with their Christmas shopping. It was a lot of fun, and I found myself sneaking around, trying to find out what size shoes Blake's girlfriend wore, and trying to discover whether Aunty Laura would like pearls or a sparkling necklace set better. Uncle Bill said that in the fifty years they had been married Aunty Laura's taste for styles had changed about fifty times, and he was a loss as to what to get her this year.

Blake told me he wanted to get his girlfriend some furry leather boots that she had been looking at and wanted me to help pick out the color. I had a great time picking out a crystal and pearl necklace and earring set for Aunty Laura—one that I had noticed her admiring a couple of times— and selecting a pair of dark brown leather boots for Blake's girlfriend. It was the most enjoyable holiday season I had ever had in my entire life, and I drank in every moment of it.

On Christmas Eve, the local family all gathered at Denise's house; I drank hot chocolate while everyone else drank wine. We watched a couple of holiday movies, and then as the clock struck twelve, Blake and Uncle Bill jumped up and down, yelling, "Merry Christmas! Merry Christmas!" I got caught up in the excitement and jumped right along with them, yelling, "Merry Christmas!" as I clapped my hands. I loved Christmas; it was my favorite holiday.

Everyone then ripped open their presents. Aunty Laura cocked her head at me suspiciously as she pulled the necklace and earring set out of the box.

"Bill, did you have Misty spying for you?" she asked as she pretended to be upset.

"Is it that obvious?" Uncle Bill frowned and winked in my direction.

Aunty Laura smiled. "It's beautiful, honey," she said as she kissed him.

I smiled. After fifty years of marriage, Uncle Bill and Aunty Laura still acted like newlyweds.

I happily opened my presents. There were a lot of them, and some were from people I did not even know. I tried not to cry, but I was so touched that so many people had thought of me. It was nice to really mean something to someone, and I felt very happy inside.

A week later, I went with Blake and a few of his friends to ring in the New Year at a friend's house. I sat on the couch as everyone drank. Blake kept telling everyone that I was his cousin and that I was leaving for a mission in a few days. The young people were very nice and asked me a lot of questions. I just smiled at them shyly, the party reminded me only too well that I was from a different world than they. I was quite awkward around people my own age and usually felt as if I were at least fifteen years older than they were. I did have some fun, though; I participated in a few of the games they were playing. They were all so nice to me, despite my awkwardness.

It was fun counting down the seconds to the New Year, and I did relent and have a few swallows of champagne. The year 2006, I thought to myself. This could very well be the best year of my life.

On January 3rd, I jumped out of bed with excitement. Everything was packed. I did not plan on coming back to Seattle. My plans were to stay on at the mission and start classes at a college nearby. I felt a twinge of sadness as I looked at the calendar. Today was Samantha's wedding day. I stood in my bedroom and shed a few tears. Then I looked at the alarm clock and saw that it was 7:30. It would be 9:30 in Wisconsin, and the wedding service would have started half an hour ago. I bit my lip. My baby sister was getting married, and I was not allowed at the wedding.

How ironic that both of our lives were taking a drastic turn on the same day. She would be joined in marriage to a man I didn't know very well, and I was leaving on a plane bound for the other side of the country, where I would pursue my lifelong dream. Two sisters that had been brought up the same way—were now changing our lives forever...on the same day. I could not help but remember the two little girls that had been trapped on the mountain, and I choked. What had happened to us was truly a crime. The happiness I had felt when I jumped out of bed seemed to float away on the morning breeze. I wondered how many children around the world were suffering as Samantha and I had suffered, children considered the mere possessions of psychotic parents or worse. I felt a tear trickle down my cheek. What about Grandma and Fanny?

Here I was, on the cusp of my lifelong dream, and I felt I did not deserve to be happy. This had always been a problem for me. Why am I allowed to be happy and they are not? Why did I escape, while Grandma and Fanny were left there? It did not seem fair that I was now safe but that there were people who were not. I knew this was just a form of survivor's guilt, but it always came over me just when I was very happy about something. The old feelings bothered me for a few minutes, until I reassured myself that I had tried to help and that sitting here and feeling sad would not help anyone.

Aunty Laura and Denise drove me to the airport. Uncle Bill hugged me goodbye at home and said he was sad to see me go. I told him I would miss him, too, and I knew that I truly would. He was one of the nicest men I had ever known.

When we got to the airport, I hugged Denise and Aunty Laura goodbye. We were all in tears, and they made me promise I would call often—even if I got stranded in the middle of an African desert. I smiled at them and thanked them for all they had done for me, and then turned and walked into the airport. Another chapter of my life was ending, and a new one was just starting. I was excited and scared at the same time. For the first time in my life, I would truly be entirely on my own.

As I walked into the airport, I felt a little sick. I had never been in an airport before, and I felt scared and unsure how to proceed. The Seattle airport was gigantic, and I stood for a moment gazing around, unable to believe that I was standing in the middle of such a modern and progressive place. This was certainly a long way from the frozen cornfields of Minnesota and my crude mountain home.

I pulled out the list of instructions Denise had given me. It was a step-by-step list of how to get from the checkpoints all the way through to boarding the plane. First, I had to go through the scanner, it said. I walked up to the moving belt and put my bag on it. When my turn came to move through the metal detector, the agent looked at me oddly. I smiled at him not realizing that my long denim skirt, waist-length hair and high collared button-down shirt might raise a few red flags. I frowned, confused, when they asked me to step to the side while they opened my carry-on. They pulled out my German song book and Bible.

"What language is this?" the agent asked me.

"It's German," I answered innocently.

I knew about 9/11 and wondered if they thought I was a terrorist. The agent just looked at me and waved me on, and I felt they had been more curious than sincerely concerned.

Since I was two hours early, I decided to stop at Subway and have a sandwich. It always felt so amazing to decide what I wanted to do and then do it without anyone there to tell me I couldn't. In fact, there was no one to tell me anything. I had gone from a life where I had zero rights to one where suddenly I was totally in charge of and responsible for my whole life. It was truly exciting, but at the same time it was a little scary.

After eating my sandwich, I sat in the waiting room, looking at magazines and newspapers. I was so anxious to get on the plane I could hardly contain myself. Finally I heard the call for my gate, so I gathered my things and made my way toward the boarding gate. I was a little worried I would get on the wrong plane, and I must have asked at least six different people to make sure I was in the right spot. Finally, I walked onto the plane and stowed away my carry-on bag. I sat in my seat and looked out the window at the gray December sky. A few snow flurries were swirling here and there, and I smiled knowing that I would soon be in Jacksonville, Florida, and would be leaving the cold Washington weather behind.

I heard a voice giving us instructions over the speakers, and I could feel the plane starting to pick up speed on the tarmac. At that moment it really hit me. I am actually doing this, I thought. The last eight months were a blur, but all of sudden here I was on an airplane, and I had truly left the Amish behind. As the plane took off, I saw flashes of my life through a blur of tears.

I marveled at the fact that the small, lonely girl that had wept and prayed while staring into a vast and unforgiving night sky as she wished on stars, was now her own person and was about to embark on her life's dream. That sad and lonely girl had been guided by a small flicker of hope. Sometimes that flame dimmed and seemed to disappear only to appear again later—brighter than ever and just in time to guide her through the roughest times.

As I wiped the tears from my face, I could not help but smile. That same girl had evolved from a victim into someone that demanded justice for victims. Although these tears held some sadness, they also held defiance and a determination not to stand by and let people get away with hurting others. No longer would this girl be submissive to a group that condoned refuge for perpetrators while innocent victims were destroyed. I imagined the shock on the Amish members' faces as that police car drove up to the Bishop's house, and as I looked down at the tears on my fingers, I smiled with a surge of satisfaction. These tears were no longer the Tears of the Silenced.

Nine years Later

"If you have a dream, don't just sit there. Gather courage to believe that you can succeed and leave no stone unturned to make it a reality."

— *Roopleen*

My stay at the mission was a great and exciting time for me. I lived in a house with six other girls and was soon submerged in the modern culture of young American women. Not long after arriving at the mission, the girls there convinced me to start wearing pants. I let them drag me to the mall and try several pairs of jeans on me. The tight jeans took a couple of weeks to get used to, but now they don't bother me at all.

While at the Jacksonville mission, I received word that Grandma had passed away from a stroke. Aunty Laura told me that while she was very sad, she was happy that her mother was finally resting peacefully. I cried for a week, and when other people at the mission asked me what was wrong I told them that my grandma had passed. They all nodded sympathetically. Little did they know the real reason for my tears...they could never understand how bad I felt for being unable to make Grandma's last days better for her.

I called Samantha several times, but each time the kind neighbor lady said the Deacon refused to let Samantha talk on the phone. I knew she was not supposed to talk to me, but I wanted to hear her voice so every week for two months I left a message for her to call me at the mission. She never did, but one day during training one of the volunteers told me that I had a call from Wisconsin. I was so happy I fairly flew out to the phone. I was disappointed when I heard the Deacon's voice on the other end of the line. He, of course, was not in a good mood and told me to quit calling. I was very sad as I hung up the phone. I had just wanted to hear her voice, but that was apparently too much to ask.

About a week later I got a letter from Samantha. In the letter I learned the good news that I would become an aunt within the next seven months. At first I was overjoyed, but that emotion soon gave way to sadness as I realized that the child would probably never really know who I was.

After three months of training at the Jacksonville mission, I went to Brazil for the outreach part of the training. Arriving at the Sao Paulo airport was a huge shock for me, as it was as for everyone else. I found the Brazilian people to be very friendly, but was shocked when I saw the ghettos as we drove out of town toward the mission. I saw little children looking out of windows in the strange villages that had been haphazardly made by stacking together wood, cardboard and whatever else people could scrounge up.

It made me sad, since I knew the children in those places were often made to prostitute themselves and sell drugs just to stay alive. Their homes were utterly filthy and unsafe. I did not understand how well-to-do Brazilians could live in this country and disregard what was taking place in their own backyards.

I came back to the United States in September and knew that one day I would return to Brazil to bring more aid to the poor people of that country. But first I decided that I needed more education. I knew this would help me get more people to listen to me, and I needed that since I had decided that I wanted to start my own foundation.

THAT DECEMBER I married a great guy that was in the missionary group with me. I had known him for less than a year, but I was sure he was the one for me. I am still convinced of that to this day.

We stayed in Florida for almost a year before moving to the southwestern United States. After we moved I began my nursing prerequisites and worked as a waitress while my husband studied to be a psychologist.

Starting college proved to be a challenging, but rewarding step for me. I still remember my very first class. It was a math class, and for the entire first day I just sat looking around the room, almost unable to believe I was there. As I got into my science courses, I marveled at the new world that was opening up before my very eyes.

Right now I am working on my Bachelors of Nursing degree and soon hope to start working on my Masters of Nursing in order to become a Nurse Practitioner. My longer range goal is to get my Ph.D. in Psychiatric medicine. I believe this will give me a well-rounded education and serve me well in the future.

I hope to start my own foundation while working on my master's degree. It will be focused on taking children and young people off the streets and helping those that come from abusive backgrounds. The goal of the foundation will be to give these young people the opportunity to get a college education, and in return, they will be expected to volunteer for at least two years at a mission. I hope to start these missions in the United States, Brazil and Africa and wherever else they might be needed.

The goal for the missions is to have them run by people that have survived extreme hardship and have bettered themselves. That way, they can fully relate to the children and or adults they will be caring for. I believe people often make excuses as to why they cannot achieve things, especially if they believe their lives have been harder than the lives of those around them. But if they can see that the people that are helping them were once in their same situation, I believe they will be less inclined to make excuses.

I also hope to start a program where I can speak to high school children on the verge of dropping out. I believe that once they hear my story, at risk children might feel less sorry for themselves; in fact, they might just be grateful for the opportunities they have been given and hopefully will try a little harder.

It has been nine years now since I left the Amish. I would say that I definitely know a lot more about the world than I did during those first few months at Aunty Laura's. But despite this, I still sometimes find myself in a group not knowing what they are talking about. Often someone will ask me, "So what high school did you go to? What did you wear to your prom?" or "Do you remember this movie or that cartoon or when this singer came out with this song?"

To these types of inquiries, I just smile and nod as much as possible, but sometimes people realize that I don't know what they are talking about. A few times I have made the mistake of telling them I was Amish; they just stared at me and began exclaiming how exciting my life must have been.

A few times I have engaged in an online discussion with people concerning the Amish. Once, I told a little of my story, and someone wrote back saying he did not believe the Amish were capable of violence. I asked, "Why not? They are people, right?"

To this, he replied that he had had Amish neighbors all of his life, and that he had never witnessed any violence. I just shook my head and wrote back that he sounded ignorant; that if he knew anything at all about the Amish he would realize that they only allowed him to see what they wanted him to see.

I do not understand why it is so hard for people to believe that the Amish are capable of horrible crimes. As I told the police, the Amish don't allow autopsies. There is no coroner, no police to investigate suspicious deaths or injuries. Most are just a bunch of people trapped in the 1600s who would rather look the other way than deal with life's major problems.

To those of you shaking your heads and scoffing at this, I would ask you, "Why do almost all of the true stories people have written about the Amish have to do with abuse—many of those stories about sexual abuse?" You can read about the case of a Wisconsin girl that wore a wire and got her entire family convicted on the internet. There have been numerous cases of children dying mysteriously at the hands of stepparents, and there was an account of a boy whose mother cut off his tongue. The boy was four years old at the time and was being punished. His mother got angry when he refused to stop sticking his tongue out, she simply chopped the end of his tongue off. Of course, there was no way to call 911 so the father cauterized the tongue with a stove iron. The boy went on to marry but had great difficulty speaking, he had only been a small boy, he had committed no crime. and yet he served a life sentence for it.(To see articles online type in (Sexual abuse in the Amish community)

Lastly I would again like to state that I do not want everyone to think all Amish are rapist and child molesters. This is not the case, in fact most Amish, while strict, sincerely do have their children's best interest at heart. But one thing reigns supreme and that is the church rules. The "bad apples" as you could call them manage to slip through the loopholes and leave a horrendous amount of pain their wake.

It is hard to explain the level of brainwashing that takes place, but sadly I can truthfully say these people believe they are doing the right thing by upholding their traditions. My wish is not to make the Amish look bad but rather to inform the public, who can perhaps in return, help the Amish see just how far down a dark road they have gone to maintain their ancient customs. Maybe and hopefully an outsider will be able to see the signs of abuse and help save someone before it is too late.

Also I would again like to stress that the more liberal Amish are not as severe as the stricter church I belonged to. I am sure if I had been in a more liberal church I would have been listened to and perhaps taken to counseling. But still there would have been the shadow of the church rules and it is unlikely to much more would have been done. But I must add that this would have been an improvement, and one cannot hope for change without improvement. If only the majority of the Amish(the stricter) would seek to become more enlightened as well.

⟁T HAS definitely been a long and painful road for me, for sure, but I feel blessed to have been given the opportunity to pursue my life's dream. I truly hope that anyone reading this book will feel inspired to pursue their own dreams and that they won't let anyone dictate to them. After all, in the end you are the person accountable for how your life turns out, not anyone else. Do not ever let anyone make you feel you are less than worthy, for every man, woman and child should have the same rights in this world. We were all born into the world the same way, and will all depart from it, one no better than the other.

If you are in an abusive relationship or situation, I beg you to take strength from my words, and find a way out. There *is* a way, even if it is scary and you are unsure of yourself. The person abusing you does not have the right to hold you captive; they are doing so to make themselves feel superior. You have the same rights as they have. Also, bear in mind that if they are harming *you*, they will most likely harm someone else as well. I still believe that the best way to stop bullies is to stand up to them and metaphorically kick them where it hurts the most.

The point of this book was not to just address problems with the Amish. I also want to touch on the subject of brainwashing because it takes place in so many of these cult-like churches. If you—or someone you know—is trapped in one of these churches, it is most likely due to severe brainwashing. From experience, I can say the best way to break the hold they have on a person is to point out the blatant inconsistencies and hypocritical teachings that are sure to be found in the church doctrine. I know, personally, that this is the only way to break free. A word of caution, though; ridiculing these practices may only give the organization a stronger hold. If the person in question can acknowledge the inconsistencies that you have pointed out, they might have a chance of escaping.

In conclusion, I am convinced that we all have the power to do better. I know there are many instances when I myself, knowingly or unknowingly made many mistakes. Many times I was not aware of the bad things that were happening until it was to late. On other occasions I know I could have stopped certain crimes had I only acted at the right time, but I did not, and cannot change that now. I can only learn from these mistakes and share the wisdom I have gathered. I strongly believe that bad people get away with heinous crimes because there are too many good people that look the other way and do not want to get involved. Just imagine the world and how much better it would be if good people stood up to the bad, instead of letting them gain power.

In reading this book, I hope teachers, police officers, nurses, doctors and anyone else that may be in a position to recognize abuse will be more inclined to report it, and not merely write it off as an accident. For anyone else out there, if you suspect child abuse, please trust your instincts and find an excuse to drop by their place of residence to see if you can gain any additional knowledge about the matter. Please, never just shrug it off and tell yourself it is not your problem. I often think it would have only taken one person to save me and my sister from our living hell. For some other little kid you could be that person. I believe that child abuse is one of the worst tragedies to plague the human race because our children are our most precious resource.

To any police officers that read this, I sincerely hope that if an Amish person makes his or her way to your station, you will listen and believe what is being said. As you can see from my account, the price an Amish person pays for going to the police is severe. None of them would fabricate a story as a way to get back at someone.

I believe I am quite fortunate to be here today. When I think back to my other life, I shiver. Sometimes, when I am alone at night and I hear the wind whistling through the trees, I remember my mountain home and how I was forgotten by the world. Many times I have to blink to drown out Aunt Fanny's face, and sometimes I can hear the screams from that mountain top so plainly that it makes me tremble. Then I think of my Amish home and the desperateness of my situation there; I am often jolted awake from a haunting dream in which I never left the Amish. My story is tragic, but it is amazing at the same time, and I truly hope it will help someone else.

To everyone out there, I wish you courage and happiness, but above all I wish for you to have the strength to stand up against the tyrants around you, those people that are bent on achieving their own desires without any regard for their fellow man. Be bold and courageous and never stop fighting for truth and justice. In doing so you will make tomorrow a better place for someone, somewhere, and may God bless you for doing so.

A sweet child is born, a little star peeps

An abused child cries, the little star weeps

A child tortured with scars and blood so red

The little star weeps and hangs its head

- Misty Griffin

Made in the USA
Middletown, DE
08 June 2017